THE HONOURABLE ARTILLERY COMPANY
1537–1987

ROYAL SIGNATURES IN THE COMPANY'S OLD VELLUM BOOK

Charles, Prince of Wales (afterwards Charles II); Charles, Elector of Palatine (grandson of James I); James, Duke of York (afterwards James II); The Prince of Orange (afterwards William III); Charles FitzCharles, Earl of Plymouth (natural son of Charles II); George, Prince of Wales (afterwards George II); and George, Prince of Wales (afterwards George IV)

THE HONOURABLE ARTILLERY COMPANY
1537–1987

by

G. GOOLD WALKER

D.S.O., M.C., F.S.A., F.R.HIST.S.

Major, late R.A., Secretary of the Company, 1922–1947

With an additional chapter covering 1947–1987 written by

COLONEL G. R. ARMSTRONG

D.S.O., M.C., T.D.

(A Bty: 1930)

With Forewords by

FIELD-MARSHAL THE VISCOUNT ALANBROOKE

K.G., G.C.B., O.M., G.C.V.O., D.S.O.

Colonel-Commandant, 1946–1954

and

GENERAL SIR RICHARD TRANT K.C.B.

Colonel-Commandant

With 5 illustrations in colour
and 93 in black and white

Published by the Honourable Artillery Company, Armoury House,
City Road, London EC1
First Published in 1926
Second Edition, 1954
Third Edition, 1986

Design and production in association with
Book Production Consultants, 47 Norfolk Street, Cambridge

Printed in Great Britain by Butler and Tanner, Frome

CONTENTS

APPENDIX

LIST OF ILLUSTRATIONS AND MAPS

COLOUR

Royal Signatures in the Company's Old Vellum Book   *Frontispiece*

Between pp. 172 and 173
The Victorious Return of the City Militia (Rowlandson, 1772)
Review of the Company in 1803

Between pp. 204 and 205
H.A.C. Infantry, 1803
H.A.C. Artillery, 1804

BLACK AND WHITE

vii

viii

LIST OF MAPS

THE AUTHOR

MAJOR G. GOOLD WALKER,
D.S.O., M.C., F.S.A., F.R.Hist.S.

Major Goold Walker served as Secretary to the Company from 1922 to 1947. Apart from writing the History of the Company from 1537, he also began the issue of the H.A.C. Journal, edited the History of the Company in the 1914–1918 war and was instrumental in the revival of the Company of Pikemen and Musketeers in the 1920s. He personally ensured that the kit, equipment and the "Posture" of the "Pike" were authentic. He joined the Special Constabulary being awarded the Long Service Medal. He was the guiding light in such activities as the Woolwich Searchlight Tattoo in 1932, organized the great Tower of London Pageant in 1935 and was responsible for the Regimental Display as the central feature of the 1937 Royal Tournament. The same year he was responsible for the many and varied functions in celebration of the 400th Anniversary of the grant of the Charter by King Henry VIII.

During the First World War he served with the Royal Artillery in France, and was awarded a D.S.O. and M.C. and was mentioned three times in despatches. During the Second World War he was first called up as Major and Senior Gun Liaison Officer with R.A.F. Fighter Command and later trained a newly-raised Light Anti-Aircraft Battery.

On his retirement in 1942, he commanded North East London Group A.A. while serving in the Home Guard. He died on 24th December, 1956.

Major Walker was an "H.A.C." man in that his father, grandfather and great-great-uncle were all members of the Company. His son, Captain I. P. Walker, who died of war wounds in 1945, was also a member.

FOREWORD TO THE THIRD EDITION

By General Sir Richard Trant K.C.B.
Colonel-Commandant, Honourable Artillery Company

The heritage of our Company, the example set by those who have served in it before us, sustains and guides us and will do the same for those who follow on after us. This heritage is to be found recorded in the Company's archives and history. The need for an up-to-date edition of Major Goold Walker's invaluable History of the Company has been manifest for a good number of years. It is most appropriate that this should be published in the 450th year of the Company's existence.

We have been particularly fortunate that Colonel Geoffrey Armstrong has kindly consented to write an additional chapter covering the forty years from 1947 to the present day. He has done this in a most meticulous and illuminating way which will greatly enhance the value of our History for the reader of today, and I am grateful to him for his efforts which have borne such good fruit.

I have great pleasure in commending the story of our great Company to all its members—young and old, active and veteran—and to those others who hold the Defence of the Realm as of paramount importance.

Armoury House

COLONEL GEOFFREY R. ARMSTRONG,
D.S.O., M.C., T.D.

Colonel Armstrong, who has written the history of the Company from 1947 onwards, has had a very distinguished career in the Company. He joined "A" Battery in 1930, was commissioned in 1935 and served with 11th H.A.C. Regiment R.H.A. in the Middle East from 1941, being promoted Major in March 1942 and serving as Second in Command to Lieut.-Colonel "Baron" Ebbels. He was awarded the Military Cross in June and finished the Knightsbridge campaign in command of the remnants of the Regiment then reduced to a single battery.

He was next appointed to command 1st Battery, 28th Field R.A. which was proceeding to Burma. In 1944 he was promoted to Lieut.-Colonel as Commanding Officer of 136 Field R.A., and was awarded the Distinguished Service Order and mentioned in Despatches.

After the war he joined Lieut.-Colonel John Barstow, D.S.O., T.D., late of 12th H.A.C. R.H.A. to help reform the 1st Regiment H.A.C. R.H.A., as Second in Command. He became Lieut.-Colonel in 1950 and Colonel in 1953. He was Master Gunner Within the Tower from 1954 to 1957, Treasurer of the Company in 1958 and Vice-President from 1962 to 1963.

FOREWORD TO THE SECOND EDITION

By FIELD-MARSHAL THE VISCOUNT ALANBROOKE,
K.G., G.C.B., O.M., G.C.V.O., D.S.O.

*Colonel-Commandant and President, Honourable Artillery
Company*

THE Honourable Artillery Company already owes a great debt
of gratitude to Major Goold Walker for the admirable history
of the Company published in 1926; he now adds to this in-
debtedness by carrying the story forward to 1947.

During this period the H.A.C. suffered a serious loss in the
death of Colonel the Earl of Denbigh and Desmond, who had
commanded the Regiment from 1893 to 1933 and had served as
Vice-President until his death in 1939. Amongst his many ties
with the H.A.C. he will be remembered by the Foreword he
wrote to the First Edition.

Under his command the Company received its baptism of
fire in modern war through the detachments of artillery and
infantry which formed part of the C.I.V. in the South African
War.

Later, when the Territorial Force was formed in 1907, it
became an integral part of this Force, and Lord Denbigh was
still in command when the Company expanded to meet the
needs of the Great War of 1914-1918 and to serve in many overseas theatres, and lived to see the second mobilization in 1939.

During this long period of Command, which ran through
momentous years, he devoted himself wholeheartedly to the
interests of the Company and the H.A.C. owes much to him.

In this second edition, as a result of many years of further
study and research into the earlier history of the Company, the
interest of the narrative as far as it concerns the first few
centuries of the Regiment's existence has been greatly increased.
The record of the services of the Company's units in the First
World War has also been amplified, whilst those of the Second
World War of 1939-1945 are fully described.

A sacred proof of the sacrifices made by the H.A.C., and a

record of its services, are provided in the Appendices, which contain the names of those who fell in action and of those who gained honours in war. These bear some testimony to the noteworthy services rendered to King and Country in recent years by this ancient Regiment.

Some further idea of these services may be gained from the fact that in each of the two Great Wars the Company produced some four thousand officers, and sponsored four or five regiments or their equivalents.

Today we still live in a troubled world, and it is indeed fitting that units of the "oldest regiment" should continue to play their part by belonging to the Reserve Army and by training to hold themselves in readiness for mobilization in the Field Force should they be called upon in a future emergency.

At the same time it is of the utmost importance that the Company should maintain its traditional structure by choosing and introducing the best material for membership in time honoured fashion.

Major Goold Walker has more than earned the thanks of the Regiment for the valuable services he has rendered; in addition to the twenty-five years which he served so ably as Secretary of the Company, he has provided an admirable and up-to-date History of the H.A.C. which must inevitably be of great service to all students of history besides being of intense interest to all members of the Company, whether serving or veterans.

In conclusion, as Colonel-Commandant, I wish to associate myself with all who have had the great honour of serving in this famous Regiment and who will, I am convinced, wish to thank Major Goold Walker for the valuable work he has done in providing a lasting record of the History and Traditions of the H.A.C.

Alanbrooke

F. M.

INTRODUCTION TO THE SECOND EDITION

THIS is the story of a corps of citizen soldiers, the oldest serving regiment in England, probably the oldest in the world. Certainly no other active military unit in this country can boast a pedigree dating back to the days when bows and bills took pride of place as the standard weapons of English soldiers, and the primitive handgun was regarded with insular suspicion as a foreign innovation.

Famous for over a century before the formation of the senior regiments of our regular forces, the Honourable Artillery Company forms the only connecting link between the army of today and the civilian levies of medieval England, whose prowess with their national weapon made them such formidable adversaries. Indeed, it is interesting to note the analogy between the old-time archer, with his peace-time training in the art of marksmanship, and the Volunteer and Territorial soldier of yesterday. The original ideal in both cases was the same—the cultivation of a nation of marksmen as a defensive force.

The complete record of a regiment four centuries old cannot be set forth within the limits of one volume, nor is it here attempted, but a need undoubtedly exists for an up-to-date history of the Company in concise and readable form, and these requirements the author has endeavoured to meet in this outline of the principal events in a long and honourable story.

The author feels bound to acknowledge the invaluable assistance he has derived from the laborious researches of Colonel G. A. Raikes, who published his monumental history of the Company, in somewhat disconnected form, in 1879. To a narrative based on the above work much illustrative detail has been added. Most of this has been extracted from the archives of the Regiment, but interesting facts and descriptive notes have been obtained from outside sources, evidently unknown to former regimental historians.

The first edition of this book, published in 1926, has been considerably amplified in the light of more recent research. It has also been brought up to date to include an outline of the Company's service in the World War of 1939-1945.

G. G. W.

CHAPTER I

THE ORIGIN OF THE COMPANY

"THE Honourable the Artillery Company's Original is time out of mind." So wrote a worthy Clerk and Adjutant of the Regiment when George I was King, and over two hundred years have failed to produce evidence for any more definite statement of the origin of this ancient corps.

There is one date to which we can refer with absolute certainty. On 25th August, 1537, King Henry VIII granted a Charter of Incorporation to a Guild or Fraternity of Saint George, which eventually became known as the Artillery Company. It is owing to the somewhat ambiguous wording of this Charter that we are left in doubt as to whether this Guild of Saint George had, or had not, an existence prior to the above date. In the preamble, the "trusty and welbiloved Servants and Subgiettes" to whom the warrant is addressed are referred to as Overseers of the Fraternity or Guild of Saint George, as if such a Guild was already in existence and was now receiving the honour of royal support. Further on in the document the same gentlemen are made Masters and Rulers of the said "Felliship of Artillary," and they, or their successors, are authorized to "begin, found and establish a certayne perpetuall Fraternitie of Saint George" to be known as "Maisters and Rulers and Cominaltie of the Fraternitie or Guylde of Artillary of Longbowes Crosbowes and Handegonnes."

Obviously this latter clause may be read in two ways. Either the four Rulers are authorized to found an entirely new institution, in which case their titles of Overseers in the preamble are premature and confusing, or, on the other hand, it may have been intended that these four Overseers of an existing Guild of Saint George were to convert a hitherto unrecognized and unofficial body of archers into a *Perpetual* Fraternity, which was to be given official sanction, endowed with many privileges, and encouraged to admit members and to exercise in arms.

1

One shred of evidence on this important point is available. The King's Roll of Payments contains several entries between 1509 and 1515 of sums of 13s. 4d. "paid to the Fraternity of Saint George's Guild." Now Guilds of that name were not uncommon in England at that period, but, having regard to King Henry's well-known love for archery, of which he was a first-class exponent, these records may well be taken to indicate royal support of a Guild of Archers and an interest which culminated later in the Grant of a Charter.

We must leave our readers to draw their own conclusions on this debatable point with the help of the copy of the Charter which is here appended:

HENRY TH'EIGHT &c To all Judges Justics Maires Sheriffs Bailiffs Constables and other oᵉ Officers Ministres and Subgietts aswell wᵗ in the liberties as wᵗout thies our Lres heryng or seyng Gretyng We late you witt that of oᵉ grace especiall certein science and mere mocion we Have graunted and licenced And by theis Pnts Doo graunte and licence for us & oᵉ heyres asmoche as in us is unto our trusty and welbiloved Sᵉvnnts & Subgietts Sᵉ Cristofer Morres Knight Maister of oᵉ Ordenncs Anthony Knevett and Peter Mewtes Gentlemen of oᵉ Preve Chambre Overseers of the Fraternitie or Guylde of Saint George And that they and every of them shalbe Ovᵉseers of the Science of Artillary that is to witt for Longe Bowes Crosbowes and Handgonnes &c whiche Sᵉ Christofer Morres Cornelis Jhonson Anthony Antony and Henry Johnson that they and evᵉy of them shalbe Maisters and Rulers of the saide Science of Artillary as afore is rehersed for Longbowes Crosbowes and Handgonnes which Sᵉ Christofer Cornelis Anthony and Henry We by thies Pnts Doo ordeigne make and conferme Foure Maisters and Rulers of the said Felliship of Artillary for and during their lyves and that the said Maisters and Rulers and their successoᵉs Maisters and Rulers alwaies beinge foure of oᵉ Sᵉvnnts Englisshemen or Denisens maye begyn founde edifie make ordeigne gadre knytte and establisshe a certeyne Ppetuall Fraternitie of Saint George and that they maye have full pouer and auctoritie to chose accepte take and admitte into their said Fraternitie or Guylde all manᵉ honeste psons what so evᵉ they be aswell being oᵉ Sᵉvnnts and Subgietts as Strangiers Denisens or not Denisens at their liberties And that the said Maisters and Rulers and suche brethern as they shall electe admitte take and accepte to them shall in thing and name be Oon Bodye and Cominaltie Corporate having succession Ppetually by the name of Maisters and Rulers and Cominaltie of the Fraternitie or Guylde of Artillary of Longbowes Crosbowes and Handegonnes And the same Four Maisters Rulers and Brethern and their successoᵉs we incorporate and make Oon Bodye by theis Pnts and that

A Grant to the ffraternity or Guild of Artillery.

2

the saide Maisters and Rulers and Cominaltie and theyr successo^rs shall implede and be impleded by the name of Maisters and Rulers of the saide Bretherhed or Guylde And also shall have power and auctoritie to chose and electe among themselfs w^t their assistence Foure undre Maisters and Rulers of the same Fraternitie or Guylde to ov^rsee and governe the same Fraternitie from tyme to tyme and to have the gov^rnaunce and custodie of suche Lands Tents Rents Possessions Goodds and Catalls as hereaftre shall happen to be purchased bequethed given graunted or assigned by any man^r Pson or Psons to saide Fraternitie or Guylde and they ev^ry yere as it shall best pleas them shall mowe ordeigne and chose successively foure undre Maisters and Rulers Englisshmen Strangiers Denisyns or not Denisens of good name and fame And they or any of them

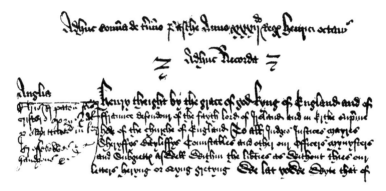

FACSIMILE (SLIGHTLY REDUCED) OF THE BEGINNING OF THE CHARTER OF 1537

if nede require to amove put out and discharge and an other in his or their name and place as ofte as shall please them to name put in electe and auctorise by the Counsaill of the Foure Maisters and Rulers and their saide Assistence AND FURTHERMORE that the same Maisters and Rulers maye have & use a Comon Seale for all things and necessaries belonging to the saide Fraternitie or Guylde And that they maye be of habilitie or capacitie in the Lawe to implede or be impleded aunswer and be aunswered before any Judge or Justice Spuall or temporall what so ev^r they be in any Co^rte or Courtes of this o^r Realme And in all and singler Accions Demaunds Quarells Plees Sutes reall or Psonall like as all other o^r Liegemen have habilitie and capacitie AND FURTHERMORE the said Maisters and Rulers and Cominaltie of the saide Fraternitie or Guylde amongs them selfs shall or maye have full auctoritie and power to make ordeigne and establisshe Lawes Ordynncs and Statutes for the good State Rule and Gov^rnaunce of the saide Fraternitie or Guilde for thencrease and good cotinuance of the same and such

Lawes Statuts and Ordynncs so made from tyme to tyme as ofte as by them shalbe thought necessary & convenient to chaunge and to transpose or kepe at their Pleas And to putt in use & execucon w^tout hurte chalenge greve or Pturbaunce of us o^r heyres or successo^{rs} Officers Ministres or subgietts or their heyres or successo^{rs} what so ev^r they be AND FURTHERMORE that the said Maister and Rulers and their successo^{rs} for the tyme beinge have full power and auctoritie to purchase Lands and Tents and other hereditaments what so ev^r they be whiche be not holden of us in Capite To HAVE AND TO HOLDE to the saide Maisters Rulers and Cominaltie and their successo^{rs} the Statute of Mortemayne or other Statute or Statuts any other thinge passed to the cotrary notw^tstanding AND FURTHERMORE of o^r habundaunt grace We have graunted given and licenced and by theis Pnts Doo give graunte and licence unto o^r forsaid welbiloved S^rvnnts and to ev^ry of them and to all and ev^ry their successo^{rs} Maisters Rulers Cominaltie and Brethern of the saide Fraternitie or Guylde that for the tyme shalbe aswell being o^r S^rvnnts and Subgietts as also Strangiers being Denisens or not Denisens being of and in the saide Fraternitie or Guylde for the better encrease of the defence of this o^r Realme and Maynetennce of the Science & Feate of Shoting in Longbowes Crosbowes and Handgonnes that they and ev^ry of their successo^{rs} honest Psons of the saide Fraternitie or Guylde for their disporte and pastyme from tyme to tyme for ev^r hereaftre and Ppetually may use and exercise the shoting in their Longbowes Crosbowes and Handgonnes at all man^r Marks and Butts and at the Game of the Popinjaye and other Game or Games as at Fowle and Fowles as well in o^r Citie of London the suburbes of the same as in all other places whersoev^r it be wthin this o^r Realme of England Ireland Calice and o^r M^rches of Walys and elleswher w^tin any of o^r Dominions Our Forrests Chaces and Pks w^tout o^r spiall warraunte and the Game of the Heyron and Fesaunt w^tin two miles of any of o^r Mano^{rs} Castelles or other places where we shall fortune to be or lye for the tyme only excepted and res^rved And also that the saide Maisters and Rulers and Brethern and their successo^{rs} and ev^ry Pticuler Pson of them maye reteigne and kepe their saide Longbowes Crosbowes and Handgonnes in their Houses Chambers and other places and their S^rvnnts to bere the same Crosbowes and Handegonnes when and as often as it shall like them at their libertie for ev^r w^tout any damage daungier penaltie losse or forfaicture to ensue unto them or any of them for the same But nevertheles the saide S^rvnnts that so shall cary their Maisters Crosbowes or Handgonnes shall not by vertue of this o^r Licence shote in the saide Crosbowes and Handgonnes at no man^r of Fowle And in case be that any suche S^rvannt be taken shoting at any Fowle w^t any Crosbowe or Handgonne the said Offender so taken to forfaicte the penaltie acco^rdinge to the Acte (this Fraternitie or Licence notw^tstondinge) And also that non other then the Fraternitie or Guylde aforesaide shall w^tin any Pte of this o^r Realme or Dominion kepe any other Bretherhed or Guylde onles it be by licence of the forsaide Maisters and Rulers of the said Fraternitie or Guyld AND FURTHERMORE of o^r more ample grace by thies Pnts we doo licence the foresaid Maisters and Rulers & Cominaltie of the saide Fraternitie or Guilde or any pticuler Pson or Psons & ev^{r}y of them to use and weare any man^r Imbrowdery or any Cognisaunce of Sylv^r at his o^r their libertie in their Gownes Jacketts Coots and Dubletts and any man^r of Sylks as Velvet Satten and Damaske the colo^{r}s of Purple and Scarlett only excepted in their Gownes and Jacketts and all and singler Furres in their Gownes or elsewhere not above Furred of Martirnes* w^{t}oute ronnying into any Man^r daungier forfaycture losse or penaltie (any Acte of Apparell or any other Acte Pclamacon thing or matier in any wise hadd made or given or to be hadd made or given to the cotrary notw^{t}standing) AND FURTHERMORE of o^r further grace especiall we have licenced And by theis Pnts doo licence the forsaid Maisters and Rulers and their saide successo^{r}s for the tyme being that they nor any of them shall from hensforthe be empanelled or copelled to be upon any man^r of Queste or Jury upon what matier soev^r it be w^{t}in o^r Citie of London or other place w^{t}in this o^r Realme And ov^r this we woll and Graunte for us o^r heyres and succeso^{r}s to the saide Maisters and Rulers and Cominaltie by theis Pnts that when and as often as the said Maisters and Rulers and Cominaltie and their successors or any of them shall use pnounce and openly speke this usuall worde comenly used to be spoken before he or they shote, that is to say this worde Faste and aftre this worde spoken if it shall happen any Pson or Prsons by the Ov^{r}sight of any Pson or Psons ronnying passing or goyng bitwen any suche Shoter and the Marke or Place wherto any suche Maisters and Rulers and Cominaltie or any of them shall hereaftre shote to be kylled or otherwise hurte So the same be a usuall and a knowne Marke sett in a open place accustomed to be shote at that then any suche Maister Ruler and Brother what so ev^r shall happen not by that occasion be attached arrested imprisoned sued vexed troubled or otherwise inquieted nor shall not be impeched nor otherwise molested or troubled for the same nor shall not suffre deathe nor lose any membre or forfeicte any man^r goods lands tents or hereditaments or any Goodds Cattells or other Proffitts for the same Any Acte Statute Proclamacion Pvision or any other Matier or thing in any wise hadd made given proclamed or provided or hereaftre to be hadd given made Pclamed or provided at any tyme to the cotrary notw^{t}stonding. AND FURTHERMORE we woll and Graunte that thies o^r Lres Pattents shall passe undre o^r Great Seale w^{t}out fyne or fee greate or small in o^r Chauncery to o^r use o^r to thuse of o^r heyres or in the Hanaper of o^r said Chauncery to be cotented or paide for the same. That expresse mention &c In Witnes &c Witness ourself at Westm^r the XXVth daye of August.

Per Bre de Privato Sigillo &c.

---

* Martens.

5

Though of official evidence of the Company's existence prior to 1537 there is none, a strong presumption of this being the case may be admitted, especially having regard to the known existence in London of bands of archers and other military bodies of similar organization for centuries before the date of our incorporation. It is noteworthy that Blackwell, writing in 1726, claims that the Artillery Company had "long before the use of Fire-arms been a Society," though he produces no evidence for his statement beyond a suggestion of records and books referring to ancient usage. Highmore, who wrote in 1804, makes no definite assertion, but offers a somewhat far-fetched conjecture as to our origin. After recording that the London Auxiliaries, "from whom in subsequent periods the Artillery Company took their rise," marched with King Alfred in the year 883 to dislodge the Danes from the town of Hertford, he adds: "In the time of William II London was infested with robbers of every description, who came forth in the evenings in gangs, and committed violent depredations; to protect both life and property against these ruffians, many of the better sort of citizens voluntarily associated themselves for the preservation of peace and good order, and the support of the civil power. The great similarity between that Association and the Company is too obvious to require the assertion of its remote antiquity."

If, then, we are to assume an earlier history, of which the authentic details have been lost in the mists of the Middle Ages, it may be of interest to glance at the scanty records of such assemblages of armed citizens as may well have included the forerunners of the Guild of Artillery.

As far back as the reign of the second Henry it was the custom of the younger citizens of London to meet together for the practice of arms, notably on Fridays in Lent, when tournaments on horseback and sham fights on the river took place. This emulation of the sports of the ruling classes appears to have provoked the derision of the nobility, for we read that, in 1253, "certain of the Court, coming with a humour of contempt and scorn to behold their exercises and giving reproachful words to those Londoners, did suffer for their derision such stripes, and wounds, that the King (Henry III) caused the citizens to pay 1,000 marks for the healing"—an early example of official discouragement applied to voluntary military training. Such arbitrary treatment could hardly have increased the King's popularity in the City, and eleven years later we find thousands of London men, headed by their own natural leaders, marching with Simon de Montfort to the battlefield of Lewes, where they were ridden down and cut to pieces by Prince Edward's mailed cavalry.

Henry III had ordered the Lord Mayor to provide a body of armed, disciplined men for the defence of the City. Such men were selected, armed and warned to muster "at the tolling of St. Paul's bell."

The same troubled reign saw the initiation of the famous "Marching Watch" in the City, a practice which was not finally discontinued until the time of Edward VI. The Watch consisted in its later days of a force of 2,000 well-armed men, clothed in white fustian, with the arms of the City on back and breast, which paraded the City streets on the vigils of St. John the Baptist and St. Peter,* bearing torches and enlivened by martial music. In 1510 Henry VIII paid a special visit to the City to see this "pompous march of the City Watch." On that occasion the Lord Mayor was attended by a giant and two pages on horseback, and the procession consisted of archers (honest persons with bows and arrows cleanly harnessed and arrayed in jackets of white with the arms of this City), pikemen, billmen, and halberdiers, with a body of demi-lances in bright armour. The pageant was lighted by 940 cressets borne aloft on poles. Eventually the Watch was discontinued on the ground of expense.

Edward I issued orders under writ of Parliament to the Lord Mayor in 1296 to send "such force as you may conveniently have" to defend the coast of Kent under the command of the Prince of Wales, and a number of citizens, well horsed and armed, performed this service. London crossbowmen were sent to defend Berwick-on-Tweed after Bannockburn, and in 1318 two hundred London men served against the Scots and were thanked by the King as "good and loyal folk." A marching watch of 200 men kept the peace of the City and four guard boats patrolled the river.

In consideration of the gallant conduct of London auxiliaries at the siege of the Castle of Leeds, in Kent, Edward II granted a special Charter exempting the City troops from service

---

* The survival of the ancient pagan feast of Midsummer Eve.

outside the City boundaries, but his successors did not always respect the terms of this arrangement. It could hardly be expected that they should.

In 1325 the City sent 140 foot soldiers to assist in the defence of Gascony, and two years later 100 City horse and 100 foot served in Scotland against Robert de Bruce. A similar force served against the Scots in 1334.

Throughout the Hundred Years War the City constantly furnished detachments of men-at-arms and archers for the King's foreign expeditions. A most interesting entry in the Memoranda Rolls records the names of the five London ships, and the numbers of men-at-arms supplied by the various wards to man them, which took part in the naval battle of Sluys (1340), in which King Edward III almost annihilated the French fleet and secured the mastery of the Channel. Another interesting entry records the names of 80 City archers, uniformed in red and white, who accompanied the King to the campaign which included the epoch-making battle of Crecy (1346).

A year before the battle of Poictiers the City presented King Edward III with the princely gift of 25 men-at-arms and 500 archers, all habited in the same uniform. This century had seen the rise to fame of the English longbow as a military weapon, and, as open spaces were required for the training of town dwellers, Finsbury and Moorfields had become the chief resort of London archers. Edward I, by the Statute of Winchester, had made it compulsory for every male between the ages of 15 and 60 to provide himself with arms according to his quality, and the bow became the standard weapon of Englishmen. The result of early and continuous training of the youth of the country in this weapon showed itself in the victories of Edward III against the French, which were almost entirely attributable to the excellence of our archery. Nevertheless it was found necessary, as early as 1363, to issue a proclamation in the City to the effect that all men strong in body should exercise the art of shooting in their leisure time and on holidays, and forbidding, under pain of imprisonment, the games of handball, football, bandyball, cambuch or cockfighting, "or suchlike vain plays, which had no profit in them."

However averse they may have been to training in peace time, the men of London were not backward when the time came for action. It was in 1359 that the French raided the coast of Sussex and burned and plundered several towns. The citizens of London, in conjunction with the men of the southern ports, fitted out a fleet of 160 sail, embarked no less than 14,000 men, and, landing on the French coast, ravaged and burnt the country at pleasure.

A pitched battle was fought in the City in 1450, when the Londoners held London Bridge against Jack Cade's rebellious Kentishmen.

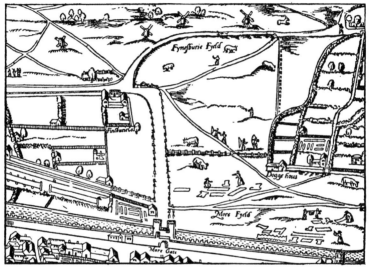

[*From the map of Ralph Agas*

FINSBURY FIELDS, *circa* 1560 TO 1570

Showing the site of the present Artillery Ground in the north-west corner of the map, between the haystack and the windmill

Throughout the Wars of the Roses, London was predominantly Yorkist. The Londoners besieged a party of Lancastrians in the Tower and forced their surrender; they held the City gates against Queen Margaret's victorious troops after the second battle of St. Albans; they fought a successful battle in the City against an attack by Lancastrians in 1471; and a body of London archers and billmen fought under Edward IV at Barnet.

In the time of Henry VII archery was on the decline and

9

from 1487 onwards a number of Acts were passed for its encouragement, with apparently little success. An Act of 1512 ordered that the Statute of Winchester should be put into execution. Every man under 60 (except the clergy, justices and judges) had always to keep and use bow and arrows; every boy had to be instructed in archery from the age of seven; butts were to be kept in repair and used on holidays. A similar Act in 1514 sought to put a stop to tennis-play and bowls, "which only lead to murders and robberies." Many of the citizens of London, however, appear to have been keen archers and jealous of the ancient rights to their shooting grounds. We learn that, in 1498, the gardens and orchards to the north of Chiswell Street were levelled and turned once more into archery fields. Again, in 1514, when the villagers of Islington, Hoxton and Shoreditch not only enclosed portions of the shooting grounds, but made a practice of forcibly seizing and destroying the bows and arrows of archers practising in their neighbourhood, something very like a riot took place. The Londoners were led by a tanner "clad in a Merry Andrew's coat," who ran up and down the city streets shouting "Spades and Shovels." The cry was understood. Citizens assembled to the number of several thousands and levelled every hedge and bank and ditch which encroached upon their archery fields.

The Wars of the Roses had seen the introduction of the handgun into England. The weapon which was to oust the English longbow was first used in this country in war by Burgundian mercenaries, but their slow and inaccurate fire excited only the derision of the English archers, and nothing further is heard of the handgun in England until 1515, when an Act of Henry VIII takes exception to its use against the King's deer, but allows such weapons to be kept for defence in all walled towns within seven miles of the sea.

We read of a meeting of archers in Finsbury Fields in 1520, and of a general muster of citizens (in white apparel, with caps and feathers of the same) in 1532. On this latter occasion the Lord Mayor was attended by "sixteen portly men, with long gilt Halberds." They mustered at Mile End and marched through the City to Westminster.

CHAPTER II

1537 TO 1601

THE suppression of the monasteries by Henry VIII had caused considerable unrest in various parts of the country, especially in the north, where a serious insurrection, known as the Pilgrimage of Grace, caused no little apprehension in Court circles. Eventually the rebellion was suppressed and the usual executions followed, but a general feeling of alarm and discontent prevailed. It was with the country in this unsettled condition that King Henry, who placed great reliance on the support of the City of London, set his seal to the Charter which incorporated for all time the Guild or Fraternity of Artillery, for the better defence of the realm by the maintenance of "the Science and Feate of Shootinge" with longbow, crossbow and handgun.

The King was not ill advised. It must be remembered that the London levies were at that time, with the exception of the King's personal bodyguard, the most efficient troops in the kingdom, and it is hardly surprising that the shrewd and soldierly monarch saw fit to bestow rights and privileges on a body of citizens which probably included, as was invariably the case in later days, the majority of the officers of the City forces, and which would, by its constitution, provide a training school for their successors.

At the time of the incorporation members of the Guild were men of substance. This is evidenced by the privilege accorded them of wearing silk and velvet, furs and embroideries. They were evidently recruited from the wealthier citizen class. Sir Christopher Morres, the first-mentioned of the four Masters and Rulers, was Master of the Ordnance and a person of considerable standing at Court. His chief function was to visit and report upon the defences of castles, such as Berwick, Carlisle and Calais. He had served at Flodden (1513), and at Morlaix in 1522 he blew in the gate and headed the stormers. Next he distinguished himself in an attack on Edinburgh in

11

1544. He was "hurt on the Brest with a Handgon" at the siege of Boulogne in 1544, but, as recorded in a Cotton MS., "he demeaned himself very valyauntly before, and killed all the Master Gonners at Bulloin." He died of his wounds and was buried in St. Peter's, Cornhill. Anthony Knevett and Peter Mewtes, also mentioned in the Charter, were Gentlemen of the Privy Chamber to Henry VIII. Mewtes was afterwards Governor of Guernsey and was killed in the defence of Calais. Thus the Court was well represented among the leaders of the Guild, and we may be sure that all the honest persons, "subgietts and strangiers, denisens or not denisens," who were admitted brethren of the Guild, were chosen as being "well affected to the King and Constitution of this Country," to use the phrase which survives to the present day in the oath administered to recruits on joining the Regiment.

It is an irreparable loss to the Company and to military historians generally that no regimental records exist of these early times and that in general we have to be content with a rehearsal of casual episodes gleaned from other sources. But by a stroke of marvellous good fortune the Company has in recent years been able to acquire a document of unique regimental importance, nothing less than the original lease of the Old Artillery Ground in Bishopsgate, granted to the Company by William, Prior of the Convent and Hospital of St. Mary Without Bishopsgate, on 3rd January, 1538, barely five months after the incorporation of the Company.

The MS. now in the possession of the Regiment is the counterpart lease which remained with the Convent and thus bears the common seal of the Company. Unfortunately, only about a quarter of this seal is intact, but sufficient remains to show on one side the royal arms of Henry VIII (the lions of England quartering the lilies of France, with a wyvern or griffin as one of the supporters). The obverse is still more interesting—a shield bearing a cross of St. George, in the centre of which a portion of a lion passant can be discerned, thus proving the existence of the Company's coat of arms at that early date. Prior to this discovery the use of our coat of arms could be traced only as far back as 1629, when it was used as the frontispiece of a military work. From the shape and size of the seal it is probable that the coat of arms then consisted simply of the lion of England on a cross of St. George, and that the feathers and portcullis on a blue chief were added at a later date as an "augmentation of honour."

The opportunity to acquire this valuable historical document arose through the dispersal of the archives of Lord St. John of Bletso, one of whose ancestors married an heiress of the Vaughan family, on whose progenitors King Henry VIII had bestowed the land and Convent of St. Mary after the dissolution of this religious foundation.

In the lease the Company is referred to by its Charter title of "Maysters Rulers and comynaltie of the Fraternitye or Guylde of Artyllary of longbowes Crossebowes and handegonnes," and the ground was let for three consecutive terms each of 99 years, at a yearly rental of twenty shillings, with a fine of forty shillings if the rent remained in arrear for three months. The Company continued to pay this rent until 1659.

On 8th of May, 1539, the citizens of London mustered in force at six o'clock in the morning in the fields from Whitechapel to Mile End and from Bethnal Green to Stepney. After being inspected to see that each man had a sword and dagger and that all were "clenely hosed and shodde" in white, 15,000 picked men entered the City at Aldgate and marched to Westminster, where they were reviewed by the King, and returned by way of St. James's Park, Holborn and Chepe. Pieces of cannon in gun-carts headed the procession, with powder and "gun-stones" (stone cannon-balls) in carts behind them. Then followed hand-gunners, bowmen, pikemen and billmen. As the musketeers passed the King they saluted him with volleys, and the great guns were drawn up and "shotte very terribly in divers places and especially before the King."

We read that the men of substance, who of course included the Guild of Artillery, "garnished their bassinets with turbes of silk set with brooches, onches and feathers." They also had breastplates decorated with silver bullion and chains of gold about their necks. Some had their poleaxes gilded. The "meaner sorte" wore coats of white cotton with the arms of the City on back and front, and "such as were not meet to be archers were turned to pikes." Every man wore splint armour under his white surcoat and a steel "scull" beneath his cap. The Wyfflers, or marshals, had feathers in their caps and chains about their necks, both they and the "Droumslades," or drumbeaters, being dressed in white, puffed out with crimson sarcenet. This review

13

was intended to impress the ambassadors of certain foreign powers, having regard to rumoured schemes of invasion, and it had its effect.

A brief passage which possibly refers to this old Company occurs in a military work published by Humphrey Barwick in 1594. Speaking of himself, he says: "And for that I entered to be a Souldier at the age of 18 yeeres, which was the second yeere of that good and godly King Edward the 6 (1548), at which time our English Archers were in force and greatly used, and Harquebuziers not as then common. For the first that ever had any whole band in England was Sir Peeter Mewtes, Knight, who had as I doo remember the charge of 500 halfe Hakes (hackbuts)." Sir Peter was the second Master or Ruler of the Guild of Artillery, the first body in England to receive official encouragement in the use of the handgun; it is therefore not beyond the bounds of probability that they were the 500 hackbutmen referred to above.

In 1554 Queen Mary issued a summons to the City for 100 "warlike men," of whom 40 at least were to be archers, to be ready to embark at Woolwich for Calais. The City Fathers unsuccessfully protested against this order as being contrary to the franchise granted to the City "by Her Majesty's noble progenitors." Again, three years later, the Queen ordered the City to furnish 1,000 able men, well armed and weaponed, horsemen, pikemen, "hagbutters," and archers, "with Captaines meet for the ordinance and conducting of the same." Doubtless the Guild of Artillery provided such Captains. These troops, uniformed in white coats, welted with green, with red crosses, formed part of the force of 7,000 English who, with their Spanish allies, defeated the French at St. Quentin in 1557.

Archery meetings still appear to have been of frequent occurrence throughout this reign. The records of Guildhall contain an interesting "Proclamacon for Shootinge in Ffynnesburye Ffelde, by the Maier," dated 1557. After calling upon every true Englishman to support and uphold the "feate of Showtinge" to the best of his power, it laid down that "he who will come thither and take a longe bowe in his hand, and fairest draweth, clensiest delivreth and farthest of grounde shootithe, shall have for the best Game a Crowne of golde." The Crown was valued at 13s. 4d. We also learn that no person was allowed to stand within 20 yards of the marks and that a trumpet was blown between each shot as a warning. There was another gallant muster of the men of the City Companies at Greenwich in 1559, when 800 pikemen "in fair corselets," 400 hacquebuts in shirts of mail, and 200 halberdiers "in almanrinets" passed in battle array before Queen Mary and the French Ambassador. It was from a body of 3,000 picked London troops, assembled at Greenwich before Queen Elizabeth on 1st May, 1572, that Captain Thomas Morgan levied "a faire company of three hundred strong," with which he proceeded immediately to the assistance of the Dutch in the Low Countries, thus forming the nucleus of considerable numbers of troops which went from England to serve against the Spaniards in that country. Their successors remained in the Dutch service until the outbreak of war between England and Holland in 1665, when they refused to serve against their mother country and were disbanded, forfeiting arrears of pay. Whereupon King Charles II took them into the English service as the Holland Regiment, which still enjoys an honoured place in the Army List as The Buffs (Royal East Kent Regiment).

The Buffs cherish their tradition of descent from the London Trained Bands, and it has become a custom for their new Colours to be presented on the Artillery Ground.

In 1578 all training in the City was suspended on account of the Plague, but was resumed by edict of the Privy Council in 1580.

During the next few years several bodies of London troops were mustered for service in Ireland under Sir Walter Raleigh and others, and in 1585 the Queen wrote to the City: "Whereas not long since we willed our pleasure unto you for the putting in order of 2,000 armed pikes and 2,000 shot *to be sorted into bands* under Captains. These shall be to authorize you to make the said levy." It is from this date that the expression "Trained Bands" came into use.

London troops sent to assist the Dutch in August of this year were dressed in red coats, "bearing the badge of the Queen of England," presumably the Tudor Rose and Crown.

From the period of the Charter onwards, the Guild of Artillery had its headquarters in the Teasel Ground, or Old Artillery Garden, off Bishopsgate. This enclosure, which is supposed to have been the site of the old Roman "Campus Martius," appears to have been used concurrently by the

Gunners of the Tower for the practice of great and small artillery. These Gunners of the Tower, under the leadership of the Master Gunner of England, taught the science of gunnery, "levelling brass pieces of great Artillary against a Butt of earth." Their pupils had to take a solemn oath neither to serve any foreign prince, nor teach their art to any alien. It was here that gunners were trained for service with the fleet, and, in 1581, the

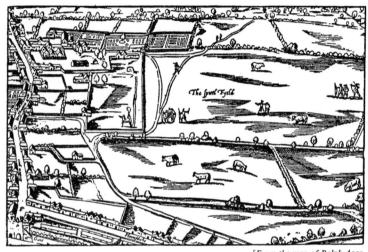

[*From the map of Ralph Agas*

THE OLD ARTILLERY GARDEN, *circa* 1560 TO 1570

Note the two members firing at a butt in the garden, and the archers practising
in the adjoining fields

Master Gunner petitioned Queen Elizabeth for authority to send deputies to the principal seaport towns to train men in the knowledge and science of great ordnance. It is to this circumstance that we owe the once prevalent tradition that members of the Company served as gunners with the fleet and so assisted directly in the defeat of the Spanish Armada. This was not the case. These men were trained by the Gunners of the Tower, while our Company at that time and for centuries afterwards concerned itself exclusively with "small artillery," namely, the longbow, crossbow, handgun or musket. We shall see later how the conflicting claims of the Gunners and the Artillery Company for the use of the Old Ground led to the removal of the Company to its present Headquarters in Finsbury.

Archery was still a popular amusement as well as a department of military training. We hear of 3,000 London archers assembling at Hodgson's Field, in Shoreditch, in 1583. The archers wore green ribbons and sashes, and the victors in the competitions were led off the field mounted on horses and attended by 200 torchbearers. Popular opinion still favoured the longbow as compared with the new-fangled firearm, and with some reason, for, as late as the year 1549, in the reign of Edward VI, the arrows of the rebellious Norfolk peasantry under Ket the tanner had driven from the field the German hackbutmen sent against them, no doubt to the secret joy of all true Englishmen.

An interesting account survives of the funeral procession at the burial of Sir Philip Sidney in January, 1587. A contemporary manuscript, "The Roll of Thomas Lant," not only describes the "Cyttizins of London Practised in Armes, about 300, who marched 3 by 3," but illustrates the actual funeral postures of the "muskiters," with rest and slow match trailing on the ground. The Captain marched first with a partisan, point to the ground. Then came the Lieutenant and three "targiters" (sword and target men), in pinked breeches. After them followed the "Muskiters 4 rancks, drums and fyfs, small shott 20 rancks, pykes 20 rancks, halberts 4 rancks," etc. The "small shott" were the caliver men, armed with a lighter piece than the heavy musket, which latter weapon required the use of a rest in firing. The men march with arms reversed and are not in step, which was possibly a funeral custom.

There can be no doubt that it is the Artillery Company which is here described. The name of "Guild of Artillery" had been definitely dropped by that time, that of "Artillery Company" had not yet become official, and our members were invariably referred to by such titles as "The Society of Citizens of London practising Arms," "The Company exercising Arms in the Artillery Garden," and similar titles. The number, 300, also tallies with other records, as we shall now proceed to prove.

John Stow, the great historian of London, writing in 1598, makes the following statement: "During the long reign of Elizabeth, the City having been greatly troubled, and charged with continual musters and trainings of soldiers, many gallant,

17

active and forward citizens, who had had experience, both at home and abroad, voluntarily enrolled themselves in the (Artillery) Company in 1585, and trained up others for the wars, so that *within the space of two years* there were about *three hundred* merchants, and others of like quality, very sufficient and skilful, to train and teach common soldiers the management of their pieces, pikes and halberds; to march, countermarch and ring; who, for their perfecting in military affairs and discipline, met every Thursday in the year, practising all usual points of war, and each man, by turns, bare office, from the Corporal to the Captain." The coincidence of the numbers in that particular year (1587) should be sufficient to prove the identity of this body of "Cittyzens practising Armes" with the body of gallant, active and forward citizens referred to by a contemporary historian as forming the body which later became known as the Artillery Company.

And now we come to an important epoch in the early history of the Company—the year of the Great Armada.

Facts, again, are scanty. Stow has placed it on record that our members "in the dangerous year 1588, had charge of men in the great camp at Tilbury, and were generally called Captains of the Artillery Garden." Maitland, writing in 1739, states that divers citizens of London, members of the Artillery Company, were chosen from it, and, to their great honour, were appointed, by order of the Queen in Council, to the rank of officers in several parts of the kingdom, and that it was by their care and indefatigable application that the Trained Bands in most parts of the country were put into a good state for defence.

The City Trained Bands of 1588 were organized in four regiments, the East, West, North and South, each comprising ten companies of 150 men (each Ward providing one or two complete companies). A MS. roll, with the names of officers and a description of the various ensigns, survives.

The camp at Tilbury was commanded by the Earl of Leicester, the Queen's favourite, who had with him John Norris, the most brilliant English soldier of his day, and other leaders experienced in war. In spite of this, the general conditions appear to have been chaotic, so much so that the veteran Norris wondered that he "could see no man in England afeard but himself." To one who was able to compare from personal knowledge our hastily raised levies with Parma's Spanish veterans, the situation must

THE ARTILLERY COMPANY ("CYTTIZINS OF LONDON PRACTISED IN ARMES, ABOUT 300, WHO MARCHED BY THREE & 3") AT THE FUNERAL OF SIR PHILIP SIDNEY, JANUARY, 1587

From the Roll of Thomas Lant at the College of Arms

19

MONUMENT IN THE CHURCH OF ST. HELEN'S, BISHOPSGATE, TO CAPTAIN MARTIN BOND, A "CAPTAIN OF THE ARTILLERY GARDEN," WHO SERVED AT TILBURY CAMP AS CAPTAIN OF THE ALDERSGATE WARD COMPANY IN THE NORTH REGIMENT OF LONDON TRAINED BANDS

have appeared serious enough, but his feelings were not shared by his men. Stow records with evident pleasure how the English troops marched into camp "with cheerful countenances, courageous words and gestures, leaping and dancing." The Englishman's incurable optimism and self-confidence on the outbreak of war was evidently as strong in those days as it showed itself in 1914. It was possibly as well that Leicester's force was not called upon for action. Fortescue, in his admirable *History of the British Army*, sums up the situation in one pithy sentence: "Ammunition was short, provisions were scanty, organization was extremely defective, and the general confusion incredible."

The City of London had furnished no less than 10,000 men "for the defence of the City and the Queen's person." They were officered mainly by members of the Artillery Garden and were admittedly the best disciplined of all the Trained Bands. After all, the blame for faulty organization and lack of supplies was none of theirs. Censure must rest where it is due, and the year 1588 provides a notable instance of typical English lack of preparedness for war, aggravated by the well-known parsimony of Good Queen Bess in military matters. The hasty assemblage at Tilbury may have been sadly lacking in military efficiency, but none can cast a sneer at those "forward citizens" who had prepared in time of peace to be the leaders of their fellow citizens when need should arise.

Little is known of those worthy members of the old Company who served at Tilbury. A list of officers of Trained Bands, with the strength of the various levies, survives, but as no regimental roll exists for that period, it is impossible to say whether all or most of these individuals were the Captains of the Artillery Garden, or not. But in the church of St. Helen's, Bishopsgate, there is a monument to one Sir Martin Bond, who was a "Captaine in ye yeere 1588 at ye Camp at Tilbury," and was afterwards President of the Company from 1616 to 1618.

The land forces did not, of course, see action, but the response of the City to the national emergency did not end with the mustering of the Trained Bands. In the Calendar of State Papers may be found a list of thirty "Ships sent forth and paid upon the charge of the City of London."

Twenty of these are recorded as "now at sea under the Lord High Admiral" on 19th July, 1588, and the State Papers also mention seven merchant ships from London at Harwich with the fleet which had the duty of blockading the coast of Flanders, where the Duke of Parma's army awaited the Armada. These seven ships eventually joined the main fleet and took part in the action of the fire-ships in Calais Roads and the subsequent chase up the North Sea.

Unfortunately, no record appears to exist of the number or names of the London soldiers who served at sea, but there must have been a complement of soldiers on each ship, and these would undoubtedly have been provided by the Trained Bands. A contemporary MS., describing a brisk action in the Channel in which the twenty London ships obviously took part, states: "The XXIII of ye same month the Spaniardes having a favourable north wind, turned sayles upon the English, the English being much readier in ye use of their shippes, sett about a compasse for ye wind; and having gotten advantage of ye wind, they came to fight on both sides. They fought a while confusedly with variable successe; whilst on ye one side the English with great courage delivered the London ships which were inclosed about by the Spaniardes."

The London soldiers who undoubtedly took part in this sea-fight must have been officered by Gentlemen of the Artillery Garden, and the suggestion that the engagement became a regimental tradition of the Company is supported by the fact that it once possessed a set of paintings depicting "The Story of the Fight, Anno 1588," which was unfortunately lost in the Civil War.

In January, 1589, soldiers and sailors were levied in London for service under Sir Francis Drake and Sir John Norris. This was the successful expedition which sacked Corunna and carried out a foray into Portugal.

After the defeat of the Spanish Armada the usual period of post-war slackness appears to have set in. It provided the occasion for the first Order in Council relating to the Company, which ran as follows:

At the Court at Whitehall, the 20th of Novembr, 1591.

PRESENT:

L. Treasorer	Mr. Vice Chamberlaine
L. Admyrall	Sir Robert Cecill
L. Chamberlaine	Mr. Wolley
Mr. Treasorer	Mr. Fortescue

A lre to the L. Maio^r of London and his Brethren. Requyring them that whereas the Artillery Yarde belonginge to the Cittie beinge erected for the trayninge of yonge gent in London firste broughte in by Mr Captⁿ Allen Lewis* servante to the L. Chancellor hathe bin of late discontynued: that the same maie forthwith upon the receipte hereof be renewed beinge a matter verie requisete and necessarie for ye benefitte of the comon weale &c."

Training appears to have been renewed.

Early in 1593 the Queen informed the Lord Mayor of the necessity for sending armed men to assist the forces in Normandy and ordered 350 men, three parts pikemen and the rest musketeers, to be chosen out of the Trained Bands and shipped to Dieppe under four Captains to be appointed by the Privy Council. Another Royal Warrant in January, 1594, levied 300 men to serve in the Low Countries.

Seven City ships served in the expedition under Sir John Norris which helped to capture the harbour of Brest from the Spaniards, 300 London troops embarking at London for this purpose. In the following year one of these ships, the *Susan Bonaventure* of 300 tons, took part in what proved to be the last voyage of Sir Francis Drake.

Four years later a further Order in Council pronounced the final doom of the longbow, which still formed the weapon of a proportion of the general levy of citizens, and ordered all bows to be exchanged for muskets and calivers. This marks the practical disappearance of the longbow from the English army, though crossbows were used as late as 1627 during the disastrous expedition under Buckingham to the Isle of Rhée, and bodies of archers were actually raised for service during the Civil War.

A letter from the Lords in Council, dated 31st October, 1596, directed the City of London to provide 3,000 men, to be led by some of the principal gentlemen of the City, for the defence of the coasts of Kent and Essex against a threatened Spanish invasion. The Lord Mayor protested, on the ground that the citizens were very dissatisfied already at the lack of profit from their investment of £19,000 in the recent successful expedition to Cadiz. The Council replied to the effect that, as the chief city in the land and by far the wealthiest, London should raise 10,000 men, as they did in 1588, for the defence of the coast.

---

* Captain Allen Lewis is named in the Roll of Thomas Lant as the Lieutenant of the "Cyttizens of London" at the funeral of Sir Philip Sidney.

At some period between 1588 and 1599 the London Trained Bands appear to have reverted to their original organization of Ward Companies of varying strength. The designs of their ensigns also underwent considerable alteration.

The Company of Citizens practising Arms in the Artillery Garden, as the old Guild of Artillery was now generally styled, continued to thrive. Many of the nobility, the Lord Mayor, most of the Aldermen, and all the officers of the Trained Bands exercised arms with the Company, which consisted in 1598 of 600 members. There is therefore little doubt that some of them saw foreign service, not for the first time, when, in 1601, a Royal Warrant levied 500 men from the London Trained Bands for service in Ireland on account of the invasion of that country by a Spanish force. The expedition embarked at Bristol in January of that year, but of its adventures we know nothing. It probably formed part of the reinforcement of 2,000 men which enabled Sir George Carew to hold the town of Cork, and, later, to assist in the final defeat of the invaders. It is interesting to note that brightly coloured uniforms had been found unsuitable for the irregular warfare of Irish campaigns, so that troops for service in that country were equipped with cassocks and cloaks of "russet, motley, or sadd grene coller"—a curious anticipation of protective colouring in uniform.

The London Trained Bands were also embodied for service in the City during the abortive rebellion of the Earl of Essex in the same year. A record exists that the City Captains and their officers received a gratuity of £200 for their services during that period. Sheriff Thomas Smyth, who, as the Captain, led the "Cyttizens of London" in the funeral of Sir Philip Sidney, was arrested for complicity in this insurrection, but was finally acquitted of treason.

CHAPTER III

1602 TO 1641

DURING the first decade of the seventeenth century little or nothing remains to be recorded of the Company's existence. There was certainly a standstill in military activity; the Company may even have been temporarily dissolved. Even so, it was not for long. Stow mentions that, in the year 1610, one Philip Hudson, with Thomas Laverock, Robert Hughes, Samuel Artois, Robert Greenhurst and others, took active measures to revive the military exercises which had been neglected for years past. This statement is borne out by the Great Vellum Book still in the possession of the Regiment, which dates from the following year. The first page is headed "A Book of such Gentlemen as have been admitted into the Artillerie Garden, London, since ye 15th Aug. 1611"; the first name enrolled is that of Philip Hudson, and the names of the remaining four mentioned by Stow all occur on the first page.

Maitland states that "all danger from the Spanish fleet having passed away, the laudable practice of instructing the citizens in the Art Military was discontinued till the year 1610, when it was revived and with it the ancient appellation of the Artillery Company." Now we have no record as to when the designation of "Guild of Artillery" gave place to the loosely applied titles of "Citizens of London practising Arms" or "Captains of the Artillery Garden"; neither is there any proof of when this alleged "ancient appellation of the Artillery Company" came into use. It is noteworthy that this title is not used at the beginning of the Old Vellum Book, which, though the Roll is dated from 1611, was not "drawne forth" till 1635. Moreover, the actual words "Artillery Company" do not appear in any of the Royal Warrants or Orders in Council, or in any other writings as applied to the Company, until 1656.

Some of the interesting variations in nomenclature applied to the Company in its earlier days are here appended:

Date	Authority	Designation
1537	Royal Charter	"Maisters and Rulers and Cominaltie of the Fraternitie or Guylde of Artillary of Longbowes, Crosbowes and Handegonnes."
1538	Lease of the Old Artillery Ground	Ditto
1544	Accounts of Roger Highme, Collector of the Rents to King Henry VIII	"Master & Governors of the Gunners."
1550	Letters Patent of King Edward VI	"Masters, Governors, Commonalty, Fraternity or Guild of the Mystery of Long-bows, Cross-bows, and hand-guns."
1551	Augmentation Office Accounts	"Master & Governors of the Gunners."
1587	Roll of Thomas Lant	"Cyttizens of London practised in Armes."
1588	John Stow	"Captaines of the Artillery Garden."
1612	Order in Council	"Companie of Cittizens of the Military Yarde."
1613	Court of Aldermen	"Societie practising Armes in the Artillery Garden."
1616	Order in Council	"Societie of Armes, Cittizens of London." "Society in Martiall Exercises."
1616	Court of Aldermen	"Societie of Cittizens of London practizinge Armes and military discipline."
1616	Richard Niccols	"London's Artillery." "London's Hopefull Infantrie."
1617	Sermon by Thomas Adams ...	"Societie of Armes practising in the Artillerie Garden."
1622	Order in Council	"Divers Cittizens of London exercising Armes in the Teazel Ground, or Artillery Garden."
1623	Sermon by Thos. Sutton, D.D.	"Gentlemen of the Artillery Garden."
1629	John Bingham	"Martiall Company exercising Arms in the Artillery Ground."
1632	Order in Council	"Companie of the Artillery Yarde." "Company of the Artillery Gardens."
1632	Royal Warrant	"Voluntary Company of the Artillery Garden."
1634	Order in Council	"Companie of the Artillery Garden."
1634	Secretary of State	"Military Company of the City of London."
1639	William Barriffe	"Gentlemen of the Artillery Garden."
1647	William Barriffe	"Ancient and Worthy Society exercising Armes in the Artillery Garden."
1656	Regimental Records	"Artillery Company."
1668	Richard Elton	"Ancient and Honourable Artillery Company of London."

A perusal of these somewhat cumbrous designations, of which there are many more slight variations, would appear to indicate that the Company possessed no fixed official title for a period of over eighty years. But there is reason to believe that the Company had been popularly known as "The Artillery Company" for some time prior to 1616. Richard Niccols, writing in that year, gives his work the title of *London's Artillery, briefly containing the noble practise of that worthy Society*. It is dedicated to "The Right Worshipfull Favourers of Arts and Followers of Armes, the Captaines of the late Musters and to the rest of the Societie of London's hopefull Infantrie." In the preface Niccols apologizes for the use of the title "London's Artillery," on the ground that "it is an impropriety of speech, not communicable to those of this praise worthie Societie," and explains that he is constrained to impose this term upon them "both because by the ignorant vulgar they are generally so called, and the French word Infantrie would be scarce intelligible to any common Reader." We may therefore consider it a matter for certainty that the designation "Artillery Company" was originally the popular rendering of the high-sounding titles then in use, and that the name bestowed on our regiment by the "ignorant vulgar" outlived all others and was adopted officially on the revival of the Company after the Civil War.

Of course, the word Artillery in the Company's title had originally no connection with guns or gunnery. It is used in its obsolete sense, meaning any missile weapon; *vide* I Samuel xx. 40: "And Jonathan gave his artillery unto his lad, and said unto him, Go, carry them to the city." The word came to be used of all "weapons of volley," such as crossbows and muskets. Barriffe's training manual, the first edition of which appeared in 1635, is called *Military Discipline, or The Young Artilleryman*, but is entirely concerned with the exercising of infantry soldiers armed with musket and pike. Our Company did not train its members as gunners until 1781, and there is no doubt that, had "the French word Infantrie" arrived in our language a little earlier, our regiment would be known to this day as the Honourable Infantry Company.

Having enrolled about seventy members in 1611, the Company in the following year made formal application to the Privy Council for permission to exercise Arms and practise Military Discipline in the Artillery Garden. Their Lordships, finding the objects of the Society commendable and worthy, and having

27

information that the petitioners generally were men of good means and otherwise well affected, "saw noe inconvenience but that said Companie of Citizens may trayne and practize Armes," but limited their numbers to 250. A weekly exercise "after the modern and best fashion and instruction" was instituted, and the numbers of the Company increased rapidly. Each new member had to be a citizen of London and approved by the Lord Mayor, who had also a final voice in the choice of officers. Captain Edward Panton was appointed Leader, and, in the following year the Court of Aldermen elected Richard Morris as Captain of the Company, and Philip Hudson as Lieutenant. This Court not only selected the officers of the Company, but paid the Leader his salary of £40 a year and gave a "free gift" of twenty marks each per annum to the Captain and Lieutenant, "for their care and pains taken with the Society."

The Military Company of Westminster was formed in 1611 under the patronage of Henry, Prince of Wales, eldest son of James I. Its original ground was in Tothill Street, but in 1635 the Company acquired land in Leicester Fields and in 1677 moved to St. Clement's Fields. As the Military Company of St. Clement's they were still flourishing in 1721. After that they disappear.

In December, 1612, the Company applied for the use of Armourer's Hall for their feasts and assemblies. This was granted at a yearly rental of £3 6s. 8d., the Company providing their own brass, pewter, spits, linen and plate.

By 1614 the numbers of the Company had increased to such an extent that there was a waiting list of "divers of the better sort of citizens of the best means and quality." The Privy Council was thereupon approached and gave its sanction to an increase of the establishment to 500, providing that none were admitted but such as were known to be of good means, well affected in religion and to His Majesty, and approved by the Court of Aldermen, who were also directed to establish good rules for the government of the Company. We have it on the authority of Stow that the Company was now grown great and in good estimation. Not only Prince Charles, but also many country gentlemen of all shires resorted to the Artillery Garden and diligently observed their exercises, which they saw were excellent; and, returning home to their own counties, practised and used the same with their trained bands. This statement is borne out by entries in the roll of members such as "William Lemmon, High Sheer* of Herefordsheere," "Thomas Skriven, Deputie Leiftennant for Salopp and Herreford and Collonell of a Regiment in the same Counties," etc.

Among the "rank and file" of the Company in the earlier years of the seventeenth century were Augustine Phillips (1614), a fellow actor with Shakespeare, and Simon Wadlowe (1612), keeper of The Devil Tavern in Fleet Street and friend of Ben Jonson, who refers to him as the "Prince of Skinkers" (tapsters).

We read in Strype's revision (1720) of Stow's Survey of London that "In the year 1614, there was a great Muster of the City, the King having appointed after Harvest a general muster all *England* over; which every Shire performed with much cheerfulness. Then did the Citizens also shew themselves very forward, as well in making new Provisions of Ammunition, as in practising all Points of War and Military Discipline; and, for the well Managing of this Muster, the Lord-Mayor and Commonalty appointed twenty Captains to be selected of the most active and able Citizens; and unto every of them he allotted 300 Shot and Pikes, *viz*, 6,000 in all for that Time, being for the most part Householders, bravely furnished—These twenty Captains performed all Things with such Expedition, Bounty and Bravery, as, except in the year 88, the like was never before; and such of them as were not formerly of the Martial Society, and Practice of the Artillery Garden, were then admitted."

This extract appears to refer to the fact that the Privy Council ordered a general muster of the Forces of the City in November, 1614, and laid down that all trained men who had served in the late reign were to be formed into companies, and any vacancies completed from householders and responsible persons. These orders having been presumably carried out, great musters were held on 8th August and 27th September in the following year. We are indebted to Richard Niccols, an accomplished writer and minor poet of the period, for a picturesque description of what must have been, on each occasion, a very martial sight. At the first muster 26 wards were represented, each "foot-band" marching under its own banner. The soldiers, "decked in bright arms," were "both for service and shew, well

---

* Sheriff.

and rightly appointed, imitating the old Romans in their garnish of feathers," which is stated, on the authority of Machiavelli's *Art of War*, to provide at once a sight "brave and terrible to the enemie, as it is goodly and delightful to friends." A magnificent sham fight took place, troop charging troop, the "strong pikes shaking with eagar ire," and the "wings of shot" delivering such thunderous volleys that men lost themselves in the smoke thereof, while scared spectators fled or lay grovelling on the ground in terror at the noise, which was heard as far as Waltham Abbey.

The review of 27th September was attended by Prince Charles, who is referred to in the poem as "that Diamond spark of royaltie, that bud of hope, Prince of great Brittannie." As the troops marched past, the masses of steel-tipped pikes waved like a cornfield, in which scarlet plumes showed up like poppies; the Captains "shone in rich gold"; and the "red, streaming crosses" of Saint George blazed above the smoke of the vollies "like bloody comets through a sable cloud." The proceedings terminated with "chearful shouts" in honour of the Prince, who sat his horse "with martiall staffe upon his princely thigh." Apart from his appreciation of the goodly scene, Niccols has his criticisms to offer. He says: "In their demeanour I noted these two defects, ignorance of order, and neglect of their Captaine's command"; and concludes that, on the whole, the troops were "more rash and turbulent, than discreet and well advised, and less instructed and trained than well furnished and appointed."

In 1616 the Privy Council ordered that the City Bands should be reorganized in four regiments of five companies each, with the Lord Mayor as their General. This was done and the regiments once more became known as the East, West, North and South Regiments respectively. A list of officers survives, and the name of every one of them can be traced in our regimental roll as a member of the Company. From this date onwards the Trained Bands appear to have been mustered for training at least once a year, as well as on special occasions.

Thomas Dekker, one of the lesser-known playwrights of the early seventeenth century, published in 1616 "The Artillery Garden, a Poem dedicated to the Honour of all those Gentlemen who (There) practize Military Discipline—*Arma viresque cano*." Only one copy is known to exist. Before the war it was in the library at Dusseldorf. The writer has seen a photostat copy.

The poem, somewhat ponderously, "consecrates to memory the worth both of Men and Military Exercises now practised in the Artillery Garden" in the following words:

> Against the day of Fight, they learne to Fight,
> And in their brave Artillery more delight,
> Than feasts or triumphes . . .
> Five hundred strong these now a march can beat,
> Their Armory as good, faire, rich, compleat,
> Warlike, and fit, as any state can boast,
> For Quantity, where Soldiers have done most.

A dispute arose about this time between the members of the Society and their Leader, Captain Panton. This gentleman appears to have been a military adventurer of more than doubtful reputation. Eventually he acquired a fortune by gambling and purchased property on which he built Panton Street and Square, near the Haymarket. In consequence of complaints by members, Panton was suspended by the Court of Aldermen, and, after lengthy bickering and an appeal to the Privy Council, was replaced by Captain John Bingham, who, at a Court of Aldermen held in March, 1618, was chosen Leader of "the Military Company exercising Arms in the Artillery Garden" by vote of the 13 Captains of the City. Bingham, a veteran of the Dutch wars, had to be made a freeman of the City to comply with the regulations of membership and was admitted into the Company of Ironmongers. The same Court of Aldermen issued the following order: "This Court doth specially devise that no man shall be admitted to that Company (of the Artillery Garden) who by reason of his abilitye and qualitye is not well fitted for the same."

While this internal dispute was in progress, a serious conflict arose between the Society and the Master-Gunner, one William Hamon or Hammond, concerning the right to use the Old Artillery Ground. As the Company held a lease of the Ground, the grounds on which Hamon based his claim is not clear. Possibly the fact that the first of the Masters and Rulers of the Guild of Artillery was also Master-Gunner of England had given rise to the use of the Ground by the Tower Gunners. However, Hammond had endeavoured to exclude the citizens from their old training ground and had forbidden their servants to "repayre to their Armoury to cleere, make cleane, and amend their Armes there," contrary to ancient usage and to the terms of the lease. Complaint was made to the Court of Aldermen, who forthwith presented a petition to the Privy Council. Their Lordships called the Master-Gunner before them, dismissed as frivolous his claim to a rent or other consideration from the Company, and ordered him not only to allow "the said Society in Martial Exercises" the full use of the ground but to do his uttermost to aid and assist them. In spite of this order Hammond continued his obstructive tactics and a further petition was put forward to the Council, who, after personal investigation, ordered that the ground be restored to the public use for the exercise of arms and artillery as it had formerly been employed. This was in 1620. Within two years we find the same obstinate Master-Gunner encroaching on the Company's exercise ground by enclosing certain cabbage gardens and thereby "restraining them from the use of a Butt with a Marke erected in the said ground and very usefull in their Exercise." The Company protested against this and at the same time sought authority to erect a new Armoury of brick and stone in the Ground, their original building being decayed and ready to fall down. The Council confirmed their former orders in respect to the use of the Ground and sanctioned the building of an Armoury "in such manner as may be Least subject to Surprize."

On 1st May, 1622, the foundations of the new Armoury were commenced, and it was completed by November in the following year at a cost of £1,000, an immense sum in those days. Henry Petowe, a member who had joined the Company in 1610, celebrated the occasion in a poem, an original printed copy of which is still in the possession of the Regiment (see pages 32 and 33). Stow relates that this Armoury was furnished with 500 sets of arms of extraordinary beauty, which were ultimately lost in the Civil War.

About this time Ben Jonson, who had himself "trailed a pike" in the Low Countries, wrote "A Speech according to Horace," afterwards published with other works under the title of *Underwoods*.

This was a poem entirely devoted to praise of the military exercises and training carried on in the Artillery Garden and to severe castigation of the vices and effeminacy of the period. He spoke of the gallant appearance of the City troops, and continued:

> Well, I say, thrive, thrive brave Artillery-yard,
> Thou seed-plot of the war! that hast not spared
> Powder and paper to bring up the youth
> Of London in the military truth.

The "paper" to which the poet refers would be the drill books written by members of the Company, including *Aelian's Tactics*, by Sir John Bingham, the newly appointed Captain of the Company.

The membership of the Company had gradually fallen from 500 in 1615 to little over 200 in 1620. This diminution had caused the expenses of upkeep, powder and shot, etc. (£250 per annum), to weigh very heavily upon the remaining members, who therefore asked the Court of Aldermen for assistance. The Court, "being desirous to encourage such a commendable exercise to be performed within this City by freemen thereof," voted an annual grant of 100 marks "for their better encouragement in that worthie exercise." This was not the only financial support received from the Corporation. On 9th May, 1620, the Chamberlain of London was ordered to pay the President of the Society £10 17s. 4d. for provisions sent into the fields on 26th April, when the "Artillery-men" mustered there, and for wine sent to the Stewards for the supper at Merchant Taylors' Hall. For many years a grant of £10 was allowed by the Corporation towards the cost of the Company's annual feast; and the following entry occurs in the Minutes of the Court of Aldermen for 30th April, 1622: "For as much as this Court is advertised that the Society practisinge Armes in the Artillery Garden doe at their owne charge make an extraordinary Feast on this day senenight and have invited to the same the Lord Mayor and divers Aldermen. This Court in token of their good respect to that Society have thought fitt to bestowe on them against that Feast One hogshead of Clarrett wyne: Thirty Gallons of Sacke and thirty Gallons of Rhenishe wyne." This admirable practice was not finally discontinued until 1669.

In 1628 Thomas Dekker published another poem with the title "Warres, Warres, Warres," the only known copy of which is in the Henry E. Huntington Library in the U.S.A. In the dedication, speaking of the Lord Mayor's "Triumph"

The foundation of the Armory of that remarkable Nur-cery of military Diſcipline, called the Artillery Garden London, *was* begun to be erected the firſt day of May, *An.* Dom. 1622. and was finiſhed the laſt day of November then next following, Co-lonell *Hugh Hammerſley* being then Preſident, *Edward Pierce* Trea-ſurer, *Henry Petowe* Marſhall, and *Iohn Bingham* Eſquire, Captaine, and one of the Councell of warre for this Kingdome.

Upon which Monument theſe Lines following were compoſed.

Londons Honour, and her Citizens approved Love, exerciſing Armes in the Artillery Garden *London.*

The Fabricke.
> THis *Architecture, Phœnix of our age,*
> (*All Europe cannot ſhew her Equipage*)
> *Is* Mars *his Miſtreſſe, which retaines the ſtore*
> *Of* Mars *his Armes, being* Mars *his Paramore,*
> *This Fabricke was by* Mars *his Souldiers fram'd,*
> *And* Mars *his Armory's this Building nam'd.*

The Souldiers Honuor.
> *It holds five hundred Armes to furniſh thoſe,*
> *That love their Soveraigne, and will daunt His foes,*
> *They ſpend their time, and doe not ſpare for coſt,*
> *To learne the uſe of Armes, there's nothing loſt ;*
> *Both time and coyne to doe their Country good,*
> *They'l ſpend it freely, and will loſe their blood.*

The Alder-mans Love.	Our City London is a Royall thing, For it is call'd the Chamber of our King; Whose worthy Senate we must not forget, Their Grant and our Request together met, They cherrish us, and wee doe honour them; Where Souldiers finde true love, they'll love agen.
The Ground.	The Ground whereon this building now doth stand, The Teasell ground hath heretofore beene nam'd.
The Donor of the ground.	And William, Pryor of the Hospitall, Then of our blessed Lady, which wee call, Saint Mary Spittle without Bishopsgate, Did passe it by Indenture, bearing date, Ianuaries third day, in Henry's time, The eighth of that name, the Covent did conjoyne,
The Vse.	Vnto the Guile of all Artillery, Crosse-bowes, Hand-guns, and of Archery,
The terme of yeeres.	For full three hundred yeeres excepting three, The time remaining wee shall never see.
The Councels confirmation.	Now have the Noble Councell of our King, Confirm'd the same, and under Charles his wing, We now doe exercise, and of that little Teasell ground, we inlarg'd Saint Mary Spittle, Trees we cut down, and Gardens added to it, Thankes to the Lords that gave us leave to doe it.
A loyall Sub-jects desire.	Long may this worke endure, and ne'r decay, But be supported till the latest day. All loyall Subjects to the King and State, Will say Amen, manger Spleene or Hate.

Mariscallus Petowe composuit.

on his accession to the mayoralty, he speaks of "*A brave Company of Gentlemen in* Armes, *were Additions of much* splendour, to *that* Day (*which of itselfe was* bright *enough,* to grace your *Lordship being at this* Time *their sole and Worthy* Colonell.*"

The poem describes drill movements, follows with a description of a battle, and proceeds to assert that the citizens of London have no need to send to foreign shores for officers to lead her troops, having plenty of capable leaders among her own sons. He then brings in the names of the twenty City Captains and their Lieutenants, all members of the Artillery Company.

The Company's troubles respecting the use of their training ground were not yet over. Master-Gunner John Reynolds, the successor of Hammond, petitioned the King on behalf of the officers of Ordnance, the "feed-gunners," and the scholars who were being trained to serve the Crown as "Canonyers." His complaint was to the effect that the citizens of London, having obtained leave to exercise a Company of Pikes and Muskets in the Artillery Garden and to build an Armoury there, had not only presumed to pull down a store-house and a proof-house, both of very ancient and necessary use, but had used threatening language to the scholars and committed other "insulteries and misdemeanours." Both parties appeared before the Privy Council and stated their respective cases. The Council once more approved the "forwardness of the said Cittizens in those so Warlike and Commendable practises" and ordered that they should have the sole use of the ground on Mondays and Tuesdays, on which days a servant of the Company should keep the door. Reynolds refusing to conform to this order, the Council confirmed their decision a month later and we hear no more of the matter. The Company, however, had already made application to the Corporation for a ground of their own.

No sooner had this bickering come to an end than some internal dissension appears to have arisen. Certain officers, who had not been successful at the annual election of civil chiefs and office-bearers, complained to the Privy Council of the "disorderly and mutinous caryages of sundry persons in the Artillery Yarde," particularly in refusing the Captain chosen by the Lord Mayor and Court of Aldermen. The Council asked for a report by the Lord Mayor on the various alleged misde-

CAPTAIN NICHOLAS CRISPE

Admitted 1621. Captain, Trained Bands, 1629-1638. Raised and commanded a regiment of Horse for King Charles in Civil War. Knighted 1641. Colonel of City of London Horse 1661. Created Baronet, 1665, The engraving (*circa* 1630) shows Crispe as a Member of the Artillery Company against a background of the Old Artillery Ground and the original Armoury

meanours (including an inquiry as to which member had called Sir Hugh Hamersley, the ex-President, a "base fellow"), at the same time requesting His Lordship to inflict such punishments, by imprisonment or otherwise, as would result in "ye repressing and beating downe of the lyke insolencies and disorders in tyme to come." The Mayoral report attributed most of the blame to the slackness and neglect of the Court of Aldermen. Correspondence on the subject finally reached King Charles, who apparently took the part of the mutineers, as he caused the following letter to be addressed to the Company:

CHARLES R.

Trustie and wellbeloved we greet you well. Whereas we are informed that the worthie and commendable institution of yor voluntary Company of the Artillerie Garden, hath been soe well pursued by yor industrious and forward endeavours that you are not only become ready and skilfull in the knowledge and use of Armes and military discipline, but that from thence, as from a fruitfull Nursery, all the trayned bands of our Cittie of London, and divers of the Companyes of the counties adjoyning have beene supplied wth fitt and able Leaders and Officers, whereby our Service hath received much Advantage, and the kingdome in generall a very great benefitt. And being unwilling that a Societie of soe good use to the publique, and of soe much safetie and honor to our renowned Citie of London should be dissolved or discontinued, as we are given to understand it is in great danger through some distractions which you have lately suffered about the Election of your Captaine. We have thought fitt hereby to will you not be hastie to disband, but if ye find that ye are molested needlessly or unjustly by any there, have recourse to us and you shall find such due encouragement as soe comendable a Societie deserves. Given att our Court at Newmarkett, the Eight day of March, in the Seaventh yeare of our Raigne.

To our trustie and wellbeloved Humfrie Smith, Ald^r president of the Company exercisinge Armes in the Artillerie Garden, London, and to the Rest of the Companie.

His Majesty's well-meant effort appears to have displeased the Privy Council. The whole matter was reopened and stoutly debated on both sides. In the end it was resolved that the King himself should appoint the Captain of the Company, the election of the President and other officers being left to the Lord Mayor and Aldermen, subject to His Majesty's approval, and with a reservation that the members of the Company should appoint the Treasurer. Instructions were also issued for the framing of Rules and Orders for the government of the Company. Accordingly the Court of Aldermen met on 12th March, 1633, and, with the advice of the previously appointed President, elected officers for the government of the Company. These consisted of a Deputy-President, twenty-two Assistants, two Lieutenants, and two Ensigns. They also appointed four Surveyors of Arms, four Sergeants, four Drummers and a Fife, an Armourer, a Gunsmith, a Clerk and a Beadle. This date marks the origin of the present constitution of the civil side of the Company. The new regulations were modified in the following year by an Order in Council which laid down that the King should appoint the Captain of the Company and the Lord Mayor and Aldermen the President, while the members of the Company should elect all other officers, and, "setting asyde all differences, speedily returne unto their accustomed exercise of Armes." Thus happily ended a dispute which at one time seemed likely to lead to the dissolution of the Company.

Throughout the reigns of James I and his successor the Artillery Garden was the recognized school of instruction for officers of the nearest approach to a standing army of the day—the Trained Bands of London and the Counties. Colonel William Barriffe, a member of the Company and a recognized expert in military training, writes in 1645:

The Grecians had their *Tactick* Masters, the Romans their *Tribunes*; and we our *Academies* and *Military Schooles* of *warre*; witnesse our ARTILLERY GARDEN, with the Military and Martiall grounds, wherein the *choice* and *best-affected Citizens* (and Gentry) are practised and taught the *Rudiments* of our *Militia*. In times of *peace* so fitting them, that they may be able to *stand* in the day of *battell*, to *God's glory*, their *owne honours*, and their *countrie's good*.

His statement is confirmed by Lieutenant-Colonel Richard Elton, a member of the rival Company of the Military Garden in Westminster, in his book *The Compleat Body of the Art Military* (*very delightful and profitable for all Noble and Heroick Spirits*), written four years later. A passage in this work runs as follows:

The great delight in handling of *Arms* in *Military* Exercises, makes the City of LONDON and the Surburbs thereof famous through the whole World, by reason, as I conceive, of those two great *Nurseries* or *Academies* of MILITARY DISCIPLINE, the ARTIL-

LERY and MILITARY GARDENS, from whom, as out of pure *Fountains*, all other our *Private Meetings* (as of *Townditch*, and *Cripplegate*, &c.) are derived.

The *Artillery Garden* deserves the first place, in respect it is the greatest meeting, from whence, as it were out of a *Nursery* have been transplanted many able knowing souldiers both at home and in foreign Countries to the great honour of our Nation. . . . . My hearty wishes therefore that all and every one of them may be propt up, and supported to all ages, that when need shall require, we may draw from these *fountains* such skilfull and experienced Commanders, and Officers as may be, as it were, a *Bulwark* to this our Nation.

A second edition was published ten years later and dedicated to Richard Cromwell, Lord Protector; and a third saw the light in 1668, this last being dedicated to the President, Vice-

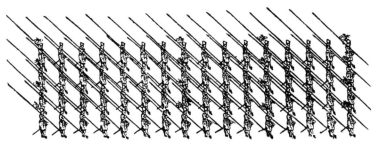

[*From a Drill Book written by a member of the Company in* 1629

A COMPANY OF PIKEMEN DRAWN UP IN FILES SIXTEEN DEEP

President, Treasurer, and the rest of the Court of Assistants of the Ancient and Honourable Artillery Company of London.

The art of war, which had been passing through a period of transition, was now becoming stabilized, and in all European countries the pike and musket had superseded all other infantry weapons. Formation, drill and other details varied with the different nations, but the theory remained the same. Each regiment of foot consisted of a phalanx of heavily armed pike-men, ranged in ranks six, eight, ten or even sixteen deep, for hand-to-hand fighting and defence against cavalry, with two bodies of musketeers, or "wings of shot." These latter were generally drawn up in equal numbers on either flank of the pikes and provided the missile action. The pikeman wore as defensive armour a breastplate and tasses (thigh guards), backplate, and morion. His weapons were a pike, varying in length from twelve to eighteen feet, and a sword. The latter was for use if the enemy broke into the ranks, when of course a long pike was merely an encumbrance. The musketeer was clad in a leather jerkin and wore sometimes a steel morion, usually a cloth hat. He was armed with the long, heavy musket, which required a rest to prop it up when taking aim. A length of slow match was carried in the hand, the lighted ends between the fingers, and a spare coil was wound round the waist beneath the buff coat. Powder cartridges were suspended from a bandolier worn over the left shoulder—sometimes as many as 18 charges were carried. The bullets were normally carried in a little bag slung to the bandolier, but when in action a few were kept in the mouth. A

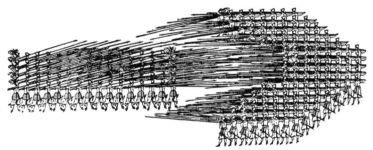

[*From a Drill Book written by a member of the Company in* 1629

A HALF-MOON OF PIKEMEN ATTACKED BY A COLUMN

pruning iron was carried for use when the bullets did not fit the bore, and fine powder for priming in a small horn slung to the side. A sword was worn for hand-to-hand fighting, but English soldiers usually preferred to use the butt in a mêlée.

The drill for pikemen consisted of a number of "postures" or manual exercises, and a complicated system of "doublings" and "countermarches," the main object of which was to enable any threatened point to be strengthened and to bring the best men to the front for attack or defence. With this purpose in view, the personnel of each file was carefully drawn up in order of precedence, the best men being placed in the front rank as "file-leaders," the next best in the rear, as "bringers-up," and the least brave or efficient where they would invariably find themselves in the centre of the body, whatever formation was ordered. In action against infantry the pikes were "charged," *i.e.*, presented horizontally towards the enemy at the level of the shoulder, while the rear ranks "ported" their pikes in readiness to step into the places of men who fell in the front ranks. For defence against cavalry, standing shoulder to shoulder in serried ranks, the pikemen in the foremost rank set the butt end of their pikes against the inside of the right foot, and, lunging forward with the pike in the left hand, presented a hedge of spear-points to the enemy. At the same time swords were drawn in case the enemy effected an entrance. The ranks in rear "charged" pikes over the shoulders of the men in front of them.

The drill with the musket was still more elaborate. To load and fire, 33 distinct orders were necessary, each order requiring several distinct motions on the part of the soldier. Here are two examples:

Order.	Motions.
"Charge with Bullet."	1. Take the bullet out of your mouths.
	2. Slip up your hands by the barrel of your muskets and put in your bullets.
	3. Clap your hands on your muskets to shake them down.
"Shorten your Scowring Sticks" (Ramrods).	1. Turn the screw-ends towards your bodies.
	2. Set the ends under your left paps.
	3. Shorten your sticks to an handful.

The musketeers, like the pikemen, were drawn up in ranks six to twelve deep. In giving fire to the front the usual method was for the front rank to fire and then wheel off to the right or left or retreat between the files to the rear. The second rank took their places, fired and followed suit, and so on till all had fired. By the time the original front rank had resumed its first position, the men had had time to reload their pieces. This plan was capable of infinite variation. When attacked, the musketeers would take refuge behind or among the pikes, and this fact probably led to the adoption of the practice of mingling muskets and pikes to meet a charge, which became eventually the standard method.

One device for obtaining increased fire power was for the front rank to kneel, the second to stoop, and the third to stand upright, all three delivering "a violent, speedy and thunderous discharge" at the word of command.

Although the bow had now been almost entirely supplanted by the musket as a military weapon, the practice of archery by civilians was still encouraged. Thorough inbred conservatism was probably the main reason, but there was quite a body of

ARCHERY IN FINSBURY FIELDS

Note the archery marks in the distance and the archer drawing to the nipple of the right breast

opinion of the older school which held that the bow in skilful hands was still equal, if not superior, to the clumsy matchlock, with its frequent misfires and varying accuracy. It was urged that an archer could loose six arrows in the time taken by a musketeer to load and fire his piece. Then, again, the cost of the new weapon, with its powder and match, placed it beyond the reach of many individual citizens, and the intricate drill necessary in loading and firing did not tend to make marksmanship with firearms the popular national pastime that archery had been. Thus we find, in 1625, a serious attempt to bring about the use of a weapon consisting of a bow and pike combined, invented by William Nead, an archer. A description of this device states that it had been in use by the Society of the Artillery Garden for over a year. At the King's express desire, a demonstration of the new invention was given by 300 members of the Company in St. James's Park and was attended by the King in person, the Council of State and the Council of War. The question was then referred to the latter body and steps were taken to bring about the general exercise of the new weapon, but, though it was definitely ordered to be practised by the Trained Bands, we hear nothing further of the device until 1644, when, in six regiments of London troops, 300 men (50 in each unit) were armed with the "combined bow and pike."

It seems that archery was still considered by those in authority to be of some military value, for, as late as 1632, Royal Letters Patent were issued for the maintenance of archery and artillery. These orders were addressed to a number of gentlemen, among them many officers of the Company, and directions were given that the ground in the vicinity of the ancient archery marks outside the City of London was to be kept open to archers.

The system of military training inaugurated in London by the Company led the citizens of other towns to follow their example. In 1621 the Bailiffs and Aldermen of Colchester presented a petition to the Privy Council to the effect that, stimulated by the most worthy example of London in her Artillery Yard, they desired permission to establish a similar organization for the service of their county. Their request was acceded to, and a similar application by the Aldermen of Bury St. Edmunds was granted in the following year. Bristol followed suit in 1625, North Yarmouth in 1626, and Chester, Ipswich and Nottingham within the next few years. Certain gentlemen founded a "Martial Yard" at Horsey Down, Southwark, in 1635.

All these institutions have unhappily failed to survive, but there is one offshoot of the old Company which still flourishes.

Originally The Military Company of the Massachusetts, it is now known as The Ancient and Honorable Artillery Company of Boston, Massachusetts, the oldest military body in the New World.

No military force had accompanied the early settlers in New England, so that each scattered community found itself dependent from the first upon its own powers of defence from the surrounding savage and treacherous Red Indian tribes. Voluntary military associations were therefore formed on the model of the English Trained Bands and by 1636 seven of these bodies were in existence—the "train-bands" of Dorchester, Charlestown, Watertown, Newton, Saugus, Ipswich and Boston, —each company having selected as its leaders the most experienced soldiers, "noble instances of sublime piety and martial accomplishments, equally qualified to adorn the church by their exemplary virtue and defend it by their valour." It was found, however, that the isolated situations of the townships and the lack of opportunity for the teaching of discipline and tactics rendered necessary the formation of a central school of training. Some of the early planters, including officers of the trained bands, had been members of the Artillery Company of London, and these, with other leading citizens, founded a new military association on the lines of their old Company. This was in 1637. The new Company addressed a petition to Governor Winthrop asking for a charter of incorporation, but their request did not at first meet with approval. Winthrop wrote afterwards: "Divers gentlemen and others being joined in a military company, desired to be made a corporation, but the council considering from the example of the Prætorian band among the Romans, and Templars in Europe, how dangerous it might be to erect a standing authority of military men, which might easily in time overthrow the civil power, thought fit to stop it betimes; yet they were allowed to be a company, but subordinate to all authority."

So the infant Company were permitted to continue their voluntary training. There is an entry in the State Records that "Captain Keayne and the Military Company have power to exercise where they please and to make use of so many of the common arms as they need." Finally they were successful in obtaining a Charter addressed to Robert Keayne, Nathaniel Duncan, Robert Sedgwick, William Spencer and others, dated

[*From engravings on the brass clasps of the Great Vellum Book*

FIGURES IN THE UNIFORM OF THE COMPANY *circa* 1635

17th March, 1638, which incorporated "The Military Company of the Massachusetts," endowed them with a thousand acres of land, and ordered that no other military training should take place on the days of their exercise.

Robert Keayne, the founder of the Military Company, was born at Windsor in 1595 and became a Gentleman of the Artillery Garden in 1623, being a freeman of London and a Merchant Taylor. He was one of the earliest settlers in Boston, where for many years he took a leading part in local government, for which service he received one of the first grants of land made by the State. Notwithstanding his reputation for piety and benevolence, he was on one occasion charged before the General Court with oppression in the sale of foreign commodities, in that he had taken more than sixpence in the shilling profit. This offence was styled a corrupt practice, the more so because the offender was an eminent professor of the gospel, a wealthy man of eminent parts with but one child, and had already been admonished by friends. A fine of £200 was imposed. On another occasion Keayne was suspected of killing for his own use a stray sow, the property of a neighbour. This case was the cause of considerable litigation, but the charge was never proved and Keayne was dismissed the case with costs.

By his will, Robert Keayne was a considerable benefactor to the town of Boston, leaving money to build a market-place, a conduit, a town house, a free school, a library and an armoury. He also left a legacy to Harvard College. To the Artillery Company he bequeathed £5 for the purchase of pikes and bandoliers, and £5 for the erection of a covered gun-platform for the training of members of the Company as scholars in Great Artillery. In addition he left the Company two heifers or cows, to be held on charge by them and the increase or profit to be laid out annually in the purchase of powder and bullets. This may sound a trivial gift from a wealthy man, but the value of a cow was £25 to £30 at that time and place. Finally the old soldier left his successors a deal of excellent advice on the management of the Company. He adds that he had in mind several other gifts for the encouragement of his beloved corps, but was deterred by the dwindling numbers which made him apprehensive of its final dissolution. "For what comfort or credit," he writes, "can a captain have to go into the field with six or twelve soldiers, and under the name of a Military or Artillery Company?"

Nathaniel Duncan, the second of those mentioned in the Charter, does not appear to have graduated with the London Company, but Robert Sedgwick, the leader of the Trained Band of Charlestown and a gentleman of education and distinction, is said to have been a member of the parent Company, though his name does not appear on the roll. He may have been a member of the rival company of the Military Garden of Westminster. However, a writer of the period observes that he was "brought up in London's Artillery Garden and furthered with sixteen years experience in New England, besides the help of a very good head-piece, being a frequent instructor of our Artillerymen." In 1652 Sedgwick was appointed to the highest military rank in the colony, that of Sergeant Major General, which office he held for one year. On the triumph of the Parliamentary cause in the Civil War he returned, with several others of the Company, to England, where he was employed as an officer by Cromwell. He served against the French and was engaged in the expedition against the Spanish West Indies which resulted in the capture of Jamaica, where he died, after having been promoted by the Protector to the rank of Major-General.

There was a William Spencer admitted to the Artillery Garden in 1611 who may have been the fourth person named in the Charter, and this supposition is borne out by the knowledge that Spencer was of advanced age at the time of the incorporation of the Military Company.

The names of several other original members of the Massachusetts Company also appear in the Old Vellum Roll. It is impossible to verify individuals and these entries may possibly refer to namesakes, but, having regard to the fact that most of them were appointed to commands on the formation of the colonial Trained Bands, it is, to say the least, highly probable that these worthies had received training at the School of War in London's Artillery Garden. Among these we find Lieutenant Richard Morris, "a very stout man and an experienced soldier"; William Perkins, Captain of the Military Band of Weymouth; Captain Richard Walker, formerly Ensign of the Military Band of Saugus; Thomas Clarke, afterwards a Captain in the Boston Militia, and others.

The Military Company of the Massachusetts continued to perform its allotted function of training citizens in the art of war, and for many years most of the officers of the New England Militia Regiments (formed in 1644 from the old Trained Bands) were selected from its ranks. The designation of Artillery Company appears to have become usual about 1657, and at the beginning of the eighteenth century the prefix of "Honourable" came into use. The prefix of "Ancient" was added *circa* 1737.

We are indebted to that energetic scribe, Lieutenant William Barriffe, for the description of an exercise performed on 18th October, 1638, at Merchant Taylors' Hall, by "Certain Gentlemen of the Artillery Garden." Eighty of these worthies took part in a military display entitled "Mars, His Triumph," which was honoured with the presence of many of the "Nobility, Aldermen and Gentry." The proceedings opened with a display and combat by eighteen "Targettiers," armed with morions, swords and targets, who "made their encounters and varied their figures all according to the distinct sounds of their musick." Then entered twenty-two members disguised as Saracens, armed with Barbary guns, cymiters and broad Turkey daggers, and "habited after the Persian and Turconian manner." We are told that "their musick was a Turkie Drumme and a hideous noise making pipe made of a Buffolas [sic] horn." These gentry went through various evolutions, their Captain "supervising them with a stately survay," then saluted the Nobility and Gentry by putting their left hands on the tops of their Turbans and bowing their bodies forward, "and so passed out at the garden doore."

Next appeared forty members "in the Moderne Armes," namely, "sixteen Musketiers in Buffe-Coats and Beaver Morians, sixteen Pikemen compleatly armed in white Corslets, whole Pikes and Morians, one Phife and two Drummes," with officers and sergeants. They marched round the hall, "the Drums beating a lofty English march," after which the drums "struck an Alt," while one of the musketeers was ushered to the front, and, "laying down his musket in a graceful manner," recited a poem specially composed for the occasion. This took the form of an appeal, addressed to the "Grave Fathers of the Citie," for the provision of a suitable ground for the Company's military exercises. The poem suggests that the whole motive of the display is to impress the Mayor and Corporation with the efficiency of the Company, and it concludes with the request that the City should

> Give your Souldiers one small piece of ground
> To shew their Arms in: else, in heaps of dust,
> Their glories will be hid, their bright Arms, rust.

The whole body then performed a multitude of "postures" of the pike and musket to a "posture tune" played by the fife. These were followed by a series of complicated evolutions, doublings and countermarchings, firings and reducements, performed to "the streyn of the Almain posture tune."

WILLIAM BARRIFFE

Admitted 1626. His book *Militarie Discipline* ran into six editions and was the recognized drill manual for both sides in the Civil War

At the conclusion of these exercises "a Sentinell gives fire without in the Yard," and "one comes crying into the Hall, Arme, Arme, the Saracens are Landed." The "Moderne Armes" are thereupon drawn up in battle array, the Saracens enter and a long and complicated sham engagement takes place. In spite of the gallantry of Mulley-ben-Achmay, the Saracen

50

chief, who, "demonstrating a kinde of haughty scorn by the gesture of his body," engages the leader of the musketeers in single combat, "intending to have stabd him with a poysoned Creese," the Turks are finally forced to surrender; their lives are spared and the display concluded with a grand march past, the officers and soldiers "doing a short Souldier-like obeysance to the Nobility as they passed by them."

Three years afterwards the Company was granted (at a rental of 6s. 8d. per annum) the lease of the uppermost field in Finsbury, next to the six windmills, known to succeeding generations as the Artillery Ground.

The lease originally granted by the Corporation was renewable every fourteen years in perpetuity, and this under the Property Act of 1922 became a lease of 2,000 years as from that date. Unfortunately this does not apply to the whole of the Ground but only to the western moiety. For some years after the grant of the lease it was found that the eastern half, plus the strip on the north (now occupied by Armoury House and its parade ground), did not belong to the Corporation but to the Prebend of Finsbury. Consequently it became necessary for the City to acquire a lease of this portion and to sublet it to the Company, which accounts for the fact that the superior landlords are now the Ecclesiastical Commissioners, who grant leases of 80 years to the Lieutenancy of London, who, in turn, sublet to the Company for a similar term.

The inhabitants of Bunhill Fields were not in the least pleased at the prospect of having the Artillery Company as neighbours and presented a petition to the House of Lords, setting forth the "evills and mischiefs to a great multitude" which would result from the "Military Gentlemen of London" having these fields for their place of exercise. Some of the alleged evils were (1) Citizens and archers passing by "to walke and recreate themselves" would be hindered and discouraged by the high wall; the pleasant passage would become a noisome lane, and the inhabitants forced to hire a scavenger to clean it. (2) Upon the building of a brick wall, 15 feet high, the passersby would lose the beauty of a delightful prospect into the fields. (3) The narrow lane would expose wayfarers to the "pill of robbers" after dark, and expose them to infection of plague, as they would "unavoydably meete with sidans carrying persons to the Pesthowse." (4) Persons sick or in childbed would be "disquietted with the shott."

The House of Lords, on receipt of this petition, ordered the building of the wall already in course of erection by the "Artillery Men" to be stopped pending the hearing of the case. A counter petition was promptly submitted by the Company and a date fixed for the hearing. No further records of the proceedings are available, but apparently the Company won the case, as they occupy the ground to this day.

It has always been the custom to call out the Trained Bands on occasions when riots or civil commotions were feared, such as when the apprentices had a holiday. For instance, on Shrove Tuesday, 1622, 800 men of the Trained Bands were mustered under eight Captains and 400 of them were directed to train in Moorfields "for preventing of riots and tumults which by the number of apprentices coming with other lewd and dissolute persons might happen to be attempted." Again, in May, 1640, 1,000 able and well-affected men of the City Regiments were embodied with orders to "suppress, slay, kill, destroy, and apprehend all persons tumultuously assembled in or about Southwark, Lambeth, Blackheath, and elsewhere in parts adjacent."

King Charles had always shown himself favourably disposed towards the Company. He had frequently attended in the Artillery Garden during his father's reign and had seen the Company pass in review before him on more than one occasion. In 1641 he afforded a further signal proof of his favour by sanctioning the enrolment of the Prince of Wales, then but eleven years old, and his brother James, Duke of York, as members of the Company. The signatures of the two Princes in the Old Vellum Book are dated 1st June, 1641. The Elector of Palatine, a grandson of James I, became a member on the same day.

A contemporary author (John Lucas, in *London in Armes Displayed*, published 1642), referring to the Artillery Company, writes: "This Corporation claims the Prioritie (as being the Univarsill Staple of Militarie Discipline) Dignified both by the Presence and Practice of Matchless Princes (viz) Charles Prince of Wales, Charles Prince Pallatine, James Duke of Yorke, all this Honble Corporation."

The words "and Practice" would seem to infer that the Royal Princes took some active part in the Company's exercises.

ENROLMENT OF THE ROYAL PRINCES IN THE GREAT VELLUM BOOK, 1641
Note.—The word "Davifer" should read "Dapifer"

CHAPTER IV

1642 TO 1659

EARLY in 1642 a reorganization of the London Trained Bands took place. The old North, East, West and South Regiments disappeared on the strength being increased to 8,000 men in 40 companies of 200 each, henceforth to be known, from the colour of their ensigns, as the Red, White, Yellow, Blue, Orange and Green Regiments, a nomenclature they were to retain until 1794. Nominal rolls of the officers of the six regiments in 1642 are available. Every one was a member of the Artillery Company.

As from January in this year the London Trained Bands supplied daily guards to both Houses of Parliament of 200 men, 100 to each House.

On the outbreak of civil war between King and Parliament in August, 1642, neither side was prepared for a campaign, and a sort of scramble ensued to obtain possession of arsenals throughout the country and to enlist the services of all available troops. These last consisted entirely of Trained Bands, in most cases hopelessly inefficient. Furthermore, they could rarely be persuaded to move outside their own counties, and in some cases lack of discipline made them more dangerous to their own officers than to the enemy. Both parties began by summoning the Trained Bands to their assistance, and both, before the war had been in progress many months, found it more profitable to relieve them of their arms and to form new armies from less unwilling material.

It is some consolation to find once more that the only troops in England of reasonable efficiency were those officered by the Artillery Company. "The one exception," writes Firth, "to the rule that the trained bands were worthless was furnished by those of London. Counting in the three regiments of the suburbs, the six regiments of the City, and the six regiments of auxiliaries, they amounted in 1643 to 18,000 men. They were the reserve on which the Parliament relied in every emergency.

PHILLIP SKIPPON
Captain of the Artillery Company, 1639-1660. Major-General of the
Parliamentary Army and later of the New Model Army
From an engraving in the possession of the Company

Without their aid, Essex could not have relieved Gloucester, nor could Waller have repulsed Hopton's invasion of Sussex. They were not very well disciplined, and were too accustomed to good food and good beds to support with patience the hardships of a campaign, but they were well drilled."

Closely connected as the Company had always been with that mainstay of the Parliamentary cause, the City of London, it is hardly surprising to find that the majority of our members supported the popular party. Consequently, though the Company did not take part as a fighting unit on either side in the ensuing long-drawn-out struggle, we find the names of very many of its members serving as officers at the relief of Gloucester and the subsequent battle of Newbury, as well as in the defence of London, the battle of Cheriton (or Alresford), the siege of Basing House, the taking of Alton, Essex's expedition into Cornwall, the second battle of Newbury, and many minor operations. Almost every individual member took part in the war on one side or the other, and their services can be pieced together from contemporary newsprints, broadsides and pamphlets.

During the twelve months prior to the opening of hostilities nearly 300 new members had been enrolled in the Company, apparently in anticipation of the conflict which appeared to be inevitable. The first year of war saw a further increase of 150, indicating that training was still carried on at Headquarters during that period. Then recruiting practically ceased. One solitary member was admitted in April, 1644, and after that our records are silent until the revival of the Company under the Protectorate in 1656.

The war service of at least one member of the Company is known to history. Captain Phillip Skippon, a veteran of the Spanish wars, had been selected by King Charles as Captain of the Company in 1639, and three years later had been appointed, in addition, to the post of Commander of the City Forces, with the rank of "Sergt-Major General." Vicars, in *England's Worthies*, states that "the martiall spirited sparkes of the famous Artillery Garden of the most renowned City of London, to his no little honour, chose him for their most pious and most expert Gimnasiarchus, or Captain of the said Garden to exercise and instruct them in the exactest rules of martiall discipline." Skippon had seen hard service in the Netherlands under the Prince of Orange, and had gained a great reputation for gallantry at the siege of Breda, where, with thirty Englishmen, he had driven off 200 Spaniards "at push of pike." At the outbreak of the Civil War the King endeavoured to secure the services of so experienced a soldier, but Skippon threw in his lot with the Parliament and was promptly appointed Major-General under the Earl of Essex, to whom he acted as Chief of Staff. As General of the Foot he saw fighting in every part of the country and was responsible for drawing up the order of battle at Naseby, where he was severely wounded. He also directed operations at the siege of Oxford. Cromwell appointed him as one of the judges of King Charles, but Skippon was no extremist and refused to act. He was a typical simple-minded, hard-fighting Puritan, firmly believing in the righteousness of his cause. In the early years of the war he published several books of devotion, such as *The Christian Centurion*, etc. Perhaps his chief claim to fame is that as Major-General of Foot under Sir Thomas Fairfax he trained and led the infantry of the New Model Army, the most efficient force that England had produced for centuries and the direct ancestor of the Regular Army of today. Historians are apt to give the entire credit for the "New Model" to Cromwell, who as Lieutenant-General under Fairfax was concerned exclusively with the horse.

The marchings, counter-marchings and skirmishings of the rival armies resulted in a clash at Edgehill, a disorderly and indecisive action of which the Royalists had somewhat the advantage. The Parliamentary army under the Earl of Essex retired hastily on London, followed, after incredible delay, by the Royal army. During their advance the cavalry under Prince Rupert turned aside to attack Windsor, which was successfully defended by the garrison under Colonel John Ven, a member of the Artillery Company (admitted 1614).

Meanwhile the City was in a panic. Shops were closed. Fortifications were hastily erected, and the Earl of Essex drew up the remnants of his army at Turnham Green, where he was joined by the whole force of the London Trained Bands. There the City troops found themselves under the eye of their old commander, Skippon, who exhorted them in a rough, blunt speech to stand firm. "Come, my brave, honest boys," said the grey-haired veteran, "pray heartily and fight heartily, and God will bless us."

The Royalists did not venture an attack but retired to Oxford, and the Trained Bands returned to their drills and exercises in the Artillery Ground. An extract from the Parliamentary Chronicle throws an interesting light on the zeal of the people of London for their cause, as well as on the utter lack of commissariat arrangements in the armies of the day. It states that the Lord Mayor of London "with some prime, well affected citizens," taking into serious consideration the fact that the soldiers at Turnham Green "could not but be destitute of victuals to refresh them," urged the clergy of the City churches to appeal from their pulpits to their parishioners "to spare some part of their diet, ready dressed for that present (Sunday) dinner, and to bestow it upon the soldiers aforesaid." The appeal was effectual. Carts paraded the City streets to collect offerings, and over a hundred loads of provisions, wine and beer, were sent to the army, "accompanied by honest and religious gentlemen, who went to see it faithfully distributed."

The City of London had already raised two regiments of horse and one of dragoons, all commanded and mostly officered by members of the Company. They now raised two more.

In April, 1643, the Common Council decided to raise six regiments of Auxiliaries (named the Red, Blue, Yellow, White, Green and Orange), but, whereas the Trained Bands were composed solely of citizens and householders, the Auxiliary Regiments were manned by apprentices, covenant servants, and the younger generation generally. Their commanding officers were selected from Captains of the Trained Bands, and almost all the officers of these units whose names can be traced are to be found in the roll of members of the Artillery Company.

In July the Royalists of Kent rose for the King, but were suppressed by a force under Colonel Richard Browne (admitted 1626) consisting of the Green Trained Bands, the Green Auxiliaries, and some troops of horse and dragoons.

Meanwhile the Parliamentary cause suffered serious set-backs in the west, where Hopton's Cornishmen won a series of brilliant victories and overran the whole countryside except for the towns of Plymouth, Lyme and Gloucester.

In August, Gloucester being closely invested by the Royalists, the London Trained Bands were called upon by Parliament to assist in raising the siege. All shops in the City were closed and six regiments were got ready for service with almost incredible speed. These troops consisted of Harvey's Horse,* the Blue and Red Regiments of City Trained Bands, and the Red, Blue and Orange Regiments of Auxiliaries. They left London on 23rd August, the Red Regiment mustering in the Artillery Ground, and joined the army under the Earl of Essex which was advancing to the relief of the beleaguered city. Some skirmishing took place, but the Royalists raised the siege on the advance of the Parliamentary army, which entered Gloucester on 7th September, and found the garrison reduced to their last

---

* Commanded by Colonel Edmond Harvey. Admitted to the Artillery Company, 1642.

barrel of powder. Essex then endeavoured, by feinting towards Worcester, to return to London without fighting, as he feared the King's superiority in cavalry, but his army was intercepted by the Royalists at Newbury. The result of the ensuing action, in which the London Trained Bands greatly distinguished themselves, was indecisive, but Essex succeeded in reaching London safely, though his rear-guard was harassed by Prince Rupert's cavalry.

Some interesting personal narratives of men of the City Regiments have survived. It appears from one of them that at the end of the first day's march several worthy citizens "who seemed very forward and willing at the first to march, yet upon some pretence and fair excuses returned home again, hiring others to go in their room." We are glad to note that at Chesham the men of the Red Regiment were "well accommodated for beer, having great plenty." At a village near Banbury, however, the troops were "very much scanted of victuals."

The first skirmish took place at Stow-on-the-Wold. The five regiments of Trained Bands formed the advanced guard, and the Red Regiment, in advance of the rest, had stood to arms in an open field all night on account of the nearness of the enemy. In the morning they found themselves all but surrounded by four or five thousand Royalist horse, but the situation was saved by the appearance of Essex with the main body of his army. As Sergeant Henry Foster puts it: "Their intent was to have compassed us in on every side, but the Lord prevented them. They might have spoiled our whole regiment, had they in the morning come down upon us when we were taking a little food to refresh ourselves." However, the great guns were brought up and opened fire. The enemy promptly retreated and the Parliamentary army followed them in battle array, five or six regiments abreast, 800 to 1,000 men in the front rank and six deep, "which goodly show did so much the more daunt the enemy that Prince Rupert swore he thought all the Roundheads in England were there." The pursuit lasted till late in the day and the Red Regiment "lay all night upon ploughed land, without straw, having neither bread nor water, yet God enabled our soldiers to bear it cheerfully." Again on the following night the same regiment found themselves acting as baggage guard on the top of Prestbury Hill, near Gloucester, "it being a most terrible tempestuous night of wind and rain, we having neither hedge nor tree for shelter, nor any sustenance of food or fire."

It speaks well for the discipline as well as for the fighting spirit of these citizen soldiers, suddenly called from the comforts of home life, that they endured these hardships of campaigning without loss of efficiency. Doubtless a leavening of religious fanaticism helped them to endure. As Foster has it, "We had by this time marched six days with very little provision. Such straits and hardships our citizens formerly knew not, yet the Lord that called us out to do his work enabled us to undergo such hardness as he brought us to."

On 8th September, the Royalists having raised the siege, Essex entered Gloucester at the head of his army. Foster relates how the cannon shot fired by the besiegers had torn up the ground "as if a bear had been rooting up the earth." The army rested for two days, then advanced to Tewkesbury and halted there while the garrison of Gloucester was re-provisioned. Essex ordered a bridge to be built over the Severn near Tewkesbury, and by this stratagem deceived the Royalists into concentrating for the defence of Worcester, whereupon the Parliamentary army turned about and made for London with all speed. After a seventeen-mile march, they reached Cirencester, surprised a small garrison of Royalists and took 225 prisoners (whom they tied together two and two with pieces of match) and 27 wagon-loads of bread and cheese, a most important and welcome prize. Proceeding by forced marches through Cricklade and Swindon, the army collected from "malignants and papists" about 1,000 sheep and 60 head of cattle. Eighty-seven sheep were allotted to the Red Regiment, but were lost at the subsequent battle. At Abern Chase skirmishing took place with the Royalist Horse, who were pressing hard on the retreating army. In this action Captain John Willett, a member of the Artillery Company admitted in 1618, was killed. That night at Hungerford, the men were much distressed from want of sleep and lack of food. It was a night of wind and rain, and they were wet to the skin.

Advancing on the following day to within a mile and a half of Newbury, Essex found that the Royalist army had intercepted him and was in possession of the town. His already exhausted troops were therefore forced once more to bivouac in the open with no shelter and little food. During the night the King's troops took up an advantageous position on high ground, where they planted their cannon and awaited with confidence the attack of their adversaries.

We cannot do better than allow Sergeant Foster to give his account of the next day's fighting: "Very early before day, we had drawn up all our army in their several regiments, and marched away by break of day; and then advancing towards the enemy with most cheerful and courageous spirits. The Lord Robert's soldiers had begun to skirmish with them before we came up to the enemy, which, we hearing, put us to a running march till we sweat again, hastening to their relief and succour. When we came up into the field our two Regiments of the Trained Bands were placed in open campania upon the right wing of the whole army. The enemy had there planted eight pieces of ordnance, and stood in a great body of horse and foot, we being placed right opposite against them, and far less than twice musket shot distance from them. They began their battery against us with their great guns above half an hour before we could get any of our guns up to us; our gunner dealt very ill with us, delaying to come up to us. Our noble Colonel Tucker* fired one piece of ordnance against the enemy, and aiming to give fire the second time, was shot in the head with a cannon bullet from the enemy. The Blue Regiment of the Trained Bands stood on our right wing, and behaved themselves most gallantly. Two regiments of the King's Horse, which stood upon their right flank afar off, came fiercely upon them, and charged them two or three times, but were beaten back with their Musketeers, who gave them a most desperate charge and made them fly. This day our whole army wore green boughs in their hats, to distinguish us from our enemies, which they perceiving, one Regiment of their Horse had got green boughs and rode up to our regiments crying, 'Friends, friends'; but we let fly at them and made many of them and their horses tumble, making them fly with a vengeance. The enemy's cannon did play most against the Red Regiment; they did some execution amongst us at first, and were somewhat dreadful when men's bowels and brains flew in our faces; but blessed be God that gave us courage, so that we kept our ground, and after awhile feared them not. Our ordnance did very good execution upon them, for we stood upon so near a distance, upon a plain field, that we

---

* John Tucker, a member of the Artillery Company since 1618.

could not lightly miss one another. We were not much above half our regiments in this place, for we had sixty files of Musketeers drawn off for the forlorn hope, who were engaged against the enemy in the field upon our left flank. Where most of the regiments of the Army were in fight, they had some small shelter of the hedges and banks, yet had a very hot fight with the enemy, and stood to it as bravely as ever men did. When our two regiments of the Trained Bands had thus played against the enemy for the space of three hours, or thereabouts, our Red Regiment joined to the Blue, which stood a little distance from us, upon our left flank, where we gained the advantage of a little hill, which we maintained against the enemy half an hour; two regiments of the enemy's Foot fought against us all this while to gain the hill, but could not. Then two regiments of the enemy's Horse, which stood upon our right flank, came fiercely upon us, and so surrounded us that we were forced to charge* upon them in the front and rear, and both flanks, which was performed by us with a great deal of courage and undauntedness of spirit, insomuch that we made a great slaughter of them, and forced them to retreat; but presently two regiments of the enemy's Foot in this time gained the hill, and came upon us before we could well recover ourselves, that we were glad to retreat a little way into the field, till we had rallied up our men and put them into their former posture, and then came on again. If I should speak anything in the praise and high commendations of those two regiments of the Trained Bands, I should rather obscure and darken the glory of that courage and valour God gave unto them this day; they stood like so many stakes before the shot of the cannon, quitting themselves like men of undaunted spirits, even our enemies themselves being judges.

"My noble and valiant Captain, George Mosse,† who was with the forlorn hope, received a shot in the back from the enemy, of which wound he is since dead. This 26th of September (*hinc illae lachrymae*) we lost about sixty or seventy men in our Red Regiment, besides wounded men; we having the hottest charge from the enemy's cannon of any regiment in the Army. Also that worthy and valiant gentleman, Captain Hunt,**

---

* *i.e.*, To "charge" or level pikes.

† Admitted a member of the Artillery Company in 1626.

** A confectioner in Bearebinder Lane. Admitted to the Artillery Company in 1631.

was slain in this battle, whose death is much lamented. These two poor regiments were the very objects of the enemy's battery that day, and they have since made their boast of it. The next day I viewed the dead bodies; there lay about 100 stripped naked in that field where our two regiments stood in battalion.

"This battle continued long; it began about six o'clock in the morning, and continued till past twelve o'clock at night. In the night the enemy retreated to the town of Newbury and drew away all their ordnance; we were in great distress for water, or any accommodation to refresh our poor soldiers, yet the Lord himself sustained us so that we did not faint under it; we were right glad to drink in the same water where our horses did drink, wandering up and down to seek for it. Our word on this day was 'Religion,' theirs was 'Queen Mary in the field.' "

If further proof be needed of the courage and efficiency of the citizen soldiers at Newbury, it is to be found in the pages of Clarendon, the Royalist historian. He pays a handsome tribute to the steadiness of the City troops in the following passage:

"The London Trained Bands and Auxiliary Regiments (of whose inexperience of danger, or any kind of service beyond the easy practice of their postures in the Artillery Garden, men had till then too cheap an estimation) behaved themselves to wonder; and were, in truth, the preservation of that army that day. For they stood as a bulwark and rampire to defend the rest; and when their wings of horse were scattered and dispersed, kept their ground so steadily, that, though Prince Rupert himself led up the choice horse to charge them, and endured their storm of small shot, he could make no impression upon their stand of pikes, but was forced to wheel about: of so sovereign benefit is that readiness, order, and dexterity in the use of their arms, which hath been so much neglected."

The return of the City Trained Bands to London was the occasion for great demonstrations of joy on the part of the inhabitants, more especially as reports had been circulated that they had been cut to pieces on the return march. The returning troops wore green boughs in their hats, as they had done at Newbury.

Meanwhile a muster of the remainder of the City Forces had been held in the Artillery Garden and adjoining fields. Complete records are available of the strength of the various regiments at this parade, with the names of the officers of all the Trained Bands at that time, compiled by one William Levett, a Royalist member of the Artillery Company. It is interesting to note, from the description appended to each name, the class of citizen of which the Company was composed at that period. We find the names of Captain William Manby, "Clerk of Leather-sellers' Hall," of whom more will be heard later, Captain John Booker, "Registrar to the Commissioners of the Statute of Bankrupts, dwelling in Wallbrook," Captain William Coleson, "of the Custom House," and many assorted merchants and tradesmen. There are at least two notorious characters in the persons of Captain Walter Lee, a haberdasher in Ludgate, who "did break the windows on Westminster Abbey," and Captain William Coleson, who "with his company carried the Statues in the church of Allhallowes to ye parliament."

Two of those mentioned afterwards became notorious as "regicides": Captain Robert Tichborne, a linendraper, who became one of Cromwell's House of Lords, and Major Owen Roe, a mercer in Cheapside, who became Quarter-Master-General of Cromwell's army in Ireland and eventually died as a prisoner in the Tower. Others are noted as "Violent O" (Roundheads). Colonel Thomas Atkins was nominated to the Court which tried King Charles, but refused to act.

The Royalists who held commissions are listed, though obviously not present at the muster, and included Colonel Thomas Adams (Pepys's "comely old alderman"), who gave large sums to support Prince Charles in exile; Lieutenant-Colonel Matthew Foster, Vintner at the Ship beyond Exchange, who is marked "put out"; Captain Richard Hacket, "now in his Majestie's service"; and Captain Newbery, who had apparently been committed to prison by his colonel.

The Royalist agent did not manage to collect all the names of the officers, but in a contemporary roll now in the possession of the Company appears the name of Lieutenant-Colonel Marmaduke Royden, a Royalist who fought for the King and later commanded the garrison at Farringdon; also that of Captain John Ven, later Colonel commanding the Parliamentary garrison at Windsor which beat off an attack by Prince Rupert, who sat at the trial of King Charles and signed the death warrant, but died before the Restoration.

It has been noted that no new members were admitted to

the Artillery Garden from April, 1644, onwards, and from the complete lack of records of succeeding years it may be assumed that the Company's normal activities ceased during the later periods of the Civil War. It was not until 1655, four years after the downfall of Royalist hopes at Worcester, that the Lord Mayor and Commissioners of Militia applied to Oliver Cromwell for leave "to revive the power of the Artillery Company, for the better disciplining of the citizens, whereby they might, upon any emergency, be enabled to act together for his defence." The Lord Protector readily agreed, took upon himself the patronage of the Company and appointed Major-General Skippon as Captain-General. It is significant that none were to be admitted members but such as were well affected to His Highness the Lord Protector.

Forthwith the Company was revived. A Court of Assistants was held in the Irish Chamber at Guildhall on 21st January, 1656, at which a Clerk and Gunsmith were appointed, and from that date the complete minutes of the Court are available in unbroken sequence to the present day. On the 28th of the same month a Beadle was appointed, whose office was to summon the whole Company and to collect moneys for the Treasurer, and at the same Court the names of the first new members to be admitted since the revival were entered in the Old Vellum Book. At subsequent meetings the Court appointed two Sergeants, a "Cloake Keeper," and two "Drums," also Gatekeepers for the Old and New Artillery Grounds.

It appears that the Company still made use of the Old Ground in Bishopsgate, but in 1658 the Company sold to the Master Gunner for £300 their Armoury and Courthouse, built in 1622 at a cost of £1,000, and all other structures belonging to the Company and situated in the Old Ground. Thus ended the century-long dispute as to priority of claim; the Gunners of the Tower were left in sole possession of the Ground in Tassell Close.

In the first Minute Book of the Court of Assistants we find the reason for the lack of all earlier records (with the exception of the Vellum Book). It appears that during the Civil War the archives and valuables belonging to the Company had been placed in charge of various eminent members. One of these, Lieutenant-Colonel William Manby, Treasurer of the Company, now refused to deliver up the plate, money, arms, books and papers in his possession. The reason for his refusal does not appear, except for the merest hint that Manby did not consider the Company, as reconstituted, to be the legal successors of the original Company of which he was Treasurer. He merely ignored all requests, orders or threats. Deputations and sub-committees waited upon the defaulter with no result; summonses to appear before the Court and before the Militia Committee were useless; a Bill in Chancery was tried in vain; petitions to the Lord Protector, to the Committee of Parliament, and later, to Charles II, had no effect. Nothing was ever recovered.

Thus the ancient archives of the Regiment, which must certainly have covered the period from 1610 to 1643, and probably went back to the date of the Charter, were irretrievably lost to posterity through the criminal stubbornness, carelessness or roguery of one individual. No traces of these records have ever come to light and it must be presumed that they were destroyed, probably in the Great Fire. Among the missing documents was the original lease of the Artillery Ground and the lost plate included a "giult standing Cupp" worth £50, also "two Silver Flaggons to the valew of 50L." The individual responsible for this irreparable loss was admitted a member of the Company in 1618 and was appointed Treasurer in 1637. At the outbreak of the Civil War he was 3rd Captain in the White Regiment of Trained Bands, and he fought with his regiment at Cheriton.

Another regimental possession which was lost in similar circumstances was "ye Storie of ye Fight Anno 1588, Painted on 8 Frames," which had been presented to the Company in 1630. These pictures had been entrusted to the care of a Mr. John Eager, of Farnham, whose connection with the Company is not clear. They were never recovered.

The first General Court after the revival was held on 26th January, 1657. This was also the first meeting on record to be held in the Armoury in the New Artillery Ground, and provides the earliest intimation that such a building existed. It appears from contemporary maps to have been situated in the north-west corner of the field. No record of its erection can be traced, but it probably dated from 1641.

At this Court Sir Robert Tichborne was elected President and Major-General Skippon, being present, "was pleased to acknowledge himselfe Captain of the Company, onely there could not bee Expected soe much from him as formerly there had, by reason of such multiplicity of business that lay upon him, but his Earnest Desire was for the prosperity of ye company." This is almost the end of the veteran General's long connection with the Company. In 1660 he was superseded in his command of the City Forces by General Monk and retired into private life.

There appears to have been some friction between members of the Company and their commanders shortly after the revival, and the Treasurer, Colonel Sheppard, was desired by the Court "to speake to ye Company and to pasyfye theyre Distempers, that noe mutiny may arise amongst them."

The ancient custom of attending the Lord Mayor on his return from Westminster was revived in 1658. Sir John Ireton, on landing at Baynard's Castle, was met by the Gentlemen of the Artillery Ground, who "accommodated his Lordship with their Company."

The earliest record of Standing Orders for the guidance of the Company occurs in 1615. On 26th April of that year certain propositions of articles were submitted to the Court of Aldermen by the Society of the Artillery Garden "to be confirmed for their better establishment and government in the practice and exercise of arms in or about the City."

The next mention of the subject occurs in 1631, when the Court of Aldermen appointed a Committee of eight (mostly members of the Company) "to carefully peruse and consider the orders (which had apparently been drawn up in 1629) to be observed by every Member of the Society exercising arms in the Artillery Garden" and to report to the Court their opinion thereon. In the following year, as no report had been received, the Court renewed its instructions, and added the Recorder of the City to the Committee to replace a member who had died. The final result, if any, of these deliberations has not survived, but in 1658 the Court of Aldermen drew up for the government of the Company a set of Rules and Orders, of which a reprint, dated 1751, is still in the possession of the Regiment.

These are believed the oldest regimental standing orders in existence, and are here set forth in full:

ORDERS

Made by the

Court of Assistants

of the

ARTILLERY-COMPANY,

And confirmed by

The Whole Society, at two General Courts, holden in the *Armory* in the *Artillery* (Ground), *viz.* the First Court on the 8th of *February* 1658, and the other Court, on the 7th *February*, 1659.

By which Orders the Company is to be governed.

IMPRIMIS, It is thought fit, and so ordered and agreed upon, that, as for the present, the Company is now ordered and governed, so it shall continue and be governed by a President, a Deputy-President, a Treasurer, and Four and Twenty Assistants, whereof four of the Assistants shall be Field-Officers, or Captains of the Trained-Bands of the City of *London*, that do pay Quarteridge, and shall continue to be of the Company, and shall be annually chosen there by the whole Body of the Company, in manner following.

II. *Item*, It is ordered and agreed upon, The whole Company shall be summoned once every Year, to meet at the *Artillery-Garden*, on the next *Tuesday* after *Candlemas-Day*; and there to nominate Three sufficient Citizens, being Freemen of *London*, and present Members of this Company, whom they shall think fit, to stand in order to Election for President, and out of them, they, or the greater Part of them, shall choose one, by holding up of Hands, to be President for the Year ensuing.

III. *Item*, It is ordered and agreed upon, That at the same General-Meeting, the Company shall every Year, in like Sort, nominate and choose, by holding up of Hands, out of such of the said Society as are Citizens and Freemen of *London*, a Deputy-President and a Treasurer, for the Year next ensuing, in Manner and Form following; that is to say, out of three Members of the said Company to be nominated, shall elect and choose one of them for a Deputy-President; who, if he refuse to hold the Place, shall pay, for a Fine to the present Treasurer, for the Use of the Company, *Three Pounds*. And out of three, to be nominated as aforesaid, shall elect one of them for a Treasurer, to keep the common Treasure of the Company for the Year ensuing. In which Nomination and Choice, it is hereby declared, that Respect is to be had to the Antientest of the Company, if they be otherwise fit: Which Treasurer so chosen, shall at the next Court of Assistants, to be holden for the Company, after his Election, put in two sufficient Sureties, such as the Court of Assistants, or the greater part of them, shall approve of, to render a true Accompt at the Years End, to such Auditors as shall be chosen by the Assistants, of what Money he shall receive and pay for the Company's Use that Year; and to pay what shall be resting upon the Foot of his Account to the succeeding Treasurer, at the Time of his Audit. And if any Treasurer, so chosen, shall refuse to hold the Place, or give Security as aforesaid, he shall pay, to the present Treasurer, to the Use of the Company, *Forty Shillings*. And for the rest of the Assistants, It is ordered and agreed, That the Treasurer for the Year past, shall be one of the Assistants for the Year ensuing; and the Company shall also choose of the Assistants that were of the last Year, Six of them, for the Year ensuing; And that the Eight Stewards, that served the presedent Year, shall be Eight other of the Assistants, for the Year following; and the rest to be elected out of the Company, until the Number of Twenty-four be made up; and if any so chosen an Assistant, shall refuse to hold the Place, he shall pay for a Fine to the Treasurer, for the Use of the Company, *Twenty Shillings*.

IV. *Item*, Upon the Nomination of Persons for Leaders, It is ordered and agreed, That the Company exceed not the Number of Eight; which Number of Eight is to be reduced, by most Voices, to Four; out of which Four to elect Two to lead, and exercise the Company in the Absence of the Captain for the Year following; the First to begin the next Training Day after the Election, and to continue till Midsummer following; and the other to begin the next Training Day after Midsummer, and to continue till the next Election. And out of Eight, as aforesaid, shall elect Two, to serve as Lieutenants for the Year following; the First to begin the next Training Day after the Election, and to continue till *Midsummer* following; and the other to begin the next Training Day after *Midsummer*, and continue till the next Election. And out of Eight, as aforesaid, to be nominated, shall elect Two for Ensigns for the Year ensuing, to bear the Colours for that Year; the First to begin the next Training Day after Election, and continue till *Midsummer* following; and the Second to begin the next Training Day after *Midsummer*, and to continue till the Second.* And shall also choose Four Surveyors of Arms, who shall look to the Arms, to see them clean kept, and in good Order; and to see that Arms be brought in according to the Order of Arms: and shall give a Note to the Treasurer, at, or before the Audit of his Accompt, what Arms be in the Garden, and whose they be, and what Arms there shall be remaining to the Company. And if any so chosen a Surveyor, shall refuse to hold the Place, shall pay for a Fine to the Treasurer, for the Use of the Company, *Ten Shillings*. And out of Two or more, shall elect One, to be Marshall for the Year ensuing. And out of Six to be nominated, shall elect Three, to be Serjeants, to supply those Places and Offices for the Year ensuing.

V. *Item*, It is ordered and agreed upon, That the rest of the Officers and Attendants, belonging to the Company, *viz.* the Clerk

---

* ? Election.

and the Beadle, &c. shall be annually chosen upon the same general Election Day, as other Officers are.

VI. *Item*, It is ordered and agreed upon, That upon the next Court of Assistants, after the General Election Day, the Leaders, the Lieutenants, the Ensigns, the Treasurer, the Stewards, and Assistants, shall give their Answer, whether they will hold their Places, or not; and if any refuse, then the Assistants, or the greater part of them, to choose others in their Places.

VII. *Item*, It is ordered and agreed upon, That any Gentleman, or Citizen, that shall desire to be admitted into this Society, shall be recommended by one or more of the Company, to whom he is known, and presented to two or more of the Assistants, and after to the Court of Assistants, and there shall be confirmed of the Company, if no just Exception be against him; and every one so admitted, if he be a Freeman of *London*, shall pay to the Treasurer, for the Use of the Company, Twenty Shillings, and Twelvepence to the Clerk for registering of his Name, and Sixpence to the Beadle for entering him into his Book; and if he be not a Freeman, he shall enter a Pike, and pay according to the rate of a Pike, and Two Shillings to the Clerk, and Twelvepence to the Beadle.

VIII. *Item*, It is ordered and agreed upon, That Every one entering himself, and using a Pike, shall pay to the Company's Use for his Admittance into the Company Forty Shillings, and Five Shillings a Quarter; and Every one entering himself, and using a Musket, shall pay for his Admittance into the Company Twenty Shillings, and Two Shillings and Sixpence a Quarter.

IX. *Item*, It is ordered and agreed upon, That no Apprentice or Covenant Servant shall be admitted into this Society, not any Person that is not known to be well affected in Religion, and not inclined to Popery; nor any that is a Bankrupt, or hath compounded for his Debts, or not of sufficient Means or Ability to spare his Time, or bear the Charge of the Company: And if any such Person now admitted, or at any Time hereafter shall be known to be such, he shall be admonished by two of the Assistants to forbear the Company; and in case he shall refuse, he shall be expulsed the Company by the Court of Assistants, if they shall think so fitting.

X. *Item*, It is ordered and agreed upon, That every Member of the Company, that is already admitted, shall before the first Day of July next; and that every one which shall hereafter be admitted into the Company, shall within two Months after his Admission, bring into the Armory in the *Artillery-Garden*, there to be kept for his Use, such Arms of his own, as shall be thought fitting by the said Captain or Leader for the Time being, his Stature considered; *viz.* Every one entered to Exercise with a Pike, to bring in his Gorget and Pike, and every one entered a Musket, to bring in a Musket with a Match-Lock and Rest.

XI. *Item*, It is ordered and agreed on, That every Musket, which shall be brought into the Garden, which hath not been tried by the Gunsmith of *London*, shall be tried by the Gunsmith of the Company, in the Presence of the Owner, and one Surveyor of Arms for the Time being, at the charge of the Owner, before the same Musket be used in the Garden, upon pain that Every one that shall offend herein shall pay, to the Use of the Company, every Training Day that he shall use it before it be tried, Twelvepence upon Demand, by the Treasurer or Collector, for the Time being.

XII. *Item*, It is ordered and agreed upon, That the next *Tuesday* after Election Day shall be a General Training Day, and so forward every second *Tuesday* after through the whole Year, upon which General Training Day every Member of the Company, being summoned to appear at the Garden, shall appear there by Two of the Clock in the Winter, between the Twenty-ninth day of *September* and the Twenty-fifth of *March*, and by Three of the Clock in the Summer Season, betwixt the Twenty-fifth Day of *March* and the Twenty-ninth Day of *September*.

XIII. *Item*, It is ordered and agreed upon, That every Officer belonging to the Company, that hath Salary, shall make his Appearance at the Garden every General Day of Training, at the Hour of One of the Clock in the Winter, and Two of the Clock in the Summer; and if in Case any of them shall come after the Hours aforesaid, he shall pay for a Fine, to the Use of the Company, Sixpence; and if he comes not at all that Day he shall pay Twelvepence, except in case of Sickness, or that he hath acquainted the Leader or Captain before-hand with his Business, and hath leave from him to be absent.

XIV. *Item*, It is ordered and agreed upon, That if any Member of this Company, being in the Garden, shall be required by the Marshal or Officers to arm himself, and shall not be armed upon any General Training Day, he shall pay for a Fine, to the Treasurer, for the Use of the Company, Sixpence, unless they can give reasonable Satisfaction to the Leader for the Time being; and if any of the Company do, upon any General Training Day of Exercise, bear Arms without a Sword or Rapier, he shall pay to the Treasurer Threepence for the Use of the Company, except he hath such as the Leader approves.

XV. *Item*, It is ordered and agreed upon, That upon the General Training Day every Member of the Company, whether he use Pike or Musket, shall be ready before the third Beat of Drum, which shall be at the Hours aforesaid, to be drawn into a File by the Officers, and shall take such Place as he shall be appointed unto; and, if any refuse to march forth in such Place as he shall be commanded, he shall pay to the Company's Use Sixpence.

XVI. *Item*, It is ordered and agreed upon, That during the Time of Exercise, there shall be a general Silence, so as no Man's

Voice be heard but the Officers, and Every one offending herein to pay Twopence to the Use of the Company.

XVII. *Item*, It is ordered and agreed upon, That no Member of the Company, during the Time of Exercise in the Garden, or in marching forth into the City-fields, or to Funerals, shall go forth of his Rank or File to shoot off his Musket, or shall do it in his Rank, without Command; and if any do so, he shall forfeit for every Time he shall offend herein the Sum of Sixpence.

XVIII. *Item*, It is ordered, &c. That no Member of this Company, being in Rank and File, shall depart from his Colours before they be lodged, without Leave of the Leader, and Every one so offending, shall pay Sixpence.

XIX. *Item*, It is ordered, &c. That no Member of this Company shall abuse any of his Fellow-Soldiers, by taking away his Powder or Match, or by shooting off his Musket, whereby any Quarrel may arise, and that the Party offending herein, shall pay for a Fine to the Company's Use, Twelvepence.

XX. *Item*, It is ordered, &c. That no Member of this Company shall, upon any General Training Day, call the Captain-Leader, Lieutenant, Ensign or Serjeants by any other Name than the Name of his Place, upon pain of Forfeiting for every Time they shall offend therein, to the Company's Use, Sixpence.

XXI. *Item*, It is ordered, &c. That if any Member of this Company shall wilfully or negligently hurt any of his Fellow-Soldiers, and be thereof convicted, he shall submit himself to pay such Fine as the Court of Assistants shall impose upon him; and if, in such cases, he shall refuse to do it, he shall be expulsed the Company.

XXII. *Item*, It is ordered, &c. That if any Member of the Company shall, at any Time, challenge any of his Fellow-Soldiers to shoot at a Mark for any Wager, without leave of the Captain, or Leader, for the Time being, he shall pay for a Fine, to the Use of the Company, Five Shillings.

XXIII. *Item*, It is ordered, &c. That if any Officer or Member of the Company shall, at any Time of their accustomed Meetings in the *Artillery-Garden*, or elsewhere, abuse the Name of God, by Swearing or Cursing, for every Time it shall be proved that he offends therein, he shall pay, to the Company's Use Twelvepence, which shall be put into a Box in the Court-House; and once in the Year shall be distributed to the Poor by the Court of Assistants.

XXIV. *Item*. It is ordered, &c. That if any Officer or Member of this Company shall abuse himself, by drinking too much, or urge any of his Fellow-Soldiers to drink immoderately at any Time, or by ill Words or other Misdemeanours, shall breed any Quarrel or Disturbance, and shall be thereof convicted at a Court of Assistants, he shall submit himself to such Penalty, as the Assistants, or the greater Part of them, in their Discretions, shall think to impose upon him, not exceeding Five Shillings; and in case any shall refuse to submit himself, he shall be expulsed the Company.

XXV. *Item*, It is ordered, &c. That if any of this Company shall come to the Garden upon any of the usual Training Days, being overseen in Drink, he shall not be suffered to bear Arms that Day; and if he shall bear Arms notwithstanding, and shall be convict of Drunkenness at a Court of Assistants, he shall pay for the first Offence Three Shillings and Fourpence, for the second Offence Five Shillings, and for the third Offence he shall be expulsed the Company; and if any Officer that taketh Salary or Gratuity of the Company, and shall offend herein, he shall pay for the first Offence Five Shillings, for the second Offence Ten Shillings, and for the third Offence he shall be expulsed the Company.

XXVI. *Item*, It is ordered, &c. That if any Officer or Member of this Company shall draw any of his Fellow-Soldiers, on any of their accustomed Training Days, or after their Training is ended to Dice, Cards, Tables, or any other unlawful Game, and shall be thereof convicted at a Court of Assistants, Every one so offending herein shall pay, for his first Offence, Ten Shillings to the Use of the Company, and for the second Offence, he shall be expulsed the Company.

XXVII. *Item*, It is ordered, and agreed upon, That if any Members of this Company shall be turbulent or factious, or a Stirrer-up of Dissension, or factious against the Peace or Welfare of the Company, and shall thereof be convicted at a Court of Assistants, and shall refuse to submit himself to the Order of the Court, he shall be therefore expulsed the Company.

XXVIII. *Item*, It is ordered, &c. That if any Difference or Quarrel shall arise betwixt any of the Members of the Company, concerning the Affairs of the Company, each Party shall submit himself to such Orders as the Court of Assistants shall set down; and if any refuse to stand on such Order, he shall be expulsed the Company.

XXIX. *Item*, It is ordered, &c. That the Company shall not be summoned to go in Arms to the Funeral of any Member of this Society except the Party deceased hath, by his Last Will or otherwise, given Ten Pounds at the least, to the Use of the said Company.

XXX. *Item*, It is ordered, &c. That if any Member of the Company shall go out of the Land, beyond the Sea, and shall give Notice thereof to the Captain-Leader, Treasurer, and Collector, for the Time being, or any one of them, he shall be freed from paying of Quarteridge all the Time of his Absence out of the Land, and at his Return, paying his Quarteridge, he shall hold his Place of Antiquity upon the Roll which he had before.

XXXI. *Item*, It is ordered, &c. That no Member of this Company shall take his Arms out of the Garden upon any Occasion, untill he hath paid all his Duties there; and if he continue of the Company, he shall bring them into the Garden again, within two Months, or else he shall pay for every Month he shall keep them forth longer, the Sum of Twelvepence, to the Treasurer, for the Use of the Company.

XXXII. *Item*, It is ordered, &c. That if any Member of this Company shall refuse to pay his Quarteridge to the Treasurer or Collector of the Company for the Time being, it being demanded by either of them, he shall pay such Fine to the Company's Use, as the Court of Assistants shall think fit to impose upon him, so as such a Fine exceeds not the double Sum of the Money then in Arrear for such Quarteridge; and any that shall be behind in Arrearage Six Months, and it being demanded, if he shall refuse to pay it, he shall, if the Court of Assistants think fit, be expulsed the Company.

XXXIII. *Item*, It is ordered and agreed upon, That once every Year the whole Company shall meet at the *Artillery-Garden* upon such a day, as the Court of Assistants shall think fit, and from thence shall go in Order and decent Manner, in their Cloaks, with Sword and Feather, to a Sermon, and so to Dine or Sup together; and every Member of the Company shall pay the Stewards, for the Time being, Two Shillings and Sixpence, Eight Days at the least, before the same Day of Meeting, whether he come to Dinner or Supper, or not; and every Captain that is at present in command of the Trained-Bands of *London*, that holds himself of the Company, shall pay to the Stewards Five Shillings, and this shall be paid by every of the Captains, whether he come or not.

XXXIV. *Item*, It is ordered, &c. That the Preacher, that shall preach on the said General Day of Meeting, shall be chosen by the Court of Assistants, and shall be paid by the Treasurer, for his Sermon, Forty Shillings.

XXXV. *Item*, It is ordered, &c. That at the same General Day of Meeting, the Eight present Stewards shall choose out of the Company, such as shall be nominated to them by the Court of Assistants, to be Stewards for the Year following; and the Stewards so chosen shall give their Answers at the next Court of Assistants, whether they will hold the Place, or not; and if any so chosen shall refuse to hold the Place, then he shall pay to the Treasurer, for a Fine, to the Use of the Company, the Sum of Three Pounds Sterling, and the Court of Assistants shall have Power to choose another in his Place.

XXXVI. *Item*, It is ordered and agreed upon, That the Assistants, or the greater Part of them, shall, at the next Court before the General Day, yearly, for the Election of Officers, make choice of six or more of themselves to audit the Accompt of the present Treasurer and Collector.

FINIS.

It was not long before the Company revived the ancient custom of the Annual Feast and Sermon. This ceremony took the form of a muster in the Artillery Ground, followed by a field exercise, after which the Company marched in solemn procession to Old St. Paul's or some other City church, where they heard a sermon preached by a dignitary of the Church specially selected for the occasion. The preacher received for his services "three broad pieces of gold." The sermons were afterwards printed and distributed, presumably for the benefit of those members who were unable to keep awake during the fifty minutes or more of their delivery. Many of these publications have survived. They almost invariably contain evidence of a strong political bias, varying with the popular feeling of the period. After the sermon the Company marched, with their guests, to the hall of one of the City Companies, usually the Merchant Taylors', where the feast was spread. The expenses were shared by the eight Stewards, elected annually from among the wealthier members, who, as recorded in the Vellum Book, "were honorably pleased to bear the charges of the Feast." They received, however, some assistance from the general fund towards the entertainment of official guests. Happily, a description of the order of march on one of these interesting occasions survives in the minute books. It is here appended.

The 18th of August 1658 The Company mett in ye Artillery Garden from thence they marcht to Pauls Church where Mr. Griffeth preacht a sermon and soe to Marchantaylors hall to dinner.

The manner of theyre march thus

Imprimis the Marshall of the Company in his Bufcoat Scarfe Sword feather Gauntlelet & Truncheon.

4 Marshalls in bufcoats Scarfes feathers swords & truncheons.

8 Stewards wth Guilt Staves swords & feathers 2 in rancke. Next place for ye Lord Mayor & Aldermen Ministers & other Guests 2 in rancke who mett ye Company att Church and after sermon marcht in theyre places to Merchantaylo^{rs} hall accordinge

to theyre degree. The Right hono^{rble} Ald^{r}man Chinerton beinge Lord Mayo^r went a foote in his Scarlett Gowne wth the Mace & sword both borne before him & ye Sherriffs & Ald^{r}men in theyre Scarlet Gownes likewise.

4 Marshalls in like habit as before.

The Right hono^{rble} ye Lord Tichborne beinge Presedent.

4 Marshalls as before.

The Hon^{le} Sr John Ireton Dep^{ty} Presedent.

4 Marshalls as before.

Coll. Matthew Sheppeard Treasurer who likewise supplied ye place of ye Capt of ye Company haveinge ye Leadeinge Staffe borne by him by another yt marcht wthout a Cloake.

The Assistants in theyre Cloaks wth swords & feathers & white staves.

The Cap^{ts} of ye trayned bands & feild officers 2 in rancke.

The Company in theyre cloakes swords & feathers 2 in rancke likewise.

The Lieuten^t in ye reare in his cloak sword & feather haveinge his Partisan borne by another yt marcht by him wthout a cloake.

The Eldest Sarjeant attended ye Presid^t ye other ye Capt:

Dinner beinge Ended they proceeded to ye Eleccon of new Stewards Every Steward haveinge two Marshalls & a drum to attend him Every Steward wearinge a Lawrell upon his head wch hee put upon ye new Elected Stewards head.

The Motto. Love hates Division.

When Oliver Cromwell died in 1658, the Court of Assistants "thought good to move the Militia (Committee) that yf the Trayne Bands doe not attend the Lord Protector his funerall, then the Artillery Company is ready to present theyre Services." The Militia Committee, thinking the Trained Bands too numerous for the occasion, requested the Company to represent the Militia forces of the City of London at the funeral, and suggested that application should be made for a convenient place in the procession to be assigned to them. Whereupon the following summons was issued to members of the Company:

Sr:

You are desired to appeare on Tuesday morninge the 9th of this instant 9ber att eight of the Clocke in the Artillery Garden compleately armed and habited wth a black feather to march from thence to attend the funerall of his late Highnes Oliver Lord Protector and not to fayle in any of the premises as you tender the honor of the Cittie & Company.

and at the same time the following orders were promulgated:

Major Randal & Capt: Best are desired to speake to the Harroulds (Heralds) to knowe ye tyme of ye Companys Comeinge to attend ye funerall & the place where they shall drawe upp.

Ordered that the Leading Staffe & Partison the heads bee covered with Sipress (cypress) and yt a ribbon bee provided for the Collours.

Ordered that there bee 10 Drums & Fifes and that the Treasurer of this Company doe provide blacke bayes (baize) for the coveringe of them.

It is unfortunately impossible to ascertain the exact design of the Colours carried by the Company at this time. Six Colours were usually used, the Colonel's, the Lieutenant-Colonel's, and one for each of the four Captains. A Colonel's Colour of this period usually took the form of a plain coloured field; a Lieutenant-Colonel's bore the cross of St. George in the first canton; the other four or more Colours were similar in colour but charged with one or more devices, such as fleurs-de-lis, roundels, crosses, mullets, caltrop, trefoils, or portcullises, for the purpose of distinction.

The following note occurs in the Court minutes of 1659: "It beinge put to most voyces whether there should bee a Cullors flyinge on the head of the Company or not upon the By Days it was carried in the affirmative and that they bee of the Companyes Cullor wth a Cross for Distinction in forme of a Lt: Collo^{lls}: Cullo^{rs}." The Company's colour, referred to above, was red. An entry in the Vellum Book records the gift, in 1635, of "red Colours with a Red Cross therein."

After nine months of troubled rule Richard Cromwell resigned the Protectorship. General Monk marched south from Coldstream and negotiations were opened with the exiled King. As a gesture in favour of the restoration of the monarchy the City, having raised the six regiments of Auxiliaries and 500 Horse, resolved upon a "sudden general rendezvous" of all their forces, "the affections of this Honourable City being so unanimous." 20,000 Trained Bands and Auxiliaries marched into Hyde Park on 24th April, 1660, "all numerous and so gallantry accoutred as did sufficiently speak both the strength and riches of the City, there being little visible difference between the Trained Bands and Auxiliaries, but only in their age." On 8th May Charles II was proclaimed King in London.

CHAPTER V

1660 TO 1701

FOLLOWING on the restoration of the monarchy, King Charles II entered London on 29th May, 1660, amid unprecedented popular rejoicings. The same City which had been a bulwark of the Parliamentary cause now took the lead in greeting the son of the deposed King. Sick of the tyranny of Parliament and a military dictatorship, the people of London threw off the trappings of Puritanism and welcomed the King to his own again with lavish display.

The Court Minutes record the intention of the Company to march on that day and to entertain General Monk afterwards. But it was not to be. The City Trained Bands were turning out in full strength and could hardly do so without officers. The records of the Militia Committee state that "the Artillery Company desiring to appear in that capacity on the day of His Majesty's passage through the City, it is thought fit that they rather appear in their proper Companies of the Trained Bands."

The Green Regiment formed a guard of honour at Southwark Bridge, where the King entered the City, and we are told that these troops, "who by the order of their Officers, had presented to His Majesty as he passed the Butt end of their Musquets, gave and discharged a great many Vollies of shot" after the royal cortège had passed. This seems to be a very early instance of the "Present Arms." The remaining five regiments lined the streets as far as Temple Bar.

The roll of membership during the two decades following the revival of the Company under Cromwell furnishes an interesting study of the trend of public opinion during that period. At first only those citizens who were known to be well affected to His Highness the Lord Protector were admitted as members, but the changed ideas which brought about the Restoration are reflected in the records of the Regiment. Naturally enough,

the verdict of the country caused certain changes in the government and personnel of the Company, due to the retirement of
fanatical Puritans and the accession of staunch Royalists, yet
the majority of the Court of Assistants and other officials
continued to serve under the monarchy and took the oath of
allegiance to King Charles. The Minute of the Court on this
subject runs as follows: *"Att a Court of Assistants of the
Artillery Company held att ye Greate James Taverne B^{pps} gate
Streete W^{th}in the 17th January 1660.* It is Ordered and agreed
upon by this Court that the Gentlemen members of the Artillery
Company doe take the Oath of Allegiance upon the General
Eleccon day."* No less than 220 new members were admitted
in 1660 against a total of 70 in the preceding year, but no
record was kept of resignations, so that it is impossible to say
to what extent the members of the Company complied with the
above order. No doubt the prominent share taken by the
Company in the several public ceremonies in the City was
partly responsible for the increase of admissions.

The general pardon granted at the Restoration to all who had
taken up arms against the monarchy did not include the
regicides—*i.e.*, those who had taken any part in the trial and
execution of King Charles I. These included a number of
members of the Company. Of those who had signed the death
warrant, Colonels John Ven (1614) and Thomas Pride (1642)
had died before the Restoration. Colonel John Barkstead (1657)
was executed. Colonels Robert Tichborne (1636) and Edmond
Harvey (1642) were imprisoned for life, and Colonel Owen Roe
(1619) was sentenced to death but died in the Tower. Colonel
Isaac Pennington (1639), Colonel John Hewson (1659) and
William Goffe (1614) fled the country.

Of officials present at the trial, Colonel Daniel Axtell (1657),
Captain of the Guard, was executed; John Cooke, Solicitor
(1643), and Edward Dendy, Sergeant at Arms (1614), escaped.

Colonel Thomas Atkins (1624) and Rowland Wilson (1634)
had been appointed by Cromwell to serve on the Court
but, like Phillip Skippon, had refused to have anything to do
with it.

For the first time we are now given an inkling of the methods
of recruiting then employed. In 1661 members of the various
City Wards were appointed to call upon "inhabitants of ancient
standing" and to invite them to join the Company. Each

candidate had to be recommended by a member, and the names were recorded in the Minute Books of the Court.

At a General Court held on 26th June, 1660, His Royal Highness the Duke of York was elected "Commander-in-Chief" of the Company, he being the first and last holder of that title. His successor, William III, styled himself Captain-General, which latter designation has survived to the present day. The Duke not only accepted the proffered rank, but took considerable interest in the Company. He almost invariably attended the annual feasts, and it was the custom for a special deputation of the Court of Assistants to report to him the results of the election of officers each year. His Royal Highness was prompt to show his displeasure when an election did not meet with his approval. In 1677 a prominent member, Sir Thomas Player, was re-elected Leader, a position he had held continuously since 1669. On hearing of this, the Duke "declared his displeasure," stating that Sir Thomas "had behaved himself so that no honest man ought to countenance him." Wherein this gentleman had offended we are not told; but he was acquainted with the royal "disproval," and never led again. In fact, from that time onward the appointment of Leader was allowed to lapse.

The King was entertained by the City at Guildhall in July of this year. On that occasion, says a contemporary writer, "the Gentlemen of the Artillery, led by the Valiant and Learned Lord Lucas, at *Cheapside*, opened to the left and right and guarded both sides of the way, while His Majesty passed through." Another chronicler relates that "after the Banquet, the Gentlemen of the Artillery, placed from the South end of the Old Jury to the West end of *Cheapside* with Trophies and Trumpets, received his Majesty." Apparently the Lord Mayor accompanied the royal procession back to Whitehall, the Company, meanwhile, "eagerly awaited his Lordship's return, which, being discovered, a volley is given, and every man departeth to his home."

In October, Sir Richard Brown, a member of the Company and a distinguished Parliamentary general who was converted by the conversation of King Charles at Holmby House and became a leading Royalist, became Lord Mayor, and the Company marched in front of his procession from St. Paul's Wharf "to shew their affection and loyalty." They were led by

Sir John Robinson, Lieutenant of the Tower and President of the Company, "in his scarlet gown and sword."

A line in the Court Minute Book of February, 1660, sanctions the payment of £3 10s. to the Armourer for cleansing a number of corselets and "one Gilt capape (cap-à-pie) Armer." This is the earliest known reference to the magnificent suit of tilting armour which is one of the two most cherished possessions of the Company. Experts tell us that the suit was wrought by Jacobe of Greenwich *circa* 1555-60 and that it is the earliest known work attributed to that celebrated craftsman. The suit is made for a man about 5 feet 8 inches in height, and is furnished with a mezail (reinforcing face guard) and grand guard (extra protection for chest and throat when jousting). The wooden tilting lance which has been in the possession of the regiment for at least two hundred years probably belonged to the original owner of the suit, but who this individual was it is impossible to say with certainty. As the suit is of the finest workmanship, he must have been a person of some importance. The writer is inclined to attribute the ownership to Sir Peter Mewtes, Master General of the Ordnance and Ruler of the Guild of Artillery about the time the suit was made. He was killed in the defence of Calais in 1558, and it is not beyond the bounds of probability that his tilting suit remained at the old Armoury in Bishopsgate, where tournaments occasionally took place. In 1658 certain officers of the Company were detailed to superintend the removal of the arms and lumber from the Old Armoury prior to its sale, and this would account for the possession of this armour by the Company in 1660. The suit has recently been valued at £25,000.

The Company having "felt some discouragement by reason of several slender musters," the Lieutenancy of London promulgated an order, dated 1662, that all Sergeants of the London Trained Bands should enrol as members of the Artillery Company for training in their duties. They were to be admitted without entrance fees, but were to pay the usual quarterly subscriptions, then referred to as "quarteridge."

In the following year the Court found it necessary to order that no apprentice or covenant servant should be admitted, and a few years later it was laid down that no person should be admitted to membership without the approval of two members of the Court. Previous to that date any member of the Company

[Photo: *Crown Copyright Reserved. Reproduced by permission of the Ministry of Works*
SUIT OF TILTING ARMOUR MADE BY JACOBE OF GREENWICH *circa* 1560,
REFERRED TO IN THE MINUTES OF THE COURT OF ASSISTANTS OF 1ST FEBRUARY
1660, AND STILL IN THE POSSESSION OF THE REGIMENT

was free to enrol anyone he wished, not always a satisfactory method of recruiting. It is recorded that one Robert Angell had his entrance money returned, "beinge a man thought fitt not to beare arms wth the rest of the Society." Stern disciplinary measures were taken by the Court when occasion arose. In 1670 Lieutenant Francis Colman had his name "razed out of the Companyes greate booke" for his "unmanly carriage" towards Captain Randall, and in the same year John Currey was similarly punished "for his unmanly action in biting of his wives nose."

The first appointment of a Surgeon to the Company was decreed by the Court in 1664, and the Treasurer was ordered to provide a scarf for that officer.*

It was the practice of the Company at this time, and apparently had been from time immemorial, to march to Balmes (often spelt Baulmes, Baums or Bawms) on one of the "General Days" in every year. On these occasions tents were sometimes pitched "in the greate Feild leading to Kingsland." Balmes House was an old mansion standing in spacious grounds in Hogsden (now Hoxton). It had originally been the residence of Sir George Whitmore, Lord Mayor of London in 1631-1632. The carriage way to the house was still in use as a private approach when the estate was held on lease by the grandfather of Cecil Rhodes and can even now be recognized as Whitmore Road, Hoxton. Balmes survives only in the corrupted name of Ball's Pond Road.

The particular reason of the Company's march to this spot lay in the fact that it occupied a central position in the old archery fields, many of the stone marks or rovers standing in its grounds. The assertion of ancient rights and the removal of encroachments were important features of the exercise, and many disputes arose in later days as brickfields, buildings and enclosed gardens began to interfere with the right of way from one mark to another.

The Company now found itself in great favour at Court, and many of the nobility and gentry of the royal household enrolled themselves as members. Prince Rupert, the dashing Royalist leader, joined in 1664, bringing with him George Monk, first Duke of Albemarle, the Earl of Sandwich, patron

---

* A surgeon wore a very voluminous scarf, which could be used in an emergency to carry a wounded man.

of Pepys and a famous admiral, and Lord Craven. These were followed shortly afterwards by James, Duke of Monmouth, the Duke of Ormonde, the Earl of Manchester (an old Parliamentary general, then Lord Chamberlain), the Earl of Anglesey and the second Duke of Buckingham. Then on the lists of Stewards for the years 1677 to 1682, eight of whom were "nobly pleased to bear the charges of the Feast" each year, we find the names of the Marquis of Worcester (afterwards first Duke of Beaufort), the Earls of Ossory, Feversham, Shrewsbury, Mulgrave, Thanet, Oxford and Arundel, with the Lords Newport, Hawley, Berkeley, Lumley, Allington, Paston and Falkland.

The signatures of all these noblemen appear in the Old

[*From the Vellum Book*

THE SIGNATURES OF PRINCE RUPERT, THE SECOND DUKE OF BUCKINGHAM, AND THE FIRST DUKE OF ALBEMARLE

Vellum Book of the Company, together with those of many other distinguished men of the period who were probably guests of honour at the Company's feasts. Among these latter are John Churchill, the famous Duke of Marlborough (who was admitted a member after his retirement from active military service in 1715); Christopher Wren, the architect; William, second Earl of Denbigh and ancestor of a recent Colonel Commandant; the Earl of Rochester; Percy Kirke, the notorious colonel of "Kirke's Lambs"; and a host of others, including practically every leading sailor, soldier, courtier and statesman of the day. Some of these distinguished personages may have been honorary members of the Company, for Sir John Reresby, the soldier and diarist, writes (under date 20th April, 1682): "His Highness (James, Duke of York) had a splendid entertainment by the Artilary Company of the Citty of London, of which I was that day made free by his Highness the Duke of York's command."

A curious account of one of the Company's "General Days" in 1665 is to be found in the Domestic Series of State Papers (Chas. II, Vol. CXX). On this occasion the troops, instead

THE DUKE OF MONMOUTH'S SIGNATURE IN THE VELLUM BOOK

of being divided into the usual sides of "Army" and "Revolting Party," assumed the titles of "Greeks" and "Romans", the officers being allotted classical pseudonyms for the occasion. The exercise was performed in the Artillery Ground and the fields and passes leading to it from Moorgate. The "Designe"

SIGNATURE OF JOHN CHURCHILL, AFTERWARDS FIRST DUKE OF MARLBOROUGH

explains that a Roman army, under Albus Regalius Turre (Sir John Robinson), is invading Greece. After forcing the passes into that country, the invaders defeat the Greek army, which retires into Dyrrachium. The Romans besiege the city, beat off a relieving army and finally carry the town by storm.

CHRISTOPHER WREN'S SIGNATURE IN THE VELLUM BOOK

Then follows "The Action." The Company march forth of the Artillery Garden, through Cripplegate into Cheapside, up Cornhill to the Lord Mayor's, whence "after the volleys Given" (the usual salute to the Lord Mayor) they proceed to Moorgate. The Romans are drawn up in the ditch outside the city wall, but the Grecians, under Philopantus (Sir George Smith), carry straight on until they come to the stile that leads into the second field, where they form up. Then the battle begins. With pike and musket the Romans "force the passes" through the fields and oblige the enemy to retire up the (City) Road. Finally dislodging the Grecian musketeers from a strong-point by the corner ale-house, the victorious Romans enter the gate of the Artillery Ground pell-mell with the flying rear-guard of the enemy. ("Noate that in this part of the action the officers are to have a greate care that no mischief is done.")

The armies are now drawn up in battle array facing one another at the full length of the field. And now, says the order of the day, "is the refreshing tyme, where the Commanders are to have a great care that noe excesse be suffered."

Having "well refresht themselves," the opposing forces fight a pitched battle for an hour and a half ("Noate, in firing the Officers are by no meanes to hurry the souldiers"), at the end of which the Greeks make good their retreat into the City. The Romans lay formal siege to the stronghold; their Pioneers throwing up lines of circumvallation, including the necessary trenches, half moons and square forts, sited with due regard to the danger of attack by a relieving force. They open fire on the town ("Noate that the Musqueteers now must load with a very full charge"), beat off an attempted relief, repulse a sally from the beleaguered garrison, and, as a grand finale, storm the citadel.

The description of the assault is of considerable military interest and merits complete reproduction:

The Storme is to be put in execution after this manner. From each quarter of the Leaguer the parties to fall on shall be thus ordered. The officer that commands the Quarter is to lead them on. First six musquetts in two files, who, in falling on, are to fire point blank: then six pikemen in two files, their Pikes comported, carrying on their Pikes each three bavins;* then two pioneers with pickaxes; then two pioneers each a ladder; then six musquetts in two files, who in falling on are to fire obliquely. The first musquetts, when they come neere the Moate, are to open outwards, and the Pikemen having taken their bavins from their Pikes are to throwe them into the Moate, over which the Pioneers passe; and having dig'd downe some of the enemy's lyne they place the ladders at the breach, the pikes and musquetts are to presse on and enter mixt.

---

* Bundles of brushwood.

The parties being all thus disposed the signal for falling on shall be a wispe of strawe flaming on the head of a Pike advanced in the South Quarter.

The Grecians, after a stout resistance, are beaten from their Out-workes; they retire into the Citty, and place themselves on the Walls, resolving to defend it to the utmost.

The Romans having thus gained the Out-workes, they make their approaches neere the Walls, whereby most of the enemy's shott are rendered uselesse. Here both parties doe liberally tosse their hand granadoes at each other for neare a quarter of am houre, during which tyme the Romans sinke a mine under the South part of the Wall; and having put all things in readinesse for a Second storme, the mine is sprung. Altus Longinus Naso, with his party presently falls on at the breach.

The other Parties of the Romans are to bring on their Ladders; the Pikemen are to mount first, armed with swords and Pistolls, or halfe Pikes.

The Grecians make a desperate opposition; but, overpowered, they are beaten, from their Walls.

The Romans enter on all Quarters, and put all to the sword but such as begg for quarter.

On 29th June, 1665, the usual drills were ordered to be suspended on account of "the great sickness" known to posterity as The Plague and which is computed to have swept away 1,000,000 persons. The arms were sent to Guildhall for safe custody, and for months the Artillery Ground was deserted. The casualties caused by the pestilence among members of the Company must have been very heavy. Of the officers elected for that year, ten are noted in the books as having died before the next annual Court.

An attempt to form a plague pit in the ground was happily frustrated by the exertions of the President, Sir John Robinson, who, for his services in this connection, received the thanks of the Company and had his name inscribed in the Vellum Book in letters of gold. The plot of land to the north of the ground was actually purchased by the Corporation and enclosed for use as a burial ground, but, the plague abating, it was not used. Later it was leased to a Mr. Tindall as a burial ground for Dissenters. John Bunyan, Daniel Defoe and several of the Wesleys lie buried there.

In the following year the exercises again suffered interruption, this time on account of the Great Fire of London, which broke out on 2nd September and laid two-thirds of the city in ashes. The records of the Company contain only the most casual references to this disaster, but most of its members were on duty with the Trained Bands for the maintenance of order and the prevention of looting. The Artillery Ground must have presented a scene of great activity for some weeks, as the Court of Aldermen gave to freemen of the city whose premises had been gutted permission to erect booths in the ground (and other places) for the pursuit of their trades. It was also ordered that all salvage should be brought to the Armoury to be sorted and inventoried for restoration to the rightful owners.

On 20th September the Court of Assistants ordered "that the breach made in the wall of the Artillery Garden in the tyme of the late dreadfull fire be forthwith made up." This breach was probably an opening made for the use of the temporary occupants of the ground. Apparently it was thought necessary at the time to remove the Company's valuables, as an entry in the cash books shows a disbursement of 10s. "for saving the trophyes" during the fire.

The City Regiments were mustered in haste when the Dutch fleet was in the Thames in 1667. The Green and Red Trained Bands joined a force commanded by the Duke of Albemarle at Rochester.

The Company appears to have almost invariably attended as a bodyguard to the Lord Mayor on the day he was sworn in at Westminster. They usually met His Lordship as he landed from his barge at one of the City wharves and saluted him with three volleys. Contemporary writing refers to the Company on these occasions by such high-sounding titles as "The Military Glory of this Nation," and "The Warlike Honour of this Nation, Bravely Reviewed." On some occasions they were accompanied by the Finsbury Archers, a body then commanded by Sir R. Peyton, a member of the Company, and who seem to have had the privilege of shooting in the Artillery Ground. This body is referred to as "a most heroic rarity; viz.: gentlemen Archers completely armed with long-bows and swords, arrows and pallisades,* with hats turned up at the outside, and tied with large knots of green ribbon." Perhaps some little jealousy was felt by members of the Company concerning this counter-attraction to the "Military Glory, etc.," for on one occasion they were asked to draw up elsewhere than in the Artillery Ground, and at another time it was suggested

---

* Stakes pointed at both ends for defence against cavalry.

that some course should be taken to hinder the Archers from marching, "but few of them being citizens." Raikes states that these Finsbury Archers were afterwards incorporated with the Company, but quotes no authority for this conclusion. The point is, at least, doubtful.

A passage in Tatham's *London's Triumphs*, published in 1664 and containing a description of the Lord Mayor's Procession in that year, states that His Lordship, "being landed at Baynard's Castle, the Gentlemen of the Artillery are there ready to receive him, Commanded by the right Worshipful and much deserving Sir Robert Peake, Knight, Vice-President of the Artillery Ground." This Robert Peake became a member of the Company in 1635. On the outbreak of the Civil War he took up arms on the Royalist side and was Lieutenant-Governor of Basing House, Hampshire, during the celebrated and protracted siege of that fortress, for which service he was knighted by Charles I in person in 1645. On the surrender of Basing House, Peake was imprisoned in London and was subsequently banished for refusing to take the oath of allegiance to the Commonwealth. At the Restoration he was elected Vice-President and Leader of the Artillery Company. In private life he was a print-seller in Holborn.

Sir Robert died in 1667. In his will, which provided for £500 to be expended on his funeral, the following paragraph occurs: "Item to the Gentlemen exercising armes upon the Artillery Grounds London Provided that 200 of them under armes doe accompany my Funerall I give Fifty Pounds to bee payd in to their President or Trer." However, in a codicil dated after the Great Fire, the expense of his funeral is reduced to £200, "it haveinge pleased God to Consume my houses and Tenements att Holbourne Conduitt . . . but still desiring my Funerall may bee attended by ye Artillery Company in armes in such numbers as they conveniently can."

The Company attended the funeral of the old Royalist at the Church of Saint Sepulchre (still in ruins from the fire), and "gave there five vollyes." The reason for the departure from the usual procedure of three volleys is not clear. Nine extra drums and a fife were used on this occasion, and twelve pioneers were employed "to clear the way with brooms for the Company to march."

The training of the Company during this period consisted

of weekly parades during the summer months, at which members were taught the postures of the pike, the musket and rest, and the musket and half pike; a number of "Ordinary Days" in the Ground, when Members of the Court of Assistants filled the post of Leader in turn; and several "General Days" in each year. These "General Days" took various forms. On one of them it was the yearly custom for the Company to march through the City "in a regimental way." This meant that the body marched as a completely equipped battalion, preceded by pioneers bearing the implements of their office and by additional drums and fifes. The principal officers were attended by marshals armed with truncheons. One of the duties of these officials was to keep the crowd from breaking the ranks, and on one occasion the Company had to pay a surgeon's bill "for cureing the man's head broke by the marshal on the last general day." But the particular feature and glory of these marches must have been the "trayne of artillery" which invariably accompanied the regiment on these occasions. In 1670 the expenses of this train, including Gunners, Matrosses and Firelocks, amounted to £20. These Matrosses (from the Dutch *matroos*) were unskilled soldiers appointed to assist the Gunners in handling their weapons. The term will be encountered again more than a hundred years later in this history. The Firelocks were the escort to the guns, armed with the new firelock or fusil instead of the musket.

In 1674 the six field guns and two wagons were attended by 24 marshals in buff coats, armed with blunderbuses, and in the same year it was ordered "that all Gent. handling muskets on extraordinary days bee desired to provide themselves with Bright Headpieces and Plumes of Red Feathers, it having bin the Ancient and constant Custom for the musketeers to march so Accoutred." This was unusual, as musketeers normally wore the slouch hat.

It is a pity that detailed accounts are lacking of the social side of the Company's activities in the reign of the Merry Monarch. It is only in the old account books that we encounter items with a bearing on the festive aspect of those days: "P^d. for wine coming back from Whitehall—2/-; P^d. coach home from the Devill taverne—1/-; five shillings given to the Yeoman of the wine seller"; such entries lend a human touch to the long list of disbursements to pioneers, drummers and the like—

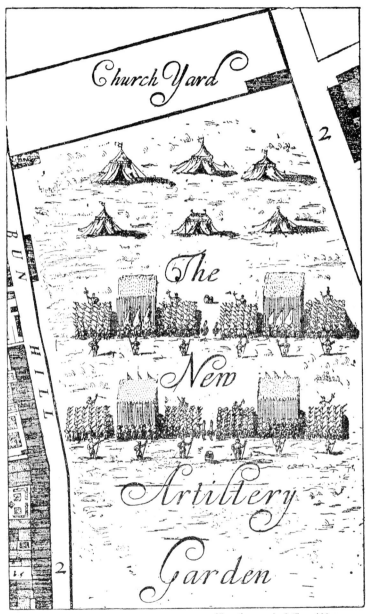

[From the survey by Ogilby and Morgan

THE ARTILLERY GROUND IN 1677, SHOWING FOUR REGIMENTS OF PIKEMEN AND
MUSKETEERS DRAWN UP IN BATTLE ARRAY
Note the old Armoury in the N.W. corner

91

and there is one which appears to refer to a good old English custom: "2/6 to Mr. Weeks his mayde Jone for kissing Sr John Robinson."

In the lists of Stewards for 1677 appears the name of "The Honble Samuel Pepys Esq. Secretary to the Rt. Honble the Lords of the Admar^{ty} of England." The celebrated diarist had already been associated with the Company for some years, as he signed the Vellum Book in 1669, the same year in which his failing sight had compelled him to abandon his famous cypher diary. The last entry in that unique specimen of literature is dated 31st May, so that he must have become a member of the Company later in that year, there being no reference to this event in his writings. If only his eyesight had served him for another few years the records of the Company would

SIGNATURE OF SAMUEL PEPYS [*From the Vellum Book*

doubtless have been enriched by his intimate descriptions of feasts and field days. But it was not to be and we must rest content with a faded signature in the Vellum Roll and the mental picture of the immortal Samuel, his full-bottomed wig crowned with a wreath of laurel, and bearing in his hand the gilded staff, emblem of his office as a Steward of the Artillery Company.

Every year the Company tendered their services as an escort to the Lord Mayor elect, and the offer was usually accepted. John Tatham, whose *London's Triumphs* consist of descriptions of the Mayoral Pageants written up year by year, records that in 1678 his Lordship landed at Blackfriars on his return from being sworn in at Westminster. There he was saluted by "the military glory of this nation, the company of artillery men, they being all in their martial ornaments of gallantry, some in buff, with head-pieces, many of them massy silver." The procession then marched to Cheapside, where several elaborate pageants were displayed, and afterwards to Guildhall, where his Lordship was saluted by the Company "with three volies more, which concluded their duty."

It seems to have been necessary to mount a guard in the Ground for the safe custody of the arms during periods of popular unrest. For example, in 1679, the year of the "Habeas Corpus" Act, it was ordered "that the Clarke procure nine men beside himselfe, to keepe wach in the Artillery ground to secure the Armes, and to pay each man two shillings and six pence and likewise to provide powder Mach and Bullett for them." This may have been a new departure, for only four years previously the Beadle had been directed to move the arms from the Artillery Garden to Guildhall "in case any Tumult bee in the Holydays."

The Annual Feast and Sermon was still the outstanding feature of the Company's activities and was invariably attended by Royalty, the Lord Mayor and Aldermen, and many of the nobility and gentry of the Court. Minutes of the Court of Assistants contain little information beyond the names of the Stewards, but an account of the Feast of 1679 happily survives in the pages of the *London Gazette* of that year. It reads as follows:

London, Octob. 21. *This day the* Artillery Company *kept their Annual Feast at* Merchant Taylors Hall. *In the morning they met in the* Guildhall, *and went to* Bow-Church, *where the Earl of* Ossory, *and the Earl of* Feversham, *out of a particular respect to the Company, met them, and after Sermon, marched with the other Stewards, which were Colonel* Legge, *Sir* Richard How, *Sir* John Chapman, *Capt.* Dodson, *for Sir* Robert Holmes, *Major* Horne, *Captain* Hudson, *with Gilt Staves in their Hands; after whom followed the Lord Mayor, the Court of Aldermen, the Recorder, and the two Sheriffs in their Scarlet Gowns, the Court of Assistants, and the rest of the Company. Being come to the Hall, they found there his Royal Highness, (whom they had prayed to Honor them with his Presence), attended by many of the Nobility, and other Persons of Quality. The cheif Officers made their Compliments to his Royal Highness, Kissed his Hand, and Presented to him, as their Captain, their Ensigns, which they first laid at his Feet. Then his Royal Highness went to Dinner at a Table at the upper end of the Hall, at which the Lord Mayor, the Nobility, and other Persons of Quality, likewise sate, the rest of the Company being at four other Tables. The Entertainment was great and splendid, and all things performed with great Order and Nobleness. Then, according to Custom, the new Stewards were chosen; which are, the Lord Marquis of* Worcester, *the Earl of* Shrewsbury, *the Earl of*

Mulgrave, *the Earl of* Berkeley, *Sir* —— Raymond, *Sir* Simon Lewis, *the Sheriffs, Sir* Ben. Newland, *and Captain* Ben. Harvey. *After Dinner his Royal Highness returned to Whitehall, leaving the Company extremely pleased with the Honor he had done them.*

So much for the official description. But the following extract from a private letter, written from the viewpoint of a disaffected citizen, throws a different light on the event and affords evidence of the growing unpopularity of the royal duke and heir presumptive:

> You may wonder, after the citizens' address to the Lord Mayor for increasing the City Guards on account of the Duke's presence at Court, that the Artillery Company, which contains about 700 citizens, should invite the Duke to a public entertainment. The Stewards chosen, both for last year and the year ensuing, consist of as many great courtiers as citizens, and, as they bear all extraordinary charges, they are at liberty to invite whom they please. How then could it be imagined that, when one-half are courtiers and the other half courtly citizens, they would omit anything which might tend to the Duke's interest, as they hoped this would prove, and it is commonly said he gave £200 towards the feast! It was stated that only 128 members were present, but some hundreds of other citizens who had paid the usual ticket money of 2s. 6d., when they heard the Duke was going, tore up their tickets; others gave them to their porters, or other mean men, and some sold them for a shilling or sixpence apiece.
>
> Amongst the healths they drank one to the happy Succession in the Right Line, and it is reported that they drank so many that one of the grave City Sirs lost his beaver hat and gold hatband, and left the greater company to sport with the foot-boys; and that the Duke promised to defend the Religion established by law, of the Church of England.
>
> On the Duke's return through the Poultry, a cry arose from many hundreds of spectators, of "No Pope, No Papist," as in the morning; when coming through Temple Bar, the people began to hiss.
>
> This shows how little was gained by this entertainment, which was no more an act of the City than if one of forty-eight Companies had invited him, and demonstrates the affection of the citizens to their Religion and Government.

It is obvious that by this time disaffection to the royal family in the City was becoming a matter for concern at Court. Steps were taken to influence the election of Lord Mayors and Sheriffs, and in this connection it should be noted that the influence of the Company on all elections in the City had become proverbial, so much so that it became the custom to ask "Who is the Artillery Company for?" Hence it is not surprising that the King, being tolerably satisfied with the existing Court of Assistants, took occasion to prevent their supersession by the issue of the following warrant suspending the right of annual election:

CHARLES R.

Trusty & Welbeloved, Wee greet you well; Whereas Wee are well satisfyed of ye Loyalty and abilities of ye present officers Employed in ye Artillery Company, and are therefore willing, out of Our concerne, and care, for ye good Governmt thereof, that noe alteracon or change bee made therein, by removing any of them out of there Employmts, or Introducing any others; Wee have thought fit hereby to Signify ye same to you, as a matter conducing to our Service, wherein accordingly Wee expect your ready comply-ance, & soe not doubting thereof, Wee bid you farewell.

Given at our Court, at Whitehall, 9th day of February, 168$\frac{0}{1}$, in ye three and thirtieth yeare of Our Reigne.

By His Majties Comand,

CONWAY.

The reading of this letter at an Annual General Court pro-voked such a storm of opposition to this withdrawal of a long-established privilege that the President adjourned the Court for a week to allow him to make sure of the precise meaning of the warrant. The King's reply was to issue a second order, explanatory of the first, signifying his will and pleasure "that all those who were in any Employment, Trust, Office or Com-and in that Our Artillery Company the last yeare, shall remayne and continue soe for ye yeare Ensuing; and in case of ye Death, or other Incapacity of any of them, that ye Court of Assistants proceed to a free Choice for supplying those Vacan-cies."

A similar warrant was issued every succeeding year during the remainder of the reign. After the first outburst the Com-pany seems to have acquiesced in the situation. Several of the Court were thrown out by vote of the remainder, evidently for political reasons, and others elected in their stead.

Here is an account, from the *London Gazette* of 1682, of another of the Company's Feasts:

London, April 20. This day the Artillery-Company kept their Annual Feast at Merchant-Tailors Hall, which His Royal Highness, upon their humble Invitation, was pleased to Honour with his

Presence. In the Morning they met, according to custome, in the Guildhall, and went to *Bow Church*, (where an excellent Sermon was Preached by the Reverend Dr. *Sprat*) and from thence to the Hall; the Stewards, which were the Right Honourable the Earl of *Tenet* (Thanet), the Lord Viscount *Lumley*, the Lord *Paston*, the Lord *Allington*, Sir *John Narborough, Philip Frowd* Esq; *John Shales* Esq; and Captain *Burden*, marching first, with guilded Staves in their hands; then the Lord Mayor, Aldermen, and Recorder in their Scarlets, and the Assistants and the rest of the Artillery-Company. About two a Clock his Royal Highness came to the City, being attended by a very great number of Nobility and other Persons of Quality, in their Coaches; In *Cheapside*, Sir *William Dodson's* Company of the Yellow Regiment of the Trained-Bands, was drawn up, and Sir *William* at the Head of it, as his Royal Highness passed by. Being come to the Hall, his Royal Highness was received by the Stewards of the Artillery Company, and by the Master and Wardens of the Merchant-Tailors Company; and after the usual Compliments and Respects to his Royal Highness, as their Captain General, and that the Assistants and others had kissed his Hand, his Royal Highness went to Dinner at a Table at the upper end of the Hall, at which the Lord Mayor, the Nobility, and the Aldermen likewise sate, there being five other Tables for the rest of the Company, which was very numerous. The Entertainment was very Great and Splendid, and the new Stewards being chosen, who are his Grace the Duke of *Albemarle*, the Right Honourable the Earl of *Arundel*, the Earl of *Oxford*, the Lord *Falkland, Henry Guye* Esq; *William Leg* Esq; Sir *William Dodson*; and *Charles Duncombe* Esq; his Royal Highness rose from Table, and retired into another Room, where a great many Persons had the Honour to Kiss his Hand; after which, his Royal Highness returned to *Whitehall*, highly satisfied with his Entertainment, and the whole management of it.

In reporting this festivity the *Loyal Protestant* records that "about 50 of the Nobility entered their Names in the Company, each giving a Guiney to the Clerk. This being over . . . several bonfires were made at night, but particularly at *Ludgate* before the *Wonder* Tavern, where were several Persons of Quality, drinking Healths to His Majesty, the Queen, His Royal Highness, and to the Prosperity of all Truly Loyal Citizens; which was pledged by them below, and answered with Huzzas and Acclamations. . . . In this manner they continued for a considerable time and some few of the Rabble presuming to cry, A Monmouth, they were sufficiently curbed for their Insolence. It's very observable that in all this Affair there was no Insolence offered to any Coach therein."

In a sermon preached before the Artillery Company at

John Jenkins
John Jenkins

Sr John Jennings
John Stroty
Buer Norton

SIR,

T is ordered, that on *Tuesday*, the 5th of this instant *September*, 1682. the *Artillery-Company* shall perform an Exercise at Arms at *Baumes*, or the fieldes leading to it. You are therefore earnestly desired to make your appearance in the *Artillery-Ground*, by Nine of the Clock on the day aforesaid precisely, in your compleatest Arms and Habit, with Red Feather. Pray fail not, as you value your own Houour and the interest of the Society.

You are desired to be punctual at the time, because the Company entends to March early.

Those Gentlemen that on that day handle Muskets, are desired to take care that their Arms are clean and well fixt, and that they bring with them fine dry Powder and even Match.

William Pemberton, Beadle.

[From an original in the possession of the Company

A REGIMENTAL ORDER OF 1682

St. Mary-le-Bow this year, the preacher, the Rev. Geo. Hickes, D.D., castigated seditious people for railing at the loyal Militia of the City, "calling them my Lord Mayor's *Janizaries* or my Lord Mayor's *Guards*."

An entry in the records of this year throws some light on

the subject of the regimental Colours in use at the time. It was ordered by the Court "that some Gentlemen waite upon the Six Colls: (of the regiments of Trained Bands) to request each of them to give a Coller for the Artillery Company: The Collers to be as the last are with Porculloses (portcullises) for the first second and third Captaines distinctions." These Colours were used for the first time when the Company waited on the Lord Mayor in 1683. It is recorded that on this occasion the members of the Company "were very gallantly and richyl habited; many of the musketeers in buff, with head-pieces of massive silver, all with red feathers, and most of the pikemen, as well as the officers, wore very rich embroidered belts."

A custom had arisen about this time of electing as Commanding Officers for each public march or exercise a General and Lieutenant-General and a Major-General. These officers would each have had their special Colour borne by an Ensign, the other three Colours being allotted to the Captains. Thus the third Captain's Colour took the form of four portcullises on a red field, with a cross of St. George in the top corner next the staff.

In July of this year (1683) the Company presented an address to the King expressing abhorrence of the recent traitorous conspiracy, a readiness to use their arms against "all Republican, Fanatical and Enthusiastick Villians and Conspirators whatever" in defence of the Ancient and Glorious Monarchy.

The expressions "Honourable Company" and "Honourable Court" were first made use of at a Court of Assistants held on 4th February, 1685. In the following year it was ordered that a certain Sam Jones Esq. should be one of the Court of Assistants of "ye Honnerable Artillery Company." This is the first use of the full title by which the Company is now known.

The Duke of York continued to evince a friendly interest in the Company, which may or may not have been due to a desire to soothe feelings which had been severely ruffled by the King's recent attack upon the City Charters. In 1684 he announced his intention of leading the Company in person on one of their General Marches. The following notice was therefore sent to all members:

HIS ROYALL HIGHNESSE having ordered the Artillery Comp^y. to march on Thursday the 26th of this Inst. June, And declared to honour the Comp^y. wth hys Royall presence, you are therefore desired By the Court of Assistance (as a Member of the said Comp^y.) To Appear in the Artillery Garden By 9 of the Clock in the morning in your Compleatest arms and habbit with Red feather.

The Company marched to my Lord Mayor's, "where they were very Nobly Entertained," and thence to Gracechurch Street, where they were drawn up to receive His Royal Highness, "who came thither about Three a Clock attended with a great many of the Nobility and other persons of quality, divers of which carried arms in the Company. His Royal Highness was pleased to leave his Coach and march on Horseback at the Head of the Company . . . His Royal Highness's Troop of Horse Guards, and several of the Nobility and Persons of Quality on Horseback, marching before his Royal Highness. . . . Being come to the Artillery-Ground his Royal Highness was pleased to quit his horse, and taking his Pike, lead the Body almost the length of the Ground. And here the Lord Mayor, the Aldermen and Sheriffs came in their Scarletts to pay their duty. . . . Then his Royal Highness and Prince George (of Denmark) were Entertained by Colonel Friend in his Tent at a very Noble and Splendid Banquet of Sweetmeats; Flutes, Hautboys and other Musick playing all the while. . . . In the meantime the Body was again drawn out to perform their Exercise, which his Royal Highness was pleased to be present at, and it being over his Royal Highness and Prince George returned to St. James' extreamly satisfied."

The orders for the reception of the Captain-General at Armoury House on this occasion throw an interesting light on the ceremonies usual in these circumstances. It was arranged that His Royal Highness "be first entertained in the Principal Tents And That the Presid Vice-Presid and Treasurer pretne to the Duke Each of them a White Staffe as usually hath bin done. And That Coll: Freind p^rsent the Leading Staffe to the Duke, Capt: Perry the Partasin and Capt: Blagrave the Colors." Forty pioneers, twenty-four drummers and six fifers were employed on this occasion.

Any satisfaction in the ranks of the Company at the accession of their Captain-General to the throne of England on the death of his brother in 1685 must have been tempered by reflections on his extreme unpopularity with many of his subjects. Diminishing musters and a steady falling off in membership were already giving cause for uneasiness, but the Court of Assistants put the best possible face on the business and voted a loyal address couched in more than usually fulsome phrases. After protesting that the Company would "with their Swords in their hands defend your Majesties Honour, Person, Crowne, title and Dignity, against all opposers to their last Breath," it concluded with the assurance that "your Majesties most duty-full Subjects do no longer expect Mercy from Heaven than while they continue firm and steady in their faith and Allegiance to your most Excellent Majesty."

King James's reply to this effusion was to issue a warrant similar to those of the previous four years, again suspending the election of officers.

On 23rd June, 1685, the Company marched through the City to pay their respects to the Lord Mayor, and afterwards "performed an Exercise in more fields (Moorfields) and the Artillery garden according to Custome."

On these and similar occasions it was usual to issue rations for the day. The exact nature of the provision is frequently recorded. For one march the Treasurer was ordered to pro-vide "a Pullet, a bottle of Canarey and a bottle of Clarett for each file, being fower deepe, that shall march on yt day." Another entry records that every four men should have "a Bottle of Sack and a Bottle of Claret a Large Fowle and The Bottle for Bread." Apparently the troops were allowed to sell the bottles and buy bread with the proceeds. If the provisions failed, the remaining files received six shillings in money in lieu of rations, and the whole supped after the exercise at the expense of the Officers for the day, each of whom paid a certain fixed sum towards the cost of the march and of the entertainment which invariably followed.

An interesting entry occurs in the Court Book under the date September, 1670, when a Committee was formed to view certain damage done in the Artillery Garden "by the throwing of Granadoes the last general day." This is the second record in the history of the regiment of the use of the hand grenade; the first mention of them occurs in the Greek v. Roman exercise of 1665, though the Westminster Trained Bands are recorded to have used them in action at Alton in 1643, when they threw "hand-granadoes" into the windows of a church defended by their Royalist opponents. Grenadiers had appeared in the French army in 1667, but it was not until eleven years later that a grenadier company was attached to each British regiment. The extracts quoted above seem to point to a more or less experimental use of the new weapon by the Company, as no record of the formation of a body of grenadiers occurs until 1686, when one Captain James Kelk applied to the Court for the necessary permission to exercise members of the Company "according to ye methods of ye Granodeeres" and was given liberty to form a Company of "such Gentlemen as are willing to Accowter themselves accordingley." They wore caps of crimson velvet, lined with fur and the colour of their uniform for many years was buff, not scarlet.

The hautboy (oboe) makes its appearance among the military music of the Company about this time. Three of these instruments were used on Lord Mayor's Day in 1686 and they continued in use for nearly 50 years. They are last heard of in 1731, when it was ordered that the Grenadiers' music should consist of "one courtail (bassoon), three hautboys and no more."

No Feasts were held by the Company during this reign. In 1685 delegates from the Court of Assistants waited on King James to know his pleasure, but were directed to defer the ceremony until further orders "as his lords who were stewards were not at leisure." The orders never came; the custom was allowed to lapse and was never revived.

There is no mention in the Company's records of the chief events of this short and troubled reign. We hear nothing of the rebellion of the ill-fated Duke of Monmouth, one of the few members of the Company to suffer death for treason; neither is there any reference to the trial of the seven bishops whose acquittal was received with tumultuous joy by the whole kingdom, nor to the rising flood of disaffection which, culminating with the defection of the army, paved the way to the bloodless revolution of 1688.

To the last King James regarded the Company, or rather their leaders, as his friends and supporters. In October, 1688, a deputation waited on His Majesty to know whether it was his royal will and pleasure that the Company should wait on the Lord Mayor according to custom. The King was graciously pleased to return this answer to the delegate: "That he was heartily glad to see him there and desired him that the Company might march by all means, for that they were honest Gentlemen and that he could trust them."

101

The Company took no active part in what Highmore styles "the justly celebrated Revolution" of 1689. This is not surprising. If we are to believe Blackwell, the Company was by this time, through the unpopular political views of its chiefs, in a declining condition, having very few members but such as favoured the Court party or "were inclined to Popery." Military training was almost at a standstill and the Company was in danger of suffering a total eclipse.

One of the first acts of King William was to issue the following Royal Warrant restoring the Company's ancient privileges, including the right of annual election of officers which had been abrogated by his two predecessors:

WILLIAM R.

Trusty and Welbeloved We greet you well. We being well satisfied of the loyalty and good affection of that Our Artillery Company, and being therefore willing to promote the welfare and preservation of it in its ancient good Order and Discipline, Have thought fitt to authorize and impower and accordingly do hereby authorize and impower you frequently to exercise Our said Company in Armes, as well in the ground commonly called the Artillery Ground near Moor Fields, as in other places where they have formerly used to exercise. And We do hereby likewise give you full power and authority to hold Courts free and publick for the annuall choice of Officers, and other occasions, as may be necessary and requisite for the better government of the said Company according to the ancient Rules and practice thereof, in such place and places, and at such time and times as hath been usuall. And for so doing this shall be your Warrant. And so We bid you farewell.

Given at Our Court at Hampton Court the 22nd day of May 1689 in the First year of Our Reigne.

By His Maj^{tles} Command,

SHREWSBURY.

This is the earliest Royal Warrant of which the Company possesses the original.

Immediately on receipt of the Warrant, the Court of Assistants met and directed that a General Court should be held at an early date for the election of officers, etc., "as formerly." It is particularly noticeable that a number of the old Court failed to retain their seats at this election. Evidently the Company was considered to have made a fresh start. Arrears of subscriptions were remitted, obviously for the benefit of members who had absented themselves from training for political reasons. Courts began to be held more frequently and were much better attended. The copy of the King's warrant in the Minute Book is referred to as "the King's Letter for reviving ye Ground." Even more significant is the fact that a debt was repudiated as having been incurred before the Revolution.

In the following year the Chiefs of the Company waited on the King and humbly entreated him to become their Captain-General. King William thereupon issued a Warrant declaring himself Captain-General and appointing Henry, Duke of Norfolk, to act as substitute during the Sovereign's absence abroad.

William III was no stranger to the Company. In December, 1670, the Company had marched forth to attend upon the

[*From a specimen in the possession of the Company*

OFFICER'S GORGET BEARING THE ARMS OF WILLIAM III
Actual size, 7 × 6¼ in.

"Prince of Orange" on the occasion of his entertainment by the City of London. After the ceremony at Guildhall the Prince had been entertained in the Artillery Ground and had signed the Vellum Book. The only details of this occasion recorded in the Company's books are the payment of the expenses of the march. These include five shillings to a "bagpipe"

103

—the only known instance of the use of this instrument in the history of the regiment.

In 1690 a grant of £10 was obtained from the Office of Ordnance at the Tower towards the cost of a new pair of gates for the Artillery Ground. This is the first and only instance of the employment of any public funds (other than those controlled by the Lieutenancy of London) in the maintenance of the Company's property.

During King William's absence in Ireland in 1690, a Dutch fleet was defeated by the French in the Channel owing to the misbehaviour of an English admiral, who lay with his squadron an idle spectator of the fight. Fearing invasion, the City Trained Bands were mustered, 9,000 strong, with six regiments of auxiliaries; but landing was not attempted.

It became necessary about this time for the Court to take steps to prevent damage to the ground and inconvenience to members caused by the practice of the game of Pall Mall. The tenant of the herbage was also warned against the admission of strangers "to try engines" in the ground.

The title of Drum-Major was first used in place of Drum-beater in 1692.

Although the Company had attained a new lease of life at the beginning of this reign, the influx of members hardly came up to expectations. This was particularly the case with regard to Officers of the Trained Bands of the City and Tower Hamlets, many of whom failed to comply with the ancient custom that they should undergo their military training in the ranks of the Company. Representations were made to the King and a Royal Warrant was directed to the Lieutenancy of London recommending "that all the Commission Officers of ye Trained Bands of oʳ said City may List Themselves members of The said Society, that so by the frequent practice of arms according to their Rules they may be the Better qualified to perform their trust, in their Respective Commands." This recommendation has been incorporated in all subsequent royal warrants to the Artillery Company up to and including that of 1863. Even the royal command did not meet with universal compliance, and for many years it continued to be a sore point with the Company that a minority of the officers of the Trained Bands declined to comply with regulations in this respect.

During the King's absence in Holland, Queen Mary reviewed

A REGIMENTAL PURSE OF CRIMSON SATIN,
EMBROIDERED WITH THE ARMS OF THE COMPANY AND OF THE
CITY OF LONDON, WITH THE DATE 1693
The original is in the British Museum

the City Forces in Hyde Park. This was on 9th May, 1692.

Six regiments of Trained Bands assembled, 10,000 strong, under the command of Sir John Fleet, Lord Mayor and President of the Artillery Company. The troops were thanked by the Queen, who expressed her confidence in the alacrity of their zeal for the Crown.

At this review the Company presented an address to the Queen, couched in the following terms:

Wee your Majestie's most loyall dutyfull and obedient subjects . . . presume to approach the Royall presence to acknowledge your Majesty's care and vigilance in disappointing the designes and mechinations of your most enveterate as well as powerfull enemie the French king, who attempted to invade your kingdoms to support a pretender, whom he hath dignified with the stile and title of King of Great Brittain, in order to amuse your subjects with Fears and jealousies. &c. &c.

The Company continued to "pay their respects" to the Lord Mayor once a year, and in January, 1694, His Lordship invited all the members to dine with him at Grocers' Hall. The orders for this occasion were as follows:

The Method of the Company's March to Dine with the Lord Mayor, as by Sir Matthew Andrews' Order.

The Beadle and Porter.
The President wth A White Staffe.
The Aldermen and Knights by 2 and 2.
The Treasurer with ye Purse & White Staffe.
The Court of Assistants by 2^s.
The Clerk.
The Two Ensignes wth Staves.
The Company Two and Two.
The Lieutenants in ye Reer of all.

The following is a copy of the ticket sent to Members for the occasion:

The forme of ye Tickett for ye Company's Dining with The Lord Mayor.

Sir,

You being a Member of The Honble Artillery Comp^{ny} of London, Are Desired to meet the Presid^t, Treasurer, And Court of Assistants and other Memb^{ers} of the s^d Society, at Guildhall, on Tuesday the 23 of This instant January at one A Clock Precisely, with your sword and Red feather, thence to march to Grocers Hall, to Dine with the Right Honble Sir Wm Ashurst, Knight, Lord Mayor of London, and Vice-President of the said Company.

Sir Matthew Andrews was then Treasurer of the Company. It was he who presented to the Company the magnificent Leading Staff (since used as a Drum-Major's Staff) dated 1693, which is still in the possession of the regiment. He had served as an officer of the Yellow Trained Bands in the Civil War.

It is not quite clear what use was made of the Purse carried by the Treasurer. From a note in the Court Minutes that "a guinea be allowed for a purse," it would seem that a purse was the official emblem of the Treasurer of the Company. This supposition is supported by the fact that the British Museum owns a purse of crimson satin, emblazoned with the arms of the Company on one side and with the shield of the City of London surrounded by trophies of arms on the reverse. It is dated 1693, and may be the actual article purchased on the above-mentioned occasion. On the other hand an earlier minute of the Court records an order "that ye Artillery Companey doe dyne wth my Lord Maior on Tuesday the 5 of May, 1685, and ye there bee a purse provided by ye Clerke to this Honble Company too putt the money in, wch is to be presented to my Lord Maior."

CHAPTER VI

1702 TO 1726

ON the accession of Queen Anne in 1702 the Company hastened to present to the "Illustrious and High Born Princess Anne" a dutiful address couched in the following terms:

Permit us, mighty Queen, to condole with the rest of your faithfull Subjects for ye death of our late most glorious and Heroick Sovereign, of immortall Memory, William the Third, the Deliverer of these Nations from impending Slavery and Superstition; the Rescuer and Maintainer of the Liberties of Europe, and Protector of the Protestant Interest in all the parts of the Earth.

But of all the obligations he laid on the People of England, what we must ever remember with the most feeling sence of Gratitude, is the preserving of your Majesty from being excluded from the throne; your Accession to which we congratulate with the greatest Sincerity having not only the most rightful and lawfull Title in the World, but as being likewise the Worthiest to succeed our Deceast Monarch, by your unshaken adherence to the Church of England, your charitable disposition to tender Consciences, your glorious Resolutions of humbling France, of Supporting your Allies, Maintaining the succession of the Crown in the Protestant Line, and incouraging the peaceable Professions of Arts and Trade in the midst of Tumultuous Wars.

According to the institution of our Company, we promise to do our best in the training your Loyall Citizens to the use of Arms, for the security of your Royal Person, Title and Dignity, and the preservation of those Blessings so much worth Fighting for, which Citizens can only enjoy in a free government, and under so excellent a Prince. And, in all Humility, we pray that your Majesty would be gratiously pleased to appoint us a General, which charge the late King did us the Honour to take upon himself, according to the example of some of your Royal Predecessors: And on our parts we shall never be wanting in Gratitude or Duty, with the Hazard of our Lives and Fortunes, to defend your Cause and Person against the pretended Prince of Wales, and all your Majestie's open or secret Enemies whatsoever.

As a result of these loyal protestations, the Queen was prompt to confirm the ancient privileges of the Company and appointed her husband, Prince George of Denmark, Captain-General. Beyond signing the Vellum Book, this Prince does not seem to have taken any active interest in the Regiment. He died in 1708, and no fresh appointment was made during this reign.

The Company appears to have been in anything but a flourishing financial condition at this time. The Clerk and other officials had constantly to petition for arrears of salary; the arms were badly in need of repair; even the rent of 6s. 8d. per annum to the Corporation was five years in arrear. The Court was thus compelled to raise a mortgage on the rent of the herbage of the ground and to obtain loans from Members (at 6 per cent.) to pay off debts. Another embarrassment was the threat of proceedings against the Company in respect of the necessary repairs to the paving of the roads adjoining the ground. After showing considerable dexterity in staving off a prosecution, the Company had this paving repaired with "good fast binding Rubbage."

This financial stringency was partly due to the neglect of many of the officers of the Trained Bands to enrol themselves as members in spite of positive orders from the Court of Lieutenancy to do so. Another cause of insolvency was the refusal of certain gentlemen, chosen as Leaders for various exercises, to accept the financial responsibility for the expenses of the occasion, thereby throwing additional burdens on the general fund. The excuses put forward in this respect are many and varied. One gentleman craved to be excused, "being to go to ye Bath" to take the waters. Another worthy Alderman refused to lead on the ground that he had no inclination to military affairs and was lame.

Finally the Court decided, with the permission of the Corporation, to lease a strip of ground 90 feet deep adjoining Chiswell Street for building purposes, leaving a space for an entrance to the ground. Advertisements were inserted in the *Daily Courant* and the *Postman*, and a board was set up at the Royal Exchange, offering the sites on 70 year leases, at 4s. per foot per annum. The ground was eventually let at 3s. per foot.

John Blackwell, the Clerk of the Company who did so much to restore its prosperity twenty years later, ascribes the unfortunate state of the Company's affairs at this period to political influences, the Court of Lieutenancy, and eventually the Company, having fallen into the hands of "the adverse

OFFICER'S CAP OF THE GRENADIER COMPANY, H.A.C., *circa* 1702

Made of leather and crimson velvet. Embroidered with a silver portcullis. On the "little flap" the cypher of Queen Anne; on the "turn-up" behind an embroidered grenade

OFFICER'S CAP OF THE GRENADIER COMPANY, 1714

Leather and tawny red velvet. On the front the arms of the Company in stamped metal and embroidery. The earliest known example of the use of a metal badge on military uniform. On the flap is the cypher of George I; on the "turn-up" an embroidered grenade

110

party." "But," says Blackwell, "the Ministry being again changed, and the Lieutenancy of this City put into the former Hands, the low Party, or *Whigs*, were resolved once more to endeavour the rescuing the Company out of the Hands of the contrary Party; and at a General Election, held *April* the 27th, 1708, gave almost a total Overthrow to them . . . whereby

ARMS OF THE COMPANY, *circa* 1702 TO 1710

In place of the usual Supporters, the Pikeman and Musketeer, the engraving shows a Grenadier and a Fusilier in the uniform of the period

From an original in the possession of the Company

the Company began again to revive and flourish; but still the adverse Party used all Ways and Means they could to depress and discourage them. So that when the Ministry and Lieutenancy was again changed after Dr. *Sacheverell's* Tryal they made the greatest Effort that ever was known to gain the Government of the Company at a General Court held *March* 20, 1710; but the honest Citizens, observing which way Things were then going, and being resolved to keep that little Privilege they had of exercising Arms, happily prevented them." Blackwell, it appears, was a Whig in politics. It is clear that the government of the regiment was a bone of contention among political factions during this reign, and that the bitterness of party strife was a potent cause of the sorry state into which the fortunes of the Company had fallen.

One regimental custom arose out of all this high feeling. In 1711 the election of officials at the Annual General Court was so keenly contested that a poll was demanded. This is the first record of the use of the ballot on these occasions, it having been the custom, from time immemorial, to vote by means of a show of hands. It is recorded that, on this occasion, "the spirit of opposition carried all parties into the labours of a scrutiny." Here we have the inauguration of the existing method of balloting and the appointment of twelve trusty "scrutineers" to count the votes.

It was also decided, in 1707, that eight members of the Court could form a quorum, elect a Chairman, and proceed to business. This rule still holds good.

An account of an exercise at arms by the Company in 1700 survives in the pages of *The Protestant Mercury*. After enumerating the various officers, it proceeds: "The General, having made a review in the Artillery-ground, orders a march to Baums, to preserve the ancient privilege; which orders are accordingly pursued, and the whole body marches in one battalion through the East gate into an open field about half-way thither, where it is drawn up, and the Lieutenant General sent with half the army to the Eastward; at which he is disgusted, and resolves to revolt, therefore possesses several passes through which the General must march to the Southward, and accordingly attacks his van by a detachment of Grenadiers and Musqueteers forcing them to give way; but they making an orderly retreat (by the advantage of a bridge thrown over a morass) gain the open field more Westward, in which the Lieutenant General also draws up in Battalia, which brings them to a general battle, in which the Lieutenant General having disadvantage, retreats to a strong pass, defending it some time, but being overpowered maintains a running fight to an eminence strongly situated, and with great celerity fortifies it, which the General attacks, and after springing several mines and carrying the outworks, prepares for a general assault, which obliges the besieged to beat a parley, and surrender upon articles."

The ancient privileges mentioned in the above passage refer to the rights of the Company, from time immemorial, to march over and exercise on all the fields extending from the Artillery Ground to Newington Butts. At this period these fields of exercise were still indicated by some 180 archery marks, stone pillars with the arms of the Company on a small iron plate and surmounted by a wooden device to indicate the individual mark. These stones served to mark ranges, being all set at known distances from each other, measured in scores of yards. They were all named. Some bore very curious titles, such as Speering Sport, Robinson's Leg, Currier's Shave, Theefe in Hedge, Piller of Powles, Maydenblush, etc. Several maps of the archery fields, showing the marks at various periods, are extant and provide an excellent field for antiquarian research.

Of the military exercises of the Company in this reign little further evidence remains. Apparently drills were not well attended, as we read of an order for the repair of 48 Pikes and Bandoliers "in case such a number should come to exercise." On the other hand, as many as 260 members voted at a General Court, showing the relative interest of the Company in matters military and political.

The Company continued to attend the Lord Mayor on the day he was sworn and usually received £30 from that official towards the expenses of the march and subsequent entertainment. In 1702 they attended his Lordship at Blackfriars Bridge accoutred in buff with silver head-pieces. The annual field day at Balmes was continued, as well as the General Marches and the "Leads" in the Ground. The Grenadier Company continued to flourish. There is in the possession of the Company a remarkably well-preserved specimen of a Grenadier's mitre cap of this period. It bears as a badge a portcullis embroidered in silver, surmounted by the crest of the Company, the cypher of Queen Anne appearing below. A similar specimen is preserved in the Victoria and Albert Museum.

It had been the custom of the Company for some years past to borrow from the Lieutenancy the necessary accoutrements for the grenadiers. In 1711, however, owing to some ill-feeling, the officials of the Lieutenancy placed obstacles in the way of the loan of the equipment for a general march. It was therefore

decided to have, instead of Grenadiers, "an advance party of
Fusiliers to march at the head of the Company on the General
Day." This is the first mention of Fusiliers in connection with
the Regiment, but by no means the last. They appear to have
taken the place of Grenadiers for a few years, and, on the
occasion referred to above, received the allowance of £4 for
drums, music, grenades, etc., usually granted to the Grenadiers.

By a stroke of fortune a reproduction of a regimental order
of this period has survived in the pages of *The Tatler* of 12th
July, 1709. It concerns an Exercise of Arms by the Company,
and reads as follows:

> *White's Chocolate House, July 12th.*
>
> There is no one thing more to be lamented in our nation than their
> general affectation of everything that is foreign; nay, we carry it so
> far, that we are more anxious for our own countrymen when they
> have crossed the seas, than when we see them in the same dangerous
> condition before our eyes at home; else how is it possible, that on
> the 29th of the last month, there should have been a battle fought in
> our very streets of London, and nobody at this end of the town
> have heard of it?
>
> I protest, I, who make it my business to inquire after adventures,
> should never have known this, had not the following account been
> sent me enclosed in a letter. This it seems, is the way of giving out
> of Orders in the Artillery Company; and they prepare for a day of
> action with so little concern, as only to call it, *An Exercise of Arms.*
>
> *An Exercise of Arms of the Artillery Company, to be performed on
> Wednesday, June 29th, 1709, under the command of Sir Joseph Woolf,
> Kt. and Ald., General; Charles Hopson, Esq., present Sheriff, Lt.-
> Gen.; Capt. Richard Synge, Major; Major John Shorey, Capt. of
> Grenadiers; Capt. Wm. Grayhurst, Captain John Buttler, Capt.
> Robert Carellis, Captains.*
>
> *The Body march from the Artillery Ground through Moorgate,
> Coleman St., Lothbury, Broad St., Finch Lane, Cornhill, Cheapside,
> St. Martin's, St. Anne's Lane; Halt the Pikes under the wall in Noble
> St., draw up the firelocks facing the Goldsmiths' Hall, make ready
> and face to the Left, and fire, and so ditto three times. Beat to Arms
> and march round the Hall, as up Lad Lane, Gutter Lane, Hony Lane,
> and so Wheel to the Right, and make your salute to my Lord; and so
> down St. Anne's Lane, up Aldersgate St., Barbican, and draw up in
> Redcross St., the Right at St. Paul's Alley, in the rear. March off
> Lt.-Gen. with half the body up Beech Lane; he sends a subdivision up
> King's Head Court, and takes post in it, and marches two divisions
> round into Red Lion Market, to defend that Pass, and seccour the
> division in King's Head Court, but keeps in Whitecross St., facing
> Beech Lane; the rest of the body ready drawn up. Then the General
> marches up Beech Lane, is attacked, but forces the division in the*

Court into the Market, and enters with three divisions while he presses the Lt.-Gen.'s main body; and at the same time, the three divisions force those of the Revolters out of the Market, and so all the Lt.-Gen.'s body retreats into Chiswell St., and lodges two divisions in Grub St.; and as the General marches on, they fall on his flank, but soon made to give way; but having a retreating place into Red Lion Court, but could not hold it, being put to flight through Paul's Alley, and pursued by the General's Grenadiers, while he marches up and attacks their main body, but are opposed again by a party of men as lay in Black Raven Court; but they are forced also to retire soon in the utmost confusion; and at the same time those brave diversions in Paul's Alley ply their rear with Grenadiers, that with precipitation they take to the rout along Bunhill Row. So the General marches into the Artillery Ground, and being drawn up, finds the Revolting party to have found entrance, and makes a show as if for a battle, and both Armies soon engage in form, and fire by Platoons.

The comments of the Editor of *The Tatler* on this quaint document are somewhat pungent:

Much might be said for the improvement of this system; which, for its style and invention, may instruct Generals and their historians both into fighting a battle and describing it when it is over. These elegant expressions, *Ditto—And so—But soon—But having— But could not—But are—But they—Finds the Party to have found, etc.*—do certainly give great life and spirit to the relation. Indeed I am extremely concerned for the Lieut.-Gen., who, by his overthrow and defeat, is made a deplorable instance of the fortune of war, and vicissitudes of human affairs. He, alas! has lost in Beech Lane and Chiswell St. all the glory he lately gained in and about Holborn and St. Giles.

The Art of subdividing first, and dividing afterwards, is new and surprising; and according to this method, the troops are disposed in King's Head Court, and Red Lion Market: Nor is the conduct of these Leaders less conspicuous in their choice of the ground or field of battle. Happy was it, that the greatest part of the achievements of this day was to be performed near Grub Street, that there might not be wanting a sufficient number of faithful historians, who, being eye-witnesses of these wonders, should impartially transmit them to posterity: But then it can never be enough regretted, that we are left in the dark as to the name and title of that extraordinary hero who commanded the divisions in Paul's Alley; especially because those divisions are justly styled brave, and accordingly were to push the enemy along Bunhill Row, and thereby occasion a general battle.

But Pallas appeared in the form of a shower of rain, and prevented the slaughter and desolation which were threatened by these extraordinary preparations.

*Hi Motus Animorum atq: hæc Certamina tanta
Pulveris exigui Factu compressa quiescunt.*

A month later the same publication waxed satirical over a gallant major of the Company who had been sent to Birmingham to buy firearms. It is alleged that when the firelocks arrived they were found to be without touch-holes.

One item of military interest remains to be recorded. In 1708 the bayonet made its belated appearance in the armoury of the Company. Invented in 1640, it had first been introduced into the English Army in 1673. Then it was withdrawn, only to be re-issued in 1686. Slow as were the Army authorities, the Company were in still less hurry to adopt the new-fangled weapon, and clung with typical conservatism to the pike.

The minutes of the Court of Assistants are disappointingly meagre during this period. Either the Company was entirely engrossed with its own petty affairs or the Clerk was a man of little imagination and less initiative. It is surprising and exasperating to find in the records of a military body no mention whatever of the chief events of those stirring days. For example, at a time when England went nearly mad with delight at the news of Marlborough's great victory at Blenheim, the first serious check to the conquering career of the French armies for nearly forty years, either the Court made no mention of the matter or the Clerk considered it unworthy of record. The minute books are full of the election of officers, deputations to wait on the Lord Mayor, and petty domestic details. Not one word of the magnificent series of victories which raised the military reputation of this country to a position it had not attained for nearly 300 years.

The science of marksmanship was not wholly neglected in these days. Leave had been given by the Court, as far back as 1664, to the Gentlemen of the Garden to set up a butt in the ground at their own expense, but unfortunately we have no record of its use. Again in 1700 permission was given to those members willing to bear the charge to erect a butt in the ground to shoot at with ball. This butt was situated in the north-east corner of the ground. It was 36 feet long and 24 feet high and was for the use of members only, "but not to be shott at in time of the Company's Tuesday Exercises."

A copy of *The Postman* dated June, 1703, contains the following notice of a competition on this range:

On Friday, the 16th of this instant, at two in the afternoon, will be a plate to be shot for of twenty-five guineas value, in the Artillery-

Ground, near Moor Fields. No gun to exceed four and a half feet in the barrel; the distance to be 200 yards, and but one shot apiece, the nearest the centre to win. No person that shoots to be less than one guinea, but as many more as he pleases to complete the sum. The money to be put into the hands of Mr. J. Jones, at the Lion and Horse-shoe Tavern, or Mr. Turoy, Gunsmith, in the Minories. Note, that if any gentleman has a mind to shoot for the whole, there is a person will shoot with him for it, being left out by mistake in our last.

A contemporary description of the Artillery Company occurs in a work entitled *A New View of London; or, An Ample Account of that City*, published in 1708 by R. Chiswell and others. Under the heading of "The Military Government of London" it is stated that "The Artillery Company are of very great authority, having perhaps been a Nursery of Martial Discipline near 2 Centuries. I find by their Constitutions, That the Company was Revived *Anno* 1610, (which implies it to have been long before). . . . Of this Company have been divers of the prime Nobility and Gentry. . . . They do by Prescription, march over all the Ground from the Artillery Ground to *Islington* and *Sir George Whitmore's*, breaking down Gates, &c. that obstruct them in such Marches. . . . They used formerly to have very splendid publick Feasts, when 4 of the Nobility and as many Citizens were commonly Stewards, to which the Principal Nobility and Foreign Ministers were invited. The Number of this Society are uncertain, but they have not long since marched 700. Those admitted pay to the Clerk a Guinea Entrance and 2*s*. 6*d*. *per* Quarter. One of the Court of Assistants leads once in a Fortnight, when it costs him in Treats about 5£. (but it seldom comes to their turn;) at other times private Persons of the Company lead, according as they are qualify'd. The Company meet every *Tuesday* in the Artillery Ground from *February* to my Ld Mayor's Day, to exercise. The Officers for the City Trained Bands are commonly chosen out of this Society, and with great reason, these being all expert in the exercise of Arms."

In June, 1714, the Court decided that it would be "for the honour and grandiour of the artillery Company to have Accouterments for a body of granadiers to march before them on general marches." This decision was probably the result of the recent trouble with the Lieutenancy over the loan of their equipment. A Committee was forthwith authorized to purchase caps, pouches, and slings for fusees sufficient to equip twenty-four grenadiers, two Lieutenants and two flankers, with caps and coats for two drummers, the money to pay for these articles to be borrowed "with the best good husbandry possible."

Blackwell states that these caps bore as a motto "The Queen and House of Hanover," thereby speaking the fears and apprehensions of the Company that too many were for *the Queen and Pretender*. He adds that this action on the part of the Company became a matter of national interest, all the newspapers being filled with it, and that "many gentlemen entered themselves members of the Company on purpose the better to qualify themselves to fight for their liberties and properties, which they apprehended were in the utmost danger."

At the death of Queen Anne all doubts as to the question of the succession were set at rest and the country prepared to welcome George of Hanover as its sovereign. Whereupon the Artillery Company resolved to draw up a memorial for presentation to the Lords Regent asking permission for a detachment of the Company "in buff coats, etc.," to march in the procession at the public entry of King George into the City. This request was complied with, and at the next Court it was resolved "that Coll. Robt. Gower, with his body of Granadiers belonging to this Company, doe march in the Cavalcade as set forth by the Earl Marshall. And whereas severall Gentlemen of this Company doe desire to march as fuziliers to joyn the said Granadiers in the sd Cavalcade, Resolved that a body of fuziliers doe march according to the said Request and that the body consist at Least of the Number of forty eight but not to exceed sixty four—provided they Equipt themselves according to this order: Clean Buffcoats: hats eged with gould: Red feathers—white stockings and black garters. The hair tied behind with red Ribbonds: Black Ribbonds before: fuzees unslung: and Cartouch boxes."

This entry is of remarkable interest as being the first record of any attempt to lay down precise details of uniform for the Company. It is also noteworthy that the red feather, for many years a distinguishing badge of the regiment, is here retained. Its use was abandoned in 1723.

As officers for the Fusiliers, the Court elected a Colonel, a Lieutenant-Colonel and three Captains, who were to march in front, and it was left to these officers to choose three Lieutenants, who were to march in the rear, and four flankers, or sergeants. The charge for drums, music and pioneers was to be paid out of regimental funds.

It appears that the Muster-Master of the City Militia, one Captain Silk, being a Jacobite, did everything possible to prevent the Company taking part in the procession and finally ventured to assert that they had no right to appear officially at the royal passage through the City. The Company at once appealed to the proper authorities, and their appeal was allowed. Further, the Company charged Captain Silk with having drunk the health of King James III on his knees, whereupon the Muster-Master was arrested, to the great joy of the members of the Company.

Shortly after this ceremony, a special Committee was appointed to draw up a digest of the memorial to the Lords Regent, with "a particular account of the applications made from time to time to procure to the Company a right of marching upon public ceremonials and the Lords Justices resolutions thereupon; and all matters relating thereto; to be entered in the Company's Book." Unfortunately, the Committee, after the manner of their kind, did not function. A note in the Clerk's handwriting under the resolution reads—"but never would meet to compleat it." Thus was posterity deprived of another invaluable regimental record.

In the same year the Company ordered "that proper application be forthwith made to the Committee of Aldermen and Common Councellmen for Twenty pounds usually paid to this Company when any King or Queen of this Realm Comes to dine in the City of London." Nothing is known of the origin of this pleasing, but long obsolete, custom.

The Clerk's salary was £20 per annum, plus £4 bonus on the rent of the herbage. In addition he was entitled to a fee of 1s. from every new member and a percentage of 2s. in the pound on subscriptions and 1s. in the pound on other moneys collected by him. As a further "encouragement to serve the Company with diligence" he received special allowance of what the Court pleased at every audit.

At a General Court held in March of the following year the Company voted a very loyal address to the King, which was duly drawn up. The Court of Assistants, with such other gentlemen as pleased, all dressed in black, with swords, went in gentlemen's coaches (at their own expense) to present the address. The Beadle was directed to take the Vellum Book for His Majesty's signature, but something seems to have prevented this and the signature of George I does not appear on the roll.

The Address was as follows:

With Joyfull hearts we adore that Almighty Providence which placed your Majesty on the Imperiall throne of Great Brittain, and with the greatest Sincerity we dutyfully own and acknowledge your Majesty to be our only rightfull and Lawfull King.

We strenuously asserted and were resolved to maintaine to the utmost of our power yor Majesty's undoubted right, and the Legall Establishment of your Succession to these Realms at a time when, by many, it was deemed a Crime to be zealous for it, but now (blessed be God) we enjoy the end of our prayers and wishes, and feel ye happy influences of yor Majesty's Just Government.

We in great humility beg Leave to assure yor Majesty yt we will chearfully concur with our fellow-Citizens, and all other your faithfull Subjects, in defence of your sacred person and Royall family (as the greatest securitys of our Religion & Libertys) against all pretenders and their open and secret abettors.

We are Religiously determined to pay a constant obedience to your Majesty, and Humbly hope you will be gratiously pleased to appoint to us a Captaine-Generall as has been done by your Royale Predecessors.

We most devoutly pray that your Majesty's reign may be long & glorious, and that the Crown may descend to your Royall Issue, & Continue in your Most Illustrious Family for Ever.

The King thanked the Company for their dutiful and loyal sentiments, and appointed his son, the Prince of Wales, Captain-General of the Company. Shortly afterwards the Prince very graciously declared his acceptance of the post and signed the Vellum Roll. It is recorded that all the members of the deputation had the honour to kiss His Highness's hand.

There was still a very strong Jacobite party in London. In 1716 some members of the Company, on their way to the Swan Tavern to drink the King's health on the anniversary of his Coronation, were insulted by a mob, who shouted "Ormonde, Bolingbroke and High Church for ever." Making their escape from the mob, two of them were arrested by a Jacobite constable of Farringdon Ward and carried before the Lord Mayor. However, both of the accused recovered costs for unlawful arrest.

Many officers of the City Trained Bands still neglected to enrol themselves as members of the Company, so the Court of Lieutenancy issued further orders in July, 1719, that all officers and sergeants of the Trained Bands not already members of the Company should enter themselves as such and perform their exercises. As an encouragement to obedience an annual payment of £78 was authorized, to be divided among those officers who paid their subscriptions to the Company and made their appearances on parade "either in person or by a fit and proper person or persons in his or their room or stead."

This practice of drilling by proxy is one of the most remarkable customs of the period. It was evidently nothing new, for in 1709 Isaac Bickerstaff wrote in *The Tatler*: "The Chief Citizens, like the noble Italians, hire Mercenaries to carry Arms in their stead; and you shall have a Fellow of a desperate Fortune, for the Gain of one Half Crown, go through all the dangers of *Tuttle-Field* or the *Artillery-Ground*, clap his Right Jaw within two Inches of the Touch-Hole of a Musquet, fire it off, and Huzza, with as little Concern as he tears a Pullet." Another instance of this curious practice, this time attended with unfortunate results, is thus recorded in *The Daily Journal* of 1731: "Mr. Longworth, who was stabbed in the Artillery Ground on Tuesday last, by a Centinel, was alive Yesterday, but in a dangerous Condition, his Wound bleeding inwardly. The Person who stabbed him, is an Apprentice in Red-Cross Street, of a good Character, *who march'd for his Master*. When the Arms were grounded in the Artillery Ground, he was placed Centinel over them, and then Mr. Longworth insulted and treated him in a very rough manner, and unhappily provoked the young Man so far as to stab him with his Bayonet."

In addition to the officers' allowance, the Lieutenancy voted a yearly grant of £72 to the Company towards the expenses of arms, powder, etc., and in consideration of the Sergeants of the Trained Bands being admitted members without any expense other than the usual fees on entrance of one shilling to the Clerk and sixpence to the Beadle.

This income, combined with the increase of membership, the rents from the building leases and the excellent management of Blackwell, so improved the financial position of the Company that, for the first time for many years, debts were paid off and the provision of more adequate accommodation began to invite consideration.

The Court of Assistants, after accepting the handsome offer of the Court of Lieutenancy, agreed to the following orders:

1. That all the Staff Officers in the Trained Bands of this City be admitted members of the Artillery Company gratis, only the payment of the Clerk and Beadle's fees upon entrance, and free from the payment of any Quarterage so long as they continue sergeants, and do march in buff on the three General Marches of the said Company, or else to have no right of voting on any election.

2. That Twenty Shillings on a Public Lead in the Artillery Ground, and Ten Shillings on a Private Lead be allowed by the said Company over and above the usual expenses of the Respective Leaders for the time being (which sum the Clerk is hereby directed to lay out on the Company's account) for the better entertainment of the Gentlemen in Arms, but always on this proviso, that there be not less than twenty-four Members in Arms on a public night, and sixteen on a private night, besides Officers.

3. That no person (members or others) be permitted (except Gentlemen of the Court of Assistants) to be at any entertainment at night after the exercise is over, but such only as have been under arms the whole time of exercise; and that the names in writing of all such be taken by the Beadle. And to take their seats at table according to their seniority of membership, except Gentlemen of the Court of Assistants and Captains in Commission.

4. That it be a standing Order and Rule—That a Public or General Lead in the Artillery Ground be not made with a less number than twenty-four Members under Arms besides Officers; and that none but Members duly qualified be permitted to Exercise on any General or Private Nights on any pretence whatsoever.

5. That four Gentlemen of the Court of Assistants on Public Leads and two on Private Leads be desired to attend in the Artillery Ground, and to go on successively according to the rotation on the Roll. The Beadle to underwrite on their summons to give them notice.

6. That no other pikes be made use of for the future in the Artillery Company, on either of their three General Marches, but half-pikes.

7. That no Marshal, "nor any other person in mean habitt," be permitted to march with a half-pike in the said Company on any of the said General Marches.

8. That one shilling and sixpence per man be paid to all the Members under Arms marching, on any of the said three General Marches of the said Company, for their entertainment.

9. That from and after the 11th of September next no member of this Company shall be allowed to re-enter by paying less than his full quarterage then due, except he lose his seniority of membership,

and take it only from such times as he doth so re-enter. This order not to extend to such Gentlemen that go out of the Land beyond the Seas, provided they conform to the 30th Order on the Roll of General Orders.

The Clerk had to certify that the officers of the Trained Bands from time to time were members, and also such gentlemen as were to have commissions from the Lieutenancy were also members; but only those who paid their quarterage were to be so certified, the Clerk receiving 6d. for each certificate for his trouble.*

The excellent Blackwell, Clerk of the Company, took over in 1719 the additional duties of Adjutant. In that capacity he prepared the schemes for field exercises and acted as Leader at Public Leads in the Artillery Ground in the absence of any member of the Court of Assistants. There can be little doubt that he knew his job on the military side, for in 1726 he published a military drill book entitled *A Compendium of Military Discipline as it is practised by the Honourable the Artillery Company of the City of London, for the Initiating and Instructing the Officers of the Trained-Bands of the said City.*

The greater part of this work is devoted to the exercise of the firelock and bayonet "as improved and practised by the Artillery Company." There are two fine plates by Hogarth, illustrating the salutes with the halbert and the half-pike, which are also fully detailed; and the letterpress includes the rules for the drawing up of regiments, with notes on the handling of colours and the various beats of the drum. But the most valuable part from an historical point of view is the short treatise on the history of the Company, which forms the preface.

The Company possesses one copy of this book, which is presumably rare, as no copy is to be found in the British Museum. There is a note on the flyleaf to the effect that the same author published a quarto volume on Military Publishments, but the writer has been unable to trace an existent copy.†

---

* It is to this circumstance that the Company owes the possession of nominal rolls of officers of the Trained Bands of London from 1719 to 1779 inclusive—most valuable and interesting records.

† A short treatise on Guards and Night Duty as practised by the Officers of the Trained Bands, dedicated to the Court of Assistants of the Artillery Company, was published by Blackwell in 1735. A copy was discovered at Armoury House in 1924.

Applebee's Original Weekly Journal for 27th August, 1720, reports that "the Worshipful the Artillery Company made a Coach-March to Tottenham High-Cross, where, being drawn out in two Armies, a bloody Battle ensued; One Party being very strongly entrench'd, were attack'd in their Entrenchments by the other, Sword in Hand, yet were obliged to retire at last, with the loss of a great many (dead Drunk) brave Officers and Soldiers on both sides." It was alleged in a later issue that on their return from Tottenham on this occasion the Company were "robb'd by a Gang of Highwaymen on Stamford Hill."

Perhaps the outstanding events in the history of the Company during this reign were the occasions on which the battalion passed in review before the King in St. James's Park. This occurred in 1722 and again five years later. On the first occasion the Company was given but two days' notice of His Majesty's pleasure and the news caused no little stir. The Court elected the usual officers and issued special orders. All officers and those members armed with the half-pike were ordered to wear scarlet coats, with white stockings and black garters. The Fusiliers were to be dressed in buff, with laced hats, wigs in black bags, white stockings or spatterdashes, and black garters. Members appearing with foul arms or habit were not to be permitted to march.

It was also ordered that the commissioned officers should wear white feathers, and the flankers red or none at all; further that all mounted officers should dismount while in the Park and march past on foot. Whether this last order was an additional mark of respect to His Majesty or merely a wise precaution does not transpire. Another innovation was the abolition of all regard to seniority of membership in drawing up the files. The officers were authorized to post every man to the best advantage, regardless of his "antiquity or dignity."

On the same day as the review the Company presented to the King the following address:

MOST GRACIOUS SOVEREIGN,

Your Majesty's Goodness and Benevolence, Your Tender and paternal Care and protection of the Laws of the Relm, and of the properties of Your Subjects, Are Vertues known to be peculiarly Inherient in Your Majesty.

[*From a drawing by Hogarth*

A SERGEANT OF THE ARTILLERY COMPANY, 1726

125

But Benevolence and Goodness, and all that tend to make a prince Beloved by honest and Gratefull Subjects, are the very things that makes him Less Feared by those that are Ungreatfull and Wicked.

Mercy and Lenity, it seems, are now the Causes and Springs of Rebelion, and Sence these are the Causes of Rebelion in Impious Subjects.

Give us Leave most Excelent Prince to Assure Your Majesty, that We are amongst the Number of Such as Highly Admire those Princelike Qualities which are so naturaly Inherent in Your Sacred Person, that by the Lustre and Excellency of them We are Incited to Assure Your Majesty that We will use Our Arms in the Defence of Your Royal Person, Crown, and Dignity, against all Popish Pretenders, and all other Your Majesty's Enemies, and their Traiterous Abettors.

His Majesty suitably expressed his thanks, and, in addition, as a testimony of his royal favour and approbation of the good order of the Company when they were reviewed by him, ordered £500 to be paid into the hands of the Treasurer for the use of the Company. This sum was invested in South Sea stock and formed the nucleus of the fund for the building of the present Armoury.

One slight contretemps marred the harmony of this eventful episode. Major Noah Delafontaine, the Captain of the Grenadiers, declared that he would not conform to the orders of the Court, but would march his men when, where and how he pleased. This was rank insubordination, and the Court retorted by issuing instructions that, if this officer attempted to march in any way but that ordered by the Court, the Company's caps and accoutrements were to be taken from him and his men. The gallant Major then saw fit to obey, but this compliance did not save him from being expelled the Company afterwards for his insolent behaviour to the Court.

Apart from this incident the review appears to have been an unqualified success. In fact, the powers that guarded the destinies of the Company on those days were so pleased with the appearance of the regiment on that occasion that "taking into consideration how handsome and uniform it would look to have all the gentlemen who carried half-pikes dressed in scarlet, and the fusiliers in buff," they ordered that for the future no member should appear otherwise than in the same order as when reviewed by the King—viz., Officers and half-pike men in scarlet, Fusiliers in buff. The Grenadiers, both officers and men, were to continue to wear buff.

[From a drawing by Hogarth

OFFICER OF THE ARTILLERY COMPANY, 1726

This decision marks another important step in the standardizing of uniforms.

The second review took place on 2nd March, 1727. This time there was more time for preparation and it was suitably employed in instruction in ceremonial. Orders were issued "that the Adjutant do ye utmost he can to instruct all ye Officers and Soldiers in all things necessary for their Compleat Marching and Direct the Several Salutes that they may be perform'd well." Furthermore, the Major-General was authorized to order a special parade of the officers for the march, and if any did not appear, or were deficient in the performance, to "put others in their room."

The same regulations held good as to dress as on the former occasion, except that commissioned officers wore laced hats with black cockades* instead of white feathers. The Captain of Pioneers was to carry a "Field Staff," and his Lieutenant a battleaxe, and they were ordered to salute with their hats only. Special notice was given that no children, servants or other persons were to march between the divisions or ranks, and any member who appeared on parade with foul arms or "mean and foul Habitt" was not to be permitted to march.

The Battalion was drawn up in files four deep in Guildhall Yard, whence the members proceeded to the Privy Gardens in coaches or by water, according to taste. The march past was in the following order:

The Order of the March of the Artillery Company before His Majesty, March 2nd, 1727

1. The Captain of the Pioneers.
2. The Company of Pioneers, with their proper Accoutrements, to clear the Route.
3. The Lieutenants of the Pioneers.
4. The led Horse belonging to the Captain of the Grenadiers, with a Groom on horseback.
5. The Servants belonging to the Officers of the Grenadiers, in a Rank, bare-headed before the King.

1. Capt. of Pioneers.

2. Pioneers.

3. Lieut. of Pioneers.

---

* The Hanoverian badge.

6. The Marshal of the Grenadiers.
7. The Grenadiers' Music, in a Rank.
8. The Captain of the Grenadiers (Major Joseph Bell) on horseback, but dismounts, and marcheth on foot before the King with his Fusil.
9. The two Lieutenants of the Grenadiers (Mr. John Lambe and Mr. Thomas Gregory), abreast, with Fusils.
10. The Company of Grenadiers, in Buff, three deep in files, with their Flankers on the Angles of the Divisions.
11. The led Horses belonging to the General Officers, with Grooms on horseback.
12. The Servants belonging to the General Officers in a rank, bareheaded, as before.
13. The Marshals belonging to the Commanding Officers, in a rank, with their hats under their left arms, before the King.
14. The Beadle of the Company, with his Staff in his right hand and hat under his left arm, before the King.
15. The Music belonging to the Body, in a rank.
16. The General (Sir William Billers, Kt. and Alderman), on horseback, but dismounts, and marcheth on foot before the King, with his Half-pike.
17. The Lieutenant-General (Lieut.-Colonel Samuel Westall) and the Major-General (viz., Major John Williams, in the room of Major Joseph Bell), on horseback abreast, but dismount, and march before the King with Half-pikes.
18. The three Captains, with the Captain-Lieutenant, in one rank—viz., Captain John Weedon, Captain William Bell, Captain Edward Raybould, and Major John Triquett.

4. A led horse.

5. Servants.

6. Marshal.

7. Music.

8. Major Bell.

9. Mr. Gregory. Mr. Lambe.

10. Grenadiers—Lt. Carter.

Grenadiers.—Capt. Tame.

Lt. Gilbert.—Grenadiers.

11. Led horses.

12. Servants.

13. Marshals.

14. Beadle.

15. Music.

Major Williams. 16. Sir Wm. Billers. Lt.-Col. Westall.

17.

Capt. Bell. Captain Raybould. Major Triquett. Capt. Weedon.

18.

19. Fusiliers.—Lt. Gregory.

19. The Front Grand Division of Fusiliers in Buff, march four deep in files, with the Flankers in Scarlet, and sashes round their waists, march on the Right Angles of the Sub-Divisions with Partisans shouldered.

20. Two Briviates, with the Bringer-up in one rank, bring up to the Front Grand Division of Fusiliers —viz., Captain John Johnson, Captain Nicholas Faulcon, and Lieutenant William George.

21. The Surgeon, Mr. Henry Middleton, with his Scarf and Arms of the Company, marcheth with his hat under his left arm, as before.

22. The three Ensigns of the General Officers—viz., Lieutenant-Colonel Peregrine Phillips, Captain Robert Anbury, and Captain George Gerrard—march in one rank, Colours flying.

23. The First Grand Division of Pikes, in Scarlet, march four deep in Files, with the Flankers on the right of the Sub-Divisions, march as before.

24. The three Ensigns of the Captains —viz., Captain Thomas Cartwright, Captain Joseph Lambe, and Captain Thomas Fulker—march in one rank, Colours flying.

25. The Second Grand Division of Pikes, in scarlet, march four deep in Files, with the Flankers on the Left Angles of the Sub-Divisions, march as before.

26. The two youngest Lieutenants, with a Briviate, in one rank, lead the Rear Grand Division of Fusiliers, viz., Captain Walter Sutton, Captain Benjamin Osgood, and Captain Samuel Saunders.

27. The Rear Grand Division of Fusiliers, in Buff, march four deep in

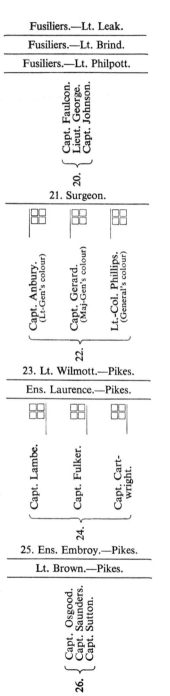

Files, with the Flankers on the left angles of the Sub-Divisions, march as before.

28. The three eldest Lieutenants, with a Briviate, march in one rank, and bring up the Rear, viz., Captain Paul Ferris, Captain William Brind, Captain Charles Thompson, and Captain John Bassindine. John Blackwell, Adjutant and Clerk, and Captain Joseph Willoughby, Assistant-Adjutant, to march at discretion.

27. Lt. Hingist.   —Fusiliers.

Lt. Woodcock.—Fusiliers.

Ens. Owen.   —Fusiliers.

Lt. Shortland.—Fusiliers.

28. { Capt. Ferris. Capt. Thompson. Capt. Bassindine. Capt. Brind.

N.B.—The Company consists of the Officers of the Trained Bands of the City of London and Suburbs thereof, and other gentlemen who are instructed in the Use and Exercise of Arms.

By approbation of the Major-General,

JOHN BLACKWELL, *Adjutant and Clerk.*

It is somewhat strange to find about one-third of the strength of the Battalion still carrying the pike at a time when it had been obsolete as an infantry weapon for nearly twenty years. During and after the Civil War the proportion of pikes to muskets in a regiment had been gradually decreasing until about 1704, by which time the pikemen had dwindled to a small body whose especial duty it was to protect the colours (hence the derivation of the word *picket*).

The reason for the retention of the pike in the Company was probably due to pure conservatism, or possibly to a dislike of handling the musket on the part of some of the worthy freemen and citizens who filled the ranks of the regiment in those days. It is noteworthy that in 1719 the Court ordered that none but half-pikes should be used by the Company, thereby discarding for all time the longer, more cumbersome, but efficient weapon.

Blackwell writes, in 1726, "The Pikes were formerly esteem'd a very useful Weapon, both for Offence and Defence, but now wholly laid aside in the Army; and not us'd any where in this Nation, except at some times in the Honourable the Artillery Company of the City of *London.*" He then proceeds to enumerate the various words of command.

It may be surmised, from the above statement, that the pike was used on ceremonial occasions at this date. The last recorded instance of its use by the rank and file of the Company occurs in 1735, when it was left to those gentlemen who marched in scarlet to use a fusee or a half-pike, "as they shall see proper." Of course, the half-pike continued to be the weapon of the officers until a much later date, and a very similar weapon was carried by sergeants, under the name of "spontoon" until mid-Victorian times.

During this period there seems to have been a growing tendency towards the laying down of dress regulations. In 1721 it was reported that some of the flankers, who were usually Lieutenants of the Trained Bands acting as sergeants, were wearing their sashes over the shoulder, contrary to the custom of the Company. The Court thereupon ordered that any flanker appearing without a sash, or who wore one otherwise than round his waist, would forfeit his allowance from the Lieutenancy for that march and would not be allowed to attend the entertainment for officers afterwards. The wearing of the sash over the shoulder was, of course, one of the marks of distinction of an officer. It was also found necessary at the same time to order an inspection before each march to ensure that the Fusiliers and Grenadiers had provided themselves with cartridges "sufficient to make good firings throwout the General Exercises." If any member had too few charges or such as were considered too small to make a good report, he was not to be permitted to march until he had produced a sufficiency. Powder and bullets were always to be had at the Armoury. The sale appears to have been one of the perquisites of the Company's servants.

The Court in 1722, appointed "an Ingenier to make their Fireworks," but it must not be assumed that this referred to the articles usually associated with the Crystal Palace and the Fifth of November, though it is recorded that the Company organized a display of fireworks within the palisades at the east end of St. Paul's Cathedral on the night of King George the First's entry into London. In the military parlance of the time the word "Fire-work" included various forms of the grenade and petard, as well as the more spectacular article.

In this connection there is the sad tale of Sergeant William Richford. It appears from a contemporary newspaper that this gentleman, a tailor in Rosemary Lane, serving as a Fusilier, met with an accident during a field exercise in honour of the anniversary of the accession of King George. It is reported that "one of the sham Bombs of about a Pound and a half Weight fell upon his head, and beat him to the Ground, then it burst and left him speechless; he continued so all the Night following; and through the Contusion and Disorder this Accident has given him, it is apprehended he will hardly recover." Apparently the unfortunate Fusilier recovered sufficiently to petition the Court for compensation on account of "the Great hurt and Dammage" he had received. In consideration of his "mean circumstances," the Company paid the expenses of his illness.

Little is heard of the Finsbury Archers during this period, though they were still in existence and usually held an annual meeting in the Artillery Ground. A newsprint of 1721 records a test of skill in the ancient science of archery to be held in the Artillery Ground "between John Smith, Master of Archery, living near that Ground, and Thomas Polington, a Devonshire Gentleman, for a Bowl of Punch of half a Guinea, where 'tis supposed most of the Proficents in that Art will be to see the Performance; Three Flights in Five are to decide the Matter."

The ground was also used at times for the trial of the latest inventions in death-dealing weapons. On a certain wet Wednesday in 1722 an experiment took place with a contrivance known as "Mr. Puckle's Machine." This was a very early type of machine gun and the newspaper report states that " 'tis reported for certain that one Man discharged it 63 times in Seven Minutes, though all the while Raining; and that it throws off either one large or sixteen Musquet Bullets at every Discharge, with very great Force."

CHAPTER VII

1727 TO 1759

THE accession of George II was not marked by the usual request for a Royal Warrant by the Company. Possibly it was thought unnecessary to petition the Captain-General of the Regiment for confirmation of the Company's privileges. More probably the matter was allowed to drift, as was the case with the address voted by the Court to congratulate His Majesty upon his accession, which was never presented.

It was in this year (1727) that the Company was granted permission to build on the west side of the Ground. It had taken four years for the concession to pass the Court of Aldermen.

On Lord Mayor's Day the King dined at Guildhall. The Court inquired if His Majesty would be pleased to receive the salute of the Company on that occasion and, having received a reply in the affirmative, applied to the Court of Aldermen for the usual grant of £20 payable to the Company when Royalty dined in the City, in addition to the ordinary charge of £30 for their attendance on Lord Mayor's Day.

A letter was received in 1728 asking permission for His Majesty's Guards on duty at the Tower to exercise in the Artillery Ground on Tuesday and Thursday mornings for two or three months. This request was granted on the understanding that the Company's tenant was recompensed for any damage to the herbage. It is noteworthy as being one of the very few occasions on which the use of the Ground has ever been granted to a unit of the regular army, though similar requests were frequent in later years.

A manuscript in the Bodleian Library describes an exercise of arms performed by the Company on 1st August, 1728, on the occasion of the annual march to Balmes. It will be noticed that the scheme still follows the idea of a "revolting Party."

THE DESIGN

Draw up the files in the Artillery Ground (three deep), extend north and south upon the lines, march the Company out at the little gate, pursue the same into Pest-house Field, and draw up facing westward.

The Field Officers, having reviewed the Body, and received the salutes of the rest of the Officers in their proper posts, then divide into two battalions, and order the Lieutenant-General into winter quarters; accordingly the Lieutenant-General takes his march northwards, and, finding the country to be barren and incommodious he draws up his men, and, by an oration he makes to them, engageth them into a revolt.

The General, by his spies, having received certain intelligence of his said revolt, sends an Officer, with a trumpeter, to know the reason of it.

The Lieutenant-General sends the Officer back in disgrace, bids defiance to the General, and said that he would give the reasons for his revolt at the point of the sword.

The General calls a Council of War, in which it was resolved to reduce the Lieutenant-General to obedience by force of arms, and therefore pursueth him with much expedition.

The Lieutenant-General draws up his forces in ambuscade, and fires upon the General on his march; upon which the General draws up his men, and returns the fire; but, the Lieutenant-General being very advantageously posted, the General could not force him, and therefore pursues his march to gain a more open ground.

The General, having gained an open country, draws up his forces to give battle to the Lieutenant-General; which the Lieutenant-General perceiving, and not willing to come to a close engagement, draws off, and gains the possession of a strong line drawn across the country, and then draws up his men, in order to defend the same.

The General marcheth his forces after him (in battalia), and being willing to prevent the effusion of blood that might ensue, sends a second summons to the Lieutenant-General to give the reasons of his revolt, or submit to his mercy at discretion, otherwise he would compel him by force of arms.

The Lieutenant-General sends word that his revolt was for want of pay, and that, if he did not send all the pay due to him, and provide him better winter quarters, he would stand the utmost extremity.

The General lets him know that all the pay due to him was ready, but that he must first execute the orders he had given him.

The Lieutenant-General, not being willing to trust to the honour of the General, fires upon him at a narrow pass in the centre of the lines.

The General returns the fire, and at last, by springing a mine, makes a breach and mounts the same, which forceth the Lieutenant-General to come to a general engagement; and accordingly both armies draw up in order of battle, which is begun by cannonading, and then to a close fight, in which victory seemed doubtful for some time; till at last the Lieutenant-General was obliged to give way to the superior force of the General, to quit the field, and to make the best retreat he could to a strong pass in his rear, where he stands his ground for some time, until the General, by sending a division, flanks him on the left, which causeth him to retire to a bar at the extremity of the said pass; but finding his army much weakened, springs a mine and throws a shoal of grenades, which disorders the General's forces, and by it gains time to secure his retreat into a strong fortress some distance southward.

The General being resolved to reduce him, orders several shells to be thrown into the place; but they not having the desired effect, orders his cannon to play (*which the Lieutenant-General answers from his batteries*) and also to scale the walls, but to no purpose; so that, after several firings of small arms on both sides, both parties desist the general fire, and only are for "birding."*

The General marcheth his forces down the great road on the east of the fortress, and draws up at the great gate leading towards the entrance of the castle, which at last is forced by him, and then draws up facing the entrance itself; and, after many firings on both sides, the Lieutenant-General's forces being beat into the place, the General prepares for a general assault; which the Lieutenant-General perceiving, and having several mines planted at the entrance of the interior polygon, springs the same with such success that many of the General's forces are slain thereby.

The Lieutenant-General observing the resolution of the General to storm the place, and his ammunition being spent, came to a resolution to try if he could gain an honourable capitulation, and therefore hangs out the White Flag and beats the "Chamade."

The General, not knowing the danger he might expose the rest of his men unto in the storming the place, therefore, upon hostages being exchanged, enters into a treaty, and after some time articles were agreed unto and signed; the Lieutenant-General marcheth out with all the tokens of honour, as drums beating, colours flying, &c., ; the General takes possession of this important place; and afterwards both armies join and march into the Artillery Ground, where they fire three volleys and lodge the colours, which concludes the EXERCISE.

DIRECTIONS FOR PERFORMANCE

1st Firing.—At the Avenue by Lady Lumley's Almshouses in Ship Field, one round, by single ranks, the Lieutenant-General making the first fire.—N.B. The ranks after their firings to wheel off to the right and left outwards, and post themselves in the rear of their own divisions, after they all have fired; then wheel off the division, that the second may advance. (So of the rest.)

2nd Firing.—At the centre of the line, between Ship Field and Rose and Crown Field (both sides being drawn up in battalia), the Lieutenant-General making the first Fire, fire once round by single

---

* *i.e.* Sniping.

ranks of each division, and then wheel off to the rear of their own divisions. Let the firings be from right and left to the centre; then the General throws a shoal of grenades and springs a mine, and forceth the Pass.

3rd Firing.—The Field Fight.—Cannonading, three rounds on each side, three rounds by platoons on each side, the General making the first fire. 1. Fire from right to left; 2. From left to right; 3. From right and left into the centre.

4th Firing.—At the Rose and Crown, where fire two rounds by divisions, the Lieutenant-General making the first Fire; the General flanks his left, and throws a shoal of grenades, which causeth the Lieutenant-General to retreat to the Bar, after he has delivered a shoal of grenades.

5th Firing.—At the Bar, where fire one round by divisions, the Lieutenant-General making the first Fire; then the Lieutenant-General throws another shoal of grenades, springs a Mine, and retires into the Castle.

6th Firing.—The Siege.—1. Bombardment (three shells); 2. Cannonading (three rounds); 3. By the Divisions of small shot (three rounds); and then Birding on each side.

7th Firing.—At the Great Gate, one round by divisions, the General making the first Fire; and then the General throws grenades and springs a mine, which forceth the Gate.

8th Firing.—At the Entrance of the Citadel, where fire one round by divisions, the Lieutenant-General making the first Fire; then the Lieutenant-General throws a shoal of grenades; after which the General springs a mine, to force the said entrance; then the Lieutenant-General springs another, to beat off the General's men, whereby many are destroyed; *and then beats the Chamade.*

The question of a new Armoury, which had been under consideration for many years, was now tackled in earnest. In 1729 a Committee was formed and plans were submitted from Mr. Stibbs and Mr. Dance. The latter gentleman was the architect of the Mansion House. After nearly three years' delay Mr. Stibbs's designs were accepted, at an estimated cost of £1,800. Then a subscription list was opened and, as an encouragement to generosity, it was decided that all who subscribed £5 should have their names inscribed in letters of gold on the panels of the Great Room. Subscribers of £10 were, in addition, to be elected to life membership of the Company; while donors of £20 were entitled, in addition to the above benefits, to be admitted honorary members of the Court of Assistants.

The Court of Lieutenancy were then asked for a grant towards the cost of the building. After inspecting the old Armoury and

deciding that nothing could be done to improve it, the Lieutenancy decided on a gift of £500. An attempt was also made,
through Sir Robert Walpole, to induce the King to give his
practical support to the project; but as nothing further is
heard of this, the effort presumably failed.

In 1734 the contract for the building of the Armoury was
advertised, and out of six tenders the Court accepted that of
Messrs. Harris & Stibbs, who offered to do the work for
£1,284. It was then found necessary to cross-plank the foundations at an additional cost of £48, so that the original Armoury
actually cost £1,332 to build. It was completed early in 1735
and was insured in the Hand-in-Hand Insurance Office for
£1,600.

The names of the subscribers to the building fund were
duly inscribed in gold on six panels and set up in the Long
Room, whence they have long since disappeared. Highmore
states that, in 1803, some of them were to be found at the sides
of the stairs leading from the Sutling Room to the Musicians'
Gallery.

Much of the decoration of the interior of Armoury House
can be traced to this period. The painting of the arms of the
Company above the fireplace at the western end of the Long
Room was presented by Ensign Wardell in 1737. That of the
Royal Arms of George II, later changed to those of George III,
at the other end of the room formed part of the original scheme.
The clock with two dials was presented by a member in 1748.
The frame and canvas for the painted frieze in the Court Room
was put up in 1751, but the paintings themselves were not
completed till eight years later. The iron gates in the entrance
hall, magnificent specimens of their kind, were erected by
subscription in January, 1746.

As soon as the House was opened it was found necessary to
regulate its use, and the following orders were drafted by the
Court of Assistants:

Ordered that the Table next the Window on the right Hand going
in, be for the Use of the Commission Officers for the Day on which
they respectively March.
That the Table on the right Hand at the Back of the Room be
for the Use of the Sergeants of the several Regiments (of Trained
Bands) as they respectively March.
That the table on the left Hand next the Window be for the use

of the Members of this Company, being Spectators, on any of the Days the Regiments respectively Muster; regard always to be had to such as are Subscribers.

That the Table on the left Hand at the Back of the Room going in, be for the Use of any Body of Volunteers who do March in the respective Regiments.

That the Room on the right Hand at the Top of the Stairs, be for the Use of any Body of Grenadiers, if any such March with any of the Regiments.

That when ever any Gentlemen of the Court of Lieutenancy please to come, they be admitted into the Room at their Pleasure, and to be seated at the Officers Table.

That no Person, on any Pretence whatsoever do presume to bring into the said great Room, any Person or Persons, not being Members of the said Company, without leave of the Field Officers for the Day first had and obtained.

That the Beadle, or his Deputy, do attend at the Door, to let in the several Members that shall desire to come in. And that the said Beadle or his Deputy, shall be supported by a good Body of Centinels to withstand any Person or Persons, who shall forceably endeavour to break any of these Orders.

That if any Person or Persons shall stir up, or raise, any Riot, Tumult, or Disturbance in the said Room, being Members or not, shall be by the said Field Officers ordered to be turned out of the Room.

That no Malt Liquors be permitted to be sold, or brought into any Part of the Armoury.

That the Clerk have the Liberty to sell Wine in the said Armoury, and all other Liquors, (Malt Liquors excepted) on the Six Muster Days only; and then to discontinue selling, and to clear the said Armoury.

That if any Member of this Company have a desire to erect a Shed or Tent, for the Selling of any Sort of Liquors on the Six Days of the Muster only (Wine excepted), may make Application to the Court of Assistants for Leave for their so doing, and that it be on the West Side of the Ground.

Shortly after this, permission was given to a Mr. Merry to erect a booth or tent against the west wall of the Ground for the sale of beer, ale, or other liquors, but not wine, during the six days of muster of the Trained Bands only, after which he was to clear the booth away and pay 3s. as an acknowledgment to the Company. His licence was renewed the following year, but only on condition that the game of skittles was not to be played. Some years later a member was summoned to appear before the Court on the charge of selling Geneva (gin) in the Ground on the day of the Regiment's marching.

The first recorded inventory of arms, armour, etc., was taken in 1738. It includes almost all the armour at present in the possession of the Regiment (with a note to the effect that it wanted painting), the old Leading Staff of 1693 and the tilting lance. It was subsequently ordered that the armour, arms, bayonets, etc., should be set up as ornaments in the Great Room.

In 1739 it was ordered that no person should be given a certificate of membership until he had been formally admitted by a Court of Assistants, and in the following year it was decided that no vintner should be admitted until it had been agreed upon at two successive Courts.

John Gittins, a member of the Company, a Captain in the Blue Regiment of Trained Bands and a Furrier by trade, published a military work in 1735. It bore the elaborate title of *A Compleat System of Military Discipline as it is now used in the British Foot with Explanations. Being a few Military Flowers Collected out of the Artillery Garden of London.* The principal dedication, to the King's most excellent Majesty, concluded with the fervent prayer "that we may never want a Prince descended from your Royal Loins to sway the Scepter of Great Britain." A subsidiary dedication to the Lieutenancy of London states that the book was printed "solely for the use of young Gentlemen and Soldiers belonging to the Honourable Artillery Company, and the Trained-Bands of this City; Which Company has always experienced your Honours Goodness towards them; and by your kind assistance, has once more raised their drooping Heads." The Book opens with a few observations upon war, such as the following: "Peace, Plenty, Pride, and War, are the four Fellies which compound the Wheel that Time turns round on: As Peace produceth Plenty; Plenty, Pride; and Pride, War; so of course, after a long Peace, War mounts the Stage." The remainder of the work consists of the exercises of the firelock and bayonet, the Grenadiers' Exercise, many and complicated evolutions, and the duties of the various ranks in all spheres of military life.

For centuries Finsbury Fields had been one of the chief centres for the national pastime of archery; and now the Artillery Ground was to become the cradle of a great English game. Cricket is heard of as a game for schoolboys as far back as Elizabethan times, but it was not until a much later

"THE GAME OF CRICKET AS PLAY'D IN THE ARTILLARY GROUND, LONDON"

Printed for Robert Sayer, at the Golden Buck in Fleet Street. From a line engraving published circa 1750. *The original painting is in the possession of the Marylebone Cricket Club*

date that it began to come into prominence as a national game for adults. Hambledon, in Hampshire, is usually regarded as the nursery of club cricket, but, in 1725, about fifteen years prior to the earliest records of the Hambledon Club, the game was being played in the Artillery Ground. It did not at first meet with official encouragement. In fact a note appears in the Court Minutes concerning "the abuse done to the herbage of the ground by cricket players." However, the rulers of the Company eventually became reconciled to the game, for *The London Evening Post* of 13th-15th July, 1738, advertises a match in the Artillery Ground between the Gentlemen of London and the Gentlemen of Chislehurst. The wickets were to be pitched at one o'clock precisely "because several large Betts are depending." The Ground was to be roped round as usual and all persons were desired to keep off the wall.

The *Daily Post* of 24th July, 1739, describes a match on the same ground between Kentishmen and Londoners, when the latter, being fifty runs down in the first "Hand," "took occasion to wrangle about a disputed Ball, and break the match off, whereby they saved themselves from being beaten, but at the same time lost their Honour."

Very heavy betting was the rule rather than the exception at this time. At a two-day match played in the Artillery Ground in 1742 between eleven gentlemen of Slendon in Sussex and eleven gentlemen of London, the stakes were £500 a side, with a forfeit of one hundred guineas if the wickets were not pitched by eleven o'clock. Another match on very similar conditions took place between the Gentlemen of London and the Noblemen and Gentlemen of the Duke of Bedford's Club.

The earliest match of which the scores are recorded is that between Kent and All England in 1744. The game was played in the Artillery Ground, Kent winning by one run. Among the representatives of England on this occasion was one Smith, known to cricket history as the "keeper of the Artillery Ground."

The *Lewes Journal* of 13th July, 1747, contains a notice of "a long-talked-of match in the Artillery Ground between the women of Charlton and Singleton in Sussex and the women of West Dean and Chalgrove, of the same County," but there is no record of the result. The "Club of the Artillery Ground" must have flourished for a number of years, as in 1765 a match is recorded between the London Artillery players and the Walworth players. The account adds that the odds were for some time in favour of the Walworth men, but at last the London men came off victorious.

Apparently the use of the ground for cricket matches ultimately became an annoyance to the Company, for in 1773 the Court ordered an advertisement to be inserted in the *Daily Advertiser* to the effect that the Company would not in future allow cricket or any other game in the Artillery Ground. This ban continued for many years. In 1834 members petitioned the Court for permission to play cricket in the ground, with a view to attracting recruits, but it was decided that the game was precluded by the terms of the leases. Another application in 1841 drew attention to a recent order emanating from the Horse Guards and directing that cricket grounds should be provided for the use of the Army throughout the kingdom. Again it was decided that a clause in the lease proved an insurmountable obstacle. Finally, in 1846, the Court yielded to pressure and petitioned the Court of Common Council that the covenants in the lease might be altered so as to allow cricket to be played.

This request was granted and a licence to that effect endorsed on the lease. The question was then submitted to the Prince Consort and, on the receipt of his sanction, subject to the necessary regulations for ensuring the general order and discipline of the Corps, a code of stringent rules for the regulation of the game and its players was drawn up. It was laid down (1) that none but members should be permitted in any circumstances to play cricket in the Ground; (2) that no member should be entitled to play until he had "passed into line," had paid his regimental subscription, and had obtained certificates from his Battery or Company Officer, countersigned by the Regimental Sergeant-Major, to the effect that he had attended a certain number of drills in the previous twelve months; (3) that every expense in connection with the game should be borne by private subscription, such funds to be properly administered by a Treasurer elected for the purpose; and (4) that the days for the playing of cricket should be Mondays and Fridays during the season, but only by special application to the Court and subject to the usual rules for the closing of the House at nine o'clock.

A most interesting account of the swearing-in of a Lord Mayor at the Tower in 1741 is to be found in the official diary of Lieutenant-General Adam Williamson, then Deputy Lieutenant of the Tower. He relates that the Lord Mayor elect had made a demand or request "to have the Liberty of being preceded by the Artillery Company, who are a body of about three hundred Men at arms well disciplined and uniformly accouter'd with a Company of Grenadiers of their owne body at their head, drums beating &c."

General Williamson goes on to say that "it was thought by the Brigadier, that when they came to the Tower ground the Militia of the Hamlets or the Warders was sufficient for his Lordships guard, and that he would be pleased to let them come no farther than Crutchet Fryers Bar, but these mermidons it seems allwais march before the Lord Mayor even to the Bar in Westminster Hall; so on the score of the Warrants saying the Mayr. 'Should be sworen in before the Constable in the same manner as he is at Westminster,' this was acquiesd with."

Then follows a description of the preparations made by the authorities at the Tower for the reception of the Lord Mayor.

"At length," continues the diary, "the Lord Mayor came in his Coach preceded by the Artillery Company as I sayd before. . . . The Artillery Company when it came to the steps of the Court wheeld to their right and as was agreed, marchd through an opening the Militia made for them, and drew up behind them streaching in to Tower Street to receive the Lord Mayor as he went home and march before him."

The account of the formalities of the ceremony, with its carefully graded scale of compliments and courtesies, is then set forth. Before leaving, the Lord Mayor inspected the Militia, the two regiments making a street for this purpose, "but should have opened it wider, for the officers had scarce room to drop the spears of their Pikes."

The threat of invasion by the Young Pretender, assisted by a French fleet, formed the subject of an address to the throne drawn up in 1744 in the following terms:

Most Gracious Sovereign,

When we reflect on the Wisdom, Equity, and Mildness of your Majesty's Government, and the known Constancy, Firmness, and Resolution, of Your Royal Mind, we could scarce have thought that any Persons either could desire or would Dare to give you any Domestic Disturbance.

But since the Eldest Son of the Pretender to your Majesty's Crown is arrived in France, and since they who have long aimed at Universal Monarchy, forgetfull of the late Glorious Victory obtained in the Fields of Dettingen by the Bravery of your Majesty's Troops Animated by your Royal Presence and Example, have now the Insolence to make preparations to invade this Kingdom, in Concert with Disaffected Persons here, wicked and Senceless enough to assist the Enemies of their Country, of their Religion, and of their Lawfull Sovereign:

We humbly beg leave with the rest of your Faithfull subjects, to approach your Throne, and, from the highest Sentiments of Duty and Gratitude, to express our just Detestation of so daring and desperate an attempt, and to assure Your Majesty That we are fully determined to sacrifice our lives in the cause of Liberty, in the Defence of your Majesty's Sacred Person, Crown, and Dignity, and in Support of the Protestant Succession in your Royal Line.

Members were invited to proceed to St. James's in coaches at their own expense to attend the presentation of this address. They were to appear in coloured coats, plain hats with a cockade, swords and white stockings.

In July, 1745, the great guns in the Ground were fired in honour of the taking of Cape Breton Island. This refers to the capture of the great French fortress of Louisburg by a hastily-raised force of colonial irregulars from New England, after an amazingly unconventional siege.

And now, for the first time for close on a century, the old Company was to have an opportunity for showing its real worth as a military unit.

Choosing a time when almost the whole of the regular army was with Cumberland in Flanders, where it had just sustained at Fontenoy the most glorious defeat in history, the Jacobite party, urged on by the French, seized the opportunity for an attempt to restore the Stuarts. Prince Charles and his Highland levies, after defeating several detachments of regular troops, marched on London. The capital was in a state bordering on panic. Trade was at a standstill; shops were closed; and there was a run on the Bank of England. Cumberland's battalions were recalled from Flanders; Dutch and Hessian troops were summoned; and desperate attempts were made, by the offer of generous bounties, to fill the depleted ranks of the few regiments in garrison at home. By the time the rebels had reached Derby the City was in a ferment of excitement. The Trained Bands of London and Middlesex were in readiness to march; watches were posted at the City gates; companies of volunteers were springing up everywhere; and the King in person raised his standard on Finchley Common and reviewed the Trained Bands and Volunteers.

In the City the alarm signal was seven cannons, to be fired every half-minute from the Tower, to be answered by the same signal from St. James's Park or vice versa. On hearing this, every officer and soldier of the six Regiments of Trained Bands, without waiting for beat of drum, or any other notice, was to repair, with the usual quantity of powder and ball, to the usual rendezvous of his Regiment—*i.e.*, the Red on Tower Hill, the Green in Guildhall Yard, the Yellow in St. Paul's Churchyard, the White at the Royal Exchange, the Blue in Old Fish Street, and the Orange in West Smithfield.

And what of the Artillery Company? Most of its members were serving with the Trained Bands, but one would naturally expect a leading part in these warlike preparations to be taken by the ancient military body whose members had so often protested their readiness to shed their blood in defence of the King and Constitution. It must be recorded that the only action taken by the leaders of the Company in this hour of trial was to order the removal of the Company's arms to the Tower for safe custody. If any other action was taken, it remains unrecorded in the archives, an almost incredible omission. There seems to have been no attempt at recruiting in face of the emergency. Either vigorous leadership was sadly lacking, or the fighting spirit of the citizens had degenerated sadly since the days of Newbury.

When the trouble was over and the rebellion had been crushed, rockets to the value of £2 16s. were fired in the Ground on the Duke of Cumberland's birthday to celebrate the victory of Culloden.

The Company gained an accession of strength during these troubles. A company of gentlemen volunteers applied for permission to join as members on the understanding that they might act as a separate division. They were allowed to do so on condition that they found their own arms and powder, and, from the colour of their uniform, they became known as the "Loyal Blue Fuzileers" of the Artillery Company. At the same time several "gentlemen of great worth exercising arms in Leathersellers' Hall" were allowed the use of the House and Ground for training purposes. This corps was afterwards disbanded, the members probably joining the Company. Later in the year it was ordered that 14 drummers should be provided with new red coats, with wings, similar to those of the Drummers of the late Gentlemen Volunteers of Leathersellers' Hall.

The following summons was issued to members for the swearing in of the Lord Mayor in 1753:

You as a member of the said (Artillery) Company, are desired to Appear on that day at the Armoury in the Artillery Ground, in your Military Habit, Completely Arm'd, Agreeable to the Character you are Appointed to March in.

The Books will be Oppened at 9 o'Clock in the forenoon and peremptorily Closed at half an hour after ten, and no Person will be Mustered after that time on any pretence Whatsoever.

By Order   WILLM. HARRIS, Clerk.

Those Gentlemen, who March with the Hanover Grenadiers, are desired to meet their Officers, at Sergeant Humphrey's, the Blue Post, in Bunhill Row, Punctually at Nine o'Clock.

The Company assembled in imposing force, having included in their ranks a body of Cripplegate Grenadiers, who acted as Fusiliers. They marched to Guildhall, where the Field Officers drew their swords and received the Lord Mayor. The procession then moved off, headed by Pioneers to clear the way, and marched to the steps of the booth on Tower Hill, where the swearing in was performed by Earl Cornwallis, the Lieutenant of the Tower. After the ceremony the Company escorted the Lord Mayor back to the Mansion House, and "after having properly lodged his Lordship and Attendants there," returned to the Armoury and dined at about four o'clock.

Not the least important feature of the Company's military exercises was the entertainment which followed, and which every member who had appeared under arms was entitled to attend. On several occasions it was found necessary to issue orders to prevent members who had not performed the exercise from sitting down to an unauthorized dinner, but an exception was made to the rule in the case of members of the Court.

It was, of course, the privilege of the Leader and other officers chosen for each particular occasion to pay for the entertainment, which accounts no doubt for a certain disinclination for high rank which occasionally asserted itself. And the Court saw to it that members received proper value on these occasions. In 1754 a special order was promulgated "to prevent the meanness that had been acted by some members of this Company." The gentlemen referred to, instead of entertaining those members who appeared under arms in the traditional manner, had apparently formed the habit of doling out a mere 20s. for a Public, or 5s. for a Private Lead. The remedy was simple. The Court agreed upon a scale of fines for Leaders who did not take upon themselves the proper entertainment of the members. Thus a Member of the Court was mulcted in the sum of two guineas, and proportionate prices were fixed for Captains in Commission, Subaltern Officers, and Gentlemen Members, while a Sergeant was let off with 10s. In order to make quite sure that the alleged "meanness" did not continue, it was clearly laid down that no entertainment of less value than the prescribed rate of fines would be accepted.

A few years later the Company found itself once more in financial difficulties owing to the failure of several Aldermen and Sheriffs to pay their proportions of the expenses of Public

Marches. It became necessary to retrench, wherefore the Court decided (1) not to have wine at any future Court of Assistants, (2) that the breakfast at future Public Marches be rolls, butter and cheese, and the wine not to exceed one dozen, and (3) that the entertainment afterwards be roast beef, without any other provision except the customary sauce, the allowance of wine not to exceed one pint to each gentleman. Then it was voted that the Grenadiers' music was an unnecessary expense and that for the future they would have to be contented with two fifes "in the Leiu thereof." On another occasion the Court ordered "that it be an Instruction to the Maj^r Genl to provide Beef, mutton, or pork, according to his Discret^n with 8 Boil'd Plumb puddings for Lord Mayor's Day next." Another effort at economy resulted in an order that the firing of the Cannon be discontinued, also that the Engineer's salary be discontinued during the silence of the Cannon. It had long been the custom to fire a salute at the drinking of the King's health, or when either of the Civil Chiefs (President, Vice-President and Treasurer) arrived in the Ground; salutes were also fired at the marching in of a regiment of Trained Bands. But perhaps the palm for rigorous economy should be awarded for the order that the lanterns and windows of Armoury House should be cleaned but once a year, "and that to be against a General Court."

In August, 1756, an unfortunate citizen named Bennett was fatally shot as he was viewing the Artillery Company exercising "by the Carelessness of one of the men in leaving his Ramrod in the Barrel."

On 19th September, 1757, the use of Armoury House was granted to the "Association of Antigallicans, at the Crown and Magpie, in Aldgate High Street," for the purpose of entertaining "the Hon. Lord Blakeney, a worthy member of this Company, it being his Lordship's birthday."

War had again broken out with France in the previous year and Blakeney had become the hero of the hour by reason of his stout defence of the Island of Minorca. Though past eighty and crippled with gout, the gallant old man had borne all the rigours of a ten weeks' siege in an ill-provided, under-manned fortress, and, after causing immense loss to the enemy, had capitulated with the honours of war. For this service he was given an Irish peerage, while Admiral Byng, who had failed to relieve him, was shot—the scapegoat of a criminally inept ministry.

It is not clear how Blakeney became associated with the Artillery Company. It may be that he was admitted an honorary member in the hour of his popularity. But he signed the Vellum Book.

In the following year a form of drill known as the "Prussian Exercise" was adopted, and a drill sergeant was employed to instruct members in the intricacies of this new system, which was stated to be that employed by the Foot Guards. However, in the following year this order was cancelled, as it appeared that the King had issued no order abolishing "the old English exercise," which was therefore restored.

The Court now gave leave to a Mr. Ladd to use the Ground for testing a machine which he had invented to travel without horses and which he could not try in any field or public place without risk of its being injured by the crowd. Unfortunately details of this invention are lacking.

The Ground does not appear to have been exclusively devoted to military purposes at this time, for complaint was made to the Court in 1758 that "Horse and Foot Races were frequent in the Artillery Ground to the great Detriment of the Gates and other Buildings by Persons climbing over to see the same." At the same Court an application from the keeper of the Pied Horse, in Chiswell Street (a tavern which still exists under the same name), for leave to give an "Exhibition of Horsemanship" in the Ground, was refused.

The Court had always been decidedly averse to allowing horses in the Ground. As early as 1673 orders were issued that horses should not be "suffered to bee ridd" in the Artillery Garden. Again in 1725 it was decided that the conduct of the person who rented the herbage in allowing horses "to ride and breathe (exercise) around the Ground" was decidedly "prejudicial to the Herbage thereof and dishonourable to this Company." One exception was made in favour of the Civic Official known as "The Common Hunt," who was permitted to graze his charger in the Ground as a special favour.

In spite of complaints, the practice of foot-racing in the Ground continued. A daily paper of 1765 records that a race was run in the Artillery Ground "by a remarkable little Gentleman, not quite four Feet high, against three blooming young

Ladies; three Heats from the Gate in Bunhill-Row, to the Gate in Bunhill-Fields; the Odds at starting were five to three against the Gentleman: The first Heat was won by one of the Ladies, with great Ease, on which the Odds were doubled; the second Heat was in favour of the Gentleman, for above Half the Course, when a Chimney Sweeper's Boy happened to fall down in the Gentleman's Way, which occasioned the Umpires to declare it foul; the third Heat the Gentleman was distanced. The Race was performed before a vast Number of Spectators and afforded uncommon Diversion." A few years later we find that "William Lodwick, of the Isle of Ely, hopp'd four miles in the Artillery Ground, for a wager of thirty guineas; he had an hour allowed him, but performed it in fifty-eight minutes!"

Even the prize ring was not considered out of place on our premises. It is recorded that, in 1772, "a severe battle was fought in the Artillery-ground, between two young men, for fifty guineas a side, when, after fighting for some time, one of them had his collar-bone broke." Apparently the gentlemen who leased the herbage of the ground was responsible for these unmilitary spectacles.

A PARADE, *circa* 1760

The engraving of which the above is a reproduction is in the possession of the Regiment. Its origin is unknown, but it gives us the earliest known picture of Armoury House and the Company on parade in the ground. Note the Grenadier Company in the distance with their drummer and fifer. This print shows the high wall, built in 1641, which enclosed the ground before any houses were built on the east side

150

CHAPTER VIII

1760 TO 1779

WHEN their Captain-General died in October, 1760, the Company decided to present loyal felicitations to his grandson, who succeeded him as George III. An address was drawn up which, after appropriate condolences and congratulations, requested the King to appoint a new Captain-General according to custom, and concluded with the usual protestations of loyalty. It was ordered that no member should accompany the President at the presentation of this address unless dressed in black, with weepers, plain hats with crape hat-bands and cockades, major or queue wigs, and black swords. Furthermore, not more than two were to ride in each private coach or chariot.

Owing to inconceivable dilatoriness on the part of the President in making an appointment with the Lord Chamberlain, this address was never presented, in spite of the repeated efforts of the Court to bring it about. Accordingly the subject-matter was incorporated in a fresh address on the occasion of the King's marriage in 1761. This second attempt, after long delay, reached His Majesty. Three years passed without any sign of a reply and the Company again approached the throne with a request for the appointment of a Captain-General. Finally, in 1766, King George issued the usual Warrant confirming all the ancient privileges of the Company and appointing George Augustus Frederick, Prince of Wales, then a child of three, to be Captain-General, a position he was to retain for sixty-three years. In the previous year the Company had celebrated the birthday of their future Commander by firing the cannon in the Ground and by the consumption of a ham and two fillets of veal, "to be eat cold in the evening and two currant tarts 4s. each."

One of the results of the long delay in the appointment of a Captain-General was that the Clerk complained that he had been for several years deprived of his usual bounty of ten guineas on rendering to His Majesty the return of the annual elections.

The early years of this reign were disgraced by a shocking act of vandalism on the part of the Court. By their order the old pattern Grenadiers' caps and slings were burned for the sake of the silver, which was sold (at 6s. 4d. per oz.) for £15 15s. 7d. The silver heads of the old Leading Staves were also sold and realized just over £4. It would seem that the Regiment is fortunate in the possession of the few remaining relics of its earlier history.

The Colours of the Company in 1771 consisted of a Union flag, charged with the Rose and Thistle, the Prince of Wales's Plume and the motto "Ich Dien," and a crimson flag embroidered with the Company's arms. By this time the number of Colours carried had been reduced to two. The field of the Regimental Colour was changed from red to blue, to correspond with the colour of the facings, in 1783.

It was in 1768 that the Corporation, anxious to do honour to the King of Denmark, requested the Company to furnish a guard of honour at Westminster, where His Danish Majesty embarked, and another guard and an escort at Temple Stairs, where he landed on his way to dine at Mansion House. It is recorded that the Company performed the duty required of them in such a manner as added greatly to the dignity of the metropolis, but the occasion has the added interest of being the first instance of what has for long been a cherished privilege of the regiment—the provision of a guard of honour on every occasion of the visit of foreign monarchs to the City.

An episode which took place in the following year has a bearing upon another of the Company's especial privileges, that of marching under arms through the City of London. The Lord Mayor wrote to the Secretary for War complaining that a detachment of Guards, returning to the Tower after suppressing a riot at Spitalfields, had marched through the City with drums beating, fifes playing, and generally making "a very war-like appearance, which raised in the minds of peaceable citizens the idea of a town garrisoned by regular troops." This does not appear to the modern idea a very terrible crime, but it must be remembered that in those days the army was exceedingly unpopular with the general public; civil authorities were particularly prone to annoy the military whenever possible; and the City of London in particular was very jealous of anything which might partake of the nature of a recruiting campaign.

His Lordship therefore demanded to know by whose orders this unusual procedure took place. In reply the Secretary for War gave it as his opinion that no troops should march through the City in the manner described without previous notice to the Lord Mayor. He promised to deal with the officer of the offending party and to prevent any just offence being given to the City or its Chief Magistrate for the future.

This is not, however, the first instance of the City's assertion of its rights in this direction. In 1746 a detachment of soldiers marching along Cheapside to beat of drum were stopped by an Alderman and desired to desist. The Captain replied, "Sir, we are Marines." "I beg pardon," replied the Alderman. "I did not know. Pray continue your march as you please."

The derivation of the City's authority to forbid the beating of drums, etc., is a matter for some doubt, but the origin of the exercise of the privilege by certain regiments can be set forth with exactitude.

According to the *Handbook of Ceremonial of the City of London* (Report from the City Remembrancer to the Privileges Committee of Aldermen, 1906), "subject to due notice being given to the Lord Mayor, the privilege of marching through the City with drums beating, Colours flying, and bayonets fixed was then enjoyed by the following regiments:

Grenadier Guards (3rd Battalion).
(Buffs) East Kent Regiment.
The Royal Marines.
6th Battalion (now 7th) Royal Fusiliers (R. London Militia)."

The privilege was extended to the whole regiment of Grenadier Guards in 1917 and to the whole regiment of Royal Fusiliers (City of London Regiment) in 1924.

In another Report in the same publication it is stated that "The H.A.C. claim and have exercised the same privilege."

Now it is matter of common knowledge that the Honourable Artillery Company have exercised the privilege on innumerable occasions within living memory, while their archives establish the fact that they had done so for centuries past.

It is beyond doubt that the privilege arose through certain regiments, shortly after the inception of the standing army, being authorized to beat up drums for recruits in the City. In some cases, but not in all, this custom, being presumably repeated from time to time, became a privilege, but always subject to due notice being given to the Lord Mayor. It has frequently been stated that the privilege entails descent from the Trained Bands, or that the regiment in question was recruited from that source, but this argument is not borne out by facts, except, of course, in the case of the 7th Battalion of the Royal Fusiliers, who are the direct descendants of the old Trained Bands. There is no evidence whatever that men of the Trained Bands were drafted into any other regiment, though it is possible that individuals may have enlisted; the regiments concerned were merely given authority to recruit in the City.

The first mention of the matter in the City Records is contained in the Lord Mayor's Waiting Book, a sort of official diary of the Lord Mayor's judicial activities, under date 1663. It runs as follows:

Theis are to authorise and permitt the bearer thereof Capt. John Mordaunt to beat up Drums within the Citty of London towards levyeing of forces for to goe in his Ma^{ty} Service under the Command of the Earle of Teviott to Tangeire without any lett or molestacon. Given under my hand this 8th of December, 1663.

ANTHO: BATEMAN.

Captain John Mordaunt was an officer of the Tangier Regiment, now the Queen's Royal Regiment, and the Earl of Teviott was Colonel of the same regiment until he was killed near Tangier on 4th May, 1664. Sir Anthony Bateman was Lord Mayor in 1663.

The first mention of the Grenadier Guards is an entry dated 21st September, 1664:

This day likewise was granted by his Lor^d to Sir Edward Broughton or to such officer as he shall appoint for the beating up of Drums in this Citty and Libtyes for fifty men Voluntiers to go on ship board under the command of his highness Prince Rupert in his Ma^{tyes} service for Ginny by warr^t under the hand and seale of his Grace the Duke of Albemarle.

Sir Edward Broughton was Captain of the 6th Company of His Majesty's Own Regiment of Foot Guards (now the Grenadier Guards), and the expedition referred to was successful in seizing certain Dutch possessions on the Guinea coast, after which it sailed across to North America and captured New Amsterdam, renaming the village New York, after James, Duke of York, Lord High Admiral of England. It is probable, however, that Broughton's company did not sail with that expedition after all, as this officer was mortally wounded in a sea fight with the Dutch on 3rd June, 1665—the great naval victory off Lowestoft.

We next come to the origin of the privilege as far as it applies to the Royal Marines. This takes the form (under date 11th November, 1664) of a copy of a warrant from the Lord General as follows:

Theis are to authorise you to beat up Drumes in . . . and other parts thereabouts for the raiseing of your Company of Foot, consisting of two hundred men for the Service of his Ma^{ty} at Sea under the Command of his Royall Highnesse the Duke of Yorke and to quarter such men as you shall raise in . . . Alehouses and victualling houses untill they be compleated and then to march to . . . And the Justices of the peace and the Constables of the severall Townes where your men shall quarter are to be assisting to your selfe and the officers employed by you in the equall quartering of your men and the officers are to take care upon the march and in quarters that the Souldiers behave themselves civilly and orderly and pay for what they shall receive from their Landlords. You are to acquaint Sir Thomas Parger (?) or Commissary Baynes when you are ready to muster and to muster first 100 men and the rest afterwards as they shall be raised. Given under my Hand and Seale at the Cockpitt the 9th of November, 1664.

ALBEMARLE.

To Coll: Sir Tho: Killigrew.

Whereupon his Lo^p graunted a license to the said Coll: Killigrew or any deputed by him to beat up Drumes within the Citty of London and Libties thereof for the purpose aforesaid.

"Sir Thomas" is evidently a mistake: it should have read Sir William Killigrew, who was commissioned on 5th November, 1664, to raise The Admiral's Regiment, which was first mustered on 16th November of that year. The above Warrant therefore marks the original formation of the Royal Marines, and it is noteworthy that there is no mention of the Trained Bands, but merely a licence to recruit in London.

Other entries in the Waiting Book refer to the Royal Marines as follows:

October 30th, 1666. Theis are to authorize you by beat of Drum to raise such Voluntiers as you shall need not exceeding 100 men for the filling upp of your Company in his Royall Highnesse the Duke of York's Regiment under the Command of Collonel Sir Christopher Wrey. And in case you shall beat upp yr Drums in the Cittye of London or the Libtie thereof you are first to acquaint the Lord Maior of London therewith. Given under my hand at the Cockpit the 26th of October, 1666.

ALBEMARLE.

To Capt. Silius Titus,
or such Officer as he shall appoint.

Sir Christopher Wrey became Lieutenant-Colonel of the Admiral's Regiment on 5th November, 1664, and Colonel on 18th July, 1665. Captain Silius Titus (author of the famous anti-Cromwell tract, "Killing No Murder") was commissioned Captain of a newly raised company in the Admiral's Regiment on 2nd July, 1666. This is the first recorded instance of the proviso that the officer must first acquaint the Lord Mayor before beating up Drums in the City, which invariably appears in subsequent warrants. It appears likely that this formality had been neglected on some previous occasion and had led to a remonstrance from the City authorities. Further warrants in favour of the predecessors of the Royal Marines were dated May and July, 1667.

The Coldstream Guards lay no claim to the privilege, but an entry in the Waiting Book dated 24th February, 1665, refers to this regiment, then known as The Lord General's Regiment of Foot Guards. It runs as follows:

Whereas his Ma^ty hath given Order for the raising of five hundred men to bee added to my Regiment of his Ma^ts foot Guards and to bee employed for sea service. Theis are to authorise and require you to beat up Drums in London and other parts thereabouts for the raysing of the said men, and to quarter them in the Quarters of the respective Companies according to the former Orders.

ALBEMARLE.

To Lieut. Col. Ethelbert Morgan
or such officer as he shall appoint.

Lieutenant-Colonel Ethelbert Morgan was the officer who commanded Monck's Coldstreamers on their celebrated march from Coldstream to London in 1659.

The next unit mentioned is the Holland Regiment, now The

Buffs (Royal East Kent Regiment). On the imminence of war between England and Holland in 1665 four English regiments in the Dutch service, the descendants of Colonel Morgan's London companies of 1572, had been given the option of forswearing allegiance to their country or immediate disbandment. Though faced with destitution, officers and men refused to take the oath of fealty to Holland and were disbanded. The English Ambassador, Sir George Downing, defrayed the expenses of their return to England and Charles II ordered the Holland Regiment to be raised from the returning troops. Wishing to recruit in the City, the officer concerned appears to have shown the Lord Mayor his commission, a copy of which appears in full in the Waiting Book under date 5th August, 1666:

CHARLES R.

Charles by the grace of God King of England Scotland Fraunce and Ireland Defender of the faith, etc. To our Trusty and well-beloved Robert Wildbore Esq. Wee doe by theis presents constitute and appoint you to be Lieutent to the Company of foot in our Holland Regim^t raised or to be raised for our service commanded by Robert Sydney Esq. whereof hee himself is Captaine. You are therefore carefully to discharge the Duty of a Lieutent by exercising the said Companie in Armes both Officers and Souldiers and to keepe them in good Order and Discipline. And wee doe hereby command them to obey you as their Lieutent. And you are to observe such Orders and direccons as you shall from time to time receive from your Capt or other your Superiour Officers according to the Discipline or Warr in pursueance of the Trust wee repose in you. Given at our Court of Whitehall the xxiii of June, 1665.

Theis are to license Robert Sydney, Esq., Collonel of the Holland Regiment and anie other person deputed by him to beate upp Drummes within this Citty of London and Libties thereof for raising his owne Company to consist of One hundred men for the service of his Ma^{ty}.

Dated this vth of August, 1666.

Entries dated 29th April, 1667, and 11th July, 1667, also refer to the Holland Regiment.

It is somewhat surprising to find a Scottish regiment recruiting in London as early as 1666, but the fact remains that on 3rd December of that year the Lord Mayor granted an order on a warrant from the Duke of Albemarle for "Lord George Douglas' Regiment," now The Royal Scots, to beat up in

Southwark, the City of London and Westminster, and to acquaint the Lord Mayor of London especially before beating. This regiment had returned to England from the French service for the second time in June of that year and was stationed in Ireland.

Finally we hear of the Royal Navy, the date being 21st April, 1668:

His Royall Highnesse haveing by his Warr^t under his hand and Seale authorized and required Sir Robert Holmes Knt Capt. of his Ma^{ts} Shipp the Defiance or his Order to beate uppe Drummes in such places as they should think fitt for the raiseing of Voluntier Seamen to serve on board the said shipp; upon request and viewe of the aforesaid Warr^t his Lo^{pp} doth License and give leave that Drummes may bee beate within this Cittie and Libties for the purpose aforesaid. The said Warr^t being signified unto his Lo^{pp} by M. Wren.

His Royal Highness was, of course, James, Duke of York. Sir Robert Holmes was a well-known admiral. Matthew Wren was Secretary to the Duke of York.

The Honourable Artillery Company has never doubted its ancient and prescriptive right to this privilege. Every year for upwards of 300 years, as its records show, it has marched through the City under arms, with drums beating, Colours flying, fifes or hautboys playing, and (since the introduction of that weapon) with bayonets fixed. This has been a matter of universal knowledge and no objection has ever been raised. The tacit consent of the City to this practice in former years is understandable, since the Company was for centuries composed of citizens and freemen of London under the control of the City authorities, and, when that connection ceased, ancient usage had been established. Consequently it was surprising to find, when the question arose in 1924, that the archives of Guildhall furnished no official record of the privilege ever having been granted to the Company. The omission is probably accounted for by the fact that none had ever questioned our rights in this matter. However, formal application to the Lord Mayor received favourable consideration, and this long-cherished privilege of the Company was officially placed on record.

An unusual form of parade took place in 1768. Parliament had been dissolved and a general election was imminent. It was debated at a Court of Assistants as to "whether it was eligible for this Company to go in a Body in their military uniform to vote for such gentlemen whom they should think proper to represent this City in Parliament." The question was decided in the affirmative, and all the members who were Liverymen, and therefore entitled to vote, paraded at Armoury House and marched to the poll at Guildhall, headed by a band of music.

The engagement of a drill sergeant from the Regular Army marked a new departure. This occurred in 1770, a "Mr. Osbourn, Drill Serjeant to the First Regiment of Guards," being engaged to attend on three days a week for three hours at a time, his duties being to instruct the Company in the exercise then in use by all His Majesty's forces. He received 4s. for each drill. Eight years later we find two Sergeants a. d two Corporals of the same regiment employed to drill recruits.

New Colours were ordered in 1771. Both were crimson—one with the Union in the first canton and the Prince's plumes and motto in the centre, the other embroidered with the Company's arms.

The first recorded regimental ball took place in 1771. From that date onwards it became an annual event and was usually held at Armoury House, though occasionally at such places as the Pantheon, in Oxford Road, or the London Tavern. The Company possesses several original copies of notices of these regimental balls, the earliest being dated 1777. It was usually laid down that "each Member be particularly attentive to the Character of the Persons he introduces, as he will be considered responsible for their Conduct," and it was invariably the rule that "no Lady be admitted in an Undress." Recently a ball ticket dated 1796 was discovered in an unopened envelope among some old papers at Armoury House.

The year 1771 was memorable in the annals of the City for the fact that the Lord Mayor and one of the Aldermen were incarcerated in the Tower for breach of privilege. The Government being the reverse of popular, they at once became the heroes of the moment. During six weeks' confinement they were lavishly supplied with creature comforts by the Corporation and received innumerable visits, addresses and letters of thanks from supporters in the City and elsewhere.

It was proposed at a Court of Assistants of the Artillery Company that an address of thanks should be sent to these gentlemen from the Company "for their steady and upright conduct in defence of the rights of Englishmen," but after a long debate the motion was negatived. However, when the prisoners were finally released, the Artillery Company, in full uniform, welcomed them with a salute from 21 field pieces and headed the procession that escorted his Lordship from the gates of the Tower to his residence.

The notorious John Wilkes was another of the popular heroes of the day, due to his strenuous assertion of the people's right to have debates in the House of Commons reported in the Press. Shortly after his election as an Alderman in 1770 he was appointed one of the Generals of the Artillery Company, but does not appear to have taken much active interest in his military duties. His exclusion by the Court of Aldermen from the Mayoralty after a tie at the polls in 1772 led to a riot at Guildhall. The Artillery Company was sent for and remained on duty there all night, for which they received a vote of thanks from the Court of Aldermen.

The scene at Guildhall on this occasion is thus described in the diary of the Duchess of Northumberland:

On the Lord Mayors Day the Mob insulted the Procession very much but it was much worse in the Evening when a number of Fellows, headed by some sailors with short Bludgeons, assembled about the Guildhall threatening all who came near them.

Many Gentlemen and Ladys going to the Ball were grossly insulted; The populace in order to get into the Hall, pull'd down the temporary works before the Portico, & set the Rails on Fire, an Engine being sent for to extinguish it, they threw that into the Flames. The Constables after a great Scuffle were obliged to take Refuge in the Hall. The populace forced open the Iron Gates, & then made an attempt upon the Door. A number of Gentlemen sallied forth with their Swords drawn but were obliged to return.

After some Time Mr. Sheriff Lewis, with several other Gentlemen with drawn Swords came to the Door & order'd it to be thrown open, then he exhorted the people to become appeas'd; otherwise he intimated that the Riot Act must be read, & the Consequences would be dreadful. The Sheriff by his conciliating words pretty well abated the Storm; & the Artillery Company soon arriving all became calm.

When Wilkes became Lord Mayor in 1774, a deputation from the Company waited on him with the usual offer of service, which was declined. The Lord Mayor evidently preferred to be attended by the Cripplegate Grenadiers, as at a subsequent Court of Assistants eight sergeants of the Trained Bands were dismissed the Company for marching in that body on Lord Mayor's Day.

The Grenadiers were still considered the *corps d'élite* of the Regiment. Only a few years before it had been decided that none but Commissioned Officers (of the Trained Bands) were to be admitted to their ranks.

In 1774 the Rules and Orders of 1658 were repealed in favour of a new code. The old orders were closely followed, but there were several important alterations. After setting forth the constitution and the list of officials of the Company, who were to be chosen by ballot "according to ancient custom," they proceeded to lay down regulations for the election of the Field Officers for each year. These consisted of the Generals, Lieutenant-Generals and Major-Generals, two or more of each rank, who performed their various duties in rotation at the various grand marches, etc. The office of General was to be confined to Aldermen; the two Sheriffs elect were to be appointed Lieutenant-Generals. On election to their respective ranks these gentlemen paid £10 each to the funds of the Company. It was further ordered that the Company should not attend any gentleman who became Lord Mayor unless he had paid these sums when due, as well as a further payment of £40 10s. for the attendance of the Company in arms on Lord Mayor's Day. Major-Generals were to be elected from the senior Commissioned Officers, and to pay £5 on their advancement.

The Rules enacted that any gentleman elected to the Court of Assistants and declining to accept office should be fined a guinea, plus 2s. 6d. to the "Poor's Box." Refusal to pay the fine was to be punished by expulsion.

Every member of the Court in rotation was obliged to take command of a public or private "Lead" and to provide an entertainment afterwards, but to safeguard the Leader from undue expense it was laid down that not more than 24 members should parade on a private, or 48 on a public lead, unless at the invitation of the commander for the evening. Further, no member was to be permitted to share in the entertainment who had not appeared under arms. A scale of fines was fixed for members of the Court who declined to take their turns to lead. Gentlemen were required to be silent and attentive on parade, under penalty of being reported to the Court of Assistants; and anyone breaking off before being regularly dismissed was mulcted of one shilling to the Poor Box.

A Lieutenant William Jewell was fined a guinea by the Court for "aiding and assisting a body calling themselves Cripplegate Grenadiers." As he not only refused to pay the fine, but called the Court to their faces "a sett of proud, arbitrary, Insolent Beggars," he was expelled the Company.

Article 29 provided that the Company should attend in arms the funeral of any member on payment of two guineas. It is noteworthy that, while the injunctions against quarrelling, profane cursing and swearing remained in force, the old rules against drunkenness and gambling were omitted.

The question of the renewal of the Company's lease of the Artillery Ground arose in 1775. After prolonged discussion it was agreed that the Company should give up the strip of land along the east side of the ground in return for the renewal of the leases for the remainder. The western half of the ground, which is the freehold of the Corporation of London, was then let to the Company for 61 years, at the expiration of which it was to be renewable every 14 years for ever. The eastern half, which the Corporation held on lease from the Prebendary of Finsbury, was leased to the Company for 83 years, commencing from 1780, and renewable without fine for all future leases taken by the City.

The year 1776 is chiefly notable for the fact that a blue uniform was ordered for the Sergeant Major, in order that he might "appear in character as Sergeant Major of this Company." It was also enacted that no gentleman should be admitted a member unless he produced a copy of his freedom of the City and was recommended by two members of the Court. The playing of cards in Armoury House was forbidden, except at the annual regimental ball, under penalty of one guinea.

In July, 1778, a company of about 50 gentlemen, who for some time had met for military exercise in Fishmongers' Hall, applied for leave to use the Artillery Ground. They declared themselves ready to become members of the Company if necessary. After consideration the Court decided that those who were freemen of the City should be admitted members, being eligible, and that those who were not freemen should be allowed the use of the ground for training for three months. This company afterwards became known as The London Association.

For many years it had been the custom for newly-elected members of the Court of Assistants to give a dinner to the remainder of the Court. This was called the Colts' Feast, or, latterly, the Stewards' Feast. In 1779 the Colts were severely censured at a subsequent Court for having, contrary to ancient custom, provided "a very coarse and indifferent entertainment," so that many members quitted the room and regaled themselves at a neighbouring tavern. However, at the next General Court this accusation was declared to be malicious and unjust and the motion ordered to be rescinded.

It was becoming not uncommon for the Company to be called upon to quell riots and disturbances in the City. In fact we are now entering upon a new phase in the history of the corps, in which its main sphere of usefulness lay in the policing of the City at a time when no other force was available to keep in check the unruly element. In 1777 the Lord Mayor and Sheriffs, fearing a disturbance on Lord Mayor's Day, requested the Company to mount guard at Guildhall. Accordingly the members assembled. Their officers were ordered to pay the strictest attention to the dress and conduct of their men, "as a considerable share of the future fame of the Company depended on the spirited execution of the guard at Guildhall." They remained on duty all night, for which they received an honorarium of £10 from the Corporation.

Whatever the value of the Company as military police, it is fairly obvious that their efficiency as a combatant unit must have been seriously open to question at this stage of their existence. This appears to have been realized by the Court in 1778, at a time when all Europe was preparing for war, for it was resolved that "as it appeared by the Charter of Henry VIII and the Patents of James I and Charles I that the Company was in those times deemed useful for the maintenance, defence and safety of the realm, and *as it might be made so again* by a proper execution of the power reposed in them by His Majesty's Warrant," it was the duty of the Company to take speedy and effectual means to encourage recruiting and to promote and enforce military exercises among its members, "as it was only by numbers and discipline that a Military Corps could be rendered formidable and respectable."

Shortly afterwards a "plan for restoring the Artillery Company to its ancient splendour and making it a most respectable Military Association" was put forward by a member. His chief suggestions were that all ranks and titles should be laid aside except such as related to the Company; that all members should be united in a body with a uniform peculiar to itself; and that non-Freemen should be admitted as members. These proposals were negatived at a General Court, but the seed was to bear fruit three years later.

The close connection which had existed for centuries between the Company and the London Trained Bands was now to be broken. For the past sixty years the Court of Lieutenancy had voted to the Company annual training grants of £78 for the Officers and £72 for the Sergeants of the Trained Bands. In 1769 the latter allowance was withdrawn at the request of the Militia Officers, who objected to Sergeants claiming equality with them as members. This action had not the desired effect, as the Sergeants were still retained as members of the Company at reduced rates of subscription. The Lieutenancy therefore issued an order that no member of the Company should at the same time be a Sergeant in the Militia, but, in order not to deprive the Company of their services, directed that the Sergeants should do duty with the Company on all grand marches and public exercises. This order carried with it an allowance of £100 per annum to the Company for training expenses, an arrangement which only lasted for ten years.

Then came the cleavage. In 1778, the Lord Mayor elect, Sir John Esdale, somewhat rudely rejected the offer of the Company's services as an escort, saying that there were very many bad customs belonging to the office of Mayor "which ought to be broke." On being reminded that former Mayors had been censured for not accepting this service, he said he did not mind censure. However, the Company furnished a Guard on Lord Mayor's Day and remained on duty at Guildhall all night. It was ordered that any member convicted of being disguised in liquor, or behaving in a riotous manner at the Lord Mayor's ball, being in regimentals, should be fined half a guinea.

The blank refusal of their services was a set-back to the Company, but worse was to come. In the following year Alderman Brackley Kennett, Treasurer of the Company, was chosen

Lord Mayor. The Company tendered their services as usual. The Lord Mayor not only declined them but refused to entertain the Company, as was customary. This decision, it would appear, was not due to meanness, as he afterwards paid £50 to the Company's funds in lieu of the entertainments. The reason lay in a desire that another military body, the Cripplegate Grenadiers, which included certain members of the Company, should act as the Mayoral escort on the day of the procession. The Court of Assistants were aware of the proposal and took great offence. Copies of their former orders, which were also the orders of the Lieutenancy, were printed and sent to every member drawing attention to the penalty of expulsion to which any member was liable who presumed to march with any other military body on such an occasion. In addition, the following advertisement was inserted in the newspapers:

HONOURABLE ARTILLERY COMPANY.

Armoury House, 6th November, 1779.

The Court of Assistants of the said Company acquaint the Public, that the Lord Mayor elect having HIRED a Number of Persons to attend him as a Military Body on Lord Mayor's day, hope that if any censure should be thrown on them, for Misconduct or otherways, it will not be imputed to the Artillery Company, they having no concern in the Management of the Business on that day.

Signed, by order of the Court,

PETER LONGES, *Clerk.*

This action had no effect. The Lord Mayor had his private bodyguard, and at the next meeting of the Court a dozen members of the Company were expelled, including the Lord Mayor himself and several officers of the Orange Regiment, of which he was Colonel. The Lord Mayor promptly laid a complaint before the Lieutenancy and this unfortunate business resulted in the withdrawal of all grants and an order that no Officer or Sergeant of the Trained Bands should in future do duty with the Artillery Company without leave of the Court of Lieutenancy or the Lord Mayor. The Company countered with a request to His Lordship for payment of his overdue fines of £10 on election to Lieutenant-General of the Company in 1766 and £10 on attaining the rank of General in 1769, informing him that it was customary to pay when in office. The Lord

Mayor replied that he did not care what was customary, but would consider it.

This undignified squabble led to practically complete severance between the military authorities of the City of London and the Company. From that day to the present time the Regiment has pursued its existence independent of financial support from the Corporation of London. Furthermore, it put an end for many years to the immemorial custom of acting as escort to the Lord Mayor on the occasion now known as "Lord Mayor's Day."

These were not the only changes in the customs of the Company that were brought about in the year 1779, which marks a turning-point in the history of the Regiment. The "Publick and Private Leads," which had been held in the Artillery Ground as far back as the records of the Company extend, were held for the last time, being discontinued after the reorganization of the following year. Even the uniform was altered. An order laid down that members should appear on Grand Marches in plain scarlet coats, blue facings and white edging, with white waistcoats and breeches, white stockings, black knee-garters, and black half-gaiters. This is the first mention of blue facings in the dress of the Regiment.

Several regimental orders for the Balmes March survive. The earliest relates to the march of 1773 and runs as follows:

London, August 4, 1773.

Sir

On *Thursday*, the 12th Instant, 1773, the Honourable the *Artillery Company* are to march to *Baums*, or the Fields leading thereto.

You, as a Member of the said Company, are desired to appear at the *Armory*, in the *Artillery-Ground*, on that Day, in your military Uniform, completely armed, agreeable to the Character to which you are appointed.

The Books will be opened at Twelve o'Clock, and the Muster peremptorily closed at Two; and no Person will be mustered after that Time, on any Pretence whatsoever.

Those, who march as Fuzileers, will not be mustered, unless they are furnished with at least sixteen Charges of Powder, a Pouch and a Bayonet.

Ordered, by the Court of Assistants, that no Officer* shall be mustered, on any Pretence whatsoever, but such only as appear in

---

* *i.e.*, of the Trained Bands.

the same military Uniform as they are obliged to do with their respective Regiments.

Those Gentlemen, who act as Sergeants, are to wear Swords, and Sashes round their Waists, but no Croslets, and march with Halberts, on the Angles of their respective Divisions.

At a Court of Assistants, held at the Armory, *in the* Artillery-Ground, November 2, 1762.

Whereas, it appears to this Court, that several Members of this Company have taken the Liberty to act as *commissioned* and *staff Officers*, on the *public Marches*, without being appointed such by any of the *commanding Officers*, who have a Right to nominate:

Ordered, to prevent the like for the Future, that whoever shall presume to march as an Officer, unless regularly appointed, shall not only lose the Benefit of his Muster,* but pay Two Shillings and Six-pence into the Poor's-Box.

And it also ordered, that every Member, whose Appearance is marked in the Muster-Book, and who doth not do the whole Duty required to be done by him, shall also not only be deprived of any Benefit from his said Muster, but likewise pay Five Shillings into the Poor's-Box.

And whereas some Members of this Company have refused, and others neglected, to pay their respective Quarterage†:

Notice is hereby given, that no Gentleman, who owes one Year at *Lady-Day* last, will be permitted to act as an Officer on a Public-March, or bear Arms at any Lead in the *Artillery-Ground*, agreeable to an Order, confirmed by a General-Court, held at the *Guildhall, London*, the 14th Day of *April*, 1720.

Neither will they be admitted to any Entertainment, either of the Company or after any Exercise, till the said Arrears are paid.

And it is ordered, that the Adjutant do make a Return, in Writing, to the next Court of Assistants, of all those who act contrary to these or such other Orders as they shall receive from the superior Officers, appointed for the Duty of the Day.

By Order of the Court of Assistants,

JOHN CROCKER, *Clerk.*

Those Majors, who have any Alteration of their Officers, in their respective Regiments, since the last March, are desired to send an Account thereof to the Clerk of the Company in Time, that the Muster-Books *may be made complete.*

N.B. A Court of Assistants at One o'Clock.

Note. No Servants or Children will be permitted to come into the Room where the Officers sup.

An order dated 1778, addressed to the Sergeants of the Trained Bands and relating to the Baums March for that year, concludes with the following warning:

---

* *i.e.*, his proportion of the Lieutenancy grant.

† *i.e.*, subscription.

If any Serjeant or Serjeants quit his or their Post (without proper Leave) before the Company is regularly discharged, or are guilty of any Misbehaviour, or shall break their Ranks on their March, or fire their Piece, or fire, fling, or throw, any Squib, Cracker, or other Fire-works, (without an Order from the proper Officer so to do,) such Person, so offending, shall entirely forfeit and lose all Advantages he may be entitled to for that Day's Duty.

It should be understood that Sergeants of the Trained Bands marched in the ranks of the Company as private soldiers.

To the PRESIDENT, VICE-PRESIDENT, TREASURER, COURT *of* ASSISTANTS, *and the Reſt of the Honourable the* ARTILLERY-COMPANY.

GENTLEMEN, *July* 25, 1777.

THE Favour of your VOTES, INTEREST, and POLL, or BALLOT, (if needful,) is reſpectfully deſired for

THOMAS MEAD,

Citizen and Girdler,

BY TRADE A

G U N - M A K E R,

To be re-elected your ARMOURER for the Year enſuing, who, (although) by the bad Effect of a very rainy Burial, after which a Complaint being made, and was extended to a Suſpenſion; but, as he has been five Times elected thereto, and near three Years thereof, the Arms of the Company is become doubled in Number, and treble the Uſes formerly made of them, which was much to his Detriment, being without any Addition of Salary as yet, — he being a ſtrenuous Aſſertor of the real Intereſt of the ſaid Company, and who, ſhould he be favoured with your Suffrages, will, by a duteous Diſcharge of the Office of ARMOURER, he humbly hopes, merit your Approbation, and an adequate Salary granted thereto.

⁂ The General-Court will be on *Tueſday,* the 29th Inſtant, at four o'Clock in the Afternoon.

FACSIMILE OF A CIRCULAR SOLICITING VOTES FOR THE POST OF ARMOURER TO THE COMPANY, 1777

They must not be confused with the members appointed Sergeants for each particular march, who marched on the angles of the divisions, as shown above. The squibs and crackers took the place of grenades in the sham fights which invariably concluded the day's exercise.

On the occasion of the last march to Balmes, in 1779, all members of the Company not Officers or Sergeants of the Trained Bands were required to parade in the newly adopted regulation uniform for the Company, viz. "A scarlet Coat, lined with white and faced with blue, the Lining to be set over the

Edges, The Breadth of the Lappels to be two Inches and a Half, to reach down to the Waist, and not to be wider at Top than at Bottom. The Sleeves of the Coat to have a small round Cuff turned up, to be three Inches deep. The Cape of the Coat to be two Inches deep, and the Buttons to be set on in Twos: Viz. Ten on each Lappel one to button through the Corner of the Cape; four on the Cuffs; four on the Pocket-flaps; and two worked Holes behind; with white Waistcoat and Breeches; white Stockings; black Knee-garters; and black Half-gaters."

The Company still followed its ancient practice of electing all officials yearly at a General Court, and it seems that those offices which carried emoluments were eagerly sought after by members. Consequently it was the custom, before the Annual General Court or whenever a vacancy occurred through death or resignation, for candidates for appointments to canvass their fellow members for votes. For instance, Captain John Crocker puts forward his claim to be continued in the office of Adjutant in the following terms:

"Having had the Honour of being elected ADJUTANT of your Company (at several General Courts), I beg Leave to solicit the Favour of your Interest and Poll, to be continued in the said Office.

"Should I be so happy as to meet with your Approbation, it shall be my constant Care and Endeavour to discharge the Duties of that Office with the greatest Fidelity.

"N.B. I have been a Member of the said Company upwards of Twenty three years."

When the Company's Messenger died in the following year there were several applications for this very subordinate position, including one from a member of the Court of Assistants as follows:

"With humble Submission, I presume to solicit the Favour of your Votes and Interest, to succeed Mr. James Hannan, your late Messenger to your Company, having been a Member Thirty-nine Years, and been on the Elective and Honorary Court of Assistants Thirty-eight Years; have served, or fined, for all Offices of the said Company: but having had very great Losses in Trade, and a Family to provide for, makes me more earnestly solicit your Suffrages for the above Office, having no Place or Emolument whatever.

"Therefore, if the Promise of Assiduity and unremitting Application to the Company's Concerns, claims your Countenance and Support on the Day of Election, I shall then have cause to hope for Success, which if so happy as to obtain, the Remainder of my Life shall be devoted to the Service of your Company; and will leave an Impression of Gratitude, which Time only can erase, on him, who, with great Respect, subscribes himself.

GENTLEMEN,
Your most obedient and humble servant,

July 7, 1779.   ISAAC DUPREE.

"N.B.   The oldest Member but Three."

The above application was unsuccessful, the appointment being given to another member, Mr. John Roake, who described himself as being "reduced by the Vicissitudes of Fortune, and the General Stagnation of Trade, from the Situation he once stood in Life."

THE LOYAL ASSOCIATED WARD AND VOLUNTEER CORPS OF THE CITY OF LONDON

The above engraving represents types of the City Volunteer Corps of 1799, and was respectfully dedicated to those Ladies who Honoured them with the presentation of Colours. In the centre of the picture, with his back to the painter, is an Infantry Officer of the Company. He appears to be wearing a "flash" similar to that still worn by the Welch Fusiliers. The group on the left consists of members of the Matross or Artillery Division of the Company. Note the civilian driver in the middle distance applying his whip to the single horse drawing the gun. He wears a grey coat faced with blue and his hat bears the monogram H.A.C. The gun is one of the original 3-pounders presented by the City of London. The bucket slung below the axle bears the Prince's plume, then the badge of the Regiment

From a colour print by M. Place after R. K. Porter

CHAPTER IX

1780 TO 1799

THE disturbances known as the Gordon Riots—a result of the repeal of certain penal statutes directed against Roman Catholics—kept the Artillery Company fully occupied during the month of June, 1780. Some 60,000 zealous Protestants, wearing blue cockades, assembled at St. George's Fields under Lord George Gordon, raised the cry of "No Popery," and marched to the Houses of Parliament to deliver a monster petition. They were joined by all the scum of London, and in a few hours a mob 100,000 strong was engaged in attacks upon the residences of leading statesmen and the chapels of foreign ministers, which soon degenerated into indiscriminate burning and looting. Rioting continued for six days. Attacks on the Bank and the Tower were repulsed by the Guards, but the prisons of King's Bench, Newgate, Clerkenwell and others, were forced, the prisoners released and the premises partly burned. Loads of chains and fetters were drawn in triumph through the streets by stolen brewers' dray-horses; fires were started in scores of places; and in every street houses were forced open and furniture thrown from the windows. The religious zeal of some of the rioters led them to attack a distillery in Holborn, where many of them perished in the flames after stupefying themselves with the spirit which was set running down the gutters.

Martial law was at once proclaimed; military were drafted into the City; and the Artillery Company and the London Association, a body of gentlemen volunteers, were called out. The Trained Bands formed themselves into a body consisting of officers and sergeants only (probably many of the hireling rank and file were to be found among the rioters). This party apparently rendered good service and suffered a number of casualties.

The Lord Mayor (Brackley Kennett) seems to have shown a remarkably poor spirit in the face of this emergency. So feeble,

THE RIOT IN BROAD STREET ON THE 7TH JUNE, 1780

Showing the London Military Foot Association (afterwards incorporated with the Company) firing on the mob at the command of Major Barnard Turner

From the line engraving by James Heath after Francis Wheatley

not to say cowardly, was his conduct, that he kept a large party of the Artillery Company, with some of the Guards, for his personal protection, instead of employing them to suppress the tumult and safeguard the lives and property of the citizens. However, parties of the Company encountered the rioters at Broad Street, the Poultry and Blackfriars Bridge, and tranquillity was at last restored. A well-known engraving shows the London Association firing on the rioters in Broad Street. It was estimated that 240 persons were killed or wounded during the riots.

During the disturbances the Prince of Wales's Dragoon Guards were quartered at Armoury House, a precedent which has been followed on more than one occasion of much more recent date. On this occasion the Company made the troops very welcome, allowing them the use of the House as well as that of the Ground. Before they went the Court entertained the officers to "an elegant dinner," but, the riots being over, they

"The Victorious Return of the City Militia after storming the Dunghill at Bunhill Fields and obliging the Garrison
to surrender at discretion,"

Showing Armoury House in the background

From the original drawing by Rowlandson, dated 1772, in the possession of the Company

INSPECTION OF THE HONOURABLE ARTILLERY COMPANY ON 22ND SEPTEMBER, 1803, BY EARL HARRINGTON

Etched by J. Mitan, aquatinted by Pickett, from a drawing by E. Dayes, Draughtsman to H.R.H. The Duke of York. Published 1804

PRIVATE, H.A.C. INFANTRY, 1798

From a coloured aquatint by Rowlandson, published by Ackermann

refused to admit a detachment of Foot Guards which had been sent to relieve the Dragoons.

Immediately after the riots, the cellars of Armoury House were used as a prison, and the Justices of Middlesex held their Rotation Office in the House for several days. This, however, was done without the consent of the Court of Assistants, who promptly met and gave orders to prevent a recurrence of this unauthorized use of the premises.

No sooner had complete tranquillity been restored than an order was issued to the Officer Commanding the forces in the City to disarm all persons who did not belong to the Militia. This was taken to apply to the Armed Associations of citizens and caused grave dissatisfaction. The London Association, in particular, had been on duty all through the period of unrest until after the execution of some of the rioters, and they resented most strongly this order for their disarming. They assembled at the Mansion House, decided that they were entitled to retain their arms under that clause of the Bill of Rights which laid down that "Protestants may bear arms for their defence," and refused to surrender them. Their officers were ordered to appear before the Privy Council, where they repeated their refusal to comply with the order and declined suggestions of compensation in the form of rank, honours or cash. Finally, to secure themselves against further action on the part of the Government, it was decided that the members of the London Association should join the Artillery Company in a body. This was done, Barnard Turner himself, in recognition of his "spirited and active part in suppressing the late dangerous riots," being admitted an Honorary Member, free of the usual fees, any former order to the contrary notwithstanding.

The complete reorganization of the Company, impending for some years, was now undertaken in earnest. It was first decided to cancel all previous rules as to qualifications for membership and manner of admission, and in future to admit any person of fair, unblemished character (being a Protestant), well affected to the King and Constitution, able to bear the expense and willing to conform to the Rules of the Company. The only stipulation was that the candidate must not be under age, or an apprentice or covenant servant. The subscription was fixed at ten shillings per annum, with entrance fees of two guineas to the Regiment, three shillings to the Clerk, two to the Messenger, and two to the Poor Box.

Every candidate was to be proposed by two members at one Court for admission at the next, and the names, addresses and occupations of candidates were to be circulated to the Court in advance. Any member so elected who was not a Freeman of London was ineligible to vote at elections or to become a member of the Court. Some months later a rule was added that candidates should appear in person before the Court. This was

AN ENGRAVING FROM THE LIST OF CHIEFS, OFFICERS, ETC., OF THE COMPANY FOR 1780
Showing the Prince's Plume, then the Regimental Badge, surrounded by Trophies of Arms, etc.

a new departure and the custom survives to the present day, exception being made in the cases of candidates on active service. Another qualification was that no one should be admitted who was under five feet two inches in height, or "from his situation in life, and make, not calculated to assume a Military appearance."

So much for recruiting regulations. On admission each member was to provide himself with arms, uniform and accoutrements. In January, 1781, the Court approved a new uniform, which followed closely the Regular Army of the period. The cost of arms and accoutrements was £4 9s. 6d.; that of the uniform £5 8s. 0d. The price of the white kerseymere waistcoat and breeches was not included in the above, as these articles, being similar to those worn in civilian attire, "could be used at any time."

Then came questions of organization. For the first time the Company was organized into a battalion on the most up-to-date lines. This consisted of a Grenadier Company, four "Hat" or Battalion Companies (so called because they wore the ordinary three-cornered hat, as opposed to the Grenadier head-dress), and a Light Infantry Company. These latter carried a shorter musket and wore a jacket instead of a coat, and a small round hat, cocked up on one side with a black cockade, a silver cord round the crown (with a tassel) and a black feather. They were selected from the most active and intelligent members. The Grenadiers were selected by the Adjutant for their size, no gentleman being admitted who stood under five feet nine inches in height. They were distinguished by wings, ornamented by loops of lace, on their shoulders, and a black feather in their hats.

Membership of the Hat Companies was decided by dividing the City and Liberties into four divisions by lines drawn through St. Paul's to the four points of the compass, the members residing in each district forming a company. These were known as the North-West, North-East, South-West and South-East Companies or Divisions. Members living outside the City were posted to the weakest companies. When a minimum of 24 members had been entered on the roll of each company, they assembled and chose their Company Officers, who afterwards settled the matter of seniority by drawing lots. Companies were also asked to agree upon a scale of fines for non-attendance at parades. Two drummers and two fifers were then enlisted and sworn in. Their pay was five pounds a year, with a new suit of clothes and a hat and feather every two years. Finally, the old titles of General, Lieutenant-General and Major-General were abolished and the Court appointed a Colonel, a Lieutenant-Colonel and a Major.

At once the Company began to improve in discipline and efficiency. Recruits were made to pass through a drill squad before joining the "New Battalion"; divisions were sized and proved before the Major took command; a scale of fines was instituted for absence from roll-call, appearing on parade improperly dressed, or talking in the ranks; and any member who behaved improperly was turned out of the Ground by the picket. As a crowning achievement the Company started musketry practice, of which nothing had been heard since the time of Queen Anne. On 21st July, 1781, the first of many annual "parties for ball-firing" took place at Sydenham. Each member was provided with eight rounds of ball and twenty-four of "blunt" cartridge. The Battalion paraded in St. George's Fields at 5 a.m. and marched to Dulwich. There the arms were grounded on the village green, colours were lodged, sentries posted and the Company breakfasted. At 9 a.m. the drums beat to arms and the Company marched to Sydenham Common, where their Colonel (The Right Hon. Sir Watkin Lewes,

Lord Mayor) inspected them. Six targets, one for each company, were fixed in the deepest ravine on the Common, to the rear of the Wells, and here the Battalion fired eight rounds per man. A spirited sham fight enlivened the march back to Dulwich. A party was sent in advance to form an ambush, complete with a masked battery of nine light cannon and three cohorns. The Battalion marched into the ambush, was attacked, recovered itself, drove back the attackers, captured and dismounted the cannon, and finally drew up on the top of a hill and fired three volleys. Then they marched into Dulwich, where they were billeted for the night. At dinner that evening, after the loyal toasts, they drank "Prosperity to the Honourable Artillery Company, and may their truly loyal and spirited example rouse the younger part of their fellow-citizens from their present indolent, and, in times like these, disgraceful pursuits after trifling pastimes and amusements."

The *Gazetteer and New Daily Advertiser* of 14th August, 1781, recorded with approval that the Artillery Company was "in such a state of progressive regulation . . . as to hold out every rational prospect that the citizens of London may never again be under the melancholy and mortifying necessity of calling in a band of mercenary soldiers" (*i.e.*, regular troops) to protect their lives and properties.

On 21st June of this year the Common Council met and passed the following resolution:

Resolved unanimously that two brass field-pieces, not exceeding the value of £150, be presented to the Honourable Artillery Company, for the signal services done by them and the gentlemen of the London Military Foot Association (now incorporated with that body), in suppressing the dangerous Riots in the month of June, 1780; and that the Committee for letting this City's Lands be desired to provide the said two Brass Field Pieces.

In the following August the Committee for City Lands asked the Company to purchase two field guns at a cost not exceeding £150. The Court decided that two brass guns already ordered should be accepted as the gift of the City, and that the resolution of the Common Council should be inscribed on the pieces, which were to be presented on 13th August, being the Captain-General's birthday. On that day the Battalion assembled in the Artillery Ground at 6 a.m. and marched over their ancient shooting grounds to Newington Butts, in order to receive the cannon in one of their farthest fields of exercise. The Lord Mayor presented the guns, as the gift of the City, "in a manly and impressive speech." The answer of the Company "was expressed by three vollies, in token of their grateful acceptance." The guns then fired a royal salute in honour of the Prince of Wales, which was followed by three volleys from the line. Then, after a march past, the Company returned to Armoury House to dinner and a display of fireworks.

It is noteworthy that the Company found it necessary to borrow two Sergeants and eight Matrosses from the Royal Artillery at Woolwich to work the guns on this occasion, also that the horses which drew the field pieces and wagons were kindly lent by Messrs. Whitbread, Calvert, Dickenson and Hale, a firm which, under the first-mentioned name, is not unknown to the present generation.

These guns are still in the possession of the Company, and are examples of what were known as "Battalion Guns," owned and used by an Infantry Regiment. They are brass 3-pounders, with a bore of 2.77 inches, and are fitted with the original tangent sights. Unfortunately, when they were recast in 1803 the inscriptions, badges, etc., were omitted.

Though the Company had for many years used various forms of light field guns for ceremonial and saluting purposes, there had never been any attempt to train a body of members in the handling of artillery. Now, however, it became necessary to make proper use of the guns given by the City, and on 22nd November, 1781, the "gentlemen practising the field-pieces" obtained the sanction of the Court for the formation of a "Matross" Division to work the new guns. This consisted of two companies, or sections, of sixteen members each, chosen from the Battalion, each company, on formation, choosing a Captain and a Sergeant. Thus the Artillery Division of the Company came into being, an event which marks an important epoch in the history of the corps. It certainly provides the earliest example of the employment of artillery by the auxiliary forces of the Crown.

Early in this year the Company disposed of its surplus equipment, selling 100 standards of arms and accoutrements, 23 good drums, a number of velvet embroidered caps and other gear which would have been of incalculable value and interest to posterity.

A new source of revenue was now discovered, and sheep were allowed to be grazed on the ground at a charge of one penny each for twenty-four hours. A little later, advertisements offered grazing for sheep or lambs at one halfpenny per head per night.

The close of the year 1781 must have seemed to Englishmen one of the darkest hours in history. Their country, chafing over the loss of the American Colonies, was at war with France, Spain, Holland, Sweden, and the newly-formed United States. In this critical situation the Company presented a loyal address to the King offering their services, without pay, in any manner His Majesty might please to command, for the defence of the metropolis. King George was pleased to approve of this address and training was carried on with increased zeal. Shortly afterwards the Court wrote to the Commander-in-Chief suggesting that some emergency might require the Company's active services, and asking "what rank His Majesty's Ancient Artillery Company holds in the Forces of the Kingdom." The reply was to the effect that the C.-in-C. was not acquainted with any rule by which a precise rank could be assigned to them, but that no doubt every proper respect and attention due to so Ancient and Honourable a Corps would be shown them.

At a meeting of members of the North-District Division of the Company on 22nd June, 1781, the following resolutions were agreed to:

I. That, to render the Knowledge they have acquired of Arms useful to their Fellow-Citizens, they will assist at all Fires that may happen within the District, to protect the Properties of the Unfortunate from the Depredations of the Rabble, and to enable the Firemen and Porters to act with greater Effect.

II. That, for this Purpose, they will immediately, on Notice of Fire, repair to the following Places of Rendezvous, completely armed and accoutred, with Ammunition, *viz.* if the Fire is in *Wood-Street*, *White-Cross-Street*, or to the Eastward of those Streets, to assemble in *Guildhall-Yard:* if to the Westward of those Streets, to assemble in *Falcon-Square*, *Aldersgate-Street*.

III. That they will remain at the Place of Rendezvous until six or more are assembled, and then act as their Officer shall direct.

IV. That the Officer leave a list at each Watch-House, of the Members residing in the respective Wards, for the Information of the Watchmen, who will be rewarded in Proportion to their Assiduity in calling the Gentlemen.

V. That, presuming an Intention to be serviceable induces Gentlemen to become Members of the Hon. ARTILLERY-COMPANY, it is hoped the Ties of Honour and Calls of Humanity will supersede the Necessity of any pecuniary Fines to compel the Attendance of the Corps on such Occasions.

Many members in addition to those of the North-District Division undertook liability for this duty, and for many years a party of the Company attended at every fire in the City and performed the duties of police.

The Company celebrated the King's Birthday in 1782 by a parade in conjunction with the London Light Horse Volunteers. They marched out of Headquarters at seven in the morning, accompanied by the two field pieces and baggage wagons, and proceeded with music playing, drums beating and Colours flying, through the City to Hyde Park, where they were inspected by General Conway. The regimental band at this period consisted of four clarionets, two horns, one trumpet, and two bassoons. There were also a drum-major, eleven drummers and ten fifers.

The following description of a duel fought by a member of the Company is culled from a daily paper dated 1783: "Yesterday I was present at one of the most valiant or murdering duels that history contains. Captain R., an Officer in the Guards, having advanced some disagreeable reflections on the Artillery Company, Mr. S., a Member, resented it with such spirit, that from my information from one of the seconds, no time was lost in appointing time and place; the back of Montagu-house was fixed on and agreed by both parties, after the usual ceremony. Captain R. fired his pistol in the air; Mr. S. returned and shot him in the arm; Captain R. fired and wounded Mr. S. in the leg; the seconds interfered, but to no purpose, for they were determined to conquer or die; the ground was changed two paces nearer; Mr. S. fired and shot Captain R. in the breast, but as he was falling into his second's arms, he fired, and the ball entered his antagonist's groin, which brought him to the ground, and no hopes of the recovery of either."

This is the only recorded instance of a pre-arranged duel fought by a member of the Company, though probably informal affrays were not unusual in those days. Here is an account of such a dispute, taken from a newspaper of 1782: "Wednesday evening an affray happened in the Artillery-ground, after the dismissing of the Artillery Company, between two gentlemen, supposed to belong to the marines. The quarrel arose from the parties having some words, in the course of which one gave the other the lye, and called him a f—l; upon which the gentleman who received the insult said to his antagonist, 'Sir, you have a sword; dare you draw it?' They both immediately drew, and after a few lunges at each other, in which one of them received a slight wound on his breast, a gentleman interfered, and put a stop to any further mischief that might have happened. Neither of the gentlemen seemed satisfied when they left the ground."

This was the period of the Regiment's greatest activity in policing the purlieus and suburbs of the metropolis. Contemporary newspapers are full of the doings of the Company in this direction. Finsbury and Moorfields had been for many years a resort of dangerous and disreputable characters, and highway robbery was frequent. In 1773 an Officer of the Company, returning home from Armoury House through Chiswell Street, was knocked down by three ruffians, who made off with his hat, his silver-hilted sword and his purse. Bunhill Row also had a bad reputation and was known colloquially as "Thieving Lane."

The *Bury Post* of 11th July, 1782, records that "a number of the Honourable Artillery Company, headed by Mr. Alderman Turner, assembled at the Artillery House, and divided themselves into separate parties, to patrole the several roads and bye ways for five or six miles round the metropolis. The party that took the road leading from Hoxton to Newington Green met a man and his wife who had just been robbed by five footpads, armed with cutlasses and horse pistols, and getting a description of their persons and the rout they had taken, immediately pursued them, and made the whole gang prisoners. The party which took the Hackney district seized the notorious Grey, with another villain, who took shelter in a house of ill-fame in Shoreditch. The other parties examined every suspicious person they met, but finding no offensive weapons upon them, suffered them to proceed. Thus, by the spirit and activity of these deserving young citizens, were seven of the most audacious offenders that ever frequented the roads assigned over to public justice, the lives and property of their fellow citizens secured from that danger, which the shameful neglect of the magistrates has exposed them to, and the mischief that must have ensued from such a desperate, armed gang of ruffians, safely prevented. They were all examined at Justice

Wilmot's office yesterday morning, when there appeared, that the five men taken near the city road, were the persons who murdered Mr. Hurd about five weeks ago in Islington fields."

On another occasion members of the Company patrolling in the neighbourhood of "Old Street Road" apprehended "seven very suspicious fellows, all well known in that part of the town, whom they secured in Clerkenwell prison." This was doubtless the outcome of a "spirited and unanimous" resolution passed at a meeting of the Fifth Division of the Company "to support the civil power in securing atrocious villains and searching suspected houses."

It seems that detachments of the Company acted occasionally as a press-gang for the Navy. On one occasion, in 1782, a detachment of the Light Infantry Company "met privately, and patrolled the roads round the metropolis till eleven o'clock, when they proceeded to the neighbourhood of Saffron-Hill; and being joined by some peace officers, made a general search through that neighbourhood, where they apprehended several idle young fellows, whom they sent to serve his Majesty."

A daily paper of 1783 records a raid by a detachment of the Artillery Company, accompanied by an Alderman and the City Marshal, on houses in Gravel Lane in a search for escaped convicts. But "after scouring the filthy habitations for upwards of two hours, no other effect followed than turning a few bunters out of bed." It seemed clear that "the neighbourhood had smoked the business, and prepared for it."

About the same time a daily paper records that "fourteen more men were taken up at a public-house, in Kingsland-road, by the Gentlemen of the Artillery Company; yesterday they were examined by the Lord Mayor, when four of them, who could give no account of themselves, were sent on board the tender, the others were discharged, on people of credit appearing to their characters."

That this work was not without its risks is evidenced by the fact that a member of the Company, Mr. Denham, was mortally wounded while on patrol duty to protect inhabitants and way-farers from the depredations of a very daring band of footpads who infested the fields near Kingsland.

On another occasion the Company was called upon by the Sheriffs to assist in the recapture of escaped convicts who had taken refuge in Gravel Lane, Houndsditch. In fact, the calls upon members at this period became so frequent that it was found necessary to lay down definite instructions as to the occasions on which the Company might properly assist the civil power. It was decided that great fires were suitable occasions, "as also congregations of robbers and other lawless or desperate men, rendering their apprehension dangerous to the unarmed civil power; or gangs of ruffians committing acts of extraordinary villainy or cruelty; but that no members should assemble in uniform except by order of the Court, and under the command of proper officers."

One other duty was performed by the Company as occasion required. It being the custom to withdraw all regular troops from the City during election times, the Company was frequently asked to relieve the Guards on duty at the Bank of England and to furnish a guard there, sometimes for as long as ten days at a time. Officers late on parade for a Bank Guard were fined a guinea; rank and file paid 10s. 6d. only, and the fine for appearing incompletely armed or equipped was 2s. 6d· All were forbidden to march in boots.

In common with Volunteers at all times and the rest of the Army at this particular period, the Company did not escape the attention of cartoonists and satirists. The Trained Bands or Militia were especially favourite butts for the shafts of these humorists, and many cartoons survive as examples of the uncouth wit that passed for humour in the good old days. A particularly fine sample is Rowlandson's "Storming the Dunghill at Bunhill Fields." It is dated 1772, and shows a regiment of City Militia marching down City Road past Armoury House. The leading company is composed of one-eyed or one-legged rapscallions, one of whom is picking a comrade's pocket as he marches; the officers (who would, as such, be members of the Artillery Company) are ridiculous figures and some are shown drinking and brawling in a tavern instead of marching with the regiment. This must have been a popular picture, as several mezzotint and line engravings were made from the original drawing now in the possession of the Company.

Another specimen of contemporary humour is culled from the Press of 1784. It runs as follows: "The Artillery Company and the City Volunteers have sent their old uniforms to be scoured, and interest is making with the City to let them have fire-arms. Proper corporals and sergeants will attend to take care they don't singe one another's eye-brows, or overload their guns. They already march to the dead march in Saul in wonderful good time. It would have frightened the French to see how highly, how widely, how boldly, and terrifically they stepped to the tune of this same march, last Monday, among the tombstones in Pancras. Scarce forty of them broke their shins, and not more than twenty fell over the graves."

Here is another example of topical wit, taken from the pages of a newspaper dated 1789: "Yesterday the City Trained Bands made a martial appearance preparatory to the Grand Procession. . . . When they were drawn up rank and file, there appeared an indiscriminate mixture of men of all sizes, with firelocks in various positions and their accoutrements equally descriptive of military uniformity. . . . On the word, 'to the right face,' being given, some went to the right, some to the left, and some to the left about, and others, more prudent than the rest, went home. The word march was unfortunately the next; of course a violent bumping of heads ensued, whilst some retreated and others advanced, but not without feeling the unfriendly effects of bayonet points in those parts most susceptible of perforation."

A still more scurrilous libel at the expense of the City Militia survives in the form of a doggerel ballad set to music for the "German Flute or Guittar." As not only a printed copy but the original manuscript draft survives among the archives of the regiment, it is possible that a member of the Company was the perpetrator of the following:

THE CITY MILITIA

You've certainly heard of that gallant Commander,
That wonderful Hero, the fam'd Alexander;
And you've certainly heard too what wonders abound
In that famous Field call'd the Artillery Ground.
    Derry down down down derry down.

Where are Soldiers whose Courage the great Globe surprizes
Of all sorts of Colours, Complections and Sizes;
Bold daring old Watchmen and wooden legg'd Sailors,
Butchers, Barbers, and Tinkers, Tomturdmen, and Taylors.
    Derry down down down derry down.

Marches, counter Marches, and grand Evolutions,
Fine Captains parading with great Resolutions,

Cannons roaring, Drums beating, and long Streamers flying,
Black-Puddings, Potatoes, and Sausages frying.
Derry down down down derry down.

In the midst of this grand, this magnificent Muster,
Says the brave Capt. Bladderem to the bold Capt. Bluster,
"A fine Body of Troops! no Flinchers or Failers;
Turn your Backsides before ye you Gentlemen Taylors."
Derry down down down derry down.

The Troops all in Order, how glorious the sight,
The pride of this Nation, its Joy and Delight;
Some Smoaking and drinking their Spirits to keep,
Some running away and some fast-asleep.
Derry down down down derry down.

Once in three Years for the Good of this Nation,
To save and protect us from foreign Invasion,
This martial Spectacle is to be found,
Shooting, Drinking and Spewing in the Artillery-Ground.
Derry down down down derry down.

P. H.

The ancient society known as the Finsbury Archers had existed in close connection with the Artillery Company for close on two centuries. Little is known of their early history, but a list of the Company's archery marks or "rovers," giving the distances in scores of yards, was published in 1594 under the title of "Ayme for Finsburie Archers." The society was revived after the Civil War in the same year as the Artillery Company; they were frequently allowed the use of the Artillery Ground to shoot in, and many members of the Company were also archers. As late as 1738 the Court of Assistants gave permission to this body to erect two archery butts in the ground, but little more is heard of them and they appear to have become extinct as a society round about 1770. The few survivors probably became members of a new body of archers formed in 1780 and which still exists as the Royal Toxophilite Society. This would account for the last-named society having in its possession some of the ancient trophies of their predecessors. These include two silver arrows, dated 1663 and 1751 respectively, given by the "Stewards in Finsbury" as prizes in those years, and the Braganza Shield, a magnificent piece of plate presented by Catherine of Braganza (consort of Charles II) to the Finsbury Archers in 1676, and worn as a badge of rank on the breast of the Marshal of that society.

In May, 1784, the Toxophilite Society, headed by the Earl of Effingham, sought permission to shoot in the Artillery Ground. After discussion, it was decided that these gentlemen should become members of the Company, retaining their uniform as archers, and forming a flank division with all the privileges of membership, including the right to elect their own officers. A set of regulations was drawn up for their guidance; among other things it was decided that they should wear "a bayonet and gaiters" when on duty. The Archers' Division apparently attended all Field Days and other exercises, as well as ceremonial occasions, but they had their special meetings or "Targets" in the Artillery Ground for the practice of archery. The Archers' Division figures prominently in a painting by Edward Dayes depicting the Company escorting the Lord Mayor in 1796.

A grand meeting of Societies of Archers was held at Blackheath in 1792 and was attended by "The Honourable the Artillery Company, in two divisions," the Surrey Bowmen, Hainault Foresters, Kentish Bowmen, Woodmen of Arden, and others. It is related that they were all dressed in green with half boots and that two persons were slightly wounded through standing too near the targets. Another account runs as follows: "Amongst those who especially distinguished themselves by gallant attention to their fair visiters, I will not omit to name the Royal Artillery Archers, whose tent was lined throughout with green silk. Their uniform also attracted universal attention, as being the most elegant and appropriate in the whole field. The honours of the day fell thick upon this society; since, out of the four prizes, they became entitled to three."

The Archers' Division of the Company lasted for twenty years, after which the members continued a separate existence and resumed their original name of the Toxophilite Society. The connection between the two bodies was resumed after a lapse of over a century, for in the year 1922, when the Archers were compelled to surrender their shooting grounds in Regent's Park, they accepted the hospitality of the H.A.C. for a season, and held their meetings in the Artillery Ground, that ancient home of the longbow.

The death of Major Sir Barnard Turner in June, 1784, as the result of a riding accident, deprived the Company of a most popular and energetic officer, to whom is ascribed a considerable

BARNARD TURNER, ESQ., ALDERMAN AND SHERIFF OF LONDON, COLONEL OF
THE RED REGIMENT OF CITY MILITIA, MAJOR OF THE HONOURABLE ARTILLERY
COMPANY, AND COMMANDANT OF THE LONDON MILITARY FOOT ASSOCIATION
DURING THE RIOTS IN 1780

From the engraving by James Walker after F. Wheatley

share in the recent reorganization and consequent increased efficiency of the Regiment. The deceased officer had acquired a high reputation for courage and energy during the Gordon Riots, and his funeral was attended by a prodigious concourse of spectators, who are said to have gathered from more than thirty miles round. The tragic nature of his death was recorded in doggerel verse in a popular broadsheet entitled "The sorrowful Account of Sir Barnard Turner, Knight; one of the Sheriffs of the City of London; Parliament Man for the Borough; who unfortunately lost his Life by a Fall from his Horse, June 12th, 1784." This poem is too long to quote in full, but the following is a fair sample:

> As Sir Barnard Turner was regailing
>   Himself with three more gentlemen,
> But on the road as they return'd,
>   Now comes on my dismal tale;
> His horse took fright all of a sudden,
>   And run with such a force and might,
> That by no means he could not stop him,
>   Foul of a chaise he run outright.
>
> The chaise it tore his thigh quite open,
>   And broke his leg quite short in two,
> What a shocking sight it was then,
>   For those that were with him to view;
> His wound immediately was dressed,
>   His friends they all assistance gave,
> But alas! it proved quite mortal,
>   None on this earth his life could save.

The Company attended the burial of their comrade (which was interrupted by the arrest of the corpse for debt), erected a tombstone to his memory, and opened a subscription list for the benefit of the bereaved family. Recently a presentation sword that had belonged to Sir Barnard was put up for auction, but, in spite of the efforts of a member to secure it for the Regiment, it found its way to the London Museum. However, the Company possesses a suitable memorial of a notable member of the Regiment in the shape of a very fine mezzotint, engraved by James Walker after Wheatley.

A special meeting of the Court of Assistants was held in August, 1784, to consider an application from a gentleman named Vincent Lunardi, Secretary to the Neapolitan Ambassador, for the use of the Ground for an experiment in aeronautics. This is not the first instance in the records of the Company of the practice of this science. In 1721 three "boloons" were provided for use at an exercise, but the nature of these appliances is a matter for considerable doubt, as even fire balloons were not invented until 1782. In 1763 an advertisement appeared in the newspapers to the effect that a "machine to sail against the wind," invented by a Mr. Higgins, was to be tried in the Artillery Ground, and the public admitted at sixpence per head. Unfortunately the Court refused permission for this experiment to take place, and ordered the machine to be removed within fourteen days, thus possibly depriving us of some interesting information on an early attempt at the conquest of the air.

Montgolfier ascended in a heated air balloon in 1782, and the first ascent in a gas-filled balloon was made in August of the following year. In November the use of the Artillery Ground was granted for the exhibition of an "Aerostatic Globe," and the following advertisement appeared in the Press:

BY PERMISSION OF THE COURT OF ASSISTANTS OF THE
HONOURABLE ARTILLERY COMPANY

On Tuesday, the 25th inst., at one o'clock precisely
(If fine weather)

Mr. Biaggini will let off his Grand Air Balloon, under the direction of Chevalier Zambeccari, from the Artillery Ground, and no person will be admitted without tickets, which are to be had of Mr. Biaggini *only* at the Lyceum near Exeter Change, Strand, and at his house No. 33, Noble Street, at the bottom of Foster Lane, Cheapside.

N.B.—The Air Balloon continues to be exhibited at the Lyceum this day and to-morrow and no longer.

This balloon was of fine silk, gilded, globular in form, and about 8 feet in diameter, but carried no aeronaut. The experiment was successful, the balloon disappearing in a southerly direction, witnessed from the Ground by a vast concourse of spectators.

A Mr. Morel applied in June, 1784, for permission to let off from the Artillery Ground "the largest balloon ever made in this country," it being 45 feet in diameter. His request was

VIEW OF THE ASCENT OF MR. LUNARDI'S CELEBRATED AIR BALLOON FROM THE ARTILLERY
GROUND, 15TH SEPTEMBER, 1784

From a contemporary print published in the "European Magazine" and acquired by the Company

refused on the plea that to employ the Ground for any other than a military purpose tended to divert individuals from their useful labour, and might interrupt the public peace.

After a violent debate, the Court abandoned this principle in favour of Mr. Lunardi, granting him the use of the Ground on condition that he gave security for £500 against damage to the Ground and also subscribed a 100 guineas to the fund for Sir Barnard Turner's family. The ascent took place on 15th September, 1784, in the presence of the Prince of Wales and a large assembly. It is notable for being the first ascent of the "first aerial traveller in the English atmosphere," as Lunardi describes himself. The balloon, $32\frac{1}{2}$ feet in diameter, was made of oiled silk in strips of red and blue, filled with "inflammable air" provided by the action of vitriolic acid on zinc. The assemblage was smaller than might have been expected, owing to the fear of mob violence in the event of the failure of the experiment. Only a few weeks before this, a Frenchman had tried to forestall Lunardi by launching a balloon at Chelsea. His balloon had refused to take the air and was thereupon torn to pieces by the infuriated rabble, who then proceeded to wreak their disappointment on the surrounding buildings.

On this occasion everything went off according to schedule, except that one of the oars, with which Lunardi hoped to be able to steer his balloon, broke off and fell to earth almost at once. Also the balloon was found incapable of carrying the second passenger, who was to have accompanied Lunardi, who had therefore to be content with the company of a dog, a cat and a pigeon, which last escaped. The balloon ascended "amid the most unfeigned acclamations and applause," and Lunardi landed safely in a cornfield in North Mimms. Rising again, he finally descended near Ware (where some farm labourers mistook him for the Devil), coming to the ground with such violence as to break up his car and shake $9\frac{1}{2}$ guineas out of his pocket.

The aeronaut became at once the hero of the hour. The Court of Assistants, in recognition of his "ingenuity and laudable intrepidity," made him a member of the Company, on condition that he took the oath of allegiance and paid the usual fees. They also granted him the use of the Ground for any future experiment. He was then presented to the King, on which occasion he wore the uniform of the Company.

It is related that one old lady was so affected when she saw the oar drop from the balloon, mistaking it for the aeronaut, that she expired. On the other hand, the ascent probably saved the life of a man who was being tried at the Old Bailey, for so anxious were the jurymen not to miss the unusual sight, that they acquitted the accused without waiting for the evidence.

Among the archives of the Company are several records of wagers among members as to the success of Lunardi's venture. The stakes were held by the Secretary, and the bets invariably took the form of bottles of wine. For instance, the following wagers were entered upon at the Paul's Head Tavern on the Wednesday preceding the ascent: "Mr. Biggs Betts Mr. Banks Three Bottles to One that Mr. Lunardi is Landed and Safe at $\frac{1}{2}$ past 8 o'clock on Wednesday evening, the 15th of Sep. 1784. Do. Do. between Mr. Bond and Mr. Clark. Hooper Betts White two Bottles to One that Mr. Lunardi lands 100 miles from the Artillery Ground," etc. The gentlemen concerned met at the Paul's Head at a later date and paid their bets "to the amount of Ten Bottles."

Lunardi made a further ascent from the Artillery Ground in May of the following year. This time his balloon resembled in shape a Seville orange and was painted to resemble the Union Flag of England. He came down in Tottenham Court Road owing to a breach in the silk. Some years later two gentlemen who had "been at some pains and expense in preparing for an experiment in natural philosophy" applied for the use of the Ground to let off two air balloons, but the Court decided that the request could not properly be complied with.

For some years concern had been felt on account of encroachments on the Company's fields of exercise in Finsbury and Islington. In 1776 the Court caused a plate to be engraved showing the positions and names of the stone archery marks which defined their ancient shooting grounds, and at the same time orders were issued to several landholders to replace certain stones which had been removed. On the occasion of the Balmes March in 1782, the Company had found a large field enclosing one of these marks, with gates locked and chained, and four men placed there to object to the passage of the Regiment. The gates were forthwith forced and the Company marched through. Two years later the Company again marched to the marks, removing obstructions and encroachments, and this time they re-named after prominent officers of the Company several of the stones whose original names had apparently been forgotten. This was excusable, even appropriate, but it is diffi- cult to forgive our predecessors for re-christening as "Major Smith" a mark bearing the quaint old name of "Egg Pye."

The encroachments continued, and two years later the Court caused advertisements to be inserted in the newspapers calling upon occupiers of land between Peerless Pool in the south, Balmes Pond in the north, Hoxton in the east, and Islington in the west, to remove all obstructions between the ancient marks of the Company. During the Balmes March that year (1786) the pioneers pulled down several fences, but afterwards found themselves confronted by a brick wall. The Company were persuaded to refrain from making a breach in the wall on the promise of the proprietors to come to terms, but a member of the Archers' Division was ordered to shoot an arrow over the wall as an assertion of the Company's rights. The gentleman whose fences had been demolished professed regret and ex- plained that he was unaware when he took the lease of his land (in Hoxton Fields, behind the "Shepherd and Shepherdess") that the Company claimed the right of "perambulating their marks in the said fields." He then offered to leave passages ten feet wide across his ground in a direct line between the old marks and to pay an annual rent of £5 to the Company. This offer was accepted, and the rent was paid for twelve years.

The Estate Committee inspected the marks in 1791 and reported that Castle Stone was nearly enclosed by a row of houses then being built "in the road leading from Old Street to the City Road." Other marks had been removed, loosened or destroyed, one in particular having been demolished by roadmakers digging for gravel on Islington Common. On the Prince of Wales's birthday in the following year the Company marched to their old marks for the last time. At each mark they halted, placed the Company's Colours upon the stone and fired a volley. Then, finding that Castle Stone had been greatly encroached upon by new buildings and gardens, they levelled several fences. The marks were then painted, restored or renewed, as necessary. Each stone had originally been sur- mounted by a device in carved wood, of geometric or heraldic design, to distinguish it, but these had all disappeared by this time. They all bore the arms of the Company on a cast-iron plate and many of them had the letters A.C. inscribed on the face of the stone.

The Company never marched to their marks again. Their fields of exercise were gradually built over and the marks destroyed. The Court appointed a Committee in 1820 to report on the condition of the marks, but nothing was done, and so the ancient rights of the Company, which had lasted from time immemorial, were extinguished. Two marks were still in position in 1858, and two others—one bearing the date 1679 and formerly known as "Jehu," the other marked "A.C. 1683"— had then been recently destroyed. Only one stone has survived. It bears the inscription "Scarlet," and was for many years built into the brickwork of the Canal Bridge in the New North Road. It was removed to Armoury House in 1888, and stands in the entrance hall—a solitary reminder of the days when the Company practised archery.

In 1788 the Company held a special church parade at St. Paul's Cathedral to commemorate the 100th anniversary of the "glorious revolution" of 1688.

Certain repairs to the Armoury were now necessary; the front wall showing signs of settlement and the roof being affected with dry rot. The front wall was taken down as far as the windows and rebuilt; and the ceiling of the Long Room was raised, the walls wainscoted and the musicians' gallery added.

The 23rd of April, 1789, was appointed to be a day of general thanksgiving for the King's restoration to health. The Company sent a loyal address, and prepared to carry out their part in the ceremony at St. Paul's. The Court of Lieutenancy inquired if the Company would be prepared to form a "gallery" from the west gate of St. Paul's Churchyard to the church door for His Majesty to pass through, and if they expected to be sufficiently numerous to prevent the crowd forcing their way into the churchyard. The Court replied that, as it was the ancient custom of the Company to provide a bodyguard for the Sovereign when he visited the City, and, as such, to precede the Lord Mayor in the procession, they were unable to waive their claim to that honour by accepting any other duty. Accordingly the Company acted as a bodyguard. The members paraded at 7 a.m., their hair dressed without side curls, that of the Grenadiers plaited and that of the Light Infantry and Hat Companies clubbed. Six pioneers marched at the head of the Battalion in blue coats faced with red, bearskin caps, and armed with "grapling balls."*

In August, 1794, the Company was called upon to aid the civil power in suppressing riots in Shoe Lane and Whitecross Street, where mobs had collected with the intention of destroying public houses in which recruits were enlisted for the army. Members paraded with twelve rounds of ball cartridge, proceeded to the disturbed areas and remained on duty for several nights. The Lord Mayor, in writing to the Court, said that the services rendered during the late riots were such as to command his warmest thanks, and to call for the grateful acknowledgment of the public. Their prompt appearance in Whitecross Street on Wednesday night had prevented a lawless mob from destroying the properties of the inhabitants, and effectually protected that part of the City from riot and destruction. His thanks were equally due for their service in repelling the mob in Shoe Lane on Thursday night, which was the last effort made by the abandoned miscreants who sought to renew the terrible riots of 1780. The Court of Common Council passed a vote of thanks to the "Gentlemen of the Honourable Artillery Company," for their readiness in assisting to suppress the late tumultuous assemblies; "assuring them that the Corporation of London will ever retain a due and grateful sense of their patriotic and meritorious services."

Later in the same year some disorder attended the trials of certain leaders of the Corresponding Society, a body which professed sympathy with the French Revolutionaries. Crowds assembled round the Old Bailey and insulted the judges and magistrates on their arrival and departure. The Company were called out on several occasions and were stationed in the London Coffee House in London Wall, ready for any emergency. On several later occasions the Company paraded for riot duty, and for weeks a guard of 32 men was mounted nightly at Headquarters. A contemporary newspaper states that the expense of the mess supper on these occasions did not exceed 2s. per man, "which is cheerfully paid by the members of the corps."

It is interesting to note that this year and for some time

---

* These were iron-spiked balls suspended by short chains from wooden staves. It was an ancient custom of the Company to have these implements carried before them on the march by pioneers. Possibly their original use was to clear a way through crowded streets.

afterwards it was considered inadvisable to print the names and addresses of members of the Company in the annual "List of Chiefs, Officers, etc." The reason was that it would be impolitic to let the public know the strength of the Company, also that in times of tumult members might suffer inconvenience if their addresses were known.

White drill jackets with blue facings and white waistcoats were adopted about this time. An undress uniform consisting of a royal blue frock coat, with black velvet collar and yellow uniform buttons, was also authorized. It was thought that this latter departure would be calculated to make the Corps more generally known, to maintain a proper confidence and zeal in the members, to inspire spirit in young citizens, induce many to join the Corps, and to impress an awe upon the minds of persons disposed to disturb the public peace.

The title of Secretary was now substituted for that of Clerk, as being more suitable to the military character and dignity of the Company.

The 19th of December, 1797, was a day of thanksgiving for the naval victories of St. Vincent and Camperdown. The King attended service at St. Paul's and was received at Temple Bar by the Lord Mayor and the Honourable Artillery Company, who preceded the royal carriage and lined the entrance to the Cathedral. In the following year a scheme for the defence of London against the threatened invasion was drawn up. The posts allotted to the Company were Armoury House (with patrols in Chiswell Street, Curtain Road, London Wall and Worship Street), and the New River Head.

Every effort was being made to increase the numbers of the Company, and the Court issued an address to the inhabitants of London, calling for suitable recruits. The address, a very lengthy one, concluded in the following terms: "At this momentous aera every zealous friend to his country is called upon to make an election of associates, with whom he can act on the spur of public emergency; and thus to discharge an immediate duty, by demonstrating a power ready to repel any danger. The Artillery-Company lifts its constitutional Banner to the observation of Merchants, Manufacturers, Persons in Office, Professional Men, and all other descriptions of good Citizens, for whose convenience, subserviently to the public-weal, its laws and regulations are ordained." The Regiment was only 300 strong; but recruiting propaganda was bearing fruit, and within a few weeks 200 new members were admitted. A subscription list was opened at Headquarters, and a voluntary contribution of £1,000 for the defence of the country was paid into the Treasury.

The Matross Division appear to have carried out occasional firing practice on Sydenham Common, and it was the custom to invite members of the Battalion to act as an escort to the guns on these occasions and to attend the dinner in the evening, at the rate of 10s. 6d. per head.

The six regiments of City Trained Bands or Militia were reorganized in 1794 in two regiments, the East and the West. Subsequently the Lieutenancy applied for the use of the Artillery Ground and Armoury for the training of the new force and the Company complied with this request on certain conditions. But the Lieutenancy claimed the privilege as a right, and this led to a legal struggle lasting five years. It is unnecessary to enter into the details of this long and bitter controversy, which at one time reached such a pitch that the two regiments of Militia were ordered to march to the Ground with drums beating and bayonets fixed and to demand admittance. However, they found the gates locked and the Company drawn up within, determined to resist any attempt at forcible entry. Finally, after the matter had been taken up in Parliament, with the usual procedure of petitions and counter-petitions, an agreement was arrived at whereby the Company retained their right to the Ground, subject to its use by the Militia on certain days while they were embodied. Instead of granting the use of the Armoury, the Company gave up a plot of ground in the north-west corner for the erection of a Militia Barracks. Each party paid its own costs.

The Company, now nearly 500 strong, was reviewed in Hyde Park by the Duke of York, then Commander-in-Chief, in the summer of 1798. His Royal Highness, the subject of the famous quatrain, was pleased to remark on the fine appearance of the "Gentlemen under Arms," and praised the performance of their exercises and evolutions. He commented particularly on the number of fine, tall men in the Grenadier Company and on the "exactness and strength" of the Matross Division. It was in this year that the latter Division applied for and were granted the right to wear on breast-plate and buttons the arms of the

[*From original specimens in the possession of the Regiment*

CROSS BELT BADGE
H.A.C. ARTILLERY DIVISION, 1799

CROSS BELT BADGE
H.A.C. INFANTRY, 1799

Office of Ordnance, as worn by the Royal Artillery at that time. This badge is still worn on the buttons of the Artillery of the Company, a distinction now shared by the Royal Army Ordnance Corps.

On 29th November, 1798, the Company attended the thanksgiving at St. Paul's for Nelson's victory at the Nile.

On 4th June, 1799, sixty-five Volunteer Corps, containing 8,000 officers and men, passed in review before King George III in Hyde Park. The Company, 421 strong, took up their position on the right of the line and received the King with a salute of 21 guns from the field pieces. The whole force then marched past, headed by the Company, and "General Officers of the highest reputation were heard to say that they never saw anything better done." This, the first of all Volunteer Reviews on a large scale, caused no little sensation at the time, and several fine engravings exist in commemoration of the event. For this review the Band was provided with new uniforms of light blue, faced with scarlet, with cocked hats, at a cost of £393.*

---

* Concerning this and succeeding reviews the Press waxed most enthusiastic. "What," demands *Bell's Weekly Messenger*, "were the raw Conscripts that won the battle of Marengo to a set of men, well fed and clothed, and inspired with a more noble and patriotic courage? What was the militia of Paris, the boasted army of the sons of anarchy and massacre, to a body of brave and enlightened men, like the citizens of London?"

KING GEORGE III REVIEWING THE VOLUNTEERS ON THE 4TH JUNE, 1799

Showing the Company marching past. Colonel Paul Le Mesurier is seen leading the Grenadier Company of the Regiment past the saluting point. The members of the royal party, from left to right, are: The Duke of Cumberland; The Prince of Wales (Captain-General of the Company, in the uniform of the 10th Light Dragoons); Lord Harrington; H.M. King George III; The Duke of York (the subject of the famous rhyme); and the Duke of Kent (father of Queen Victoria)

From an engraving by S. W. Reynolds after R. K. Porter

A few weeks later the same regiments were inspected by the King at their respective posts. The Company was drawn up on the north side of Finsbury Square; the Prince of Wales, as Captain-General, took command and received His Majesty, afterwards signing the parade state and expressing himself as highly gratified to have appeared at the head of so very respectable a Corps. Another review of Volunteers was held in Hyde Park in June, 1800, at which the Company was commanded by the Prince of Wales in person.

Arrangements were made about this time for members to be instructed in "the Science of the Broad Sword, a Knowledge both useful and necessary to Gentlemen of a Military Profession." The lessons were given under the direction of a Mr. Patterson, "a Man very competent to the Undertaking."

199

ROYAL REVIEW OF VOLUNTEERS IN HYDE PARK, 4TH JUNE, 1799
Panoramic view showing the Company leading the March Past

Drawn and etched by Robt. Smirke, Jun., aquatinted by R. Earlom

CHAPTER X

1800 TO 1836

IN 1800 Napoleon's scheme of Armed Neutrality against this country was bearing heavily on British trade, with the inevitable result that food prices had risen to unprecedented heights. Consequently riots in the metropolis were not uncommon, and the Company were frequently called upon to prevent the mob from looting provision stores. In the following year information was received that one of the plans of the disaffected was to seize the arms and ammunition at Armoury House; wherefore a guard was mounted nightly for some weeks. In July the Company was inspected in the Artillery Ground by the Earl of Harrington, commanding London District, who expressed his satisfaction with the steadiness and excellent conduct of the members on parade. The firing was very good, the marching excellent, and he could only lament that the weather had been so unfavourable as to deprive him of the opportunity of seeing a greater number of their very handsome corps. The summons to this parade concluded with these words: "And the Court rely on the Spirit and Feeling of every Member of the Company for a numerous, full, and respectable, Appearance, on an Occasion in which the Honour, Character, and Fame, of the Hon. Artillery-Company are most essentially committed."

A silver-gilt shooting medal presented to the Regiment by King George V bore the inscription: "Honbl. Artillery Comy. South East Division. Adjudged to Mr. Wm. Lyon for the best shot with ball 100 yards distance at Highbury, 24th Sept. 1801." This is not quite the oldest shooting medal of the Company known to have existed, two others bearing the dates 1793 and 1800 respectively. It seems that similar trophies were presented for other forms of efficiency at this period, the Company's collection including one awarded "for services" in 1791 and another "for merit" in 1803. Unfortunately, the whole valuable and unique collection was stolen from Armoury House in 1938.

SILVER-GILT REGIMENTAL SHOOTING MEDAL
"Adjudged to Mr. Wm. Lyon for the best shot with ball 100 yards distance at Highbury, 24th Sept., 1801"
Presented to the Company by His Majesty King George V

The Peace of Amiens, signed in 1802, was proclaimed in the City by the Lord Mayor, escorted by the Company and several regiments of City Volunteers. However, war broke out again in the following year, and the Lord Mayor asked the Company to maintain a night guard of 50 men at Armoury House until the attempt at invasion had been abandoned. This guard was continued for nearly two years.

A Volunteer Corps known as the River Fencibles had been organized to deal with the transport of troops and military stores to any threatened point, and the Company carried out several manœuvres in conjunction with this body—practising embarkation and disembarkation at various points on the river. The Company was again inspected by the Earl of Harrington at Headquarters in 1803, a review which formed the subject of a well-known engraving.

Two brass six-pounder guns were now presented to the Company by the President, Alderman Sir William Curtis, and

ARMOURY HOUSE, 1815

ARMOURY HOUSE, 1851

From the water-colour drawings by T. H. Shepherd in the Crace Collection of Drawings, Print Room, British Museum

203

the Matross Division was accordingly doubled. These guns, exceedingly handsome pieces, engraved with the Prince's Plume, the arms of the Regiment and those of the donor, are still in the possession of the Company.

Extensive repairs to Armoury House became necessary in 1802. They were carried out at a cost of over £700, and the curious flag tower on the roof was added at this time.

The uniform of the Company was changed in 1803, and the Regiment is fortunate in possessing fine engravings showing both that of the Infantry and the Artillery under the new regulations. In this year the threat of invasion brought about a considerable increase of membership, as many as 117 being admitted at a single Court, while the total for the months of July and August was 639.

The following account of a field day at Sydenham Common—a sham fight between the Light Infantry and the South-West Division of the Company—occurs in the columns of a contemporary newspaper:

Yesterday morning at eight o'clock two Divisions of the City Artillery, viz., the South-west and the Light Infantry, met at the Greyhound, Dulwich, from whence they proceeded with their Ammunition Waggons and Camp Equipages to Sydenham Common. On entering the wood, the Bugle sounded to extend. The Infantry commenced firing on the Battalion, the Battalion halted, and fired several vollies on the Light Infantry; the Bugle sounded for the Infantry to retreat to their encampment, at which time the Battalion, with fixed bayonets, made a charge down the hill on the Infantry, until they received orders to halt, and shoulder their arms, and to retreat to their own camp; after which a target was placed at upwards of 100 feet, as a mark, at which the Divisions fired, by single files, for two most beautiful sabres, which were won by Mr. BURROWES, of Capt. BESSEL'S Company of Light Infantry, and the other by Mr. GWINNELL, of Capt. HATCH'S: the former hit the target three times out of six, and the latter shot through the bull's eye the first shot. After which they grounded their arms, and partook of a cold collation, which each man had provided in his knapsack, and of which several Ladies partook. The day being fine, the whole formed a charming *coup d'oeil*.

It was now decided to add to the Battalion a Rifle Company one hundred strong. The rifled musket was by this time no novelty, though the Army authorities clung to the old smooth bore for another forty years. Two regiments only had been armed with the new weapon. The 95th, or Rifle Corps, after-

H.A.C. Infantry, 1803
The building on the left is the old Militia Barracks

From a coloured engraving by E. Walker

ARTILLERY DIVISION, H.A.C., 1804

From an engraving by Hill and Hopwood, after James Green

"Representation of a Target shot at the Practice Ground of the Royal Artillery at Woolwich, the 10th day of October, 1823, by a section of the Jager Riflemen of the Honourable Artillery Company of London"

This engraving shows a section of the Jagers firing "from the spot" (*i.e.*, at the halt in extended order) at a target 5ft. 6in. high by 15ft. long, which has been well covered. Nine men were stationed at 250 and eight at 200 yards. Every man loaded with loose powder and ball. The period allowed for firing was 30 minutes, during which time 580 balls struck the target

wards to become famous in military annals as the Rifle Brigade, had been formed in 1800 as a corps of marksmen, and was at this time undergoing the special course of training at Shorncliffe under Sir John Moore which laid the foundation, in drill and discipline, of the famous Light Division of the Peninsular War, possibly the most efficient troops England has ever produced.

The new Rifle Company of the Regiment was dressed in dark green, with braidings of black mohair. A pelisse was adopted in 1815 and worn over the jacket by all ranks. The Company still possesses a complete uniform of this type, including the curious undress cap—dark green, leather lined, and shaped very like the conventional nightcap. The Rifle Company was originally formed by allowing 50 members of the Light Infantry to transfer, the remaining vacancies being filled from the "Hat" and Matross Divisions. In the following year the new unit became known as the Yager Company, which title it bore until it was disbanded in 1854. It rapidly became a *corps d'élite* in the Regiment, its members paying particular attention to marksmanship, for the encouragement of which the Court provided them with two iron targets at a cost of £50. We read that a trial of skill lasting eight days was held in 1805 between the different Rifle Corps in the neighbourhood of London. "The following," says the *Morning Post*, "is a correct return of the firing, as collected from the minutes of the different umpires:

> Duke of Cumberland's Corps of Sharp Shooters, 81.
> Hon. Artillery Company's Yagers, 57.
> Hackney Riflemen, 46.
> 8th Loyal London Riflemen, 37.
> Duke of Sussex's Loyal North Britons, 33.
> Loyal Southwark Riflemen, 21."

The Yagers also accepted a challenge in 1811 issued to all England by the Nottingham Riflemen, a corps consisting for the most part of gamekeepers. The match took place at Stamford in Lincolnshire. Unfortunately the result of this meeting is unknown, but it is recorded that the Yagers, at considerable expense and sacrifice of time, supported the skill and military reputation of the Company.

On another occasion they challenged the 95th (Rifle Brigade) to a shooting match, which was declined by the officer commanding that regiment on the ground that it was contrary to etiquette for a regular regiment to enter the lists against a volunteer regiment.

The Company possesses a curious engraving showing a detachment of Yagers shooting on the ground of the Royal Artillery at Woolwich in 1823, with a diagram of the target. It is recorded that nine men fired at 250 yards range, and eight at 200, using no cartridges, but loading with loose powder and ball.

They fired for thirty minutes, during which time 580 balls struck the target, which was 5 feet 6 inches high and 15 feet long, representing nine files of men. This must have been considered a remarkable feat, or it would hardly have been commemorated by an engraving. An unusual use of the bayonet

COLONEL PAUL LE MESURIER, H.A.C., 1799

Served in the ranks of the London Association during the riots of 1780; admitted a member of the Company, 1781; successively Vice-President and President, Major and Lieut.-Colonel of the Company; Alderman of London, 1784, and Lord Mayor, 1793. Took an active part in the preparations against threatened French invasions and in the suppression of civil commotions

From a coloured engraving by Charles Tomkins, published as a frontispiece to "The British Volunteer"

is to be seen in this picture; one of the marksmen, having stuck his side-arm in the ground, is using the crosspiece of the handle as a rest for the barrel of his musket. The bugler (or "horner") wears a scarlet jacket, with green sleeves. The Yager Company appear to have carried Colours when on detached duty, a decided departure from the prescribed practice of riflemen. They produced their own book of "Regulations of the Yager Company," in which it is stressed that the Yager must be "distinguished by superior life, animation and ease in every action."

City Volunteer Regiments were brigaded for the first time in 1804, and it was agreed that the Honourable Artillery Company was entitled to be the first battalion of the first brigade. A court-martial under the new Volunteer Act was assembled at Armoury House to try a drummer for absence from duty. He was found guilty and sentenced to 50 lashes. The prisoner was marched into the drill shed, stripped and tied to the halberts. He received 10 lashes, the remainder of his sentence being remitted at the request of the Commanding Officer. Similar punishments were frequent during the next few years, as many as 100 lashes being awarded for absence from duty. One drummer got off with 20 lashes on account of his previous good conduct; another was convicted of theft and sentenced to be drummed out of the Regiment with a label on his back and breast bearing the words "Notorious Thief." With a halter round his neck, the delinquent was marched down the line, the band playing "The Rogue's March" before him. There seems to have been considerable slackness in attending drills. In a circular letter Colonel Le Mesurier remarks: "I am sorry to notice the shamefully bad musters we have had of late, as also many Absentees on the *Night Guard*, and beg you will understand, that from this time I shall cause particular Notice to be taken of those who neglect that very important Part of their Duty." The punishment for failure to attend drills was expulsion, names being read out on parade and posted at Headquarters. This does not appear to have been an effective deterrent, wherefore, in consequence of several discreditably small musters, the Court ordered that the names of members so expelled should be advertised in the Press, which was done in many instances.

In 1804 Anthony Highmore, a solicitor and a member of the

South-East Division, published *The History of the Honourable Artillery Company of the City of London from its earliest annals to the peace of* 1802. This work is the first serious attempt at a complete regimental record. Highmore's narrative of the period within living memory at the time of writing is valuable, but his accounts of earlier times are distorted by political bias. He endeavours to connect the history of the Company with current events by quoting long extracts from Hume and Smollett.

The concentration of troops by Napoleon at Boulogne for the invasion of England naturally necessitated active preparations for defence, and the following special summons was circulated to members:

SIR,

BEING commanded *in Brigade-Orders* to notify to you the Possibility of the Corps being speedily called upon for Service, "in Consequence of Intelligence received by Government of the Embarkation of large Bodies of Troops in Holland, of a Fleet of Men of War being ready to sail from thence, and the increased Preparations of the French at Boulogne and its Neighbourhood," I have to desire that you will appear in the Artillery-Ground, *next Wednesday,* and every succeeding Wednesday, Afternoon, in *marching Order:* viz. with Knapsacks, Havresacs, and Canteens, or with such of those Articles as you are provided with. You will also bring in your Knapsac your Trowsers and Foraging-Cap, in order to ascertain how far you are complete for Military Duty, and you will be acquainted by your Officers with what farther Articles you ought to be furnished with, in Order to be reported for Service.

I am, SIR,
Your very faithful Servant,
PAUL LE MESURIER.
Col. Hon. Artillery-Company.

Armoury-House,
August 12, 1805.

This order was followed by another which laid down the articles required for service, and which is worth reproduction:

Head-Quarters, Armoury-House,
15th August, 1805.

G.O.

YOU are desired to appear here in SERVICE ORDER on Wednesday the 21st Instant, at Half past Five o'Clock in the Afternoon, M.T. and to hold yourself in readiness to muster, at any

future period, at the shortest Notice, in the same Order, viz.
*Haversack, *Canteen, and *Knapsack,—the latter to contain,

1 Shirt,	1 Flannel Nightcap,
1 Pair of Stockings,	1 Black Silk Handkerchief,
1 Pair of Shoes,	1 Pair of Trowsers,
2 Flannel Waistcoats, to	1 Great Coat and Foraging
cover the Loins.	Cap,
	1 Pair of Gaiters.

Pipe Clay, Blacking Ball, Pouch Ball, Oil (in a Tin Case) Tow, Flannel, Rags, and Sponge, Emery and Buff Leather Sticks, Brushes for Cloaths, Shoes and Buttons, Razor, Combs, Soap, Towel, and Sponge; Knife, Fork, and Spoon, to be packed in as small a Compass as possible, and also a Turnscrew, Brush and, Pricker, and some spare Flints (in the Pouch)—*Marching Order* will be regulated by Circumstances.

At the present Crisis it will be impossible to dispense with your regular Attendance unless satisfactory Reasons are assigned to me.

PAUL LE MESURIER,
Colonel, Honorable Artillery Company.

N.B. The Articles marked thus (*) may be had by applying at the Armory-House.

As everyone knows, the attempted invasion was rendered abortive by the victory of Trafalgar, and on 5th December a General Thanksgiving Service for "the late Signal and important Victory obtained by His Majesty's Ships of War, under the Command of the late Vice-Admiral Lord Viscount Nelson, over the Combined Fleets of France and Spain" was held. On this occasion an anthem was performed before the Lord Mayor, Aldermen, and Corporation of the City of London, His Royal Highness the Duke of Cambridge and Staff, and the Hon. Artillery Company, "The Music by George Frederick Handel Esq."

Reviews and inspections were of common occurrence, but in January, 1806, the Company attended on an historic occasion. This was the funeral of Lord Nelson, when the Company took the right of the line of all troops on parade and lined Ludgate Hill, with their flank on the Cathedral. Contemporary prints show the Company in this position with the funeral car, escorted by bluejackets, passing their ranks. A paragraph in the *Morning Post* some days before the event states that the Prince of Wales, "if prevented by *etiquette* from attending the funeral of Lord Nelson as chief mourner, intends taking the command of the Honourable Artillery Company, of which he

THE H.A.C. (*in right and left foreground*) LINING LUDGATE HILL AT THE FUNERAL OF LORD NELSON

From a contemporary print

is Colonel, on the day the remains of his Lordship are to be interred."

The difficulty of persuading members to attend parades is constantly in evidence. In 1807 the Commanding Officer implores members not to allow him, as Colonel, to appear at the head of a Company, instead of a Regiment, and adds a promise that the convenience of the Corps, while on duty, will be studied as much as the nature of the Service will admit. In the following year he adds a rider to a summons to parade to the following effect: "It grieved me much to be obliged to make a return of the attendance on the last inspection; and, I am sure, those members, who were not present, did not consider the honour of the regiment was at stake, or they would have attended in defiance of the weather."

At a Court of Assistants on 27th July, 1808, seven members who had failed to attend the summons of the Court to account for neglect of duty were summarily expelled the Company.

A scheme for shooting prizes was inaugurated in 1811. It was laid down that every member attending two-thirds of the field days (or special musters on occasions of public emergency) should be entitled to fire for prizes of the value of £10 each,

THE DUKE OF SUSSEX REVIEWING THE HONOURABLE ARTILLERY COMPANY, 1828
From a coloured aquatint by R. Havell, Jun., after G. Forster

allotted to each division in proportion to its numbers, but not exceeding ten in all. Under these conditions 87 members made themselves eligible; a prize meeting was held at Hampstead; and four silver cups were given as prizes. One of these trophies is still in the possession of the Regiment.

The targets fired at were 30 inches in diameter, and the range for Battalion Companies was 80 yards. It was considered that a range of 100 yards would throw the chance of a prize into the hands of a few—moreover, regular troops only fired up to 60 yards. The winners on this occasion were to be those who put in the greatest number of shots *without reference to the target fired at.*

At the conclusion of hostilities in 1814 all Volunteer Corps were disbanded. Through an official mistake the Honourable Artillery Company actually received an order from the Office of Ordnance stating that the Home Secretary had directed that the Company was to be discontinued and all arms, accoutrements, etc., sent to the Tower. This matter was quickly adjusted, and the Company soon found itself employed in its time-honoured duty of keeping the peace of the City. For the next few years meetings of distressed artificers, discharged mariners and would-be reformers necessitated the frequent attendance of the Company; one of their duties was to guard the Debtors' Prison in Whitecross Street, presumably in anticipation of an attempt to release the occupants.

In connection with a threatened continuation of these disturbances, Colonel Curtis, commanding the Company, took it upon himself to report to the Home Secretary that he did not consider it safe to leave the Company's arms unprotected. At his request a party of Coldstream Guards was sent from the Tower to act as a guard at Armoury House. The Court of Assistants were highly incensed at this action on the part of the Commanding Officer, considering his application to Government for a guard highly derogatory to the Company and calculated to subject the Regiment to the contempt of the public. The Guards were refused admission to Armoury House; a guard of members was established and maintained; and the Court passed a resolution to the effect that it would be better if superior military officers were to consult the Court before communicating with the Government on such matters. The Colonel then wrote stating that "as personal allusions were so much indulged in as to give him, as Colonel, a very unpleasant feeling," he thought it only consistent with his views to resign. His resignation was accepted, and the Court decided to offer the vacant post to the Duke of Sussex, the youngest son of King George III. His Royal Highness was first nominated for admission as an ordinary member, according to immemorial custom; he passed the Court, answering the usual questions; was balloted for; paid his fees; and at the next Court was appointed Colonel.

It was not considered necessary to apply for the usual Royal Warrant on the accession of the Captain-General, and an Address to the Throne from a military body was considered unsuitable, despite numerous precedents. The Court therefore contented itself with recording expressions of sorrow, loyalty and congratulation. The necessary alterations on the Colours and appointments were authorized and effected, the Prince of Wales's feathers giving place to the royal crest, which has been borne ever since. It was then decided, in order that the Company might make a good appearance at the Coronation, that every member should have a new uniform at the expense of the general fund, and two hundred members were so equipped at a cost of over £2,000, the buttons, lace, etc., being of gold instead of silver. The finances of the Company were in such a flourishing condition that it became the custom for the dinner after field days to be paid for out of regimental funds.

On the day of the Coronation the Company assembled at Armoury House at midnight and marched to the Privy Gardens, where they were due to parade at 3 a.m. They were stationed in Parliament Street with their flank two paces from the platform on which the actual ceremony took place. It is surprising to find that on this important occasion the Company could muster only 179 members, of whom 52 were Yagers.

The Yagers appear to have been the crack company of the Regiment at this period. They frequently went to Woolwich by water and marched to Plumstead for ball practice, and they appear to have reached a very high standard of marksmanship. In 1823 a member of the Yager Company decided a wager made at their mess table "by ascending the Monument steps, 310 in number, in two minutes and a half, which he compleated within the time."

The Yager Company ran their own mess, and the Company still possesses a pair of large port decanters engraved with the royal crest, interlaced Y's and the motto of the Yagers, "Vis Unita Fortior."

A petition was now presented to the King praying that he would issue a warrant authorizing the use of the coat of arms of

COMPANY COLOUR OF THE YAGER COMPANY, H.A.C., 1821 TO 1830
Carried on detached duty only

the Company, of which no record existed in the Herald's College. It is noteworthy that the arms include the use of "Supporters," an honour usually reserved for Peers of the Realm, Knights of the various Orders, or "Proxies of Princes of the Blood." These supporters take the form of a pikeman and a musketeer, and their equipment and clothing in the earliest-known reproduction lend colour to the assumption that they were added in the early years of the reign of James I. However, the coat is a pleasing heraldic composition and a most honour-

[*From an engraving by Wenceslas Hollar*, circa 1635 *to* 1640

ARMS OF THE ARTILLERY COMPANY

216

able one, bearing as it does the badges of England and various royal devices. The crest—an arm in armour, grasping a leading staff, between the dragon's wings of London—is equally appropriate and significant; indeed the whole "achievement" is one of which the Company may justly be proud.

In compliance with the Company's petition, His Majesty issued a Royal Warrant to the College of Arms directing the Heralds to confirm the armorial bearings "for centuries borne" by the Company. Accordingly the ancient arms of the Regiment were duly exemplified according to the laws of arms and recorded in the Herald's Office. The official grant of the arms is dated 30th April, 1821. In it the arms are described as follows:

Argent a Cross Gules (being that of St. George) charged with a Lion passant guardant Or (being part of the Royal Arms of England) on a Chief Azure a Portcullis of the Third between two Ostrich Feathers erect of the Field. And the Crest following Vizt. On a Wreath of the Colours A dexter Arm embowed in Armour the gauntlet grasping a Pike in bend Sinister Or between two Dragons Wings Argent each charged with a Cross Gules as the same are in the margin hereof more plainly depicted and I the said Garter do by these Presents exemplify to the said Artillery Company the Supporters following that is to say On the dexter side A Pikeman armed and accoutred supporting with the exterior hand a Pike erect proper And On the sinister side a Musketeer with his Matchlock Bandileers and Rest all proper as also depicted in the margin hereof the said Arms Crest and Supporters together with the Motto "Arma Pacis Fulcra" to be borne and used for ever hereafter by the said Artillery Company of London upon Shields, Banners, Seals, Regimental Colours or otherwise according to the Tenour of His Majesty's said Sign Manual and the Laws of Arms.

As far back as 1749 a committee had been formed for the purpose of instituting a search for the Charter of Incorporation and other early records of the Company, but nothing further had happened. In 1823 a special committee was appointed to inquire into the rights and privileges of the Company. This committee inaugurated a search for the Royal Charters and Letters Patent then supposed to have been granted by Henry VIII, James I and Charles I, but of which no enrolments were known to exist. A year later it was reported that none of these documents had been found, but that a large number of grants under the Privy Seal had lately been discovered and that it would take considerable time to go through this mass of documents. Finally, after long and patient search, the original Charter of Henry VIII was found in Rolls Chapel on St. George's Day, 1829. The finder was one Thomas Hart, a member of the Company, to whom the Court passed a vote of thanks and a sum of £50 for his services. On application to the Master of the Rolls, directions were given for the enrolment of the Writ of Privy Seal thus discovered, and for an exemplification to be made, it not having been enrolled in Chancery, as it ought to have been.

Another worthy member, Quartermaster R. S. Kirby, presented to the Regiment in 1825 an Index to the Court Minute Books from 1657 up to the current year. For this monumental piece of spade work "equally marked by industry and judgment" he received the thanks of the Court and a piece of plate of the value of 50 guineas.

In consequence of great want of uniformity in the colour of trousers worn by members on parade, it was decided to issue regulation cloth gratis, but shortly afterwards the old tight pantaloons and long gaiters were abolished and each member was supplied with two pairs of white drill trousers.

The first action of the Company on the accession of William IV was to approach His Majesty with a petition setting forth that the Company was a military Society of great antiquity, of great use in times of tumult in the Metropolis, and that previous sovereigns had confirmed the privileges of the Company and even declared themselves Captain-Generals; and that his late Majesty had "occasionally condescended in person to take command of the Battalion," wherefore they prayed His Majesty to confirm their ancient rights and privileges, and to honour the Corps by placing himself at their head.

At a Court of Assistants in September, the Duke of Sussex presented the new Royal Warrant, in which the King appointed himself Captain-General. In accordance with the royal wish, the Vellum Book was to be taken to him for signature. The Duke also produced a letter expressing the King's "entire approbation" of a proposed new uniform for the Company.

This refers to the order of King William that the Company should in future wear a uniform similar to that of the Grenadier Guards, but substituting silver lace for gold. But though the King actually issued the order, as a distinguished mark of royal favour, and was sufficiently interested in the matter to command that a private's coat should be made especially for his inspection, it is without doubt due to the influence of the Duke of Sussex that the change was brought about. This is proved by a letter from His Majesty's private secretary to the Duke, which speaks of the new uniform "which you propose for the Royal [*sic*] Artillery Company."

The King further commanded that the whole corps should be clad in scarlet. This order gave great offence to many of the Yager Company, who were so ill pleased at their uniform being changed from green to scarlet that the Captain, Lieutenant, and seven members resigned. The Artillery Division were also turned into red-coats. The Band was also dressed in red, instead of the old blue coats with scarlet facings. A complete issue of the new uniforms was provided at the expense of the Company, the cost being £8 6s. 5d. per head; but officers and N.C.Os. paid the extra cost of their dress over that of a private. In consequence of the great cost of the officer's coats, they were allowed to follow the example of officers of the Line and wear blue frock coats, braided with black, on ordinary musters.

There is no doubt that King William took considerable interest in the Company and gave them every possible encouragement. Thus we learn from a newspaper cutting dated 1830 that "the King has signified to the Honourable Artillery Company, of which he is the Captain-General, that they are to consider themselves in future his body guard, by whom alone, it is expected, his Majesty will be attended in the City at the civic festival."

A proposed visit of His Majesty to the Guildhall in November, 1830, was postponed at the last minute through fear of popular tumult. The Company had already paraded as a guard of honour, and promptly tendered their services to the Lord Mayor. At his request they remained under arms until two o'clock next morning, when, all being quiet, they were dismissed though a guard was maintained at Armoury House for a few days. For this service they received a vote of thanks from the Court of Aldermen "for the very handsome manner in which they tendered their Services in aid of the Civil Power."

The ten dwelling-houses belonging to the Company in Bunhill Row, adjoining the west gate, were rebuilt in this year. The yearly subscription for members, reduced to one guinea in 1816, was again raised to two guineas. It was once more reduced to a guinea in 1834 and increased in 1858 to two guineas, at which figure it has remained to the present day.

The date of the Coronation having been fixed, the Duke of Sussex wrote to the Home Secretary, Lord Melbourne, offering the services of "this Ancient Volunteer Body." The offer was accepted, and the Company was stationed in the Churchyard of St. Margaret's, Westminster. Lieutenant-Colonel Cox, who commanded the Company, received a gold Coronation Medal.

Frequent instances occur about this time of a very ancient privilege of the Company. It was enacted by the Charter of Henry VIII that no member of the Guild of Artillery "shall from hensforthe be empanelled, or copelled to be upon any man^r of Queste or Jury upon what matter soev^r it be wthin o^r Citie of London, or other place wthin this o^r Realme." Whether exemption from such service was now claimed by members on the authority of the recently discovered Charter is not clear, but many individuals were certainly discharged from service on all sorts of juries on production of their certificate of membership of the Company. The following certificate of exemption was granted to a member:

This is to certify that the Members of the Honourable Artillery Company being liable to be called upon in their Military Capacity at any time, at the shortest notice, to aid the Civil Power in quelling any tumultuous Riots or Disturbances that may take place; they the said Members of the Honourable Artillery Company aforesaid are exempted from serving upon any Jury or Juries, and from serving the Office of Constable, Special Constable, and Head Borough [Constable?]. And he, the said Joseph Sparrow, is hereby discharged from his attendance at the Old Bailey Sessions accordingly.

GEORGE POTTER,
For the Secondary of London.
Dated at the Sessions House in the Old Bailey, London,
this 1st of December, in the Year of our Lord, 1831.

A memorial to revive the practice of archery in the Ground was presented to the Court in 1835, and it was decided to allow those members who had taken part in field days to use the ground for this purpose. However, at a General Court the proposal to adopt the regular practice of archery was negatived.

In 1837 there was a proposal to celebrate the three hundredth anniversary of the Incorporation of the Company by Royal Charter. This suggestion was considered by the Court in the light of existing information, and was negatived, on the ground that it was not possible to identify the Honourable Artillery Company with the Guild of Artillery of the twenty-ninth year of King Henry VIII. The report of the Committee of Privileges on this matter states that "although there were many and strong grounds of inference that an Association for the practice of Arms did exist during the reign of Henry VIII (under what precise title did not appear), yet, as the first formal recognition of the Company which the Committee had been able to discover was the Order in Council of the 3rd July, 1612, they thought it would be highly inexpedient to make arrangements (as had been proposed) for the celebration of an anniversary with which they were then unable to establish any identity by proof or good evidence." Any doubt which may still have remained on this point was set at rest by the discovery of the original lease of 1538, which identifies the Company most conclusively with the Guild of Artillery of 1537.

King William IV died on 20th June, 1837. On the day of his funeral the Artillery Division paraded at Headquarters and fired minute guns from 9 to 10 p.m.

CHAPTER XI

1837 TO 1880

IMMEDIATELY on the accession of Queen Victoria the Company presented a petition on the usual lines setting forth the claims of the Corps to royal recognition, quoting precedents of encouragement by former monarchs, and praying for confirmation of ancient privileges and the appointment of a new Captain-General. The answer was prompt. On 31st August, 1837, the Duke of Sussex laid before the Court a Warrant under the royal signature confirming all former privileges of the Company and appointing him Captain-General and Colonel. This is the first instance of the combination of these two ranks, an example followed until 1936, when King Edward VIII allowed the original title to be revived.

In September of this year the Court approved plans of a church in the north-west corner of the ground, on the understanding that the windows should not grow into ancient lights. Later it was decided that the Regiment should pay £65, being half the cost of facing the south and east sides of the church with stone. The object of this was to ensure the erection of an edifice more or less in keeping with the Armoury.

On the first occasion on which the young Queen visited the Guildhall, the Company's privilege of providing the guard of honour whenever the City was visited by Royalty was confirmed. It was ordered that the Lieutenant-Colonel and Major should wear their gold sashes, King William IV having granted them that distinction when in attendance on his person. This latter point was the subject of an official letter from the Duke of Sussex, as there appeared to have been no former record in the Court Minutes of this "act of royal grace." The Company furnished a guard 250 strong, each man with six rounds of ball cartridge. They were stationed in Guildhall Yard, and it is recorded that the procession took an hour and a half in passing.

By a special alteration in the Rules and Orders, a Veteran

Company, limited at first to 30 members, had been established in 1804. In the following year the first member had been admitted to this body; later, a Captain and a Sergeant were elected. It had been decided in 1833 that Veteran Members had the right to appear in uniform, and that they should fall in on parade for the purpose of being included in the returns, being then appointed to such duties as might be required. These duties seem to have included the policing of the ground at ceremonial parades.

Regulations regarding admission to the Veteran Company were now amended, and it was resolved that officers and N.C.Os. who had held rank for not less than fifteen years, and been members for not less than thirty years, might be admitted into the Veteran Company, nominally retaining their rank, provided the Military Committee reported to the Court that such member, by zealous discharge of his duties, had merited such distinction. These rules were again revised in 1841, the period of service being reduced to twenty years, including ten years in commissioned or non-commissioned rank. In 1854 the period of service necessary for the retention of rank was reduced to five years. Four years later a uniform of blue faced with red for Veteran Members was suggested, but the recommendations of the Military Committee were not approved and it was decided that members should wear the uniform of their rank at the time of retirement, with a plain cocked hat for officers and a regimental forage cap in the case of other ranks. This headgear was altered in 1860 to a regulation Line shako.

Prior to the Coronation the Duke of Sussex drew the attention of the Home Secretary to the fact that at the last two coronations the Company had had the honour of being placed next the Guards in the lining of the streets. He therefore requested that the Regiment might render a similar service at the approaching ceremony. This offer was accepted, and the Company was stationed in Parliament Street between the 1st and 3rd Battalions of the Grenadier Guards. They were on duty from 4 a.m. till 6.30 p.m. The Queen afterwards offered knighthood to Lieutenant-Colonel Cox (the well-known banker), an honour he felt compelled to decline, to the disappointment of members of the Company.

About this time the Company subscribed fifty guineas to

the Nelson Memorial and a similar sum towards the statue of the Duke of Wellington.

The Company continued to provide a favourite mark for the shafts of satire, and the following extract, from a weekly paper of 1840, affords not only a fair sample of the wit of the period, but gives an insight into the manners and customs of our predecessors of early Victorian days. After a poem which commences:

> Hero! renowned in battle's strife,
> *Horrida bella's* on thy brow;

an illustration shows a pot-bellied officer of the Company, his sword on the wrong side, taking a glass of wine in front of one of the fireplaces in the Long Room. Then follows a description of the Regiment, some of which is worth quoting and much of it mere balderdash:

Our pencil this week portrays, in all his martial glory, the officer of the Honourable Artillery Company, who, if he cannot boast of a participation in the deathless fame of the field of Waterloo, can urge many acts of valorous enterprise in checking civil commotions in this vast city. . . . His daring and courage seem oozing from the very interstices of his portentous pantaloons; his visage is adamantine, and the soul of Alexander the Great is buttoned up beneath his belligerent coat. . . .

The Honourable the Artillery Company was instituted many years since, by charter; that charter enables the body to purchase lands in mortmain, and their estates are now of considerable value. His Royal Highness the Duke of Sussex is the captain-general and colonel of this corporation. The uniform (which is red) is the only military costume to which his Royal Highness is entitled. In this dress he appears on state occasions, and wore the same on the recent nuptials of the Queen with Prince Albert. The second in command is denominated the lieutenant-colonel. Charles Cox Esq., the army agents, fills this distinguished post. The third in rank is the major, James William Freshfield, Esq., joint solicitor to the Bank of England and member of parliament for Penryn. The officers and privates are young men of respectability, who are admitted by ballot; they are at the expense of their dresses, and amount in number to between six and seven hundred. One division of the regiment consists of artillery-men, many of whom are very expert in the management of the engines of war. . . . The company meets every Thursday, at the artillery ground, to drill and take lessons in the art of war; they do not muster very strongly, which, perhaps, arises from their having no pay. . . . The armoury is well worthy the investigation of the curious, as it presents some of the most grotesque habiliments of war that ingenuity could devise or imagine.

In cases of civil commotion, this corporation is eminently in request; it also is called out on the happenings of great conflagrations, and other momentous occasions; the members likewise display themselves on coronations, and other national events. On any outbreak taking place . . . the corporation meet day and night, and mount guard as regular troops. They have arms and ammunition for nearly a thousand men. In the lamentable riots of 1780, this body of men were called into active service; and in old Broad-street, wherein the mob had evinced a most determined and destructive spirit, eight members of the Artillery Company lost their lives, while mounting guard. . . . Their energies and courage are sustained by a plentiful allowance of brandy and wine, which is of the choicest character, being imported by themselves, and deposited in the cellars beneath the mansion in the artillery ground. . . . On field days, which are now few, but which, in the time of George the Third, were many (that monarch frequently reviewed the company), the troop cut a pretty considerable figure, and, in their indulgencies and tastes, combine very felicitously the *civil* and the *martial* character. They sport the eye-glass, the perfumed handkerchief, and not a few do duty in spectacles. The *regular* troops may smile, perchance, at a soldier carrying an umbrella, and, in the event of a shower of rain, beholding a long continuity of expanded ginghams held up by a company under review. The late Charles Matthews . . . describes many of this company, when a review was over, as depositing their arms in the toll-house at Kilburn, and proceeding homeward by the Paddington stage, confessedly a somewhat novel movement in military tactics.

The corporation meets frequently in the year, at their house in the artillery grounds, to enjoy the luxury of a good dinner, and to broach the choice wines before alluded to. These *feeds* are paid for out of the revenues of their estates, entailing no expense whatever on the consumers thereof. Once in a year, moreover, the company do the gallant, and the ecstatic, by the celebration of a ball. On these occasions, the members execute the magnificent, shining, like a host of *Marmions*, in the full blaze of a galaxy of beauty. A ball without a military *cove* is as "flat, stale, and unprofitable" a thing as a "fish dinner at Blackwall without the fish," as Sir William Curtis once remarked. . . . But we must conclude by observing that, in the months of summer, an evening promenade is established in the rural grounds of the Artillery Company, in which the fair lasses of our eastern empire are wont to disport their lovely forms. On these occasions, the sons of Mars go through their varied evolutions, looking as fierce as soldiers ought.

Now occurred the first of several serious collisions between the civil and military authorities of the Regiment. Some suggestions for improving the military efficiency of the Company emanated from a private meeting of some forty members, one proposal being that Sergeants of the Line should be appointed as Drill Sergeants. The Court considered these suggestions and approved some of them. The Duke of Sussex was most indignant at this interference by the Court in purely military affairs, and expressed his opinion at a subsequent meeting in no measured terms. He styled the meeting of private members to discuss subjects of military discipline as "an irregular, most unmilitary, and even mutinous proceeding," and censured the Court for having received a deputation and considered their suggestions. His Royal Highness at the same time expressed warm attachment to the Company, and stated that his whole anxiety was for the maintenance of a state of discipline which should earn for the Regiment the confidence and good will of the Sovereign, the esteem of the civil and military authorities and the regard of their fellow citizens.

The Court expressed gratitude at the interest taken in the Company by their Captain-General, whose remarks they discussed at a later meeting. Finally a letter was drafted expressing regret at the misunderstanding which had arisen, and assuring His Royal Highness that the suggestions complained of had been received by the Court, not as the resolutions of a body of members, but as suggestions for the improvement of the Company from numerous and respectable individuals (a somewhat ingenuous quibble), it having been the custom from time immemorial for members to submit respectful suggestions to the Court on such matters. They added that members of the Company, being citizens of respectable rank in society, expensively equipped at their own cost, could hardly be governed by the same rigid rules of obedience as were rightly enforced in a regiment of the Line.

Fuel was added to the fire by a resolution of a General Court to the effect that it was essential that regular N.C.Os. should be employed in drilling the Regiment. On being informed of this, the Duke wrote regretting that, after his expressions to the Court of the necessity for separating the military government of the Company from its civil management, a resolution completely at variance with his opinion should have been passed by a General Court. His Royal Highness added that he now considered it his duty to report the situation to superior powers, but offered to allow sufficient time to elapse before doing so to enable a Special General Court to consider the situation. A Special General Court was called and decided that, under existing Rules and Orders, it was an undoubted right and privilege of members, when not on military duty, to deliberate individually or collectively upon the affairs of the Company, and to express such opinions to the Military Committee; which Committee had been appointed, and could also be abolished, by vote of the members. In asserting these rights the Court made no pretension whatever to any right to dictate to the military officers of the Company concerning the exercise of their military commands, but unreservedly acknowledged the duty of implicit obedience on all occasions of the Company being under arms. The only object they had in view was the improvement of its military discipline, efficiency, and character; and they were deeply mortified to find His Royal Highness laying upon the Corps the imputation of irregularity, insubordination, and mutinous conduct, and respectfully disclaimed such imputations as injurious and entirely unmerited. The Court also resolved that while it felt incumbent upon them to adhere to the principle of self-government, conferred on them by so many successive Sovereigns, they were ready to take into consideration any suggestion from His Royal Highness for the revision of any of the rules with a view to improve efficiency and military discipline.

Thus the civil and military authorities found themselves at complete variance on a question of discipline. The former, it is clear, were acting in perfect accordance with the Rules and Orders, but the military side had stronger backing than that afforded by those time-honoured regulations. The Duke sent in a report, and the Chairman of the Court was requested to attend at the Home Office. There he was informed by the Home Secretary that a serious view was taken of the fact that a civil court had attempted to control a military body; that the opinion of law officers of the Crown had been taken; and that if it was found necessary to lay the matter before the Crown, he (the Home Secretary) would have no alternative but to advise the breaking up of a Corps where such improper notions and feelings were entertained. At the same time he expressed his readiness to afford an opportunity to the Company to consider its irregularity and to endeavour to place itself on such a footing as would prevent a recurrence of the trouble.

The Court of Assistants had now no alternative but to assure their Captain-General of their desire to give the fullest effect to his recommendations. A conference followed, which had the result of bringing about certain alterations in the Rules and Orders, by which the separation of the civil and military concerns of the Company was effected. Shortly afterwards, in 1842, the appointment of Field Officers and Adjutant was reserved to the Crown, and so the matter ended for the time. This constituted the first serious breach between the civil and military sides of the Company. We shall see later how history repeated itself on more than one occasion.

The flint-lock musket, with which the Company had been armed for nearly 150 years, now became obsolete, and in 1840 percussion muskets were provided, similar to those in use by

SHOOTING WITH THE REST   SHOOTING SITTING WITH REST
Yager Company, H.A.C., 1843

regiments of the Line. About the same time it was ordered that no members should wear spectacles when under arms.

In April, 1843, the Duke of Sussex died. The Artillery Division fired seventy minute guns at Headquarters on the day of his funeral, and the Court afterwards voted one hundred guineas to the fund for erecting a memorial to his memory. This took the form of a wing to the Royal Free Hospital in Gray's Inn Lane.

His Royal Highness, from the time he became Colonel in 1817, had taken a very active part in the affairs of the Company. He frequently presided over the Military Committee, which generally assembled at his quarters in Kensington Palace, and on occasion he took the chair at Courts of Assistants. Though he had differed strenuously from the general feeling of the Regiment on certain points, it is beyond doubt that he had the well-being and discipline of the Company always at heart, and it has been shown that he was always foremost in claiming and maintaining regimental rights and privileges.

The Prince Consort expressed his willingness to accept the vacant post, but as it appeared that all former Captains-General had been selected from members of the Company, the Home Secretary suggested that it might be desirable to admit His Royal Highness a member prior to his appointment. Prince Albert was therefore formally proposed and admitted, and a new Royal Warrant confirmed his rank as Captain-General and Colonel of the Company.

The first occasion on which the new Captain-General saw his regiment on parade was at the opening of the Royal Exchange, when the Company provided a Royal Guard. His Royal Highness wrote from Windsor Castle that he had been impressed with the appearance of the guard, and looked forward to seeing more of the Company.

At this juncture both the Lieutenant-Colonel and the Major of the Company resigned from the active list after forty-six years' service in each case. Both received permission to continue to wear their uniform "on festive occasions and at Court." Under the new regulations their places were filled at the nomination of the Crown, but both officers attended and were admitted members of the Company on appointment.

In 1846 the Company were successful in defeating a scheme of the Eastern Counties Railway for the formation of a railway terminus in the Artillery Ground.

The part assigned to the Company at the time of the Chartist Riots was to occupy Guildhall and to defend Southwark Bridge. It is a matter of history that the great Chartist meeting on Kennington Common came to nothing, but it was regarded with great anxiety at the time. The Company mustered in the Artillery Ground at 7 a.m. on 10th April, 1848. Only three members were absent, one being seriously ill and the other two on the Continent. Every man was provided with forty rounds of ball-cartridge; and before leaving the ground Lieutenant-Colonel FitzRoy addressed the men in a short, spirit-stirring speech, calling on them to be firm—to do their duty—to stand by one another, and to fire low, picking off the ringleaders. A hearty cheer was the response, and at nine o'clock they marched out, with Colours flying, to the tune of the "British Grenadiers."

The Honourable Artillery Company, under the command of the Duke of Sussex, assembled for Ball Practice at Child's Hill, Hampstead, 1831

From a coloured aquatint by R. Havell, Jun., after G. Forster

The streets were filled with a hooting, cursing mob, and matters for a time looked serious, especially when missiles began to fly. Exercising admirable forbearance, the Company eventually reached Guildhall, which they proceeded to barricade. Most alarming rumours arrived from time to time, but finally it was announced officially that the Chartists had dispersed without disturbance, evidently awed by the preparations of the authorities. After that the Company did ample justice to an excellent cold collation liberally provided by the City, and then marched back to Headquarters. There was again some hooting, but nothing like the disturbance of the morning. For their services the Company received votes of thanks from the Court of Aldermen and the Common Council.

In connection with these disturbances a most interesting correspondence took place between the Prince Consort and the Duke of Wellington. The Duke wrote on 6th April as follows:

The utmost anxiety is felt by those interested in the peace of the Town, in consequence of the position of the Guns to which this Company is attached in the Artillery Ground. They are liable to be seized by one of the Monster Mobs going about at any time. The Artillery Company could not be expected to protect them from being seized. He understands that they are ready with their ammunition and drag ropes to be moved at once. There are no Troops nearer to the Artillery Ground than the Tower. It had been suggested that the Guns belonging to the Company should be placed in the Tower. As the Constable of the Tower The Duke of Wellington certainly should object to the Artillery Company forming a part of its Garrison. The late Duke of Sussex referred to The Duke some questions respecting its discipline, and sent Him Papers respecting the constitution of its formation and existence, of which He does not exactly recollect the details. But as well as He recollects, it was established in the Reign of Charles 1st, during the Rebellion, and its Officers and Men are appointed by the Corporation of the City of London, or the Officers by self-election confirmed by the Corporation. But whether in the one way or the other, the Corps is of the nature of a National Guard: the Men not Soldiers by profession, but Citizens; and Soldiers only when under Arms. The Officers elected by themselves or by the Corporation of the City of London. This Corps must therefore be considered as a deliberative Military Body, liable to all the impressions of the population among which stationed, and whose existence is calculated to produce effects similar to those which the existence of the National Guard did at Paris, and will produce wherever a Corps formed on such principles will be established.—He therefore would represent the inconvenience attending the reception of the Officers and Men of the Artillery

OFFICER AND PRIVATE, H.A.C. INFANTRY, 1848

From a coloured engraving by J. Harris after H. Martens, published by R. Ackermann

Company as part of the Garrison of the Tower.—They ought not to be allowed to accustom the Non-Commissioned Officers and Soldiers of the Guards, or other Troops which they might meet in that Garrison, to deliberate upon the Orders which they may receive. At the same time He apprehends that the Artillery Company will not consent to deposit their Guns and Ammunition in the Tower, and to resume their Station at the Artillery Ground; and indeed He doubts whether Your Royal Highness could order that such a disposition should be made of the Guns and Ammunition without the consent of the Corporation of the City of London.

All which is submitted to Your Royal Highness by Your Royal Highness' devoted Servant,

WELLINGTON.

Apart from its quaint literary style and the complete ignorance shown of the history of the Company, the above effusion throws an interesting light on the opinion of the peculiar constitution of the Company entertained by the higher military command at that time. Evidently the Duke had in mind the trouble of 1842, and it is not surprising that the "self-election" of officers should appear to him a dangerously democratic principle; but it is amazing that an official of high rank should have been so uninformed as to stigmatize the Company as a body of men likely to contaminate the discipline of the Guards or to emulate the disloyalty of the National Guard at the time of the French Revolution.

The reply of the Prince Consort to the Duke's letter is perhaps a little disappointing, as he entirely ignored the suggestions of possible disaffection in the Company. It runs as follows:

BUCKM PALACE,
April 6, 1848.

Prince Albert has had the Honor of receiving F.M. the Duke of Wellington's Letter of this date, and begs to state in answer to it that Lt.-Col. Bryce Pearse of the Honble Artillery Compy., not considering himself sufficiently experienced in military matters, has two days ago placed his resignation in the Prince's hands and that He has therefore recommended the Honble. Henry FitzRoy, who formerly served in Her Majesty's Army, to the Queen for the Lt. Colcy. of that Corps, who has been graciously pleased to appoint him by warrant from the Secretary of State for the Home Dept.

The Artillery Company was chartered by King Henry VIII, manages its affairs by a Court of Assistants, composed of the Superior Officers and the Treasurer, and is entirely independent of

H.R.H. THE PRINCE CONSORT REVIEWING THE COMPANY, 1848

the Authorities of the City of London, to the best belief of the Prince.

If the D. of W. wishes it, the Prince will consider the communication which he has received, as an intimation of the desire upon the part of the Commdr. in Chief that the Guns belonging to the Honble. Artillery Company be deposited in the Tower of London for safety, and will desire the Lt. Col. to put himself in communication with the Duke, as Constable of the Tower, for that purpose.

The Prince can see no reason why the Regt. should found upon this, a desire to be stationed in the Tower as part of the Garrison.

ALBERT.

Captn. Genl. & Col.

Hon. Artillery Compy.

The Duke replied the same night, promising "to give orders to the Officer Commanding in the Tower quietly to make preparations for the reception and safe keeping of the guns in question in the Tower, which shall be of a Nature to render it convenient for the persons attached and their Officers and Artilly Men to visit them occasionally and keep them in order, whenever it may prove not otherwise than convenient to admit these Men into the Fortress."

Later in the year the Prince Consort inspected his Regiment for the first time. We are told by a contemporary weekly that the Company paraded 300 strong, with four well-mounted pieces of ordnance and ten rounds of ammunition per man. After the general salute "the line walked and marched past in slow and quick time" and subsequently "fired in line and in square with much precision and accuracy." The same paper goes on to refer to a musketry practice which took place later in the same week. "The illustrious Prince having issued orders to the hon. company to proceed to Charlton for a series of ball practice, they on Thursday morning again assembled on their parade ground, commanded by their colonel, the Hon. Henry FitzRoy, M.P., and marched to the Eastern Counties Railway, *en route* to Charlton. There was a capital muster. Headed by their fine band, they passed through the various streets and created abundance of astonishment; many being the surmises as to where they could be going. Arrived at Charlton, they marched to the ground at the back of the White Horse, halted, and again formed into companies, and commenced firing individually from right to left, and then in sections, at targets, the distance being from 80 to 100 yards. Each man fired six

235

rounds, and it is the unanimous opinion that they acquitted themselves with most admirable precision. Officers and non-commissioned officers also fired, and told nearly every time, till at length the bull's-eye was completely riddled. The company again formed with that 'good digestion' which 'waits on appetite,' and marched for the White Horse, and made a very severe attack upon a cold collation that had been prepared for the occasion; after which they returned to town by the same route. It ought to be stated that all are *gentlemen* who belong to the Honourable Artillery Company."

In consequence of a considerable increase of membership during this year, the number of companies was increased from six to eight. Shakos were also provided, and red piping was worn on the seam of the trousers for the first time. It is also on record that a private was severely reprimanded by the Court and fined ten guineas for leaving the ground without leave when on parade at an inspection by Prince Albert. The fine was paid.

On 4th June, 1849, the formation of a Masonic Lodge for members only was sanctioned. This organization survives as the FitzRoy Lodge, having derived its title from the Lieutenant-Colonel.

A change of importance in the history of the Company took place in 1849, the appointment of all officers being reserved to the Crown by Royal Warrant. It seems that this alteration was due to the opinion of the Government of the day that the Rules and Orders, particularly those which laid down that officers should be elected by vote of the members, were inconsistent with the preservation of military discipline. The announcement of this order gave great dissatisfaction to the Court of Assistants and to a considerable body of members, who looked upon it as an infringement of their ancient privileges. A requisition signed by 68 members proposed that the Court should be the supreme authority in all cases, civil and military, and that no officer should sit upon the Court who had not been elected by ballot. These proposals, which would have deprived officers appointed by the Crown of any real authority, were carried at a General Court, though by very small majorities, and a new Court was elected which included the leaders of the malcontents. This new Court drew up a petition to the Queen, praying for the restoration of the ancient privilege of the election of officers, or, in other words, the annulment of the late Warrant.

The Company was thus divided into two contending parties, the one ready to recognize and receive the new Warrant as an honour and mark of royal favour, the other striving to retain the elections in their own hands. Several of the latter, however, were afterwards offered, and gladly accepted, commissions from the Queen. Each party drew up an Address on the subject to Prince Albert—the one signed by 126, and the other by 190; the two parties being thenceforward known as "The Hundred and Twenty-six" and "The Hundred and Ninety."

The Captain-General replied to the 126 Malcontents with a threat of resignation, and a stern warning that, if they persisted in their opposition, it would become a question for Her Majesty's Government "to consider how far their duty to the Country would justify them in permitting the existence, in the heart of London, of an Armed Military Body entirely free from those established and fixed rules of discipline, and power of enforcing it, without which the Constitution of this country does not sanction the maintenance of an armed force, even by the Sovereign."

To the 190 Prince Albert expressed his pleasure at their willingness to obey the Queen's Warrant.

The two Addresses, with the Captain-General's replies thereto, were laid before the Home Secretary, and Colonel FitzRoy shortly afterwards reported to the Court the opinion of that official, namely: "That the effect of the resolution passed by the Court appeared to be to render null the authority of the officers to be appointed by the Crown, and replace them exclusively under the jurisdiction of the privates. That if these resolutions were persevered in, indicating as they did a disposition to resist the Royal authority under which alone the Company could have any existence as a Military body, he should feel it his duty to advise the dissolution of the Company."

Having regard to the Address signed by the 190 contented members, the Home Secretary promised to delay his report to the Crown in order to enable the Court to reconsider the position. Thus far it is remarkable how closely the dispute followed on the lines of the previous trouble of 1841. This time, however, the Court were not disposed to accept defeat. They presented a memorial to the Lord Mayor and Court of Aldermen, invoking their assistance in obtaining from Her Majesty the restoration of their privilege of electing officers. This was followed by a counter-petition from the contrary party. After considerable discussion and a division, the Court of Aldermen carried a proposition regretting the dissensions in the Company, which they feared might lead to a suspension of their military functions, "thus depriving the citizens of London of a useful and effective defence," and recommending that a deputation wait on the Secretary of State to urge that the right of electing their own officers might be restored to the Company. The deputation,

Review of the Company by H.R.H. The Prince,
Captain-General and Colonel, 1852

consisting of the Lord Mayor, the Town Clerk, the Remembrancer and the Recorder, stated their case, concluding with an earnest request on behalf of the Lord Mayor and Aldermen, that the services of so constitutional and effective a body for the protection of the peace and property of the City should not be lost to the citizens of London.

The Home Secretary, in reply, stated that he could not hold out any hope of alteration being made in the last Warrant.

238

This decision should have ended the matter, and it certainly led to the Rules and Orders being amended by a General Court in accordance with the requirements of the Home Secretary. Unfortunately, a small body of "die-hards" continued to make trouble, while the Court do not appear to have accepted their defeat with a good grace. They sent yet another deputation to the Home Secretary, with no result, and then indulged in a series of petty attacks on Colonel FitzRoy, an officer whose methods appear to have roused great antagonism. Finally, a serious and most discreditable disturbance took place at the annual dinner in celebration of the Prince Consort's birthday. The Court, obviously with malice aforethought, had departed from the invariable custom on these occasions that only those who had previously appeared under arms should attend the dinner, and had ordered that the dinner should be open to all members and that uniform should not be worn. Consequently many members attended parade and then dined elsewhere. On returning to Headquarters, still in uniform, some of them passed through the Long Room and were hooted and hissed by the diners. Missiles were thrown, and an attempt to eject some of the members in uniform resulted in a scuffle, in which swords were drawn.

With the feelings of the opposing parties at such a pitch, it speaks highly for the tact and conciliatory powers of the Prince Consort that he was able eventually to put an end to this unfortunate state of affairs. By his personal intervention he succeeded finally in restoring harmony, and at a General Court in December, 1850, all the most active in the recent contest against the military authorities were rejected, and a Court was elected containing only nine of the old Court, whose term of office had led to such deplorable occurrences.

Making all allowances for the feelings of those who felt that a long-cherished privilege was being reft from the Regiment, it is difficult to find excuse for the fatuous policy of the Court of Assistants, which, for the second time in ten years, brought the old Company to the brink of destruction. The conduct of the opponents of the Royal Warrant provides only too sound an argument for the urgent necessity for discipline and control other than that vested in officers elected by their fellow members.

On the other hand it must be admitted that Colonel FitzRoy

UNIFORMS OF THE COMPANY, 1853-1855

From left to right : Captain, Artillery Division; Captain, Battalion; Captain, Rifle Company; Driver, Artillery Division; Private, Battalion (Drill Dress); Lieutenant, Light Infantry Company; Sergeant, Artillery Division; Corporal, Rifle Company; Private, Battalion (Full Dress, off duty)

From a lithograph by John King

had acted throughout in a somewhat high-handed manner, and had on several occasions treated the Court with studied contempt. No doubt there were faults on both sides, and it would have been pleasanter to have ignored the whole sorry business. This would certainly have been done, but for the necessity for a complete and impartial account of this crisis in the affairs of the Regiment.

The Artillery Division had worn scarlet coats on ceremonial occasions ever since William IV had changed the old uniform of the Company to one similar to the Grenadier Guards. They had, however, continued to wear their blue uniforms for drill and undress purposes. It was now ordered, in 1851, that they should be allowed to wear blue on parade when the Commanding Officer should so direct.

In 1852 a covered shooting gallery, 110 yards long and 17 feet wide, was constructed at the back of Armoury House, with the consent of the Corporation, at a cost of £350. This range was allotted to companies on certain nights and rules were drawn up to regulate its use. Among other things it was directed that no smoking or refreshments would be permitted while firing.

Uniform greatcoats were worn by the Company for the first time this year. They were of the same pattern as those of the Foot Guards, but with bronze buttons and without the blue facings then worn. Officers wore blue cloaks instead of greatcoats. The broad red stripes on the trousers of Infantry officers and all ranks of the Artillery Division also made their appearance in this year.

The year 1853 was chiefly notable for a presentation by the Prince Consort of new carriages and limbers for the two 6-pounder guns. This date marks the formation of the old Field Battery, which survives as "B" Battery, H.A.C. Up till that time the Artillery Division had consisted entirely of Foot Artillery, the guns being moved with drag-ropes, except on special occasions, when horses were provided for a "march-out." Lieutenant W. H. Tatham, a member of the Veteran Company with 56 years' service, now offered to write a history of the Company in continuation of Highmore's work of 1804. For some unexplained reason the Court declined the offer. Only a few years later several petitions signed by large numbers of members were presented to the Court asking that a succinct history of the Company should be written and placed on sale, but no one was found willing to undertake the work. About the same time the Court prohibited card-playing in Armoury House, it being considered highly detrimental to the best interests of the Company.

The Grenadier Company of the Regiment, in continuous existence since 1686, was abolished in 1854. Its fate was shared by the Yager or Rifle Company, the Infantry being reduced to six Battalion Companies and a Light Infantry Company armed with rifles. At the same time a new rule was passed requiring members to perform at least twelve drills a year. This regulation appears to have been very necessary, as some members had done no drills at all for several years. Some months later seventeen of these gentlemen were expelled for non-attendance.

The Court of Assistants, though shorn of much of its former power, still meted out justice to delinquents for purely civil offences. They fined a sergeant £5 for assaulting a boy by throwing him downstairs, and ordered the sentence to be posted in the Sutling Room. In December, 1845, they voted 100 guineas to the Royal Patriotic Fund for the alleviation of the sufferings of the troops in the Crimea.

Bearskin caps were first worn by the Infantry in 1855, when they took the place of the old shakos. The last occasion on which the Company paraded in the old head-dress was at a royal guard of honour at the Crystal Palace, when the Queen was accompanied by the Emperor and Empress of the French. The Emperor, says *The Times*, "could not fail to be struck with the imposing air of this celebrated Corps."

The lease from the Lieutenancy of the eastern half of the Ground was renewed for another term of 99 years as from June, 1855, on payment of a fine of £3,000, and the surrender of the plot of ground now occupied by the yard of Finsbury Barracks.

The average age of members at this period must have been somewhat advanced. Only a few years before, the age at which gentlemen might be admitted members was raised from 35 to 40. Captain Bossy resigned after 52 years' service, during 17 of which he had held the office of Adjutant; and when Captain Samuel Barnard retired into the Veteran Company in 1856, he had already served 53 years on the active list, having been admitted in 1803. This officer's tunic, with many articles of equipment, was purchased at a sale in recent years.

In connection with a review in Nazing Mead, in 1856, *The Herts Guardian* stated that "the Hon. Artillery Company has achieved for itself a character for military appearance and discipline when on duty, inferior to no regiment in the service. All those who saw them this day would bear testimony with pleasure to their steadiness, precision of march, and manly, soldierly appearance; and we are bound to add, that in all the manœuvres in which they were engaged, it was impossible for the spectators to distinguish their performances from those of troops of the Line."

At the outbreak of the Indian Mutiny the Court caused recruiting advertisements to be inserted in the papers setting forth the advantages of a practical military training such as would fit recruits for service in the Regular Army or Militia. It was stated that during the Crimean War thirty or forty mem-

HORSE ARTILLERY, H.A.C., 1860
Known as "Jay's Troop." Formed in 1860, abolished in 1869

bers of the Regiment had obtained commissions in the Militia and many of them subsequently transferred to Line regiments.

The first occasion on which a detachment of the Company left London for training was in August, 1858, when the Light Infantry Company went to Seaford for a week. It is recorded that "the duties of guard-mounting, company and light infantry drill, though especially heavy work for the latter over the hills, proved the men to be possessed of great endurance, and truly fit for active service anywhere." Great praise, the account adds, is due to the men for their quiet and orderly conduct. From that year onwards camps were an annual fixture for a detachment of the Company, if not for the whole body. The Horse Artillery Troop, formed in 1860, encamped at Seaford for ball practice in 1863, and were successful in sending through the target 14 out of 30 shots at 700 yards. The weapons were 6-pounder smooth-bore guns.

The white fatigue jacket and forage cap came into use in this year.

Two hundred Enfield rifles were supplied by Government in 1859 to encourage long-range shooting. It therefore became necessary to find a suitable range, and, after some difficulty, arrangements were made for the use of a range at Hornsey Wood.

Early in 1860 Lord Colville of Culross was appointed Lieutenant-Colonel on the death of Colonel FitzRoy. A considerable increase in membership took place at this time, so much so that it became necessary to enlarge the Armoury by the addition of the present drill hall. The Battalion Companies were increased from six to eight, and a "spirited attendance at drill" on the part of members is reported.

The Company was now transferred from the jurisdiction of the Home Office to that of the Secretary for War. It appears that the War Office, noting that the Regiment was referred to in all its Royal Warrants under the old title of "The Artillery Company," thought fit to omit the time-honoured prefix of "Honourable" from the name of the Company in the Army List. However, the Prince Consort brought the matter to the notice of the Queen, who was graciously pleased to command that, as the Artillery Company of London had always been known under the name of the Honourable Artillery Company, that title should be officially borne by the Regiment.

The officers' privilege of wearing gold sashes, which had been conferred upon the Company by William IV, was now withdrawn. The Captain-General issued an order that the gold sash was reserved as a distinctive dress for the Brigade of Guards and military members of the Queen's Household. Ten years later the Prince of Wales authorized the wearing of a crimson and silver sash, similar to those used by the Foot Guards, but substituting silver for gold.

In view of the still increasing strength of the Company, it was decided, in April, 1861, to add a squadron of Light Cavalry to the establishment. At the same time two additional companies were added to the Battalion, and the distinctive title of the Light Infantry Company was abolished, being no longer in use in the Army. A suggestion to raise two Engineer Companies was negatived at a General Court. The Light Cavalry wore a magnificent uniform of blue faced with scarlet and heavily adorned with silver lace. For some years the squadron appeared at guards of honour, reviews and other functions, until in 1891 it was transformed into a Battery of Horse Artillery, taking precedence of the Field Battery as "A" Battery, H.A.C.

The Prince Consort died in December, 1861, and the Company lost a fine commanding officer and a good friend. On the day of his funeral, the Artillery Division fired forty-three guns in the Ground, and a service was held at Headquarters, the new drill hall being used for the first time. The Court subscribed £100 to a memorial, and decided that the drill hall should be known henceforth as the Albert Room.

At the entry into London of H.R.H. Princess Alexandra in March, 1861, thte Company was allotted a prominent part The Infantry Batalion formed a guard of honour at London. Bridge; the Light Cavalry, with the Horse and Field Artillery,

H.R.H. Review of Volunteers at Brighton, 1866
The Prince of Wales passing the saluting-point at the head of the
Honourable Artillery Company

were drawn up in King William Street, the number on parade being nearly 600.

The Queen signified her intention to appoint the Prince of Wales Captain-General and Colonel of the Company, this being one of very few instances in which Her Majesty consented to fill a vacancy caused by the death of the Prince Consort. The Prince was formally proposed for membership and admitted to the Company, after which a Royal Warrant confirmed his appointment. From the first His Royal Highness took the keenest personal interest in the Regiment. He led the Company past the Commander-in-Chief at the Hyde Park Review of 1864; he was present when the Princess of Wales presented new Colours in the same year; and he commanded the Company at the Brighton Review in 1866.

In consequence of Fenian outrages in London, night guards were maintained at Headquarters for several months in 1867. The records of this period include a succession of reviews and royal guards which it would be tedious to enumerate; but the strength of the Company was gradually declining, and in 1869 the number of companies was reduced from ten to six and the Horse Artillery was disbanded on account of its expense.

Some City Volunteer Regiments, not unnaturally, cast envious eyes upon the Company's Ground, with the result that a communication was received in 1871 from the Lieutenancy of London asking if the Company would permit certain regiments to make use of the Ground for drill, in such a way as not to interfere with the Company. The Court, having regard to the future welfare and prosperity of the Company, were of opinion that the Ground should be maintained for the uses to which it was dedicated. The Lieutenancy decided not to proceed further, but a Member of Parliament gave notice of a motion to introduce into a Bill a clause giving the City Volunteers the rights and privileges enjoyed by the ancient Trained Bands, which would have given them the right to use the Ground. This motion was never brought forward; but in 1873 the Court resolved, of its own initiative, to consider terms upon which the Company might invite the City Volunteers to use the Ground for military purposes, providing the leaseholders would give the necessary consent. Their deliberations were cut short by the receipt of a letter, signed by the Commanding Officers of four City Volunteer Regiments, who, claiming to be the successors of the London Trained Bands, demanded an appointment "with a view to arrange for the use of the Ground and Premises at Finsbury, now occupied by the Honourable Artillery Company," by their respective regiments.

The Court declined to receive this letter, in consequence of the most offensive and unwarrantable terms in which it was written; the resolution of the previous Court in favour of considering the admission of the City Volunteers was rescinded; and it was decided to defer any further consideration of the subject until the letter referred to was withdrawn. At the same time the Commanding Officers of five City Regiments had petitioned the Court of Aldermen for assistance in obtaining for their regiments the use of the Artillery Ground. However, after some correspondence, the officers concerned apologized, and made a full and complete withdrawal of any legal claim to the use of the Ground.

One more attempt was made on their behalf. The same Member of Parliament brought forward a resolution requesting the Government to take steps to obtain the use of the Artillery Ground for the City Volunteers; but the Government declined to be a party to any invasion of the rights of property, and the motion was withdrawn. The Company had already taken the advice of the Attorney-General and another eminent counsel as to whether the City Volunteers had any right whatever to use the Ground. The answer was an unqualified negative.

The Prince of Wales now suggested that the uniform of the Company should be changed from red to blue. In this he was backed by the Commander-in-Chief. The Court of Assistants replied thanking His Royal Highness for the interest he had ever taken in the Company, but pointing out that the change would involve members in considerable expense and would probably cause resignations. At the same time they submitted that the Infantry of the Company felt a sincere attachment for the colour of the uniform they had the honour to wear. Nothing further is heard of the suggestion.

Captain G. A. Raikes, Instructor of Musketry to the H.A.C., published in 1879 *The History of the Honourable Artillery Company* in two volumes, a compendious work which will long remain a standard book of reference on the Company's history. The amount of research involved in this production must have been enormous, and the result is an immense mass of facts relating to the Regiment tabulated in the form of a yearly diary, somewhat difficult of assimilation, but invaluable as raw material for a more discursive narrative.

CHAPTER XII

1880 TO 1914

LIEUTENANT-COLONEL R. J. LOYD-LINDSAY, V.C., M.P. (afterwards Lord Wantage), had commanded the Company since 1867. He had won the Victoria Cross as an Ensign of the Scots Fusilier Guards at the battle of the Alma. In his memoirs it is recorded that he threw himself with energy into the task of bringing the Company up to the standards of modern requirements, and did his best to grapple with the peculiar difficulties presented by a body "to a great degree independent of ordinary military regulations, partaking of the nature of a club for social purposes as well as for military training." But he found the task no easy one and felt compelled to inform the Secretary of State for War that the Company "fails to comply with what is required of it." His object, he declared, was to prevent what he considered the finest military volunteer body in England being reduced to the level of a mere club, and he desired to see its funds devoted to military rather than to social purposes. On these lines he worked assiduously for fifteen years, but though his efforts were crowned with considerable success, the feeling of the Regiment in favour of the old order of things proved too strong to be efficiently broken through. Nevertheless, he achieved many improvements and always looked upon the Regiment as a unique body of men possessing great capabilities for utility and expansion.

Lord Wantage now retired and was succeeded by the Duke of Portland, a young Guards officer, who was duly admitted a member before being gazetted to the command.

In the same year objections were raised to the appointment of Lord Headley to command the Light Cavalry Troop on the ground that he had not been a member for six months before promotion. However, the technical breach of Rules and Orders appears to have been passed over in this case.

It was the custom at this period to summon before the Court

all members who did not succeed in making themselves militarily efficient for the year. Their explanations were heard and they were excused, censured, fined, asked to resign, or expelled, according to the merits of each individual case.

After protracted debates it was now decided that the qualification for membership of the Veteran Company should be ten years' efficient service in the ranks, or five years' service in commissioned or non-commissioned rank. Some years later this was reduced to eight years' efficient service in any rank, a qualification which held good for service in time of peace until 1931, when, in regard to the greatly increased military activities then appertaining to membership, the qualification was reduced to five years.

The centenary of Vincent Lunardi's balloon ascent was celebrated on 15th September, 1884, under the auspices of the Balloon Society of Great Britain. Three large balloons ascended from the Artillery Ground in the presence of a large concourse of spectators.

In November the Company presented a lifeboat to Walton-on-the-Naze. This boat, purchased with funds raised by the regimental Dramatic Society, was christened "The Hon. Artillery Company" and launched in the presence of a guard of honour of the Regiment. The general finances of the Company were not at this time in a flourishing condition, the Regiment being £4,000 in debt.

The question of the precedence of the Company arose at a review in 1887, when the Royal Naval Artillery Volunteers (a corps long since extinct) claimed the right of the line by virtue of their connection with the senior Service. The point was decided at the time in favour of the Company, but the decision was questioned in Parliament. The answer was that the Honourable Artillery Company, in consideration of its antiquity, was given precedence immediately after the Regular forces and before the Militia and Yeomanry by a general order of 1883. The right of the Royal Navy to take the right of the line over all land forces was not disputed, but, as the Militia and Yeomanry were senior to all Volunteers and the Royal Naval Artillery Volunteers came under the latter category, it followed that the H.A.C. took precedence over that body.

As representatives of a military unit which has survived since the days of Queen Elizabeth, a detachment of the Company was present at the Tercentenary Commemoration of the defeat of the Spanish Armada at Plymouth in 1888. Two years later the Armada Memorial on Plymouth Hoe was unveiled. The heraldic emblems on this monument include a shield bearing the arms of the Company, in recognition of the fact that members of the Regiment served at Tilbury Camp and at sea in 1588. Detachments of all arms of the Company attended the opening ceremony.

In the following year a remarkable and unprecedented position in the affairs of the Company arose with little warning, and rapidly developed into a situation of extreme anxiety. For some years the state of affairs at Armoury House had not been entirely satisfactory. In the first place it had been discovered that the one sure road to promotion to non-commissioned rank was by way of a suitable gratuity to the Regimental Sergeant-Major, who, with his subordinate Drill Sergeants, was paid by the Company. The same official was also found to be making a profit on the sale of equipment, uniforms, etc., and both matters were dealt with. The salary of the Adjutant (Colonel Borton, a retired Army officer) was also paid from the civil funds of the Regiment, voted by the Court of Assistants and subject to revision by the general body of members. The defects of this arrangement are obvious, as an officer largely responsible for the discipline of the unit was thus virtually in the pay of the privates. This might have led to no evil results but for the fact that the Duke of Portland took little interest in the Regiment, leaving the command almost entirely to his Adjutant, to the exclusion of the Field Officers. Colonel Borton appears to have been somewhat inactive and decidedly unpopular. Rightly or wrongly, he was alleged to have shown favouritism in the selection of officers, choice of whom was practically entirely in his hands. With matters in this unsatisfactory condition a proposition was made at a General Court to reduce his salary. The motion appears to have been the outcome of a private feud, and it was defeated; but the incident not unnaturally rankled in the mind of the Adjutant, and was not calculated to improve an already strained relationship. His opponents argued with some point that they had recently raised Colonel Borton's salary, without reference to any higher authority, and therefore had a right to reduce it; but the incident doubtless formed one of the charges to be preferred against the discipline of the Company.

At this time the Prince of Wales was endeavouring to induce the Company to place itself under the provisions of the Volunteer Act, and at a Special General Court held in November, 1888, this was unanimously agreed to, the members accepting His Royal Highness's assurance that he would do all in his power to ensure the retention by the Company of its old precedence and the control of its property. It was also agreed that an annual fixed sum should be placed at the disposal of the Commanding Officer for military purposes.

Then came the crisis. At a General Court held on 6th December, 1888, a vote of £500 to the Commanding Officer for military expenses, which apparently included the Adjutant's salary, was not passed, but an amendment "that, as the vote of a fixed sum to be paid to the Commanding Officer to cover military expenses forms part of the new and incompleted arrangements suggested by H.R.H. the Captain-General and Colonel, the consideration of this Resolution do stand over until the proposed alterations in the constitution of the Company have been submitted to the members," was carried by thirteen votes.

To the impartial observer this resolution may appear vexatious, but does not strike one as amounting to rank insubordination or mutiny. However, the Duke of Portland, who was not at the meeting but presumably acted on the advice of the Adjutant and without further inquiry, promptly reported to the Captain-General that the Company was "in a most unsatisfactory state as regards discipline." Representations were then made to the Secretary of State for War, and an order was issued for the withdrawal of the Company's arms. At the same time the resignations of the Prince of Wales, the Duke of Portland, and Colonel Borton were officially announced. To say that the members of the Company were stupefied by the sudden and drastic nature of the blow that had fallen upon them would not understate the case. For a certain hesitation in passing a vote for £500 out of the Company's private funds, they had been punished with a severity, not to say ignominy, which would have been adequate for a mutinous and thoroughly disloyal regiment. It was felt that the sentence was not only unnecessarily harsh, but actually unjust, and immediate steps were taken to put this view before the proper authorities. In the meantime the guns had been delivered by the Field Battery to

Woolwich and the rifles and ammunition removed, so the Company continued to drill without arms.

The situation caused extraordinary interest throughout the country. The Press took sides—the majority supporting the Company—and the matter was discussed with considerable fervour, in some cases amounting to virulence. Caricatures, some of them not particularly respectful to eminent personages, appeared in many periodicals; correspondence columns flourished amazingly on the subject; even the Continental Press had its comments to make. Some individuals with private axes to grind hailed the supposed break-up of the old Company with delight, and many were the suggestions put forward as to the disposal of the Company's property. It was publicly reported that members of other, and less wealthy, volunteer corps were "rejoicing with an unholy joy at the downfall of the haughty occupiers of the drill-ground in Moorfields."

It transpired that the Prince had been informed that the mention of his name had been received with jeers at that eventful General Court. This incident was alleged to have occurred during a heated discussion on a motion to repudiate the suggestion of a spirit of insubordination in the Regiment, a charge which had been made by an officer of the Company (Captain C. Woolmer-Williams) in an abridged version of Raikes' History recently published by him. The Court of Assistants took prompt steps indignantly to deny this abominable slander, and to assure the Prince of Wales of their unswerving loyalty. It is beyond doubt that there had been either misunderstanding or deliberate misrepresentation on this point. There had obviously been moments of excitement during the debate, and some members had given vent to their disapproval of certain statements; but that any mention of His Royal Highness's name was the cause of such expressions of feeling was simply not in accordance with fact. The discipline of the Regiment may have been, nay, undoubtedly was, of a type peculiar to itself; but of the complete loyalty and devotion of its members to the Throne and to their Captain-General there was never the faintest shadow of doubt. The indignation of the members at this assertion knew no bounds, but the mischief had been done, for it was probably on this statement, rather than on the withholding of the supplies, that the charge of insubordination and indiscipline had been based. It is a matter for the greatest regret that the Commanding Officer failed to handle the matter with greater tact. Had he instituted a court of inquiry before reporting to the Captain-General, the whole unfortunate occurrence of the resignations and disarming might never have taken place. Even as things happened, it is impossible for the unbiased historian to fail to compare the hasty procedure on this occasion with the tact and judgment displayed by the Prince Consort in similar circumstances forty years before.

Meanwhile deputations waited on the Secretary for War; questions were asked in Parliament; a petition was presented to the Queen; and every possible step was taken to ensure the continuance of the Company, which once again seemed to be threatened with annihilation. Finally the matter was brought to a close by the issue of a new Royal Warrant, dated 12th March, 1889, which cancelled the previous warrant of 1863. Under the new Warrant the appointment, not only of officers but of Sergeant Instructors, was reserved to the Crown; the Regimental Sergeant-Major was to be selected by the Captain-General; N.C.Os., except the Sergeant Instructors, were to be chosen by the Commanding Officer from members of the Company. The numbers of the Company were limited to 2,000, and authority was given for the discharge of any member for neglect of duty or misconduct. Furthermore, it was laid down that the Company might be called out for service in Great Britain by Royal Proclamation; and the Secretary of State for War was given authority to issue such further regulations as might be necessary for the better government, discipline and efficiency of the Company. At the same time the civil rights of the Company were adequately safeguarded.

Viscount de Vesci, a former officer of the Coldstream Guards, was then appointed Lieutenant-Colonel and Captain Labalmondière, of the Royal Artillery, was gazetted Adjutant. Shortly afterwards a new Regimental Sergeant-Major and three permanent Drill Instructors were appointed, all paid by Government. In the following year the Secretary for War, by virtue of his powers under the new Warrant, ordered the Light Cavalry Troop to be converted into a battery of Horse Artillery.

Although the Company had accepted the new Royal Warrant without demur, the Prince of Wales did not immediately withdraw his resignation. For several years the Regiment was without a Captain-General, until, early in 1893, a petition was drawn up and signed by the Civil Chiefs, the Court of Assistants and all the officers of the active list, assuring the Prince of their continued loyalty and requesting him to accept the ancient and distinguished post of Captain-General and Colonel. His Royal Highness was graciously pleased to accede to this request, and on 10th June, 1893, was again appointed to the command of the Company. Lord de Vesci at once began the task of reorganizing the Regiment as a useful military body, which it certainly was not in those days. The Field Battery had never done any gun practice and the newly formed Horse Artillery for several years could only turn out two guns. The infantry could drill and there were individuals good at musketry, but that was all.

Lord de Vesci, with his home in Ireland, found it impossible to give sufficient time, and in 1893 the Earl of Denbigh and Desmond, who had five years previously retired as a Captain from the R.H.A. and R.F.A., in which he had served ten ears and seen service in the Egyptian Campaign of 1882, was offered the command and, having been admitted as a member, was gazetted as Lieutenant-Colonel. He at once took an active part in trying to make the Regiment efficient and soon represented strongly to the War Office the futility of trying to improve the artillery with its ridiculous and obsolete armament of 9-pounder muzzle-loaders. It was not till 1898 that it was possible to obtain 15-pounder breech-loading guns, with which the Regular Army had been re-armed.

The old question of the precedence of the Company cropped up again in 1892. At a field day at Chatham the Officer Commanding the Field Battery found his claim to lead the march past contested by officers of Yeomanry on the ground that theirs was a senior service to the Volunteers and that cavalry always took precedence of field batteries. It was pointed out that by ancient custom, confirmed by Royal Charter, the Honourable Artillery Company took precedence after the Regular Army and before all Militia, Yeomanry or Volunteers. The General Officer Commanding recognized the Company's claim, and the Field Battery took the place of honour at the head of the column.

In 1899 the Field Battery was turned into Horse Artillery, and the two Batteries then became known as "A" and "B."

The Regiment, still sadly under strength, held its annual camps, sometimes as a complete unit; at other times the

Batteries proceeded to separate training grounds. Reviews were frequent; guards of honour were provided as occasion required; and the Company was invariably well to the fore in shooting competitions. The ceremony of Trooping the Colour was held every year at Headquarters, and was usually attended by a member of the Royal Family.

The outbreak of the South African War in October, 1899, had no immediate effect on recruiting as far as the Company was concerned. Only 15 new members joined during that month, 23 in the following month, and 15 in December. The rush came in January, after volunteers had been called for to take their places in the fighting line. In that month 182 members were admitted, and for some time afterwards an average of 60 to 70 recruits a month was maintained. The slackness in the early days was probably due to the misplaced optimism which looked upon the war as a sort of punitive expedition, a state of mind encouraged by the first reports of minor successes.

Then followed those dark days in December, 1899, when the country learned with amazement and dismay of successive defeats suffered by the three principal British armies—Stormberg, Magersfontein and Colenso. All notions of a triumphal march to Pretoria vanished; the Press-begotten ideas of a cowardly enemy gave place to a realization that our armies had to face a stubborn foe—a nation in arms, consisting of well-mounted marksmen, provided with up-to-date munitions and operating in a vast country admirably adapted for defensive tactics. Foolish optimism vanished, and the country settled down to its task.

It was now realized that our Regular forces were not sufficiently numerous for the successful prosecution of the war, and there was a call for volunteers, both at home and in the Colonies. The Honourable Artillery Company had already offered to provide a battery of artillery and a company of infantry, but the former was declined on the ground that there was a sufficiency of Regular artillery. As regards the infantry, it was proposed that the Company should send their quota of 40 men towards the Infantry and Mounted Infantry of the City Imperial Volunteers, the formation of which had just been announced. Within a day or two the required number was selected from numerous volunteers, and two officers, a surgeon, and 41 other ranks of the Company were sworn in as C.I.V.

Only a few days later Lord Denbigh read that a battery offered by the Elswick works had been accepted and at once inquired if the previous decision had been altered. He saw Lord Wolseley, who laughingly remarked, "We progress here," and accepted a 4-gun field battery from the H.A.C. Lord Lansdowne, Secretary of State for War, next day handed Lord Denbigh a cheque for £17,000 to buy what was necessary. War Office consent was obtained for acceptance of an offer by the City to provide a complete equipment of four quick-firing 12-pounder guns, which Messrs. Vickers had just made. These were the first quick-firers with "fixed ammunition" used by a British force in the field. Following this welcome decision came a proposal to incorporate the Battery in the C.I.V. The offer was accepted, and the Battery, though the Company remained responsible for its personnel and equipment, became technically a branch of the C.I.V., enjoying the privileges of that corps and sharing in the funds subscribed for it. The Artillery Division of the Company at that time numbered 180 men, a majority of whom, with a considerable number from the Battalion, at once volunteered for service. Eighty-four were selected. From this number all the combatant officers, sergeants and corporals of the new Battery were chosen, while the remaining personnel were recruited by selection from various corps of Volunteer Artillery, with a sprinkling of Regular soldiers.

The final contribution of the Company to the City Imperial Volunteers, including drafts, was 154 men. Of these 26 served in the Battalion, 30 in the Mounted Infantry, and 98 in the Battery. The latter may be regarded henceforth as an H.A.C. unit, having been created and organized by the Company, which also supplied all the officers and two-thirds of the personnel. The cost of equipping the Battery was borne partly by Government, partly by the Lord Mayor's C.I.V. Fund—to which the Company had officially subscribed £1,000, and members of the Company, by private subscription, another £1,500—while certain articles of equipment were provided by the generosity of individual members.

After only three weeks' intensive training, the Battery sailed for South Africa, landing at Cape Town on 28th February, 1900. After a spell on the lines of communication, it was sent to the front, and fired its first shots in the relief of Lindley, after which it formed part of a force which followed up De Wet and compelled him to evacuate Bethlehem. Some spirited actions were fought during this advance and in the subsequent operations against Prinsloo, which resulted in the surrender of that General, with 4,000 Boers, at Fouriesburg. The Regiment treasures a Boer flag, presented to the Battery by General Paget in recognition of its services at the taking of Bethlehem. The remainder of the Battery's service was spent in guerilla warfare in Northern Transvaal.

The C.I.V. Mounted Infantry, of which the Company provided No. 1 Section of No. 1 Company, landed on 29th January, 1900, at Cape Town, where they were equipped, and were sent to the front in time to take part in the general advance under Lord Roberts. The H.A.C. detachment received their baptism of fire at Jacobsdal and were present at the surrender of Cronje at Paardeberg. They shared in numerous small actions during the advance on Bloemfontein and were among the first troops to enter Johannesburg. After the capture of Pretoria, the C.I.V.M.I. took part in the great concerted movement which led to Prinsloo's surrender.

The Infantry Battalion of the C.I.V. landed in South Africa in February, 1900. After service on the lines of communication they joined in the advance to Pretoria and behaved with gallantry in the spirited action of Doornkop. Hard and continuous marching was the lot of the infantry soldier in South Africa, and that the C.I.V. did their share is evidenced by the fact that at one period they covered no less than 523 miles in 40 marching days. In addition to desultory fighting, convoys and garrison duty, the Battalion served with distinction at the battle of Diamond Hill.

The return of the C.I.V. to London ranks as a landmark in the history of the metropolis. The enthusiasm was unprecedented, the returning troops being acclaimed and fêted in a way unique in military annals. There was some excuse for this ebullition of feeling. After forty years of discouragement and derision, Volunteer soldiers had proved themselves willing to undertake active service and worthy of taking their places in the fighting forces of the country. They came of a generation unaccustomed to war, to whom every soldier in the field was a hero; they had volunteered for active service and had acquitted themselves with credit. Again—possibly the potent factor—they had a very good "Press." Hence the immense crowds, the fervid acclamations, and the fulsome leading articles, which, to the present war-hardened generation, seem out of proportion to their services, and were certainly galling to the Regular soldier, who had borne the brunt of the war and was to receive no such reception on his long-delayed return.

The feelings of the men themselves can best be conveyed by a quotation of the closing passage of a book—*In the Ranks of the C.I.V.*—written by that ill-fated member of the Company, Erskine Childers (who served as a driver in the Battery):

The interminable day of waiting; the landing on the quay, with its cheering crowds; that wonderful journey to London, with its growing tumult of feelings, as station after station, with their ribboned and shouting throngs, flashed by; the meeting at Paddington with our comrades of the Honourable Artillery Company, bringing us their guns and horses; the mounting of a glossy, smartly-equipped steed, which made me laughingly recall my shaggy old pair, with their dusty, travel-worn harness; all this I see clearly enough. The rest seems a dream; a dream of miles of upturned faces, of dancing colours, or roaring voices, of a sudden dim hush in the great Cathedral, of more miles of faces under gaslight, of a voice in a packed hall saying "London is proud of her——," of disconnected confidences with policemen, work-people, street-arabs, and finally of the entry once more through the old grey gateway of the Armoury House. I expect the feelings of all of us were much the same; some honest pride in having helped to earn such a welcome; a sort of stunned bewilderment at its touching and passionate intensity; a deep wave of affection for our countrymen; and a thought in the background all the time of a dusty khaki figure still plodding the distant veldt—our friend and comrade, Atkins, who has done more and bloodier work than we, and who is not at the end of it yet.

In addition to those with the C.I.V., some 60 members saw active service with other units. Fully a third of these had originally been members of the C.I.V. and, on the return home of that unit, had transferred to other corps. Others joined individually or in small groups, mostly in the Imperial Yeomanry, and served till the end of the war, many ultimately receiving commissions. During the war 33 members of the Company held commissions on active service, of whom 8 were promoted from the ranks for service in the field. About the same number were given Regular commissions.

In all 193 members served in South Africa, of whom 4 were killed or died of wounds, 2 died of disease and 30 were wounded or invalided home. The honours and distinctions awarded to members included 1 C.M.G., 1 D.S.O., 3 D.C.Ms., and 18 mentions in despatches.

For their part in the South African War the Company received the Battle Honour, "South Africa, 1900-02."

This employment of the H.A.C. on service gave a great fillip to the Corps. As one result the Batteries were soon provided with their own artificers. Prior to the South African

OFFICER, C.I.V. BATTERY AND PRIVATE, C.I.V. INFANTRY, 1900

OFFICERS, HONOURABLE ARTILLERY COMPANY, 1908, ARTILLERY AND INFANTRY

War it had been the custom to borrow artificers and shoeing-smiths from the Regulars when in camp. This was a great advance in efficiency, which steadily progressed at each annual camp, commanded in person by Lord Denbigh, who, at the outbreak of the Great War, after commanding twenty-one consecutive trainings, was able to show that a useful military force, animated with a splendid *esprit de corps*, had been gradually evolved.

For the Coronation of its Captain-General in 1902 the Company claimed its ancient privilege of attending the ceremony in full strength and of being posted next to the Guards. This right was conceded, though subsequent events necessitated a

259

reduction of numbers to 200. The Battalion was posted between Parliament Street and the House of Commons, the Batteries being drawn up on Horse Guards Parade.

For some 200 years no communications appear to have taken place between the Company and its offshoot, the Ancient and Honorable Artillery Company of Massachusetts. Probably each had forgotten the existence of the other. It was not until 1857 that correspondence was opened between the two corps which developed into a regular interchange of courtesies. Copies of records were exchanged, and the Prince Consort, Captain-General and Colonel of the H.A.C., was elected an honorary member of the A. & H.A.C., the same compliment being extended to the Prince of Wales on his succession to command of this Company. Then occasional visits of individual members on both sides paved the way to more extensive fraternizations, until, in 1887, a party of 11 members of the Boston Company assisted to celebrate the 350th anniversary of the incorporation of the parent body. In the following year 21 members of the London Company returned the visit for the celebration of the 250th anniversary of the American corps.

These preliminary visits were productive of such mutual good will that the A. & H.A.C. decided to visit England in a body, whereupon the Company seized the opportunity to arrange a suitable reception for the first American military body to set foot in the Old Country. The visit took place in 1896 and was most happily timed. The Venezuelan crisis had been acute in the previous year; feeling between the two countries—or rather between the Politicians and Press of the two countries—was somewhat strained; and the visit accordingly assumed an international significance of some importance. The Ancients, as they were called, wished to land as an armed force in uniform and march through the streets with swords drawn. This request had to be forwarded through the British Ambassador at Washington and it came before the Cabinet. Having regard to the friction of the year before, the Prime Minister (Lord Salisbury) thought that the arrival of the American force would be a good opportunity for a display of official friendship, and he informed Lord Denbigh that the Government would make the visit an official function and take over most of the entertaining. The A. & H.A.C., 170 strong, were warmly welcomed and suitably entertained by the Regiment. This was only as it should be, but a far more extended programme had been arranged. The American unit was reviewed by Queen Victoria at Windsor and by the Prince and Princess of Wales at Marlborough House; a review at Aldershot was arranged for their benefit; and they were entertained at the Royal Artillery Mess at Woolwich. Quite apart from official courtesies, the reception accorded to the Americans by the public and the publicity it evoked in both countries could hardly have failed to exercise a beneficial effect on the frayed international relationship.

Our Boston friends lost little time in issuing an invitation to our Regiment to visit Boston in 1900. This invitation was accepted, but the South African War intervened, rendering postponement unavoidable. Finally, on 23rd September, 1903, a detachment of the Company, 163 strong, under Lord Denbigh, left for Boston, where they were accorded a wonderful reception and almost overwhelming hospitality. Our members were escorted through five miles of decorated streets by an imposing military force amid scenes of popular enthusiasm; they were feasted and fêted; receptions, church parades, banquets followed in rapid succession; and whenever the Company moved its line of march was one triumphal progress. They then visited Providence (Rhode Island), where they were hospitably entertained by the First Light Infantry Regiment of Providence.

Special trains and steamboats had been chartered by their energetic hosts, and the Company, attended by an equal number of their comrades of Boston, were taken on a week's tour of 1,850 miles, during which they visited New York, West Point, Niagara Falls, Toronto and Montreal. The visit to the Military College at West Point was most interesting. On arrival the H.A.C. marched past the cadets to the parade ground, where the cadets then formed up and invited Lord Denbigh to inspect them and take the salute. They afterwards gave a wonderful exhibition of their marvellous precision of drill. At New York the Company were escorted and entertained by the Old Guard of New York.

The next landmark was a visit to Washington, where the detachment was entertained at the White House by President Roosevelt, who affixed his signature to the list of famous names in the Vellum Book. Returning to Boston there were more banquets. The Company entertained their hosts and the

British residents of Boston entertained the Company. Then came the leave-taking. Docks and shipping were black with people; the Union Jack waved beside the Stars and Stripes from the Bunker Hill Monument; bands played; factory whistles and ships' sirens sounded a farewell; and tens of thousands of spectators took up the cadence of the "Regimental Fire"—that ninefold shout peculiar to the Company and of which the origin has been forgotten.

So ended a remarkable experience for all privileged to take part. The American visit certainly provided a fair example of what may be done by such intercourse towards the promotion of good fellowship and understanding between communities so closely allied by blood and tradition as are the two great branches of the English-speaking race.

Lord Colville of Culross, a member of the Company since 1859, who had served in succession as Lieutenant-Colonel, Vice-President and President, died in 1903. Shortly after his death the King issued a Royal Warrant expressing his will and pleasure that in future the office of President should be combined with that of Commanding Officer. Lord Denbigh thereupon assumed the dual office, which is still held by the Colonel-Commandant.

It is not generally known outside the Regiment that King Edward bestowed on the Company the distinction of a special ribbon to the Volunteer Decoration and Volunteer Long Service Medal, which extends to the same medals under their Territorial designations. This ribbon of red and blue, edged with narrow yellow stripes—King Edward's private colours—has been a cause of mystification to many Regular officers who have noticed it on the breasts of members. The grant was promulgated by Army Order 257, dated 1st November, 1906.

By the Territorial and Reserve Forces Act, 1907, the Volunteers were reorganized as Territorials, and the H.A.C., who had occupied an independent position in the Volunteer Force, were now invited to join the Territorial Force. At a general meeting of the Company it was unanimously decided to join if the Government would pass a special Act of Parliament excluding the property of the Regiment from the provisions of the Territorial Act and confirming the civil rights of the Company. A special Bill safeguarding the property and ancient civil rights and privileges of the Company was therefore passed in the following year under the title of "The Honourable Artillery Company Act, 1908." Shortly after this Bill received the Royal Assent, a notice appeared in the Gazette to the effect that, His Majesty the King would continue to remain at the head of the Honourable Artillery Company of the Territorial Force, as its Captain-General, on its transfer thereto and conversion from the Honourable Artillery Company of London.

The immediate result of the transfer of the Company to the Territorial Force was a considerable influx of recruits, 553 new members being admitted in the following year, whereas the yearly average had been about 70. The strength of the active list in 1909 was 1,066 all ranks, 97.6 per cent. of whom were returned as efficient for the year.

King Edward died in May, 1910. Throughout the 37 years of his connection with the Regiment his interest never failed. Before his accession to the Throne he had been a frequent visitor to Armoury House, attending parades, balls and smoking concerts with impartiality. In later years he held inspections of the Company, the last review having taken place in Buckingham Palace Gardens the year before his death. The Company, who were in camp at Bulford, journeyed back to town for the funeral of their Captain-General. Three officers and 50 other ranks of the Battalion formed part of the escort, while the remaining 650 lined the side of the Mall. Later in the year His Majesty King George V signified his pleasure to assume the title of Captain-General and Colonel.

When preparations for the Coronation came under consideration, representations were made for the Company to be allotted its traditional position next to the Brigade of Guards, but it was decided that the Corps did not enjoy the prescriptive right to a position other than that conferred by precedence in the Army List. The Regiment was thus deprived of its time-honoured position in Parliament Street and placed between Whitehall and the Admiralty Arch on the day of the Coronation. On the occasion of Their Majesties' procession through London the Infantry were placed between two Battalions of Guards in Trafalgar Square.

A detachment of the Ancient and Honorable Artillery Company of Massachusetts visited London in 1912 at the invitation of the Company. The celebrations in their honour included a Trooping of the Colour at Armoury House and a visit to

King George V with the Ancient and Honorable Artillery Company of Massachusetts, at Buckingham Palace, 1912

Windsor, where a memorial tablet was placed on the old house of Robert Keayne, the founder of the American branch. Finally, both Regiments were inspected by King George V at Buckingham Palace.

In August, 1914, came the first great test, and the Honourable Artillery Company rose to the occasion. The Batteries and Battalion were mobilized at once; old members flocked to rejoin the active list and Armoury House was besieged by thousands of young men eager to join so famous a corps. How many hundreds were turned away after the existing units had been brought up to strength will never be known, but after some delay permission was obtained to recruit two 2nd line Batteries and a 2nd Battalion. As the war went on, so the Company continued to expand, until eventually it comprised four Horse Artillery Batteries, a Siege Battery and two Battalions overseas in the fighting line, with two Reserve Batteries, a Reserve Battalion and a Depot at home. In all, some 14,000 men passed through its ranks; every one was admitted through the Court of Assistants in the time-honoured manner.

Inspection of 1st and 2nd Battalions H.A.C. by H.M. King George V, 12th September, 1914

CHAPTER XIII

1914 TO 1918

THE 1st Battalion, recruited up to war strength, was inspected by His Majesty King George V in the Artillery Ground on 12th September, 1914, and sailed for France on the 18th. After several weeks of guard duties and musketry practice, the Battalion was engaged in trench digging near Les Lobes, and here came under fire, suffering several casualties on 13th November. On the 21st the H.A.C. went into the line for the first time, attached by companies to Regular units of the 3rd Division.

The Battalion was again inspected by the Captain-General on 3rd December. It was the first time a King of England had been with his army in the field since Dettingen (1743). Senior Regular officers present were somewhat shaken by the "Regimental Fire" given to His Majesty by companies as he passed down the lines.

The Battalion won its first honours (M.C. and D.C.M.) the same night, when two companies were supporting the 2nd Royal Scots. Then on 9th December the 1st H.A.C. went into the line as a battalion, taking over trenches in front of Spanbroek Molen. The trenches were shallow, mud-filled ditches, dominated by the German line; the parapets were often only breast high; the approaches were open and bullet-swept. It rained incessantly, with frost and snow at intervals. Three days and nights of this cost the Battalion 12 officers and 250 men in casualties, mostly from exhaustion, exposure and frostbite.

Throughout the remainder of this winter of almost unimaginable hardship and misery for the troops in the line, the H.A.C. took their turns of trench duty in the areas of Spanbroek Molen, Kemmel or St. Eloi. Sometimes during the period of so-called "rest" out of the line, the men would be engaged all night on fatigue parties carrying material up to the trenches. Casualties mounted steadily, and were replaced on 13th January, 1915, by the first draft of 4 officers and 300 men from the 2nd Battalion.

By this time the H.A.C. had already been called upon to produce officers for the battalions of their brigade. On one occasion early in January, 23 H.A.C. privates just out of the line were ordered to report to the Worcesters, Wiltshires, South Lancashires and Royal Irish Rifles as Platoon Commanders. Several of them were killed before their gazettes came through.

The Battalion were in the line at St. Eloi during the first German gas attack on the north side of the Ypres Salient, so were only on the fringe of the area.

HONOURABLE ARTILLERY COMPANY INFANTRY IN FRANCE AND FLANDERS, 1914

HONOURABLE ARTILLERY COMPANY ARTILLERY IN EGYPT, ADEN AND PALESTINE, 1915 TO 1918

On 5th June the 3rd Division moved into the ill-omened Salient, and on the 8th the H.A.C. found themselves in the Hooge pocket, with the enemy on three sides of them. During this three-day tour they were extremely lucky, both in the line and during the almost equally dangerous marches in and out of the Salient.

An attack to straighten the line between Hooge Château and Railway Wood was now ordered for 16th June, and the task of the H.A.C. was to follow up the 1st Lincolns, occupy and reconstruct the captured trenches, and dig a communication trench back to the old front line. This was carried out with great dash and gallantry, but at a cost to the Battalion of 15 officers and over 200 men killed or wounded, a regrettable waste of potential officer material which should never have happened. These casualties were replaced by another draft of over 300 from the 2nd Battalion.

Again and again the H.A.C. took their tour of duty in the trenches of Hooge, St. Eloi and near Wieltze below the Pilckem Ridge. While holding the Hooge crater area for six days from 18th September onwards, during the bombardment preliminary to another attack, over 100 casualties were suffered, including 4 officers killed by a single shell. The Battalion, reduced to 150 men, plus 60 survivors of the Liverpool Scottish, was rushed up into the Salient by daylight on 30th September. The Germans had exploded a mine in front of Sanctuary Wood and occupied the crater, from which they were subsequently driven by bombing parties of the Royal Scots and H.A.C., the regimental party being led by Sergeant A. O. Pollard, who won a D.C.M. in this action.

In October the H.A.C., after a quiet spell in the trenches at Armagh Wood, said good-bye to their comrades of the 3rd Division and travelled by motor-bus to Blendecques, near St. Omer, and became H.Q. troops. Here for five months the Battalion trained, provided various guards, and sent 20 or 30 men a week to the Army School for Cadets near by. These losses were filled by drafts from home, and in a few months very few of the rank and file had any actual experience of warfare. This was, however, rectified by sending 250 men for attachment to the Wiltshires of the 3rd Division for a tour of trench duty in December.

In March, 1916, the Battalion moved to Hesdin to prepare the new G.H.Q. in that town and Montreuil. Here practically the whole personnel were required each day for guards at the C.-in-C.'s château and other places. On 1st July the H.A.C. handed over their duties at G.H.Q. to the Artists Rifles and marched towards the line to join the recently constituted Army Brigade of the 63rd (Royal Naval) Division. A tour of duty followed in the Calonne sector, and the Division was then withdrawn for training at Marquay preparatory to being thrown into the holocaust of the Somme battle.

After a seven-day tour of duty in the trenches of the Redan, which included a good deal of patrol activity, there was a period of fatigues, cable-burying, salvage work, etc., not without casualties, and on 3rd November the Battalion went into the line at Hamel for three days.

It now became known that the Battalion was to take part in an attack on Beaucourt. Zero hour was 5.45 a.m. on 13th November, and, after a barrage from 1,000 guns, the H.A.C. went in in dense fog. The fact that the right flank rested on the River Ancre enabled the attack to maintain direction. "A" Company, H.A.C., and a company of the Hood Battalion advanced a mile and a quarter, and when the fog lifted the H.A.C. were digging in in front of Beaucourt and were fired upon by Germans 800 yards to their left rear. The rest of the Division, with "B" and "C" Companies, H.A.C., were held up opposite the original front line and lost heavily. "D" Company, H.A.C., following up the Hoods, mopped up pockets of Germans which had been overlooked in the first rush, and eventually "B" and "C" joined up with "A." The attack was resumed next morning. "A" Company and some of the Hoods, advancing under heavy machine-gun fire, got into Beaucourt itself and finally attained the high ground beyond, which was their first objective. The H.A.C. had done well, but at heavy cost. The operation cost the Battalion 81 killed and 184 wounded.

After a period behind the line the H.A.C. went in again on 27th January, 1917, for five days in the same sector. This time a line of outposts constituted the front line, and one of these posts was raided by the enemy and several men captured. During their next tour of duty, in the Pusieux line, the Battalion lost their commanding officer, who was killed outside his dug-out on 7th February. The Battalion then attacked, captured and held Baillescourt Farm and adjoining trenches, taking 86 prisoners. The weather was bitterly cold and the ground hard as flint. Enemy shelling was intense and sometimes it was impossible to relieve the outpost line in their shell-holes more than once in 48 hours. The Battalion, which had suffered heavy casualties from shells and exposure, was relieved on 14th February.

The H.A.C. had one more turn in the Pusieux line from 21st to 28th February, during which they attacked and carried Beauregarde Dovecot and Gudgeon Trench. The February

H.A.C. ADVANCING TO THE ATTACK AT GAVRELLE

From a drawing by Adrian Hill

operations had cost the Battalion 39 killed and 100 wounded. After a further three weeks of road-making in the Thiepval and Miraumont areas, the Battalion went out with the Division for training.

The 15th April, 1917, found the H.A.C. in the line north-east of Arras. Here they were to take part in an attack on the strongly held Oppy-Gavrelle defences, a part of the Hindenburg Line, on 23rd April (St. George's Day). The Battalion was to support the 7th Bn. Royal Fusiliers (the old London Militia, our neighbours of Finsbury Barracks) and the 4th Bedfords. The barrage opened at 4.45 a.m. and the first attack was a costly failure, the Fusiliers being reduced to about 70 men. The Bedfords, however, managed to secure a footing in Gavrelle village on the right flank. "A" Company, H.A.C., were sent forward to support the Fusiliers and, after severe fighting, entered the German front line. "B" Company then advanced and cleared the enemy support trench. By this time the whole of Gavrelle village had been captured, but on the left the Division's attack had failed disastrously and "B" Company found themselves in touch with Germans occupying the same

271

CAPT. A. O. POLLARD, V.C., M.C.,   CAPT. R. L. HAINE, V.C., M.C.
D.C.M.   35th Sikhs, I.A. (Formerly 1st H.A.C.)
1st H.A.C.

trench. The H.A.C. could do nothing but consolidate their gains. During the night "C" and "D" Companies relieved "A" and "B."

In the morning two battalions of Prussian Guard counter-attacked, but were partly broken up by our artillery fire and the remainder were dealt with by the H.A.C. It was estimated that the enemy suffered 3,000 casualties, and the result for them was utter failure. At night the Battalion, reduced to about 40 effectives per company, was relieved.

A further attack was organized for the 28th. While other units delivered a frontal attack, "C" Company, H.A.C., was to work to the left along the old German front line, where a strong-point had proved very troublesome. "D" Company were to work left along the German support trench. The frontal attack met with determined resistance, but "D" Company bombed up the support line for some distance, and "C" Company (led by Lieutenant R. L. Haine) succeeded, after three costly failures, in carrying the strong-point. Then a strong enemy counter-attack forced "C" Company to relinquish their gain and retire along the trench. The Germans followed up their initial success with seven desperate attacks by Prussian

Guards at intervals throughout the day, all of which were driven back by the Lewis gun and rifle fire of the H.A.C.

Nightfall brought a lull in the fighting, but early next morning Lieutenant Haine led the remnants of "C" Company in a fresh attack on the strong-point, which was captured with 50 prisoners. "B" Company (under Lieutenant A. O. Pollard) now passed through "C" and established a post farther along the trench. The Germans soon attacked this post, but Lieutenant Pollard was personally an excellent bomber and reached the enemy with his bombs before they could reach him. He checked the attack and as they retreated he advanced, his men keeping him supplied with bombs. In this way he cleared no less than 300 yards of trench. As he advanced he posted men to man the trench, while "A" and "D" Companies spread out to occupy the increased front. Thus Pollard achieved the remarkable feat of capturing and holding a system of trenches which had held up the frontal attack of a whole brigade. For this he was awarded a V.C., and the same decoration was given to Lieutenant Haine for his gallant and finally successful assaults, against tremendous odds, on the strong-point which had dominated the situation.

When the Battalion was relieved it handed over more than 2,000 yards of captured trenches and marched out about 120 strong, the survivors of the desperate fighting of the last 48 hours.

The Battalion had a fairly quiet five-day tour in the Gavrelle trenches towards the end of May and later put in a night's digging in Oppy Wood. Then they were ordered back to G.H.Q. for guard duties at G.H.Q., with the view of supplying officers to replace the enormous casualties among the commissioned ranks of the army. In addition to training for commissions, it was decided that the H.A.C. should supply a nucleus of highly-trained demonstration platoons to assist in the training of other units. This was done and the H.A.C. demonstrated "The Platoon in Attack," "The Platoon in Defence," "March Discipline," "Fire Discipline" and the like, both in England and France, not only to formations of the British Army but to many units of the newly-arriving American forces.

During the great German offensive of March, 1918, the C.O. of the Battalion asked that the H.A.C. might be sent into the line, but this request was refused on the ground that the provision of officers was of too vital importance. But when the German drive had been checked and their armies were in retreat, the Battalion was ordered to join the 4th Guards Brigade in a specially mobile formation intended to support the Cavalry Corps in a break-through. The H.A.C. embarked in buses on 8th October to follow up the advance of the Fourth Army. At Belle Eglise the convoy was bombed, causing a number of casualties. But the enemy were fighting a stubborn rear-guard action and the cavalry could not advance against machine guns. The Battalion then returned to G.H.Q. and on 11th November came the news of the Armistice.

Both "A" and "B" Batteries marched out of Armoury House early in August, 1914, but were allotted to different formations for training. However, they both sailed from Avonmouth early in April, 1915, as part of the 2nd Mounted Division and disembarked at Alexandria. The Yeomanry regiments of the Division were sent (dismounted) to Gallipoli, but the Batteries were relegated to the defence of the Suez Canal, "A" at Kantara, "B" just north of Suez.

Towards the end of June news of a minor disaster outside Aden caused the hasty formation of a relief force which included "B" Battery, who embarked on 14th July on an exceptionally trying, though mercifully short, voyage, landing at Aden on the 19th. At Sheikh Othman, a village which had just been recaptured, the men suffered severely from heat, dust, flies, skin disease and a scanty supply of evil-smelling water, but the Battery saw action against a Turkish reconnaissance in force on 24th August, and two days later in an attack on a village 12 miles away.

Early in September "B" Battery was relieved and returned to Egypt. In December "A" Battery embarked at Alexandria for Mersa Matruh to join an expedition against the Senussi tribe, who were giving trouble and had cut the communications between Mersa and Egypt. One section was engaged in a spirited action near Bir Shola, checking enemy infantry at ranges as short as 1,000 yards under machine-gun fire. The Battery returned to Alexandria by road at the end of February, 1916.

Both Batteries had now sent a large number of men home for commissions and were busy training reinforcements. Also a School of Instruction was started at Zeitun for training candidates for commissions and giving "refresher" courses generally. The School was staffed entirely by H.A.C. officers for the first two years of its existence.

The Batteries, after spells at Mena Camp, near the Pyramids, were, to their bitter disappointment, sent back to the Canal Defences, "A" to Ayun Musa, south of Suez, "B" to Ballah. Here they remained champing at their bits for another summer, while more and more of their original personnel left for commissions.

In November, 1916, "A" Battery moved to Kabir and in February, 1917, to Ismailia, where it joined the 4th Brigade, Australian Light Horse, with which it served until the end of the war. Pedrails and extended draught bars for use in soft sand were fitted to the guns, and the Battery marched to Kantara, where the force for the invasion of Palestine was assembling. Meanwhile "B" Battery had remained at Ballah, missing both the disaster to their Yeomanry Brigade at Katia in April, 1916, and the subsequent victory of Romani in August. However, on 16th October, 1916, they advanced to Kantara and on across soft sand to Romani—a most exhausting march, during which it took seven hours to traverse 12 miles.

On 6th December, "B" Battery advanced to Bir el Mazon, and on 3rd January, 1917, marched with the 5th Mounted Brigade to El Arish, the Turks having retreated to Rafa. There about 2,400 Turkish infantry were strongly entrenched on a hill, but almost all were killed or captured in a spirited action on 8th January. "B" Battery was in the thick of this engagement, one of its sections advancing at a gallop across open plain and going into action in a sunken road within 2,000 yards of the enemy, from which the guns enfiladed the Turkish trenches, assisting materially in the success of the assault.

"A" Battery marched across the Sinai Desert to El Arish early in March, 1917, and joined "B," forming, with the Notts and Berks R.H.A., the artillery of the Imperial (later known as the Australian) Mounted Brigade. "A" supported the 4th Australian Mounted Brigade, "B" the 5th.

On 24th March, 1917, the army advanced to attack Gaza, an operation which resulted in complete disaster. Though our cavalry encircled the town and actually entered it from the north, the two infantry divisions failed and suffered severely in the frontal attack, and, owing to inadequate communications, a retreat was ordered when ultimate victory was still possible. A very disorganized retreat followed. "B" Battery fought and marched for 28 hours on end, at the end of which horses and men were equally dead-beat.

The second attempt on Gaza started at dawn on 19th April. "A" Battery was in action all day in support of their Brigade, heavily engaged in a holding attack, and finally withdrew under heavy fire when it was known that the main attack, over a bare glacis against strengthened defences, had failed. "B" Battery were in action with the 5th Brigade, who eventually found their flanks in the air, and "B" was called upon to cover their retirement while under concentrated fire from 5.9 howitzers. A third of the gunners were hit (by some miracle none fatally), but the guns continued to fire out of the smoke of bursting shells until ordered to retire, when guns and ammunition had to be man-handled to a wadi where the teams waited.

For some months the Batteries led an arduous life of constant movement on reconnaissance, patrol and outpost duties, or as escort to demolition parties, in waterless country and subject to continual harassing from Turkish guns and aeroplanes. Then came the attack on the enemy left flank at Beersheba. Both Batteries were in the force which, after forced marches aggregating 70 miles, launched a successful attack on 31st October. "B" Battery galloped into action under considerable fire to cover the attack on the entrenched hill of Tel el Saba, which was then rushed by New Zealanders. "A" Battery and the Notts R.H.A. galloped across the open to support the mounted charge of the 2nd Australian Light Horse, who, leaping the enemy trenches, carried the town.

Troops were then concentrated for the attack on Sharia and Hareira on 7th November, in which both Batteries took part, and next day the Cavalry Corps started in general pursuit of the beaten enemy across the Plain of Philistia. The Turks put up stubborn rear-guard actions and frequently our troops had to fight for water. On two occasions "B" Battery's horses went for 76 hours without a drink. Often a whole night was spent watering horses by canvas bucket from a deep well, of which the lifting gear had been destroyed, and sometimes a whole night was spent in an unavailing search for water.

Both Batteries were involved in stiff fighting when the Turks counter-attacked heavily near Balin on 12th November, some

"A" Battery, H.A.C., advancing from Sharia to Huj with Australian escort, November, 1917

of "B" Battery's guns being in action at a range of 300 yards. Next day, however, the advance was continued until the mounted divisions reached the line of the Jaffa–Jerusalem road where they remained until the infantry moved up and entered Jerusalem on 9th December. The Batteries had borne a full share of the fighting, marching and counter-marching in these operations, frequently under conditions of great hardship, and now underwent a period of bitter weather with incessant rain until the end of December, when they moved south of Gaza to rest and refit.

On 1st April, 1918, their division marched to Selmeh, near Jaffa, and then past Jerusalem to Jericho. The Turks had been driven out of the lower Jordan valley and a bridgehead had been established on the east bank of the river. It was now proposed to launch a raid in strength across the river to destroy a viaduct. The task of the Australian Mounted Division was to cross the river at midnight, march north for 15 miles, hold the ford and bridge at Jisr-el-Damieh, and capture Es Salt. However, the bridge proved to be too strongly held to be rushed, so the 4th

Brigade took up a position covering the bridge and remained there all next day, while other troops moved towards Es Salt. But the Turks had thrown a pontoon bridge over the Jordan farther north; over this a whole division passed and counter-attacked early on 1st May. The 4th Brigade, with "A" Battery and the Notts R.H.A., had taken up a position along a range of foothills, with impassable rocky ground in their rear. "B" Battery was in action farther south. A wave of 4,000 Turkish infantry came on in open order. The three Batteries opened fire and broke up the frontal attack, but bodies of the enemy started working round both flanks. "A" Battery was ordered to retire by sections through very broken ground. Six-horse teams were useless, so the wagons had to be abandoned and an attempt made to save the guns with 14- and 16-horse teams. One gun overturned in a steep wadi and had to be abandoned. The enemy were now within 400 yards and the leading gun-teams were mown down by machine-gun fire. Further progress was impossible; the remaining teams were unhooked and horses and men withdrew to cover. The Notts R.H.A. were also forced to abandon all their guns.

Meanwhile "B" Battery, who had sent all their spare men to help the hard-pressed front line, fired until their ammunition was almost exhausted and then retired by sub-sections under close-range rifle and machine-gun fire. One gun overturned crossing a steep ravine. A party of men tried to get it away, but Turks opened fire and killed nearly all the horses and the gun had to be abandoned. The other three guns of "B" withdrew safely and took up a position farther south. Support now arrived and the line held firm, repulsing three determined attacks. Next day the enemy renewed the pressure, but the line held, covering the retreat of the force which had taken Es Salt, but later had been forced to relinquish the town under heavy pressure. "B" Battery's three guns covered the whole front till nightfall, when the force withdrew through a brigade of infantry. Later a Court of Enquiry found that the Batteries were not to blame for the loss of their guns.

On 21st May, having received new guns, the Batteries took up positions in the Wadi Aujah and endured for two months the blazing heat, dust, snakes and scorpions of the Jordan valley in full summer at 1,200 feet below sea-level. The heat killed even the flies eventually. There was considerable artillery activity and the Batteries helped to repel a determined attack by Turks, supported by Germans, on 14th July. At the end of July the Division was relieved and both Batteries crossed the mountains to camp near Jaffa.

Preparations were now well in hand for the Great Drive. Each Battery sent up a section to the front line to register for the barrage and then remained in the shelter of olive trees and orange groves, in which the concentration of cavalry was well hidden. "B" Battery was then transferred to the 5th Cavalry Division, as there were only enough guns for two batteries for each division. On the night of 17th/18th September the guns moved into front-line positions near Arsuf, and at 4.30 a.m. on the 19th the barrage opened from 400 guns and five infantry divisions attacked across the 10 miles of coastal plain. The enemy were taken entirely by surprise and our infantry broke through with hardly a check, wheeling right and pinning the whole Turkish right wing against the hills, while behind them the cavalry swept through.

5th Cavalry Division, followed by "B" Battery, went first along the sea-shore, brushing aside slight opposition. The rest of the cavalry followed, fanning out behind the old Turkish line and giving the impression to the enemy that a landing on the coast had taken place. "A" Battery followed their brigade to Jericho, where 7,000 prisoners were taken, and on through Tiberias to the Jordan, where they met the first real opposition at the bridge of Benat Yacub, 80 miles from their starting point. The bridge had been demolished, but the Battery went into action and at dusk the cavalry forced a crossing. The guns forded the river and the advance proceeded, with considerable local opposition. At Kaukab, 10 miles from Damascus, about 2,500 Turks were entrenched. "A" opened fire at 2,400 yards. The Turks streamed out of their trenches as the shells crashed among them and two cavalry regiments charged with drawn swords, with the Battery firing over their heads till the last moment. It was a grand finish, for these were the last rounds fired during this war by the Battery.

On 2nd October the Battery took part in the ceremonial entry into Damascus. The Division then pushed on northwards, but at Homs the news of an armistice was received.

Meanwhile "B" Battery had followed the 5th Cavalry Division over Mount Carmel on to the Plain of Armageddon. It had taken part in the capture of Nazareth and then supported the 15th Cavalry Brigade's spirited actions which led to the taking of Haifa, firing their last rounds in action as the cavalry charged home. The last few days had witnessed the destruction of all enemy forces west of the Jordan; the cavalry had cut their lines of communication and in every defile the retreating Turks were bombed by the R.A.F. Across the Jordan the Turkish 2nd Corps had been cut off and surrendered at discretion, but were allowed to retain their arms for their own protection against massacre by our Arab allies. "B" Battery went on to Damascus, but the war had resolved itself into the collection of prisoners and their protection from the fury of the local populace. The Armistice found "B" Battery at Aleppo.

War Office authority for the raising of a 2nd Battalion was obtained before the end of August, 1914, and within a few days it was recruited over strength with magnificent material, on a nucleus of officers and men surplus to the 1st Battalion. Training in England was impeded by the frequent provision of heavy drafts to replace casualties in the 1st Battalion and by a constant drain of the best men to commissions in other units. Conversely the Battalion was strengthened by the posting from time to time of officers and men of the 1st Battalion on recovery from wounds or sickness. It formed the garrison of the Tower of London for six months in 1915, also providing the Bank of England Guard, and returned there to mobilize for service overseas in August, 1916. Even at that late hour nearly 300 men were transferred to the Artists Rifles for future commissions.

On 1st October, 1916, the Battalion marched out of the Tower for embarkation at Southampton, and soon found itself with the famous 7th Division in the line at Ploegsteert. Enemy trench mortars were active and the Battalion sustained its first casualties.

The Division then moved south to the Somme battlefields, and on 29th November the Battalion took over a sector of the line at Beaumont Hamel which consisted of a badly damaged German trench and an outpost line in shell-holes. The mud was knee deep in the trench and waist deep in the outpost line. Six men were killed and several wounded during the relief, but when in reserve the entire Battalion was accommodated in a vast dugout in the former German front line, complete with fitted bunks and electric light. Several tours of front-line duty followed under appalling conditions, and the casualty list mounted steadily.

On 15th January the Division was relieved, but went in again on 25th February on the news that the enemy were retiring. The Division followed up in face of stubborn rear-guard actions, and the 2nd H.A.C. made an unsuccessful attempt to carry Bucquoy. The Germans retired again, devastating the countryside completely, and our line advanced towards Ecoust. Here the Germans counter-attacked and captured an H.A.C. advanced post. Two attempts to recapture it failed in face of well-sited machine guns and the Battalion suffered nearly 200 casualties. The enemy were then thrust back to their main new defence line, resting here on the village of Bullecourt. After a short rest the Battalion moved up again, and on 3rd May the H.A.C. and 1st Royal Welsh Fusiliers were ordered to recapture Bullecourt, which had been won and lost again by another division.

The starting positions were being swept by shell fire, but the attack went in against concentrated machine-gun fire and through tangled wire. Two companies of H.A.C. reached their first objective and cleared a trench in hand-to-hand fighting, taking 50 prisoners, and the other two companies then passed through them, but found their right flank in the air through the enforced retreat of another unit. Eventually both the H.A.C. and the R.W.F. in the village were forced to withdraw to the trench first captured. Very heavy fighting continued and our supply of bombs failed. Finally the H.A.C. were ordered to withdraw, as two fresh battalions were about to attack. One of these was almost annihilated by shell fire on the starting-point; the other reached the enemy wire, but could make no progress. The 2nd H.A.C. then withdrew, having lost 11 officers, 6 of them killed, and well over 200 men.

One party of ten men under a Corporal was unable to withdraw from Bullecourt, but remained in a ruined house for three days and four nights, beating off all attacks and supplying themselves with ammunition, food and water from the dead. When the village was finally taken on 7th May by another brigade they were found there. All were awarded Military Medals.

The remnants of the Battalion (now only 250 strong) relieved another unit in front of Bullecourt on the night of 14th May and had just got into position when an enemy counter-attack developed. Pressure was severe but the attack was beaten off except on the left, where one company was almost annihilated and the Germans pushed a wedge into our lines. A counter-attack retrieved the situation, but the Battalion was now reduced to 4 officers and 94 other ranks.

During an all too short period of rest the Battalion was brought up to strength by drafts and went into the line again at Bullecourt from 25th June to 1st July, losing 2 officers and 7 men killed. Then came a tour of duty in support, while carrying parties and trench digging added more casualties, and then back to the line again. But on 8th August the Division was relieved and the H.A.C. went into training well behind the front. This had hardly commenced when the Division was ordered to the ill-omened Ypres Salient, where the long-drawn struggle for the Passchendaele Ridge was raging. Here the 2nd H.A.C. was to undergo another terrific ordeal, and on the night of 7th October the Battalion moved into the water-logged forward area in heavy rain, losing many men from shell fire on the way up. The barrage on our back areas was heavy and persistent. One fatigue party of 26 men sent back to bring up stores was wiped out except for one N.C.O.

On the early morning of the 9th the H.A.C. attacked and carried the village of Reutel, but at a cost of 8 officers killed and several wounded, 49 other ranks killed, 189 wounded and 42 missing (almost all later reported killed). Despite its losses the Battalion was sent up to the line again on 26th October, this time with the Royal Welsh Fusiliers to relieve two battalions which had been shattered in an attack that morning. The mud was worse than ever—waist deep in places—and the doomed battalions had been quite unable to keep up with the barrage, so were mown down by machine guns as they floundered through the morass. There was no line to take over, the relieving battalions having to search for the few survivors among the mass of waterlogged shell-holes. Through the night the H.A.C. were chiefly employed in rescuing wounded bogged in shell-holes. Forty or 50 of these were brought in. On the evening of the 28th the Battalion, which had suffered another 40 casualties from shells and snipers, was relieved.

After these experiences the order for the 7th Division to move to Italy came as a joyful relief, as nothing could be worse than Bullecourt and Passchendaele. The Battalion was brought up to strength by drafts from the 1st Battalion and entrained for Italy, passing through Genoa on 24th November. After a period of training, the Battalion took over a sector of the line at Nervesa on the River Piave—a great contrast to the Belgian front, with posts along a cliff and Battalion H.Q. in a farmhouse. Then came orders to return to France, cancelled at the last moment. Instead, after training for hill fighting near Padua, the Division moved to the Asiago mountains. Here action was mainly confined to patrolling, during which the H.A.C. inflicted many casualties on a party of Austrians at Stella Fort. Several tours of duty were carried out in this sector, during one of which a patrol from the Battalion was almost wiped out by machine-gun fire. There was also a raid, in which 29 of the enemy were killed and 2 captured for a loss of one killed and 15 wounded.

Then it became known that the Army in Italy was to attack. The 2nd H.A.C. moved to the banks of the Piave, sent out a reconnaissance party dressed in Italian uniforms, and was told that it had been assigned the difficult and honourable task of forcing a passage of the river in full flood, with the enemy strongly entrenched on the farther bank and on the small island of Papodopoli. Twelve flat-bottomed boats, manned by Italian watermen, were to be used to ferry over the assault parties after dark on 23rd October, 1918. The bayonet alone was to be used in the first assault.

The night was overcast and at first all went reasonably well. Two boats were swept downstream by the swirling torrent, but the remainder landed their first loads and the nearest Austrian defences were rushed with the bayonet. Then the alarm was given and within a few minutes a barrage fell on the beach, crowded with men embarking. The moon came out from behind clouds and machine guns opened fire on the boats and on the men wading ashore. But the embarkation proceeded and the force on the island advanced, with parties of Royal Welsh Fusiliers mopping up behind them. Nearly 300 prisoners were taken before the enemy fully recovered from his surprise and after brisk fighting the main objectives were secured. Next morning brought heavy shell fire on the captured positions.

Steady rain fell; the river rose and the main attack was postponed. However, supports and supplies were ferried across to the island during the night.

On the evening of the 25th the H.A.C., supported by the R.W.F., opened an attack on the remaining Austrian positions on the island, and early next morning the two battalions threw back counter-attacks from the north bank of the river after heavy fighting. The capture of the island was now complete and it became the jumping-off place for the general attack which swept the Austrians out of Italy. The enemy losses in the attack on Papodopoli included about 100 dead and 600 prisoners. Those of the H.A.C. were about 120, including one officer and 16 other ranks killed.

The Battalion was in action again on the banks of the Tagliamento, but on 4th November the Austrian request for an armistice was conceded and the war on this front was over. The 2nd H.A.C. formed part of the Army of Occupation, being stationed at Imst in the Austrian Tyrol, where it acquired a high reputation for its discipline and good behaviour.

Formed in November, 1916, the 309th (H.A.C.) Siege Battery landed in France on 26th April, 1917, and early in May went into action among the ruins of Ypres in solid established gun-pits which withstood several direct hits from 5.9 shells. From 10th May onwards the Battery took part in the artillery preparation for the attack on the Wytschaete–Messines Ridge, that model example of a successful attack on a limited objective.

After this initial victory the Battery moved out of Ypres to the Château des Trois Tours and prepared a new, well-camouflaged position, whence they put in steady and prolonged firing in preparation for the next offensive. The firing was not all on our side, however. On 15th July the enemy put 200 rounds into 309's position and knocked out one gun.

At 3.50 a.m. on 31st July the greatest cannonade hitherto known commenced and at first the attack went well enough. But the weather broke and rain fell day after day. The guns moved forward and 309 had eight days of steady shooting at Essex Farm and then moved forward again to a position among shell-holes and waterlogged trenches at Burnt Farm. Langemarck was captured on 16th August and 309 advanced to Turco Farm on the lower slopes of Pilckem Ridge, where for two months the Battery was employed in counter-battery work, while casualties from the enemy's return fire mounted steadily. After four months in action the Battery was given a four-day rest behind the line.

After the capture of Poelcappelle on 4th October the Battery moved up again some 1,200 yards into a morass of mud and fired heavily and continuously, especially for the attack on 26th October, on which day the guns were in action continuously from 5.45 a.m. till nightfall.

Early in November the Battery tried to prepare another position about a mile farther forward, but the working parties were driven off by shell fire day after day, and the ground was so cut up by craters that it was finally abandoned. Another spot was selected across the Steenbeke to which the guns were finally drawn by teams of heavy horses from 60-pounder batteries, as tractors were useless in the swampy ground, the gunners man-handling the guns for the last 200 yards across shell-holes. The first time the Battery opened fire from this position (28th November), the enemy replied with a salvo round the guns, followed by a heavy bombardment for fifty minutes. This treatment was repeated every two days. Still the Battery carried out the usual harassing fire and supported a futile attack on the night of 1st December. On 21st December 309 was relieved, after eight months of continuous service in the Passchendaele offensive.

After a period spent in digging rear positions in the Ypres sector (which came in useful next spring) 309 was transferred to the Fifth Army, being reinforced by an additional section of two guns.

When the great German counter-offensive broke on 21st March, 1918, 309 Siege were hurried to the Somme front, which they found in a state of considerable flux. After receiving orders to take up positions in several villages already in German hands, the Battery retired across the Somme at Cappy and went into action at Curlu Corner. All through their second night without sleep the gunners toiled at getting the guns into action and at dawn opened fire, while tanks in retreat clattered past and columns of very weary infantry plodded forward. Orders for retreat came at 10.30, and that day the Battery occupied four successive positions, firing steadily through the next night from the last, at Bronfay Farm on the Maricourt–Bray road.

All next day the guns fired and at night made a quick get-away just in time, going into action again at Laviéille. But the retreat was now over and the Fifth Army was holding the line of the River Ancre. Artillery on both sides was still very active, and 309 had casualties almost every day.

Early in April the Battery was sent to Bonnay to help stem the expected enemy attack on Villers Bretonneux. This materialized on the 24th after a violent bombardment in which 309 sustained casualties from shells and gas. The Germans carried the village, but it was retaken by Australians the same evening, the heavy artillery receiving especial praise for their barrage work. After this the Battery returned to its old Brigade, the 47th.

309 supported the capture of Ville-sur-Ancre by Australians on 19th May and of Hamel on 4th July.

"At 4.20 a.m. on 8th August," wrote Earl Haig, "our massed artillery opened intense fire on the whole front of attack, completely crushing the enemy's batteries, some of which never succeeded in coming into action." This was the prelude to the great British attack which ended the war in three months, and from this time onwards 309 was on the move almost daily, their 6-inch howitzers doing the work of field guns as the German line reeled back. Buire, Dernancourt, Méaulte, Fricourt, Carnoy, Maurepas, Forêt, the Drocourt-Quéant Switch, Bouchavesnes, Moislains, Templeux le Fosse—all these places saw 309 in action in support of our ceaseless attacks.

Then the Germans stood fast at Epéhy and repelled repeated attacks. The Battery was in action near Villers Faucon and came in for considerable enemy attention, suffering a number of casualties, until on 18th September Epéhy was taken and the line moved forward again. The enemy was now in the main Hindenburg Line and the guns were in action at Ste Emilie for nearly a fortnight, firing over 2,000 rounds at trenches and strong-points which were later found to have been completely obliterated. 309 co-operated in attacks on 3rd, 5th and 8th October which carried the Hindenburg Line and crossed the River Scheldt, and then the German retreat became so rapid that a minimum of heavy artillery could be employed in the pursuit. The Battery therefore had a short rest and then advanced again to take part in the attacks on Le Cateau on 17th and 18th October. The guns were in action in Le Cateau itself for another attack early on 23rd October and came under heavy fire from heavy and light artillery and even from machine guns. This was the Battle of the Selle, which the Siege Battery was thus instrumental in placing on the Colours of the Company, together with those of "Amiens", "Albert, 1918", "Somme, 1918", "Bapaume, 1918", "Epéhy", and "Cambrai, 1918", in all of which 309, alone of the units of the Regiment, had taken part.

The guns advanced again and on 4th November the Battery took part in its last action, putting up a creeping barrage over the great Forest of Mormal.

During its eighteen months of active service, the H.A.C. Siege Battery lost 32 killed or died of wounds and 70 wounded out of an establishment of 140.

"2/A" and "2/B" Batteries were formed at Headquarters in September, 1914, on a nucleus of officers and N.C.Os. from the reserve and first-line units. Both Batteries were speedily recruited to full strength from the waiting list and started training on obsolete guns (including those used by the H.A.C. Battery in South Africa).

The Batteries separated and continued training in various parts of England and Scotland for over two and a half years, but came together, re-armed with 18-pounders, as part of 126 Army Field Brigade in May, 1917. During their training period the Batteries had suffered repeated loss of N.C.Os. and men who, restless at being kept at home so long, applied for and obtained commissions. In fact, by the time the Batteries went overseas each had sent nearly twice its original strength for commissions in other units.

126 Brigade sailed for France on 22nd June, 1917, and arrived in the Ypres Salient in time for the great attack of 31st July, which was to have carried the ill-fated Passchendaele Ridge. After a period of attachment to batteries in the line and the usual routine of digging fatigues, "2/A" and "2/B" took over positions in what had been "No man's land" before the attack, in the area of Admiral's Road. The weather had broken badly and the ground was one expanse of water-logged shell-holes. Roads were non-existent and for a time rations and ammunition had to be brought up by pack-horses. The one redeeming feature of this position was the presence of German concrete dugouts for accommodation and shelter from the persistent shelling.

The guns were employed in nightly tasks of harassing fire, averaging 600 rounds per battery per night. On the early morning of 20th September they fired the preliminary barrage for an infantry attack—4 rounds per gun per minute for many hours—in conjunction with countless other batteries on either hand. Limited objectives were gained and for the next few days the guns dealt with persistent counter-attacks, as many as eleven in one day, and with enemy concentrations, which were often broken up before the attack could be launched. Another short advance on 26th September was preceded by the usual intensive bombardment and resulted in a further gain of shell-torn, water-logged ground. Then the guns were ordered forward and new positions were found, "2/A" at the apex of the triangle on the St. Julien–Poelcappelle road, "2/B" on the Steenbeke. The Batteries pulled in on the night of 3rd October (in a south-westerly gale and a downpour of rain). The sites chosen were merely the least swamp-like patches in the general morass; flash cover was non-existent; and it was impossible to dig dugouts or shelter trenches, as any depression filled immediately with water. Casualties were mounting up. "2/A" had already had two Battery Commanders severely wounded.

The time chosen for the attack on the following morning happened to be that at which the enemy had also arranged to attack. So just before our opening barrage was timed to begin the guns came under heavy and continuous shell and machine-gun fire. In a few minutes every gun detachment in "2/A" had sustained casualties; "2/B" were later reduced in some cases to one man per gun. German prisoners began to trickle back in in small unescorted groups and one German N.C.O. organized stretcher parties and assisted in carrying "2/B's" wounded to the dressing station. However, the requisite barrage was fired in spite of everything, and this attack succeeded in gaining a foot-hold on the main ridge. Over 5,000 prisoners were taken.

The weather now became even worse, but every day barrages had to be fired and night harassing fire went on as usual. Ammunition supply became a nightmare. The ground near the guns being impassable, even for mules, hundreds of rounds had to be dumped at the side of the nearest road by night by drivers running the gauntlet of the nightly barrage. Then the gunners salved such as had not been blown up or buried by shell fire, and manhandled it on a light railway to the gun positions. All this activity took place under a practically continuous dispersed barrage, for the enemy, having lost his observation posts on the high ground, resorted to a perpetual harassing fire of all calibres distributed over the entire battery area, as well as on all roads and tracks. Also he was retiring on his ammunition dumps and anxious to use them up before they fell into our hands.

Another attack launched on 9th October resulted in some further gain, and the Batteries were filled with pride on learning that the 2nd H.A.C. of the 7th Division had captured and held the non-existent village of Reutel, though at heavy cost. Again on the 12th our infantry attacked. This time the Batteries were called upon to fire an especially long and complicated barrage, starting at a range of 2,700 yards and going up to 5,650, with 52 "lifts," lasting nine hours. It was opened in heavy, driving rain, and the enemy countered with a heavy barrage of gas shell. The attack was largely "bogged down" in impassable ground, but some little progress was made.

The persistent wet weather now made it impossible even to hope for a break-through. The army could only have advanced with the greatest difficulty if the Germans had gone home, for the battlefield was one vast morass—an unending series of huge, intersecting craters filled with liquid mud, around the rims of which occasional greasy duckboard tracks meandered crazily. Attacking infantry struggled forward knee deep or more; sometimes the wounded drowned where they fell before the devoted stretcher-bearers could reach them. The survivors perhaps reached their first objectives, only to encounter such concentrated shell fire that supplies could not reach them, and the survivors would crawl back to their starting point. Still the Higher Command, from their distant château, ordered attack after attack, and division after division went into the line, lost half its effective strength in a few days, and was relieved.

The Gunners, though they were not called upon to face machine guns in an attack, had perhaps more than their share of the shelling. Never before had the Boche devoted such a heavy proportion of his fire to counter-battery work. Living conditions for the artillery were almost as bad as those for the infantry in front, and furthermore they were kept in the line for weeks and even months on end. The gun line lived under a perpetual barrage, while the drivers faced nightly the menace of the shell-swept roads and tracks.

"2/A" and "2/B" were relieved for ten days in October, but on the 28th returned to the battle. "2/A" took over a position near Langemarck—a two-hour walk by duckboard from the nearest practicable road. Here four of the six guns had been knocked out and the single officer and three men remaining of the battery to be relieved were in a dazed state after a particularly severe shelling. "2/B" were on what had been the Langemarck–Keerslaare road, only twenty-five minutes' walk by duckboard from a passable track. Conditions were so severe— the gun detachments had to be issued with waist-high rubber waders—that it became necessary to combine several batteries and organize a system of frequent reliefs at the gun-lines, while the remaining personnel recuperated in the comparative comfort of the wagon-lines. However, night firing continued, ammunition arriving by pack-horse, and barrages were fired in support of operations on 30th October and 6th November, the latter resulting in the capture of Passchendæle village by Canadians.

The guns were then moved up again into the devastation which had been Poelcappelle and later to Voorst Farm. But the battle was dying down, though harassing fire continued on both sides. On the evening of Christmas Day both batteries pulled out into rear positions and the men were employed in fatigues and the relief of other batteries until 27th January, when they left the Salient for a well-earned rest.

The great German offensive of 21st March, 1918, found the Batteries in reserve near Bethune behind the Portuguese. The Brigade moved south and then north, and went into action in the Loos sector. Here on 6th April, "2/A" was subjected to a very severe bombardment by gas shell lasting seven days. Four officers and 80 other ranks had to go to hospital with gas poisoning, of whom three died. Rear positions were now being prepared in anticipation of a German attack which never materialized in this sector. "2/B" had a forward gun in Loos which caused the Germans much annoyance at the expense of some casualties among drivers taking up ammunition. "2/B" was then swept by an influenza epidemic, among those who died being their Battery Commander.

Early in July the Batteries changed positions with another

brigade and found themselves in a quiet spot in Maroc, but the wagon lines at Boyelles were much harassed by night bombing. In August the Batteries went into action in open ground in the Tilloy area in front of Arras, where dozens of batteries were dug in at 15-yard intervals all along the valley, 1,000 yards behind the front line of the Canadian Corps. On 26th August the barrage opened and the Canadians attacked, capturing Orange Hill and Monchy-le-Preux. The guns at once advanced. Day after day the attack continued, the infantry pressing forward and the guns following—in some cases they were in action only 600 yards behind the front line. 1st September found the Batteries at Vis-en-Artois, where two officers of "2/A" and one of "2/B" were killed, and two more officers and several men wounded.

At 5.30 the next morning the barrage opened for the great attack which broke the Drocourt-Quéant Line, one of the most successful actions of the war, the enemy being forced into precipitate retreat from this elaborate system of trenches and strong-points over a front of 33 miles.

126 Brigade now went into action north-west of Dury, firing north-east, where the enemy were putting up a stubborn resistance. German counter-battery fire and night bombing were severe, and on the 9th "2/B" wagon lines were badly shelled, 6 men and 40 horses being killed and a number of drivers wounded. On the following day both Batteries moved to positions near Pelves, from which they supported several attacks, the last of which carried part of the amazing system of defences known as the Hindenburg Switch. The Batteries now crossed the Scarpe. "2/A" cut wire for an attack on the 7th and supported another attack on the 10th. By this time the enemy were retreating so fast that formidable positions were occupied without resistance. The gunners next underwent the exhilarating experience of following up the swiftly retreating enemy. Soon the devastated area was left behind and the troops were gladdened by the sight of clean country and unharmed villages, and gratified by the eager hospitality of the remaining population. Positions were occupied, only to be abandoned before a shot had been fired. A few hundred rounds were fired by "2/A" at Ommaing and by "2/B" near Quarouble on 6th November, and on the following morning barrages were fired at extreme range to cover an attack by Canadians—the last

rounds to be fired in action. Both Batteries advanced slowly along congested roads, much impeded by demolitions and craters, and were in action near Mons and waiting to open fire on the morning of 11th November when the Armistice came into force and the Batteries had the proud experience of taking part in the triumphal entry into Mons.

In addition to the services enumerated above, over four thousand members of the Company were given commissions in various fighting units. Honours and decorations won by members of the Company in the War of 1914-18 included 3 V.Cs., 3 C.Bs., 6 C.M.Gs., 46 D.S.Os., 23 O.B.Es., 17 M.B.Es., 2 D.S.Cs., 459 M.Cs., 10 D.F.Cs., 5 A.F.Cs., 25 D.C.Ms., 129 M.Ms., and 60 foreign decorations. The names of 1,600 members are recorded on the Roll of Honour.

CHAPTER XIV

1919 TO 1939

WHEN the question of battle honours for the Great War came to be considered, the Company found itself in a unique position. It is well known that the Royal Artillery carries no battle honours, its service in every theatre of war for well over two hundred years being covered by the word "Ubique." But here were five batteries not wearing the "Ubique" badge and not units of the Royal Regiment, but very definitely part and parcel of a much older corps, the Honourable Artillery Company. It was therefore suggested that these batteries should be considered eligible for the award of battle honours, to be borne, with those gained by the infantry, on Colours which, it was submitted, were those of the Company, not merely of the Infantry Battalion. The War Office, aghast at such an unprecedented request, boggled for a time, and suggested, as an alternative, that the batteries of the Company should be allowed to wear the "Ubique." This honour was declined; and eventually the Company carried its point, and its batteries now possess the distinction, unique in this country at that time, of eligibility to win and bear distinctive battle honours.

The honours awarded to the Company for the Great War were as follows:

THE GREAT WAR—3 Infantry Battalions and 7 Batteries of Artillery.

"Ypres, 1915, '17," **"Somme, 1916, '18,"** "Ancre Heights," **"Ancre, 1916,"** **"Arras, 1917, '18,"** "Scarpe, 1917, '18," "Arleux," **"Bullecourt,"** "Pilckem," "Polygon Wood," "Broodseinde," "Poelcappelle," **"Passchendaele,"** "Amiens," "Albert, 1918," "Bapaume, 1918," "Drocourt-Quéant," "Hindenburg Line," "Epéhy," "St. Quentin Canal," "Cambrai, 1918," "Selle," "Sambre," **"France and Flanders, 1914-1918,"** "Piave," **"Vittorio Veneto,"** "Italy, 1917-18," "Rafah," "Egypt, 1915-17," **"Gaza,"** "El Mughar," **"Jerusalem,"** "Jordan," "Megiddo," "Sharon," "Damascus," "Palestine, 1917-18," "Aden."

[The battle honours selected to be borne on Colours are printed in heavy type.]

In 1919 Lord Denbigh suggested to the Authorities the formation of an H.A.C. Division of Special Constabulary. About 150 members joined and soon won the particular praise of the Police authorities for smartness and efficiency.

In 1922 "A" and "B" Batteries, H.A.C., were brigaded with the City of London Yeomanry Battery as the 11th (H.A.C. and City of London Yeomanry) Brigade, R.H.A., T.A. The Infantry at the same time became the senior battalion of the 2nd London Infantry Brigade of the 56th London Division. In this year the Battalion took part in a parade of Territorial Infantry on Horse Guards parade ground and received the King's Colour of the 2nd Battalion, H.A.C., which now hangs in Armoury House. The whole Regiment took part in a Royal Review of London Territorials in Hyde Park on 22nd June, taking the right of the line and leading the march past according to ancient custom.

On 4th July in this year H.R.H. The Duke of Connaught unveiled the War Memorial to the Fallen in the War of 1914-18, a stained glass window embodying the figure of St. George and the Company's coat of arms, on the great staircase in Armoury House, with a Roll of Honour in a vellum book in an oaken recess below.

As part of the economy campaign which swept through the Army in 1924, the small detachment of Royal Artillery which almost from time immemorial had been stationed at the Tower of London was abolished, and it was decided that the Artillery Division of the H.A.C. should take over the duties of firing salutes from the Tower guns. This was done for the first time on 6th May of that year. Then, in 1931, the Tower authorities proposed to revive the ancient appointment of Master Gunner of the Tower, but, this suggestion meeting with disapproval from high Army authorities, the Constable of the Tower asserted his prerogative of supreme command, under the King, in his own domain, and appointed the senior artillery officer of the H.A.C. to the post of "Master Gunner *Within* The Tower." This appointment has since been held in rotation by senior officers of the Artillery Division of the Company.

Early in 1925 sanction was given by the Court of Assistants for the formation of a Company of Pikemen for purposes of regimental pageantry. They were to be dressed in the uniform of 1641 (the year in which the Company took over the present

H.A.C. ARTILLERY FIRING SALUTE AT THE TOWER OF LONDON

Ground) and exercised in the "postures of the pike" and other drill of the period. It was originally envisaged that they should take part in regimental pageants and attend as guards of honour on suitable occasions at Armoury House. Since then, however, in addition to the above activities, it has become customary for this body, to which a number of musketeers were added a few years later, to attend as a bodyguard to the Lord Mayor in the procession and at the Guildhall banquet on Lord Mayor's Day each year, and on other ceremonial occasions.

Under the Law of Property Act, 1922, as amended in 1924, the Company's lease from the Corporation of London of the western half of the Ground, which had been renewable every fourteen years in perpetuity, became a lease for 2,000 years. The commutation of the fine of £100 payable by the Company for each renewal, together with compensation to the Corporation for the loss of the possible right of re-entry on the Company's problematical failure to renew the lease, was amicably settled in conference with the City Lands Committee of the Corporation.

Considerable activity prevailed at Headquarters during the General Strike of 1926. A half battalion of Scots Guards was encamped in the Ground; the active list of the Company provided day and night guards; and the Special Constabulary, rapidly expanding from about 150 to 600 strong, were constantly on duty "maintaining tranquillity."

Since 1889 the appointment of Regimental Adjutant had always been held by an officer of the Royal Artillery, who was *ipso facto* responsible for the training of the Infantry Battalion. In the reorganization of 1921 the Batteries had become part of the 11th Brigade, R.H.A., which formation had an Adjutant responsible for the training of the R.H.A. batteries, while the Regimental Adjutant administered the Batteries and trained and administered the Battalion. In December, 1927, an Infantry Adjutant was appointed from the Brigade of Guards, the Artillery Adjutant becoming Adjutant of the Artillery Brigade. The senior of the two acted as Regimental Adjutant.

The Company had possessed a shooting pavilion at Bisley for over twenty years. The original wooden building was now found to be unequal to the requirements of the Regiment. Wherefore a new lease of the ground, with some additional space, was obtained from the National Rifle Association, and a new "Bisley Hut" in solid oak-framed Tudor style was erected at a cost of over £4,000, which was raised by subscription among members.

On 25th June, 1928, at a parade in the Artillery Ground, the Prince of Wales presented new Colours bearing the battle honours won in the Great War of 1914-18. After the Trooping of the new Colours His Royal Highness attended a specially summoned meeting of the Court, became a member of the Company, and signed the Vellum Book. This occasion was the subject of a painting by Gilbert Holiday which now hangs in Armoury House.

Following a precedent established in 1906, and in view of a special connection between the City of London and a distinguished regiment which traces its origin to the old Trained Bands of London, the use of the Ground was granted in July, 1928, to the 2nd Battalion of The Buffs on the occasion of the presentation of new Colours by the Lord Mayor of London. After the ceremony the officers and sergeants of The Buffs were suitably entertained in Armoury House.

Blue caps were now authorized for wear with khaki service

dress on ceremonial occasions both by the Artillery and Infantry of the Company and white belts by the Infantry. They were worn for the first time on 9th November, 1928, in the Lord Mayor's Procession.

The lease of the eastern half of the Artillery Ground, including the site of Armoury House, was due to expire in 1954. In 1930, however, after negotiations initiated by the Lieutenancy of London, the Ecclesiastical Commissioners offered a new lease of 80 years, at the same rent but with a fine of £20,000, of which the Company's share was £6,666 13s. 4d. After obtaining legal advice, the Company accepted the new lease on these terms.

In 1931 the Company's right for its members to wear the special regimental ribbon (granted by King Edward VII) with the Territorial Efficiency Decoration (T.D.) and the Territorial Efficiency Medal was confirmed by War Office Letter of 25-3-31, 68/Gen/5455 (A.G.4. Medals).

The Regiment was invited by the Royal Artillery to take part in a Tattoo at Woolwich in July, 1932. The idea was received with enthusiasm, and detachments, including both active list and veterans, gave displays illustrative of the long history of the Company.

After having commanded the Regiment for forty years, including the most eventful period in its long history, Colonel The Earl of Denbigh and Desmond resigned the appointment of Colonel-Commandant in 1933 and was shortly afterwards elected Vice-President of the Company. Colonel The Viscount Galway, D.S.O., O.B.E., who had recently commanded the Life Guards, was appointed Colonel-Commandant.

A new departure in military training was inaugurated in the spring of 1934, when some sixty officers and other ranks took part in a week-end tour of northern France to study on the ground certain actions of the 1914-18 war, the phases of which were explained in detail by members of the Staff and in some cases by officers who had taken part in these battles. The students were then formed into syndicates and asked to formulate the decisions they would have made in similar circumstances. This highly popular and interesting method of training became an annual feature.

For several years both Batteries of the Regiment had entered for the King's Cup Competition for batteries of Territorial Artillery in an exercise illustrative of "fire and movement."

For some years the Company failed to achieve the chief honours, though "A" Battery won the Prince of Wales's Cup as runner-up in 1929. At last, in September, 1934, "B" Battery were successful and brought home this coveted trophy. They were the only horsed battery in the finals. In 1938 both Batteries were mechanized.

For many years, both before and after the war of 1914-18, the Company was well to the fore in various rifle shooting (and machine-gun) competitions among all units, Regular and Territorial, in the London District, especially in the yearly competition for the "Daily Telegraph" Cup, which originally involved a forced march of 11 miles, followed by firing on the Pirbright ranges. The Regiment had won this trophy in 1910, 1911, 1914, 1922, 1923, 1924, 1927, and 1928. In 1929 the conditions were altered to correspond more closely with modern conditions of warfare and the competition became a rapid advance over a comparatively short course, followed by fire and movement with rifles and Lewis guns. The Company won again in 1930, but in 1935 it was decided that the segregation of a number of the keenest and most efficient members of the Battalion for the period of training was not in the best interests of the efficiency of the Battalion as a whole and, in consequence, the Company did not enter a team. Meanwhile the Regiment had won the Dewar Machine-Gun Trophy several times, and also made a habit of annexing a very fair percentage of the trophies in the divisional and decentralized competitions.

For some time the insufficiency of accommodation in Armoury House for the military needs of the Company had been acutely felt. In particular the miniature range in the Drill Hall was wholly unsatisfactory and inadequate; there was a sad shortage of lecture rooms, offices and stores; and the dressing rooms were seriously overcrowded.

In the summer of 1933 the church of St. Paul in the northwest corner of the Ground had been condemned as unsafe and demolished. After protracted negotiations the War Department acquired a lease of the site of the church and of the adjoining vicarage. Building operations were started. The old vicarage was adapted as store-rooms, offices and the like, while on the site of the church arose a new building, the ground floor of which was a gun-park, the basement a miniature range, and the upper floors a series of lecture rooms, two of which were made capable of being used as squash racket courts by the application of money from the Denbigh Memorial Fund. A tablet recording Lord Denbigh's long service as Colonel-Commandant was affixed to the wall outside the squash courts.

In February, 1935, the Colonel-Commandant, Lord Galway, was appointed Governor-General of New Zealand and left to take up this important appointment. He was succeeded in the command by Colonel The Earl Fortescue, M.C., formerly of The Scots Greys, and more recently Colonel of the Royal Devon Yeomanry.

At the Silver Jubilee of King George V the Company, in conformity with its ancient privilege, provided a guard of honour when the King visited St. Paul's Cathedral for the Thanksgiving Service on 6th May, 1935. Detachments of the Artillery Division lined the steps of St. Paul's and the churchyard. The remainder of the Battalion lined the upper part of Ludgate Hill.

In late May and early June of 1935 a Tower of London Pageant was held in the Tower Moat under the ægis of the Tower Hill Improvement Committee. The Court of Assistants complied with this Committee's request that the Secretary of the Regiment might be permitted to act as honorary producer of this pageant, which was an ambitious effort, involving an expenditure of well over £20,000 and the attendance nightly of over 2,000 unpaid performers. The active list of the Company were unluckily in camp at the time, but some hundred veteran members took part and reproduced, among other episodes, a representation of the historical pageant "Mars, His Triumph," originally performed by members of the Company before the Lord Mayor and City Corporation in 1638. In spite of the expense and not too clement weather, a substantial sum was handed over for Tower Hill Improvements.

On 6th July, 1935, the Duke of Gloucester reviewed the Regiment in the Artillery Ground. After the Inspection and the Trooping the Colour, His Royal Highness honoured the Company by becoming a member in due form.

A regimental unit of the Royal Defence Corps had been formed in 1934. This Royal Defence Corps was now replaced by National Defence Companies, T.A., linked with units of the Territorial Army. It was laid down that the role of the N.D.C. would be to protect important points in Great Britain on the threat of, or during, war. The personnel were to consist of ex-members of H.M.'s Forces between the ages of 45 and 60, or under 45 if unfit for more active service. The regimental unit was recruited from veteran members to a strength of 80 of all ranks.

On the death in 1936 of King George V (whose memory was perpetuated by a full-length portrait by St. Helier Lander—subscribed for by members—of His Majesty in Garter robes) King Edward VIII assumed the title of Captain-General and Colonel of the Company. It was decided, however, to make representations that His Majesty might wish to bear the more ancient title of "Captain-General" only. This had been borne by successive Royal Commanders from James, Duke of York (afterwards James II) to William IV. Then, when the Duke of Sussex succeeded William IV, being already Colonel of the Regiment, he added the title of Captain-General to the rank he already held. Later another Colonel was appointed and there was therefore no reason for the Captain-General to retain the dual rank. As a result of the representations from the Company, King Edward was pleased to relinquish the designation of Captain-General and Colonel, and to assume the title of Captain-General. This same title was assumed by King George VI after his accession in December, 1936.

To mark its 400th anniversary in 1937 the Company was asked to produce the central pageant for the Royal Tournament at Olympia. This took the form of a representation, as far as the limits of the arena would allow, of a regimental field day in 1829, the last year in which the H.A.C. wore its own distinctive uniform. The Artillery Division, Grenadiers, Light Infantry Battalion and Rifle Companies were represented, and some members, mostly from the active list, devoted themselves to the intricacies of period drill, including the loading and firing of Brown Bess muskets and brass muzzle-loading cannon. Great pains were taken to ensure correctness in dress and equipment. The Colours carried were replicas of those of the period and even buttons were faithfully copied from the originals. At the actual performances the troops went through a series of highly complicated evolutions with admirable steadiness and precision. The King is reported to have expressed the opinion that it was the best turned-out display of the kind he had ever seen.

The regimental celebrations of the 400th anniversary of the Charter, which were attended by a strong delegation of the

Ancient and Honourable Artillery Company of Boston, included a Regimental Ball at Armoury House, a Garden Party and Pageant, also at Headquarters, a Church Parade at St. Paul's Cathedral, a Regimental Banquet at Grosvenor House, attended by the Duke of Gloucester and a very distinguished assembly, a return banquet given by the A. & H.A.C. at the Mayfair Hotel, a most lavish reception by the City of London at Guildhall, and culminated in a Review of the Regiment by His Majesty The King in the Artillery Ground. The "Ancients" presented to the Company an oil painting representing their first muster on Boston Common in 1638.

1937 was also marked by the affiliation to the Regiment of the Transvaal Horse Artillery, a unit of the Defence Forces of South Africa of very similar standing to the H.A.C. Following on the official announcement, members of the T.H.A. visiting England for the Coronation were entertained at Armoury House, and members of the Company resident in South Africa have since maintained close touch with the Regimental Headquarters of the T.H.A. at Auckland Park, Johannesburg.

Despite vigorous protests, the Company has suffered grave disappointments in departures from precedent on official excuses of expediency as to its representation and position at Coronation ceremonies since the spacious days of King George IV, King William IV, Queen Victoria, and King Edward VII, when the Battalion had the honour of parading in full strength and was stationed next to the Foot Guards in Parliament Square. At the Coronation of King George V, however, the Company was deprived of its traditional position next to the Guards in Parliament Street and was stationed between Whitehall and the Admiralty Arch. At the Coronation of King George VI the Regiment was indeed represented in the Royal Procession by detachments of the Batteries in full pre-war dress, but the Battalion was allowed only one officer and three other ranks, who marched, for some inexplicable reason, in the *rear* of the London Division of the Territorial Army. Another party of two officers and 25 other ranks, with the King's Colour, helped to line the street at the junction of the Embankment and Northumberland Avenue. In addition the Saluting Party from the Batteries duly shot off 62 guns at the Tower of London.

Following the adoption by the Company at this time of an officer-producing role, it was decided in very high quarters that it was desirable that the democratic custom of the Regiment—a relic of the days when officers were elected annually by the votes of members—under which all ranks intermingled, drank and dined together when off parade, should be modified to some extent by the formation of an Officers' Mess, a thing hitherto unheard of except in camp or on active service, though for a good many years regimental officers had had the sole use of an officers' ante-room (and made very little use of it). The duty of enforcing these orders fell on Lord Fortescue, who invited the support of the Court of Assistants, setting forth the reasons of the military authorities for the innovation.

Two rooms on the ground floor (including the former officers' ante-room) were therefore set aside as an Officers' Mess and ante-room. All members, active or veteran, who had held commissions were eligible for membership of the Mess. The new departure met with considerable disapproval from sections of the Company, not least among some of the officers. But it was an order and it was obeyed.

The 300th anniversary of the foundation of the Ancient and Honorable Artillery Company of Massachusetts was celebrated in 1938 and a delegation 84 strong, representing all units of the parent Company, proceeded to Boston for the occasion. On the eve of sailing the officer in command of the delegation and the senior veteran officer had the honour of being received at Buckingham Palace by His Majesty.

The delegation disembarked at Quebec, where they were welcomed by representatives of the A. & H.A.C. and the Mayor of Boston, and were entertained by the military authorities and the Royal 22nd Regiment of Canadian Permanent Militia. At Montreal they were the guests of the Canadian Grenadier Guards and the Queen Victoria Rifles of Canada. Crossing the border into New Hampshire, they were met by the Governor of that State, hospitably entertained and taken by road through the White Mountains to Swampscott, Mass., where the main body of the Ancients were waiting to receive them with their well-known hospitality.

On the following morning the delegation donned their uniforms (blue undress) and made their formal entry into Boston, escorted by a strong turn-out of the A. & H.A.C., and, headed by several bands, including a pipe band, marched to Faneuil Hall for the official reception by the Ancients. Later the party were received by the Governor of Massachusetts at the State House and by the Mayor of Boston at the Town Hall. That evening there was a resplendent military ball at the Armoury of the First Corps of Cadets.

The next day was devoted to a visit to Plymouth, Mass., where the party inspected the Pilgrims' Memorial and sat down to a "clam bake," afterwards viewing the original Plymouth Rock, alleged to be the exact spot where the Pilgrim Fathers landed. On the way home there was a tea party at Cohasset which will be remembered by members of the delegation for the amazing pulchritude of the young ladies who had been gathered to help entertain them. That evening there was a banquet given by the Governor of Massachusetts.

The 6th June was the actual 300th Anniversary. After lunch at Faneuil Hall the delegation joined the procession of many units and marched to the Old South Church for the usual service and then on to Boston Common. Here the time-honoured ceremony of the Drumhead Election took place and the new Commanding Officer was installed. The senior officers then planted a young oak tree from Windsor Park, presented by the King, and the procession moved to the Copley Plaza Hotel for the Anniversary Banquet.

On the following day the party visited Newport, Rhode Island, where, after a route march round the town, they lunched, and then left for New York, where several days were spent in sightseeing, including a visit to West Point Academy, where a parade of 2,000 cadets provided an inspiring spectacle.

As some little acknowledgment of the most lavish hospitality they had received, the delegation left with the Ancients a silver statuette representing their founder, Robert Keayne, in the uniform of the Company of 1623 (the date he joined the old Company).

During the years following the Great War the Company had frequently been called upon to exercise its ancient privilege of mounting guards of honour in the City to members of the Royal Family and foreign Royalties (or other Chiefs of States). These occasions included guards to the King and Queen, the Prince of Wales, the Duke and Duchess of York, the Duke of Gloucester, the Duke of Kent, the Duke of Connaught, the King of the Belgians, the King of Roumania, the King and Queen of Italy, King Fuad of Egypt, the King and Queen of

KING'S GUARD OF THE H.A.C. MARCHING INTO BUCKINGHAM PALACE
6TH JULY, 1938

Afghanistan, Prince and Princess Takamatsu of Japan, the President of the French Republic, and the Premiers of Great Britain, Canada, Australia, New Zealand and Newfoundland.

A signal honour was accorded the Regiment when it was ordered to mount the King's Guard at Buckingham Palace on 6th July, 1938, this being the first time that the duty had been performed by a unit of the Territorial Army. The Guard was a credit to the Company and was congratulated on its turn-out and bearing by the Captain-General, who watched the mounting from a balcony in the Palace. The Guard also received many other messages of congratulation, including a much appreciated one from the Warrant Officers, Staff Sergeants and Sergeants of the 2nd Battalion Grenadier Guards, then on duty in Wellington Barracks.

A "State of Emergency" was proclaimed on 26th September, 1938, as a result of what became known as "the Munich Crisis." Orders were received as to the "obscuration of light" —a dreadful bit of officialese which eventually reverted to the plain English of "black-out." Fire-fighting measures were initiated, hampered by a general lack of equipment and a certain amount of contradictory advice as to how best to deal with incendiary bombs. Meanwhile shelter trenches were dug in the ground (carefully avoiding the cricket pitch); a totally inadequate issue of sandbags arrived and were filled; gas masks and steel helmets were issued; and a rush of recruits set in.

But the orders for embodiment never came and the crisis passed—for a while.

Presumably as a result of the defenceless state of the metropolis against air attack which was all too evident at the time of the Munich Crisis, it was decided early in 1939 to form a number of Territorial anti-aircraft units. Accordingly, in March, the Company acceded to a request from the War Office to undertake the formation of a Heavy Anti-Aircraft Regiment. This consisted of three batteries (Nos. 273, 274 and 275) and became the 86th (H.A.C.) H.A.A. Regiment, R.A. The original officers were mainly provided by the Regimental Reserve of Officers or by promotion from the ranks of the active list. The personnel were selected with care from several thousand men of a very high type who presented themselves, including a number of veteran members and ex-members. Almost all the original rank and file eventually obtained commissions.

Later in the year the decision was announced that the existing Territorial Army was to be duplicated. As a result cadres of two new batteries of R.H.A. were thrown off by "A" and "B" Batteries, H.A.C., and were recruited up to strength. "A" and "B" now formed the 11th (H.A.C.) Regiment, R.H.A., and the new batteries, "C" and "D", became the 12th (H.A.C.) Regiment, R.H.A.

During the above expansions over 2,000 applicants had to be rejected during the process of selection for the new units.

The Infantry Battalion, being entirely an officer-producing unit, was not duplicated, but recruited up to full strength, and the considerable wastage caused by other ranks receiving commissions in other units was made good.

The Company's historical role of officer-production was now well to the fore. In addition to new commissions in the Regiment to officer the new units, by the end of July some seventy members had received commissions in other regiments. Though these were eminently qualified for such promotion, a somewhat paradoxical situation arose as war appeared almost inevitable. The majority of members, who had worked and qualified

Photo: "The Times"

H.A.C. Infantry Battalion marching through the City,
5th September, 1939

for the "Officer's Certificate," remained in the ranks expecting to be commissioned immediately on the outbreak of hostilities. On the other hand, a minority, who for reasons of their own had not undertaken the special training devised especially for officer production, presented themselves at the headquarters of other London units and, on the strength of their service with the H.A.C., were immediately granted commissions in the new T.A. battalions or batteries. Thus the uncertificated were in many cases the first to be commissioned, an outcome of the Regiment's new role which can hardly have been envisaged by the authorities. Contrariwise, many who had won their "O" Certificate were fated to undergo months of training under war conditions before receiving the commissions for which they had qualified in peace time.

The outbreak of the World War on 3rd September, 1939, found the 86th H.A.A. Regiment already manning A.A. defences in the London area, while the H.A.C. Defence Companies, now part of the 13th (Home Defence) Battalion The Royal Fusiliers, had already been called up to man vital points in the London docks. The H.A.C. Special Constabulary also took up their police duties attached to Commercial Street Police Station.

The officer-production unit which the 11th Regiment had maintained, in addition to its combatant role, formed the 121st (H.A.C.) O.C.T.U. (Artillery) at Aldershot. The Infantry Battalion found itself converted into the 162nd (H.A.C.) O.C.T.U. and stationed at Bulford.

CHAPTER XV

1939 TO 1947

At the outbreak of war the 11th (H.A.C.) Regiment, R.H.A., consisted of "A" and "B" Batteries, with Regimental H.Q. These at once left Armoury House and went into training, which at first was considerably hampered by the necessity for guarding vulnerable points, and later by the assumption of defence roles on the coast against the threat of invasion. There was also a steady drain of men for commissions, so much so that long before the Regiment went overseas the great majority of the original personnel had been commissioned and had been replaced by "intake" from all parts of the country. In November, 1940, a third Battery was formed and named "E".

The Regiment was finally armed with tractor-drawn 25-pounders and attached to the 1st Armoured Division, with which it completed its training, and eventually embarked at Liverpool in September, 1941, and after a protracted and rigorous voyage disembarked at Port Tewfik on 6th December. The Regiment formed the artillery of the 2nd Armoured Brigade, "A" Battery supporting The Queen's Bays, "B" Battery the 10th Hussars, and "E" the 9th Lancers.

After ten days in the desert near Alexandria the Division was hurried to the front, then in the area of El Agheila. Here the Division was split up, the Batteries being attached to various small reconnaissance columns whose object was "to harass the enemy." The results were disastrous. On 21st January, 1942, the column to which "A" Battery was attached came under heavy shell fire and was simultaneously attacked by over forty tanks. Retreat was inevitable, but large belts of soft sand made the going very difficult and the column was several times dive-bombed by Stukas. As a result six guns and many vehicles were lost. The retreat continued, but on the afternoon of the 23rd "A" Battery's two remaining guns were ordered to cover the retreat of other units. They were attacked by 36 tanks and the gun detachments were mown down by machine-gun fire. The guns were then manned by officers, most of whom were killed or wounded, and the guns were knocked out.

Farther south "B" Battery had been engaged in a similar running fight. On 21st January they had engaged a mass of enemy vehicles, scoring many hits, but were forced to retire across sand-dunes and had to abandon two guns hopelessly bogged.

"E" Battery had opened fire on the 21st to cover "A" Battery's withdrawal. During the subsequent retreat their column was twice heavily dive-bombed in a defile between sand-hills. The Battery put up spirited rear-guard actions, but lost three guns bogged in sand. On the night of 23rd January the column was still retreating, with German flares going up on all sides, but were able to get clear, and at dawn on the 24th hit back by engaging two enemy leaguers, doing considerable damage and inflicting (as it was afterwards learned) over 200 casualties. But later in the day the column's "B" Echelon was ambushed in a steep wadi and "E" Battery alone lost 54 vehicles, while some 70 men were either casualties or prisoners.

Eventually the three columns rejoined the main force on the Gazala line. The 11th Regiment had been extremely unfortunate on practically its first introduction to desert warfare to run into what proved to be a powerful German counter-offensive.

Early in March "H" Troop of "E" Battery, while on detached duty with the Free French, was attacked by some 30 tanks in the open. The detachments were shot down by machine guns and three guns were knocked out, the survivors being captured. General Koenig afterwards drew attention to the heroic conduct of the detachments in fighting their guns to the last, thus allowing the escape of the remainder of the column. He recommended all who took part for the award of the Croix de Guerre, but the awards never materialized. "H" Troop was re-formed forthwith and about this time 239 Anti-Tank Battery was added to the strength of the Regiment.

In the battle of Knightsbridge the 11th were very heavily engaged, but it is impossible to describe succinctly the very confused and bitter fighting which ensued. For the first three or four days Rommel's attack was held. The armoured regiments, each supported by its particular battery, engaged in a series of desperate battles with the opposing armour. 239 Anti-Tank Battery were shot to pieces in an action against enemy tanks, most of the men dying round their guns, the remnants being gallantly rescued by a party from "A" Battery. The 9th Lancers were so reduced by casualties that they were ordered to hand over their few remaining tanks to The Bays and were withdrawn for re-equipment.

The Germans now brought up a number of 88 mm. guns, and these, added to the superior fire power of their tanks, began to turn the tide against us. The battle reopened with renewed fury. "E" Battery fought till it was reduced to a single troop, which was then combined with the remnants of "I" Battery, R.H.A.

The Regiment was now ordered to hold a ridge to cover the withdrawal of the 50th British and 2nd South African Divisions. "B" Battery put up a terrific defence over open sights against a semicircle of enemy tanks and guns. The three remaining guns of "F" Troop were knocked out one by one, but no orders had been given to retire, so the survivors of the detachments still stood to the wrecked guns and the Germans were afraid to close in. The other troop was eventually ordered to withdraw under a smoke-screen fired by "A" Battery and went into action again farther east. The Queen's Bays and "A" Battery fought stubbornly to cover the retreat and at nightfall the results could be seen in a semicircle of burning German tanks.

The remnants of "A" and "B" then leaguered with 1st Rifle Brigade, whose O.C. gave orders for a night march to escape from the enemy, who were by this time on all sides except the north. The only way of retreat lay over the rocky escarpment of the Acroma Ridge—an almost precipitous descent among jagged boulders, followed by an equally steep climb, and then an easier descent. The gradient was about 1 in 2, but by some miracle, aided by the efforts of the gunners with pick and shovel, the column got through without serious mishap and was able to follow up the retreat past Tobruk.

As a result of these actions the Brigade Commander wrote to Lord Galway: "I would like to let you know how magnificently the 11th (H.A.C.) Regiment, R.H.A., fought with my brigade for twenty continuous days. The courage of every gunner was beyond reproach and the skill of the Battery Commanders and Troop Leaders was worthy of the best traditions of the R.H.A. The example of 'F' Troop, on 14th June, who kept in action till every piece was hit, will go down in the annals of your Company's history. I am more than proud to have had them under my command and their comportment has been an example to the Brigade Group."

What remained of the Regiment concentrated at Sollum, where "B" and "E" Batteries became a composite unit. On the fall of Tobruk the army again retreated and the Batteries dug in near Mersa Matruh. When retirement to the Alamein line was ordered, the 11th were again in the rear-guard, this time attached to 50th Division. For two days the guns were in action, with the enemy drawing ever closer to their positions and occupying the high ground all round them. Then it was decided that the trapped force should divide into eight groups and try to break out by night. "B/E" Battery, escorted by East Yorkshires, was in the first group which forced a way through the enemy by hard fighting under heavy fire from all sides. The fifth party included "C" Troop of "A" Battery and also got clear without great loss. The rest of "A" Battery was in the last group to move; their infantry escort went on without them, and they suffered severe losses in killed, wounded and prisoners. The total casualties of the 11th Regiment in the battle of Knightsbridge and subsequent retreat were 9 officers and 54 other ranks killed, 18 officers and 159 other ranks wounded, 10 officers and 201 other ranks captured, or total losses of 37 officers and 414 other ranks. Furthermore, 50 of the prisoners, mostly of "B" Battery, were afterwards drowned by the torpedoing of the ship in which they were being taken to Italy.

No sooner had the exhausted remnants of the H.A.C. collected behind the Alamein line than they were formed into a composite H.A.C. Battery, and next day marched back into the line. South African troops had dug in on the northern sector, and New Zealanders, just arrived from Syria, were holding the southern defences, but between them lay a gap of 14 miles in which a scratch force was awaiting the inevitable onslaught of Rommel's victorious Panzers. Day after day for a fortnight the Germans attacked, but were broken up and hurled back by the fire of the guns until the defensive finally prevailed. It was the turning point of the war.

When the line was at last solidly held the H.A.C. were

relieved. Reinforcements arrived, and then the Regiment was given the signal honour of being the first to be armed with the new self-propelled guns, 105 mm. gun-howitzers on Grant tank chassis, known as "Priests." 239 Anti-Tank Battery now left the Regiment. The 11th trained behind the lines with these weapons, and the 1st Armoured Division (whose armoured regiments had been armed with Sherman tanks) was then given the task of making the actual break-through at El Alamein.

As the tremendous barrage opened at 2140 hours on 23rd October, the three armoured regiments, each attended by its appropriate battery, passed through three parallel lanes cleared through the mine-fields. Dawn broke when they were 500 yards short of the third mine-field, and enemy shelling at once grew intense and the battle began in earnest. The Batteries went into action actually in a mine-field and there were soon many blazing German tanks on the slopes ahead. Our tanks advanced, but two more mine-fields were found beyond. The Queen's Bays and "A" Battery checked a counter-attack by German tanks. All next day the fighting continued, 9th Lancers and "E" Battery attacking in the afternoon. All Batteries had sustained direct hits on their Priests, involving a number of casualties, but the bullet- and splinter-proof armour afforded protection to at least some of the detachments. On the 25th the 10th Hussars charged through the fourth mine-field, struck the fifth but found a way round it, losing five Shermans in the attempt. That night the infantry advanced again. 1st Rifle Brigade of 1st Armoured Division fought a most brilliant action and installed themselves with anti-tank guns in a commanding position. The guns advanced and caused great havoc in the German gun lines and infantry positions. The battle raged on.

On the 28th 2nd Armoured Brigade was withdrawn for rest, but went in again on the next evening through the New Zealanders. The slogging match continued as before. The ninth day seemed easier and on the morning of the tenth day 2nd Armoured Brigade crashed through the remaining defences and advanced for six miles before running into a rear-guard of tanks and anti-tank guns. The Batteries dealt with this opposition. 10th Hussars captured the German Commander-in-Chief, General von Thoma, and by the end of the day the Brigade had advanced 10 miles. Next day tanks and guns advanced another 20 miles, turned north, met and over-

11TH H.A.C. AT EL ALAMEIN

whelmed another rear-guard, and eventually cut the coast road. That night the Brigade was sent on a detour south through the desert to cut off the retreating Afrika Korps near Mersa Matruh. But the weather broke. Heavy rain fell; the tanks had heavy going through deep mud; and the supply trains with petrol could not get through. The attempt at encirclement failed.

1st Armoured Division was ordered to Tmimi for rest and training, where they remained until 21st February, 1943, when they left for the front and the Regiment went into action in front of the Mareth line. Then the Division was sent on a detour of 300 miles across sandy desert to join the New Zealand Division south of El Hamma. Next day, 26th March, the New Zealanders attacked, and after dark 2nd Armoured Brigade advanced through the mine-fields and penetrated two miles into the enemy lines. When the moon rose the Brigade advanced in column of squadrons, The Bays and "A" Battery leading, and charged forward astride the road, shooting down all opposition, for nearly 20 miles, halting two miles short of El Hamma. Here there was heavy fighting for three days against anti-tank guns and tanks, while the divisional artillery and the New Zealanders came up. The enemy were routed and 1st Armoured Division swept through El Hamma and across a broad plain up to the rocky ridge of El Akarit. British and Indian infantry brilliantly stormed this position, and the armour swept through and dealt with enemy tanks near Mezzouna. After another 40-mile advance and another brush with a rear-guard, the Division was withdrawn to rest.

The 11th H.A.C. were now loaned to the First Army and the Regiment set out on a 300-mile march to join 6th Armoured Division at Le Kef, where it met the 12th H.A.C. Within a few days the 11th went into action alongside the 12th. "A" was allotted to 17th/21st Lancers, "B" to the 16th/5th Lancers, and "E" to the Lothians and Border Yeomanry. "E" Battery had to fight some German paratroops for their gun position.

The attack went in and the armour, supported by the 11th, swept forward through the infantry and engaged in a tank battle, in which "A" Battery knocked out two German Mark VI tanks.

Meanwhile 1st Armoured Division had advanced on the left and the 11th were now relieved by the 12th and ordered to rejoin their own Division. The advance was held by the defences of the Djebel Kournine and, after several days' slogging, the armour was withdrawn, but went in again at dawn on 6th May after an infantry attack during the night, the 11th being once more attached to 6th Armoured Division. This attack went well after a stiff preliminary encounter, 100 German A.A. gunners surrendering to "E" Battery. All Batteries put in good work destroying 88 mm. guns and blasting a path for the tanks. On 7th May units of both 6th and 7th Armoured Divisions entered Tunis, but the 6th swung east towards the Cape Bon peninsula and was given the difficult task of forcing the Hammam Lif gap, a strongly defended three-mile ledge between mountains and sea. This they carried out most brilliantly, supported by 11th H.A.C., on 9th May. The armour crashed through the bottleneck, the last defensible enemy position, and "B" Battery had an infantry action clearing houses of snipers.

6th Armoured Division now wheeled south towards Hammamet to cut off the German forces facing the Eighth Army at

Enfidaville. The enemy were surrendering in droves. An officer of the 11th was the first man to gain touch with the Eighth Army, and the Regiment was present at the surrender of their old enemies of the Afrika Korps.

Hardly was the victory celebrated than the 11th H.A.C. were ordered to join 51st Highland Division for special training for the landing in Sicily. This took the form of amphibious exercises in L.C.Ts., in one of which "A" Battery suffered shipwreck.

The Regiment's guns were the first to land in the invasion of Europe, going ashore (some through five feet of water) at the southern tip of Sicily on 10th July, practically unopposed. The guns joined 50th Royal Tank Regiment and advanced northwards. There was fighting at Palazzolo, Vizzini, Francoforte, Scordia, Gerbini Airfield, Sferro, Catenanuova, Scalpello, Centuripe and Miletto, some of it very tough, with bombing from the air at intervals. Eventually the Germans were pushed into the north-east corner of the island, but got away to the mainland by delaying the pursuit with road mining and demolitions.

The only part taken by the Regiment in the invasion of Italy on 3rd September was in the preliminary bombardment, using an enormous Italian coast defence gun, which had with difficulty been persuaded to function. Their Priests were almost all worn out, and officers and men were going down with malaria as the long-continued strain began to tell. On 8th September Italy surrendered and the Regiment was ordered to rejoin its own Division, leaving Syracuse on 21st September for Bizerta.

That winter the 11th lay in farm billets near Algiers and later visited various training areas as new equipment became available. Towards the end of May, 1944, the Division was ordered to Italy and disembarked at Taranto. Here the Regiment's Priests were replaced by Sextons, a Canadian tank mounting a 25-pounder gun.

1st Armoured Division was suddenly rushed up to the front through the Apennines and arrived exhausted and sleepless after a week of movement, concluding with two consecutive night marches. Orders were to follow up an infantry attack on 3rd September and pass through the 46th Division. Wherefore, after another night march over tortuous mountain tracks, 2nd Armoured Brigade attacked across the River Conca. But the terrain was difficult and the tanks were halted by *nebelwerfers*, anti-tank guns, bazookas, snipers and mines. A full-scale attack, supported by the Batteries, met with only limited success. The Brigade also came under heavy and persistent shell fire by day and bombing by night. Successive attacks made slow progress, and on 12th September there was again a full-scale attack. The Regiment fired heavily for 24 hours, 225 rounds per gun during the night alone, and the San Savino–Passano ridge was captured early next day. The Regiment's O.P. tanks had a particularly strenuous battle. The advance was maintained in spite of severe casualties and the guns went into action on the captured ridge and supported further attacks. The Brigade advanced into the bridgehead which had been formed over the River Marano, and the weather broke in heavy rainstorms, which converted fields into treacherous bogs.

Orders were now given for 2nd Armoured Brigade to attack at dawn on 20th September. An optimistic view had been taken of the situation. It was said that "the door was wide open" and there was talk of 1st Armoured Division advancing even to the Brenner Pass (with airborne supplies). But the German resistance was far from broken. The Bays, leading the attack, were trapped in a wadi exposed to enfilade fire and lost 24 tanks, with many casualties. "A" Battery's O.P. tank with them was hit and the officer and all the crew killed. The Batteries fired 3,022 rounds of high explosive and 710 of smoke shell that day. The infantry went in again at night and crossed the River Marecchia, but rain fell again heavily and the Batteries were bogged down trying to advance.

Distressing news was now received that 1st Armoured Division was to be disbanded owing to lack of reinforcements. However, 2nd Armoured Brigade was to retain its identity and was to be used as an independent unit. During the next few weeks the army pressed steadily forward, 2nd Armoured Brigade supporting 4th, 58th and 56th Divisions alternately. The battle went on week after week; river after river was crossed— the Rubicon, the Savio, the Ronco, the Mentone, the Rabbi, the Bolzanino, the Marzena and the Lamone. Town after town was captured—Santarcangelo, Savignano, Montalbano, Montegallo, Longiano, Celincordia, Cesena, Forlimpopoli, San Martino Forli, Villagrippa, Castiglione, Belvedere, Pideura, Celle and Faenza. These rivers and the ridges between them

provided a series of magnificent defensive positions and continuous, desperate, hard fighting was necessary to eject the
stubborn German rear-guards from them, and in every action
the 11th H.A.C. bore its share in close support of the armour
by laying down barrages for infantry attack or by frustrating
counter-attacks. Sometimes over 5,000 rounds a day were
expended. And most of this happened in abominable weather.

During January, 1945, the Regiment enjoyed a brief rest at
Pesara, but on 2nd February went into the line near Villanova
in static warfare. Then came a move to the coast to support a
successful amphibious landing by No. 2 Commando on The
Spit on 2nd April. Leaving The Spit on the 5th, the Regiment
supported the initial crossing of the River Reno south-west of
Lake Comacchio. After firing 280 rounds per gun in this operation, the 11th moved to Cotignola to support the main crossing
of the River Senio under heavy shelling, with trouble from mines
and machine guns. D Day was 9th April, and, after heavy air
bombardment of the enemy positions, the Batteries contributed
over 13,000 rounds to the barrage. Next day the 11th returned
to 2nd Armoured Brigade.

Each Battery supported its own armoured regiment at the
crossing of the Santerno and the ensuing rush for the Argenta
Gap in a battle which developed into a very considerable
victory and the complete rout of the German forces south of the
River Po. During the advance the Batteries were engaged in
many spirited actions and fired over 46,000 rounds, the last
being fired at the retreating enemy across the Po on 25th April.
Later that day came the order to cease fire.

The outbreak of war found the 12th (H.A.C.) Regiment,
R.H.A., complete in personnel but without either vehicles or
guns. The Regiment went into billets at Boreham Wood, and
during the first winter of the war its men were mainly occupied
in guarding vulnerable points (V.Ps.) in the London area, while
training was carried on in the intervals on such equipment as
could be improvised or extracted from dumps. The Regiment
was soon trained to employ 13-pounders, 18-pounders and 4.5
howitzers. It has been well said that the manning of V.Ps.
during the extremely cold winter of 1939 was the best possible
training for war. Nothing that followed could compare with it
for discomfort and boredom, and in the most disagreeable

[Photo: Bassano, London

THEIR MAJESTIES KING GEORGE VI AND QUEEN ELIZABETH WITH THE OFFICERS, 11TH H.A.C. REGIMENT, 30TH JULY, 1941

battles in Africa or Italy spirits could be raised by comparison with the experiences of "Battersea 1939" or other engagements with the hostile forces of Nature and London District.

In April, 1940, the Regiment moved to Skegness and shortly afterwards received a further eight 18-pounder guns with which to repel the threatened invasion. The Regiment's transport consisted of a motley collection of requisitioned cars, commercial vans and brewery lorries. After several moves during the summer, the first pair of 25-pounders arrived on 1st August, and by the end of October the Regiment possessed sixteen assorted weapons and an increasing proportion of W.D. vehicles. The Regiment was in succession attached to 56th London Division and 2nd Armoured Division for training, and in August, 1940, was posted to support 1st Armoured Reconnaissance Brigade, consisting of 4th/7th Dragoon Guards, 12th Royal Lancers and East Riding Yeomanry. These regiments were armed with a small quasi-armoured vehicle called a Beaverette, and they did numerous counter-invasion exercises in the narrow lanes of East Anglia. The brewery lorries, with 13-pounders and 4.5 howitzers attached, pounded cheerfully in the rear. It was good training in mobility and in improvisation, if not perhaps in serious gunnery.

During this period and simultaneously with the duties and the training, the Regiment subjected itself to a constant sorting of personnel by interviews and Boards, and drafts of potential officers were dispatched at short intervals to the various O.C.T.Us. that were being established. The places of the officer candidates were filled by various drafts, some of which also contained potential officers, and the sorting process of both H.A.C. personnel and draftees continued. By November, 1940, practically the whole N.C.O. and other rank personnel of the H.A.C. Regiment which had embodied in September, 1939, plus a number of others, had been posted to one or another O.C.T.U., with the exception of a few individuals who had determined to remain and serve in the ranks of the H.A.C. From this policy the nation derived a steady flow of officers who had received their initial training in the ranks of the Company, greatly to their own advantage and to that of their subsequent units. The Regiment had the good fortune to attract back to its officer ranks many of the best of its own officer candidates, and, whatever may have been the feelings of individuals at the time, or of the Battery Commanders who were constantly being ordered to post what they considered were their key men, there was very little wastage of talent. Since the postings were spread over a period of twelve months, much of the spirit and traditions of the Company were transmitted to the new recruits drafted to the Regiment, and the great benefit of this was seen when the Regiment went into action.

In November, 1940, the 12th came under command of 6th Armoured Division, with which it was to serve until the end of the war. The Regiment were the supporting arm of 26th Armoured Brigade, consisting of 16th/5th Lancers, 17th/21st Lancers and Lothians and Border Horse. Training proceeded at an increasing pace; equipment was completed in March, 1941; firing practice camps and large-scale exercises such as "Bulldog" and "Bumper" followed. The Regiment were stationed first in Oxfordshire, then in Cambridgeshire and last at Ayr. Finally the Division was inspected by His Majesty the King, and "C" Battery sailed from the Clyde on 1st November, 1942, as part of the leading elements of Operation "Torch" (the invasion of North Africa), and the remainder of the Regiment followed on 14th November.

"C" Battery landed at Algiers on 12th and 13th November as part of "Blade Force," an armoured regimental group which had been detailed to make a dash for Tunis. This involved forced marches of some 500 miles over mountain ranges. The Regiment was armed with towed 25-pounders, and the armour consisted of Valentine and Crusader tanks armed with 6-pounder and 2-pounder guns. The Germans had reacted promptly and strongly to the invasion, and had an easy task in reinforcing by air and sea from Sicily, with the result that Blade Force and the leading elements of 78th Division were held up well west of Tunis. "C" Battery saw considerable fighting and suffered a number of casualties, mainly from dive bombers.

Meanwhile the remainder of the Regiment had disembarked at Algiers on 22nd November and a few days later re-embarked for Bone, thence marching to the area of Teboursouk, where 6th Armoured Division were concentrating. There they were rejoined by "C" Battery, and the story of the next three months was one of constant defensive fighting and movement in foul weather and under the worst conditions. The Germans had complete air superiority during this period and all movement and supply had to be done at night. The German Pz. Mark III and Mark IV were superior in gun power and armour to the Valentines and Crusaders and in performance in the muddy going. While the build-up in the rear was going on, the initiative passed to the German forces and their thrusts had to be successively parried in heavy fighting at Bou Arada, Robaa and Sbiba, and Thala. At Robaa the Germans for the first time produced the Mark VI Tiger tank, and in a most exciting two-day battle it was proved, contrary to the expectations of experts, that the 6-pounder anti-tank gun sited in enfilade could at short range knock out this formidable monster. In each of these battles the 12th took a very active part, sometimes as a regiment and often in detached batteries or even troops. At this time the First Army consisted solely of 78th Division and 6th Armoured Division, with U.S. forces of approximately a corps strength operating in the south and some scattered and ill-armed French units. Formations soon became broken up and, as the situation became more confused, regiments and even batteries and troops were detached to deal with some fresh crises. Although the forces involved were comparatively small in number, the country was large and the stakes were high. A battery or troop commander would often find himself C.R.A. of an area separated by 100 miles and a range of mountains from any neighbouring unit. The Commanding Officer would constantly have to travel 200 miles to visit all his batteries. Round any corner might be met a German armoured car; O.P. parties would ambush each other and a G.P.O. escape after capture by enemy infantry. This period provided considerable excitement, wonderful experience, and showed how very valuable and how imaginative had been the training which the Regiment had received from the Regular officers who had commanded and trained it during the three years' preparation at home.

At Thala on 23rd/24th February, 1943, "F" Battery put up an exceptional performance in holding the road against German armour and infantry which had broken through the Americans in the Kasserine Pass. This action is described in the Royal Artillery Commemoration Book. For a night and a day the guns were in the front line with no support behind them, but they destroyed several enemy tanks and held the road until relief arrived. After this the Regiment was switched back to the north to Bou Arada and thence north again to assist in the support of 46th Division, which had now arrived and been subjected to heavy attack at Beja, and then north again to the coast at Sedjenane. At length on 22nd March the Regiment was withdrawn to a concentration area at Sakiet Sidi Youssef, where 6th Armoured Division was being concentrated. 26th Armoured Brigade were now rearmed with Sherman tanks and this created a complete change of the tactical situation.

On 9th April the Regiment supported the forcing of the Fondouk Gap by 26th Armoured Brigade and then advanced with their armoured regiments, forcing back the enemy rear-guards to Kairouan and Sbiba, where junction was made with the Eighth Army. 6th Armoured Division were then withdrawn to prepare for the attack upon Tunis and concentrated in the area of Bou Arada.

For the first phase of the attack on Tunis 6th Armoured Division was joined by 11th H.A.C., from the Eighth Army, with their self-propelled Priests, and during the concluding stages of the campaign the two H.A.C. Regiments on several occasions were in action next to one another. After some preliminary fighting, during which the Germans made a night attack which almost reached the gun areas, the British attack was launched on 22nd April. An infantry brigade of 46th Division made the initial attack supported by 12th H.A.C., and when the objectives were reached 26th Armoured Brigade with 11th H.A.C. in support went through. On the following day the 12th relieved the 11th and took part in further advances, which were eventually held up two days later by the defences of the Djebel Bou Kournine. During these attacks the Regiment suffered a number of casualties, principally caused by heavy shelling.

The 6th Armoured Division and both the 11th and 12th were then withdrawn to prepare for a new attack south of Medjez. Four infantry divisions made the initial assault, after which the 6th and 7th Armoured Divisions passed through, 11th H.A.C. supporting 26th Armoured Brigade and 12th H.A.C. supporting 201st Guards Brigade (attached to 6th Armoured Division). This attack, launched on 6th May, was successful. Tunis was entered by patrols on the 7th, and on the following day the 11th and 12th, by-passing Tunis to the south, took part in 6th Armoured Division's attack on the defile of Hammam Lif, a seemingly impregnable position between the mountains and the sea, which was brilliantly carried. The 12th and 201st Guards Brigade then made a night advance across the base of the Cape Bon peninsula to cut the enemy's lines of communication and take the forces opposing the Eighth Army in the rear, and the guns of 12th H.A.C. were in action at Bou Ficha when the remainder of the German Army surrendered. A few days later 11th and 12th H.A.C. dined together at Hammamet.

A period of rest and training in North Africa followed. 12th H.A.C. were stationed at Robertville, near Philippeville, and were issued with the American S.P. 105-mm. gun or "Priest" which 11th H.A.C. had employed so successfully in the Desert. The 12th were the second regiment in the African theatre of war to be issued with Priests, and much work had to be done in devising, in consultation with the 11th, the best establishment of vehicles and men and in experimenting with the tactical handling of these excellent weapons as well as in the purely technical problems of training men to use U.S. weapons, sights and ammunition. A firing range was established a few miles from Robertville and a great deal of firing, course shooting and fire and movement took place. The Armoured Brigade were stationed near by and numerous schemes in co-operation with the respective regiments were organized. In the intervals of training there was magnificent sea bathing to be had at Philippeville and near by, and for some there was leave in Algiers and for a very few "compassionate leave" in England. Visits to the Base Hospitals in Algiers resulted in the return to the Regiment of nearly all the wounded through channels more effective than official. When 11th H.A.C. returned from their successful campaign in Sicily there was a further exchange of visits for training and social purposes between the two Regiments.

In March, 1944, the 12th moved to Italy, landing at Naples and moving to a concentration area near Alife. The campaign in Italy differed in many ways from that in North Africa. The forces engaged were larger, the country was more confined, mobility was restricted and obstacles natural and artificial more numerous. The Allied forces continuously held the initiative and enjoyed air superiority (although the losses suffered by 12th H.A.C. in Africa from bombing by the German Air Force differed little from that inflicted on them by the U.S. Air Force in Italy). But the 12th entered the campaign with great advant-

12TH H.A.C. BELOW MONTE CASSINO

ages. Successful experiences in North Africa had produced fine teamwork and mutual confidence in all ranks; the S.P. gun was extremely satisfactory, and the possession of an adequate establishment of Sherman O.P. tanks was an enormous gain. There was a very high standard of technical skill among signallers and specialists. Co-operation between Batteries and the Armoured Regiments of 26th Armoured Brigade was developing into a mutual friendship and respect which by the end of the campaign had firmly linked "C" Battery to 16th/5th Lancers, "D" Battery to The Lothians and "F" Battery to 17th/21st Lancers. During the two major battles of the campaign at Cassino in May, 1944, and at the Senio in April, 1945, the Regiment took part in the preliminary bombardments upon an Army or Corps plan and was switched with great rapidity from the support of one division to another before eventually reverting to 6th Armoured Division for the decisive armoured battles. Between the two major battles the Regiment was continuously in action with 6th Armoured Division in the advance up Italy, supporting in turn the Armoured Brigade and 1st Guards

Brigade and the Brigade of Rifle Regiments. From 6th May, 1944, the Regiment was continuously in action, moving almost every day. The German rear-guards fought skilfully and tenaciously and made great use of demolitions and of natural obstacles, which were numerous in a country where the mountains were high and tank-proof and the valleys constantly intersected by streams or deep, dry water-courses, bridges, culverts, and aqueducts, all of which were blown. Progress became a constant series of short advances. Sometimes the advance would be 5 miles, sometimes 25 miles, but invariably it would end at an obstacle for which Sapper assistance and the cover of night was necessary. Each morning the advance to contact would start again at or before first light. The Regiment's guns were continually deployed and close up with the leading armoured regiment, usually advancing by leap-frogging and under the centralized control of the C.O. and Second-in-Command. The high mountains gave the enemy much advantageous observation, and had they been better served in ammunition supply our losses from hostile shelling must have been even more severe. G.P.Os. developed great skill in hiding their positions in the most forward areas, and Troop Leaders and Battery Sergeant-Majors were expert in bringing up their guns and supply lorries by covered routes; while the American flashless propellant of 105 mm. was invaluable, the extra smoke that it gave being readily acceptable on a battlefield filled with dust and smoke. O.Ps. remained with their armoured regiments for weeks at a time, and B.Cs. would only occasionally be able to slip back to their Command Posts for a hurried visit to their Batteries. The strain on O.P. officers and crews and their tanks was heavy, but occasionally they could get a day's rest and maintenance while another armoured regiment took the lead; but the gun groups, the G.P.Os. and Regimental Headquarters were never out of action. In spite of this efficiency was maintained, leave rosters were operated, and morale remained first rate if one accepts the evidence provided by the wounded, who seemed invariably to struggle to return and to succeed in getting back to the Regiment.

After some weeks at Alife engaged in concentrating after the crossing from North Africa and in further practice of close co-operation between infantry, tanks and artillery, the Regiment moved into silent positions below Monte Troccio ready for the attack on Cassino and the crossing of the Gari river. The Regiment supported 8th Indian Division in the initial assault and then was switched to support 4th Division and 78th Division in their advance beyond the river. A week's very hard fighting followed. The armoured regiments were acting in close support of the infantry battalions of 4th Division, and the O.Ps. were deployed with their armoured regiments. Progress at first was at the rate of a few thousand yards a day. The enemy counter-attacked, and shelling, particularly of the bridges over the Gari, was very heavy until the fall of the Monastery, which was taken by the Poles after severe fighting. The Regiment's guns were the first to cross the river, and gradually the advance was maintained until after eight days' fighting the enemy withdrew behind Acquino to what was known as the Hitler Line. This obstacle was forced in another major attack by the Canadian Corps, and 6th Armoured Division, which had been reconcentrated south of Acquino, took up the advance towards Rome, forcing the crossing of the Melfa and driving back the German rear-guards in the manner described. Rome was reached and by-passed to the east and the advance continued up the Tiber valley to Perugia in continuous stiff fighting. In July the Division attacked and captured Arezzo, and next day one of the Regiment's O.P. tanks was the first to cross the Arno. The advance continued through beautiful but difficult country, filled with orchards and vineyards, by Pontassieve, passing Florence, which was captured by 6th South African Armoured Division. On 28th August for the first time since the battle opened on 11th May all units of the Regiment were simultaneously out of action, the wireless silent, and Battery and Troop Commanders assembled for a meal at Regimental Headquarters. But in two days the Regiment was on the move and in action again until relieved early in December.

By now the advance had reached the Apennine mountains, where the Germans had been working to establish their winter position, the Gothic Line, during our progress up the leg of Italy. The defiles grew ever narrower and the positions more difficult as the Regiment went into action near San Benedetto Boccone and finally near Castel del Rio. The weather broke in early November and the Armoured Brigade was withdrawn to rest and refit, many of the men being employed as stretcher-bearers, carrying parties, etc., for 1st Guards Brigade and the battalions of the Rifle Brigade who took the lead in the mountains. 12th H.A.C. remained in action until 27th November when the Regiment was relieved in order to hand in the 105-mm. Priest and draw instead the British S.P. 25-pounder "Sexton," as a measure of economy to save the dollars involved in firing American ammunition. The merits of the 25-pounder are well known, but the heavier shell, the accurate air-burst fuze and the flashless propellant of the 105-mm. had won it many friends, not to mention the useful white phosphorous smoke which had come to the rescue of many a puzzled O.P. officer.

The next two months were spent in rest, retraining on British equipment and calibrating the Sextons. A festive Christmas was spent at Monte Lupone, and leave in Rome or Florence was enjoyed by nearly all. There was a memorable party when officers and sergeants from 11th H.A.C. came on a visit. There were some amusing brushes with the rear echelons of the Eighth Army, which moved the Regiment back and forth over the Apennine mountains and enabled them to show that they had lost none of their cheerful mobility. Organization and efficiency had reached a pitch where one could rely upon the Regimental Canteen being open for business within an hour of arriving in new billets.

Early in April, after the usual careful reconnaissance, the Regiment moved up to take part in the final offensive of the campaign, which was to commence with the crossing of the River Senio. The Regiment was again initially in support of the attack of 8th Indian Division. O.P. parties crossed the river with 6th Lancers, the Armoured Car Regiment of the Indian Division, and advanced to the River Santerno. During this period the Regiment's gun group reconnaissance parties suffered sad casualties as a result of bombing by U.S. heavy bombers. On 15th April the Regiment was switched at the shortest notice to support the New Zealand Division in the successful crossing of the River Sillaro, and immediately back to rejoin 6th Armoured Division, which had been held in reserve for the decisive blow. O.P. parties had been slipped to their armoured regiments some days before, but the gun groups and R.H.Q. had to make a difficult night march across the main supply routes of II Corps. However, by first light all were in position. The Division moved up to the Argenta Gap, which 56th Division had opened in heavy fighting, and advanced through difficult country against stiff opposition from S.P. guns, tanks and bazooka parties, with numerous irrigation canals and embankments as natural obstacles. On the following day Traghetto was cleared and the advance continued on flat ground interspersed with farms, orchards and vineyards, with canals or rivers (with blown bridges) every few miles. The water obstacles delayed the advance but could not stop it. There was tough and confused fighting in Poggio Renatico, which was finally cleared by 17th/21st Lancers, supported by "F" Battery. On the 22nd "C" and "D" Batteries crossed a canal (the Fossa Cembalina) on a Bailey bridge and followed their armour in a good day of firing and movement, with some hard fighting for Mirabello and Bondeno.

On the morning of the 23rd the Lothians and "D" Battery reached the River Po and engaged German boats and ferries crossing the river. The 16th/5th Lancers and "C" Battery also advanced and engaged targets on the other side of the Po. The 17th/21st Lancers and "F" Battery advanced to San Agostino and there established touch with New Zealanders and Americans. In the evening the Regiment concentrated in the area north of Porporana, within 1,000 yards of the Po, and this proved to be the end of the campaign for the 12th. During the night 1st Guards Brigade crossed the river and bridge building commenced, but the 12th with the Armoured Brigade were not allowed to cross, priority being given to the New Zealand Division whose task was to rush for Trieste, and to the motor battalions of 6th Armoured Division who followed the Derbyshire Yeomanry in pursuit of the beaten enemy into Austria. "D" Battery's O.Ps. went forward in support of the Derbyshire Yeomanry and crossed the Adige river. At this point the German Army in Italy surrendered.

The final phase in Austria deserves mention since for many it will remain longest in their memory of 1939-1945. The Regiment moved up into Austria on 12th May. For a few days the situation was tense, since Yugoslav Partisan Forces were attempting to annex the country. But the Rifle Brigade had established themselves in the key buildings of Klagenfurt and other places, thanks to their Colonel, who had served with Tito's Partisans and knew their method of operation, and in a few days' time the Partisans were forced to withdraw. German forces withdrawing from the Balkans had to fight a pitched battle with the Yugoslavs in order to reach 6th Armoured Division area and surrender. But after this there was no further trouble. As a result of good luck and good reconnaissance, 12th H.A.C. were able to obtain a delightful area in Carinthia about 30 miles north of Klagenfurt in the valley of the River Gurk. There the Batteries settled down in the little villages of Strassburg, Gurk and Weitensfeld to a happy summer in beautiful surroundings. The sun shone, the river was full of trout, the ban on fraternization was lifted just in time, bathing in the Wortersee was superb, there were horses to ride and shooting in the mountains. There were plenty of German volunteers to maintain vehicles and do the menial tasks of cook-house and hygiene, and all ranks enjoyed a holiday such as is given to few in their lifetime. It had been well earned and it was well enjoyed. In spite of the absence of work and the easy-going mood of everybody there was no relaxation of discipline, no crime whatsoever, turn-out remained excellent, and relations with the civil population were uniformly good. For some weeks the Regiment had to look after the horses—over 3,000 of them— of a Cossack Brigade which surrendered. The horses were sorted and drafted to sundry units and the majority to Italy to replace the shortages there. Each Battery and Regimental H.Q. started a Riding Club and many beginners learnt to ride. The river, too, provided unlimited sport for the keen angler and many new recruits to the sport were made. Wireless aerials made excellent rods and Italy was ransacked for lines and tackle. Trout were sufficiently numerous and co-operative, so that wholesale poaching methods were never necessary and a suffic-ient bag could always be achieved with rod and line. The 6th Armoured Division constructed an excellent racecourse on which were held race meetings which attracted horses and riders from Italy and Germany as well as local talent. 12th H.A.C. had to organize and run the Totalisator, which was successfully done although not without some headaches to the responsible organizers. It was not altogether surprising that when regular service of leave in England was started there were occasional cases when those who had been fortunate in the ballot were prepared to give up their vacancy in order to remain in Austria. In August demobilization by age and service groups commenced, and during the autumn the more senior officers and men began to leave. In September the 11th and 12th were merged into one

Regiment and the separate story of 12th (H.A.C.) Regiment, R.H.A., comes to an end. In its time it had earned the respect of those who fought with it and the affection of those who fought in it.

The 13th (H.A.C.) Regiment, R.H.A., was formed in November, 1940, on a cadre of 5 officers and 38 other ranks from the 12th H.A.C. and became a unit of the newly formed 11th Armoured Division. Officers and rank and file alike were posted from anywhere, so that for a time the leavening of H.A.C. personnel was small, but later most of the officers applied for membership of the Company.

Intensive training started at once. It was expected that the Division would go to North Africa, but the orders were changed when the first-line reinforcements had already sailed and so were lost to their units. Training recommenced. The armoured regiments received Sherman tanks and the 13th H.A.C. were armed with self-propelled Sextons—25-pounder guns on Ram chassis. There was much practice in "waterproofing" and "wading" as befitted units earmarked for a sea-borne invasion.

The Regiment eventually embarked with the rest of the Division at various London docks, and landed on the Normandy beaches (practically dry-shod after all the practice in waterproofing) on 15th June, 1944—D Day plus 9. The Regiment was part of 29th Armoured Brigade, "G" Battery supporting 23rd Hussars, "H" Battery the 3rd Royal Tank Regiment, and "I" Battery the 2nd Fife and Forfar Yeomanry.

The Brigade saw its first action on 26th June at the crossing of the River Odon and the capture of the high ground beyond. The Batteries fired 150 rounds per gun that day and were well to the fore, incurring casualties from snipers when they moved into close country of copses and standing corn. In the second day's fighting the 13th lost three O.P. tanks, the officers and crew of one of them all casualties. Fighting continued for five days, when the armoured regiments were relieved, but the guns remained in the line, moving their positions eight times in fourteen days.

After a few days' rest the H.A.C. took part in an attack by three armoured divisions, led by 29th Armoured Brigade, on the high ground round Bourguebus. On 18th July, after a preliminary bombardment of the enemy positions by the R.A.F., the armour attacked under a barrage, 3rd Royal Tanks, followed by "H" Battery, leading, followed by the Fife and Forfar with "I" Battery and 23rd Hussars with "G". Two more armoured Divisions (Guards and 7th) followed and a very stiff battle developed. The Fife and Forfar and "I" Battery came under very heavy fire and lost many tanks; two of the Regiment's F.O.O. tanks were hit; and "H" Battery took 75 prisoners. Objectives were finally reached and the Batteries went into action and repelled a counter-attack that evening. The advance continued next day and two villages were taken. Enemy shelling developed considerable strength, but a useful advance had been made, the battle won, and the Division had pushed back the 1st S.S. (Adolf Hitler) Division.

After two days' rest the Division was switched to the Battle of the Bocage, and on 30th July went in to the attack, the Regiment supporting from a position near Caumont. For two days the guns moved forward with the advance against stubborn enemy resistance in very difficult enclosed country, and then for six days dealt with persistent German counter-attacks and infiltrations. For two days every spare man of the Regiment was out on patrol against infiltrating "thugs."

The Battle of Normandy had now been won. On 13th August the Regiment moved forward and then began the chase of the retreating Germans, a matter of overcoming rear-guards, bridging rivers and speedy movement over roads made difficult by mines and demolitions, blown bridges and booby traps. At L'Aigle the 13th had two days' rest and then moved on to Vernon on the Seine. On reaching this place orders were received for the immediate crossing of the river to Tilly, and from there to continue the advance at first light next morning; objectives—Amiens and the crossings of the Somme.

The next day (29th August) it poured with rain for 24 hours, but the Brigade advanced 25 miles in face of some stiff opposition. On the 30th the weather was little better and there was more delaying action by the Boche, so that at dusk the spearhead was still some 30 miles short of Amiens. Wherefore, after an hour's halt, the Brigade thundered on through the darkness, villagers turning out in the pouring rain to cheer them on. A solitary tank and a column of horsed transport were met and dealt with, and an hour and a half before dawn Amiens was reached. The Germans, who had intended to hold the line of the Somme, were taken completely by surprise; fortified positions were not manned; and the German Commander was surprised at breakfast. The town was captured and the bridges secured intact after a little lively scrapping by all arms.

The advance continued next day (1st September). Opposition was light and patchy; the Brigade covered between 25 and 30 miles and halted for the night astride the Arras–St. Pol road. Next day there was a shorter drive over Vimy Ridge and into Lens, where the enthusiasm of the populace was tremendous. On the 3rd the Brigade advanced through Tournai and across the Belgian frontier, and Antwerp was reached on 4th September, small groups of the enemy putting up determined resistance in the outskirts, where the Regiment suffered several casualties from snipers. The troops had a terrific reception from the inhabitants, though shells were still falling, and for two days the fêting of the liberators continued. For the Regiment it seemed an adequate reward for their years of training.

On 7th September the Regiment moved on, and on the 9th crossed the Albert Canal, but an attempted advance next day was held up by anti-tank guns and bazookas, several of the latter being put out of action by "G" Battery's F.O.O. tank. On the 11th the infantry came up and the advance was continued. Some days later the Regiment crossed the border into Holland and found the country very marshy, with small copses liable to contain snipers. Progress was now very slow, with intervals for mopping-up, but on 25th September "H" Battery fired its first salvo into Germany. The Regiment now supported several Divisions in limited advances before bad weather brought operations virtually to an end and the line settled down to more or less static warfare for the winter. The conditions were very rigorous for the troops; snow and extreme cold from the third week in December till the end of January was followed by a thaw and heavy rain in February, which made the roads almost impassable.

After a short spell of rest and training, the 13th moved towards the Rhine, and on 23rd and 24th March fired 16,800 rounds to cover the crossing of the Rhine and the establishment of a bridgehead. Support was continued until the Division had advanced out of range, and then, on the 28th, the Regiment crossed the Rhine to begin the final victorious advance on the following day.

11th Armoured Division was now regrouped as follows: 23rd Hussars and 8th Rifle Brigade, with "G" Battery in support; 3rd Royal Tanks and 4th King's Shropshire L.I., with "H" Battery; and "I" Battery spare. After some hectic fighting on 30th March, the bridge across the River Ems was blown in the faces of the foremost attackers, but on the 31st the river was bridged three miles to the north and the Division crossed and advanced to the Dortmund-Ems Canal, which was crossed on 1st April—a great achievement—after very brisk encounters against determined rear-guards. Next day the Division cleared Tecklenburg and pressed on through the night to capture intact the bridge at Eversheide, just north of Osnabruck, early next morning. Then on to Osterkappeln and on again next day against stiff resistance, especially in one village, where 600 prisoners were taken. "I" Battery took a separate road through thick woods and brought in 100 prisoners at the rendezvous next morning.

On 5th April the Division reached the Weser and a bridgehead was formed. Here there was much trouble from dive-bombers and enemy guns. "G" Battery broke up three counter-attacks by S.S. troops against 8th Rifle Brigade in the bridgehead.

Three days later this bridgehead was abandoned and the Division crossed the river by a bridge higher up. The advance continued; over the Leine to the Aller, crossed at night by the K.S.L.I. Then followed two days' bitter fighting in the bridgehead among thick woods and swamps, in which many tanks were bogged.

The Division moved east and on the 15th captured, occupied and passed the unbelievable horror of the infamous Belsen Camp. The guns were very active on the 17th helping to overcome enemy rear-guards. On the 18th the Division liberated 500 British prisoners of war, and next day reached the Elbe at Luneburg, where an attempt at bridging was unsuccessful. However, a crossing was accomplished on the 29th by 15th Scottish Division, supported by the guns of the Regiment, which crossed the river next morning with the 11th Armoured Division and passed through the Scots in a dash for Lubeck, which was reached on 2nd May. There the most amazing thing happened. "G" Battery in one night took 600 prisoners, including a U-boat commander and his crew, "I" Battery took 800 prisoners, and the Division altogether about 15,000. That evening the 13th suffered casualties from enemy fighter-planes.

Next day the Regiment moved on to Zarpen, north of Lubeck, and at 1800 hours on 4th May all German resistance ended.

At the outbreak of war the 86th (H.A.C.) H.A.A. Regiment, R.A., was already deployed at action stations for the defence of London, and during the period of the "phoney" war training was continued, with frequent changes of station at the whim of the authorities. 273 Battery engaged a lone raider over London on the night of 23rd August, 1940, and thus was the first unit of the H.A.C. to engage the enemy in this war. The long period of watching and waiting brought about a certain amount of restlessness among both the officers and men of the Regiment. Some volunteered for transfer to units already in France; others applied for commissions in all branches of the service. Thus it came about that, though not officially recognized as an officer-producing unit, in the first year of the war the 86th sent over 700 men to O.C.T.Us., besides nearly 100 who received direct war emergency commissions from the ranks. Altogether the Regiment produced no less than 1,019 officers, including 138 to Infantry, 28 to the Royal Armoured Corps and 9 to the R.A.F. Of these 43 fell in action or died of wounds.

The German Luftwaffe first attacked London in strength on the night of 6th September, 1940, with a raid by 68 aircraft. This was followed by attacks by over 300 each night, and for nearly two months an average of 200 bombers attacked London every night. For the first three nights the defences were silent, orders being that no battery was to engage the enemy unless they could be picked up by searchlights, to enable the height-finders and predictors to be brought to bear. In actual practice it was found that the Luftwaffe preferred to fly above cloud, or, if the sky were clear, to take violent evasive action when the searchlights strove to pick them up. Then Mr. Churchill is said to have spoken his mind, and on the following night the guns roared incessantly, and though the gigantic expenditure of ammunition resulted in few enemy casualties, the morale of the general public benefited prodigiously. A claim by 275 Battery to have brought down a bomber on the night of 9th/10th

EVENING: CHADWELL READY FOR ACTION

September was eventually substantiated, and the Regiment put in several later claims which were classed as "doubtful." There were also a number of daylight raids, and, after the first concentrated "blitz" on London had come to an end, there were still sporadic attacks, some of them very heavy, notably on the night of 29th December, 1940, when much of the City was burned, and on 15th May, 1941. The Regiment's casualties throughout in the defence of London were 1 killed and 17 wounded.

In November, 1940, a new Battery, numbered 383, was formed on a regimental cadre and eventually joined the 86th. Another battery, formed in June, 1941, and numbered 446, was regimented to the 86th in September of that year. In October, 1941, 275 Battery left the Regiment.

Early in 1942 the 86th were placed on the Army Troops Reserve Roster and were eventually relieved from their static operational positions for training in mobile warfare. In July, 446 Battery left the Regiment. On 1st December, 1942, the Regiment came under Home Forces Command. Training was continued, with many moves to all parts of the country, and included anti-tank shooting, infantry training, sea target practice, firing in a field role and a number of combined exercises.

Finally, in May, 1944, the Regiment moved to its concentration area at Aveley, Essex, and on 2nd June embarked at Tilbury on landing craft as part of the force for the invasion of Normandy. The 86th was the first Heavy A.A. Regiment to land on the Normandy beaches, elements of the Regiment disembarking on D Day, and the remainder during the next two days. During the first month of the battle of Normandy the guns were in action almost every night and occasionally by day, their Brigade being credited with 87 aircraft destroyed. The second and third months were quieter, the main task being to engage enemy mine-laying aircraft, which usually kept out of range. 383 Battery were twice employed in a field role, first at the taking of Carpiquet Aerodrome and later in the pursuit of the retiring German army.

In September the Regiment moved to Honfleur, across the water from Le Havre, and were given the role of neutralizing enemy A.A. batteries during raids by our bombers, and also that of preventing any escape by sea by enemy forces. The neutralizing of the enemy batteries was an outstanding success. Only three gun flashes were observed from approximately sixteen enemy gun positions. This enabled the R.A.F. to carry out four major raids in daylight at 3,000 feet practically unmolested. Then for six weeks the Regiment was in action at Dieppe in a combined A.A. and coast defence role, while providing working parties for unloading ammunition at the docks and practising a defence scheme for "containing" 30,000 German prisoners (guarded by only 120 British soldiers) in case they broke camp.

At the end of October the Batteries were issued with the latest type of American radar and predictors and, after two weeks' training, were deployed under American command for the defence of Brussels against flying bombs. This proved to be a difficult and harassing business, as the flying bombs would come over unexpectedly at any hour of the day or night, at a very low height, generally at extreme ranges and travelling at 350 to 400 miles per hour, so that a good night's rest was out of the question. However, the Regiment had several successes.

274 Battery shot down two during the first two days of November, and during the remainder of that month and up to 23rd December the Regiment was credited with another 21 successes. During the night of 20th/21st December, flying bombs were coming over at the rate of one every ten minutes. One Battery fired off its entire stock of ammunition and many were shot down.

When the Germans broke into the Ardennes in December, 1944, the Regiment was partially deployed in an anti-tank role near Tirlemont, where the enemy were infiltrating, dressed in American uniforms. The movement was carried out in dense fog and the guns waited expectantly for the appearance of German tanks. However, the enemy advance slowed down and reinforcements arrived to take over.

On Christmas Eve the Regiment was ordered to move to positions north-east of Antwerp for the defence of that port against flying bombs. Here there was constant action and also preparations for the defence of the town against ground attack. On 27th February, 1945, the 86th moved into Holland, and, though the Luftwaffe had now almost ceased to function, there was almost continuous action until 15th March, as the enemy were loosing off everything they had from the launching sites in the neighbourhood of The Hague; sometimes as many as 100 flying bombs came over in 24 hours. From 10th to 14th March about 35 flying bombs were engaged, and at the finish the Regiment's percentage stood at 53 for the whole period. When the end came, as the sites were captured, the troops were weary but very proud of their collective achievement, with other units, of destroying 2,183 "doodle-bugs," whereas only 211 got through. One of the fly-bombs crashed on 274 Battery's position, inflicting several casualties and wrecking twelve vehicles. On another occasion several men were wounded by 3-inch mortar fire as a result of a mistake by Commandos undergoing instruction preparatory to the crossing of the Rhine.

When the flying bomb menace had ceased the Batteries moved to Flushing for coast defence and to South Beveland in an A.A. role, but had no further action. The Armistice found them still in these positions, with one battery at practice camp at Ostend.

[Photo by courtesy of the Sunday Graphic

THE ARTILLERY GROUND, MARCH, 1941

275 (H.A.C.) H.A.A. Battery, after leaving the 86th Regiment, became a unit of 165 H.A.A. Regiment, sailed for France on D Day plus 3, and was at first deployed for the protection of air-strips in the beach-head, only 1,500 yards from the enemy. On 23rd June, 1945, the Battery was relieved from its A.A. duties and allocated to a Heavy Regiment for operations in a ground role. It helped to support a Canadian attack south of Caen, on 21st July, and was subjected to repeated shelling, suffering some casualties. After reverting to its A.A. status, it was again employed in a ground role to support the break-through at Caumont.

The Battery followed up the advance into Belgium and was attached to the Guards Armoured Division. It was in action in a ground role in the attempt to break through to Arnhem, and one troop was stationed on the bridges at Nijmegen for defence against M.T.Bs. etc. The Regiment was cut off in the "corridor" by a German counter-offensive and provided infantry platoons to support a successful counter-attack with tanks. The river defence sections came under persistent shell fire and suffered many casualties.

The Battery then supported attacks by the 3rd (British) Division at Venraig, Overloon, etc., and at the end of October, 1944, moved to Deurne to support a counter-attack by 15th Scottish Division.

When the German Ardennes offensive started, 275 moved to protect Louvain and later the bridges over the Meuse at Dinant. Later it supported the attack of the 1st Canadian Division to clear the ground between the Meuse and Rhine, firing in 22 days 16,349 rounds in a ground role. At the crossing of the Rhine the Battery fired in the barrage and then crossed the river to take up an A.A. role. After a brief interlude of sundry duties, it was deployed in the defence of the Elbe bridges and fired its last rounds at 0435 hours on 4th May (Armistice Day).

446 (H.A.C.) H.A.A. Battery, R.A., which left the 86th in July, 1942, was retained in a home defence role, and saw action in the suburbs of London before ultimately being sent to defend the Orkney Islands. It was disbanded in 1945.

The H.A.C. National Defence Companies, attached to the 13th Bn. Royal Fusiliers, were stationed from the commencement of hostilities in the London docks area, with a company

THE HONOURABLE ARTILLERY COMPANY

H.A.C. GUARD OF HONOUR AT ST. PAUL'S CATHEDRAL ON OCCASION OF
THE SILVER WEDDING OF THEIR MAJESTIES KING GEORGE VI AND QUEEN ELIZABETH,
26TH APRIL, 1948

Members of the Company of Pikemen in the foreground

at the Bank of England and for a time Headquarters at Armoury House. They were thus in the very thick of the air raids of 1940 and 1941 and sustained a number of casualties in the course of their indispensable guard duties, to which were added fire-fighting and training for the defence of the Port of London against invasion. Finally, in 1942, the 13th Fusiliers, re-numbered the 30th, became a General Service unit, and the majority of the H.A.C. personnel were discharged on account of age or medical category.

The H.A.C. Special Constabulary, the only unit of the Company which from first to last was manned exclusively by members of the H.A.C., carried on throughout the war with their unspectacular but indispensable and, during air-raids, distinctly dangerous, duties with their customary phlegm and fidelity.

Meanwhile Armoury House had miraculously survived the enemy bombardments, suffering the minor casualties of broken windows and roof damage. Though some eight incendiary bombs fell on the building at various times, the resulting fires were dealt with in time by the loyal and gallant efforts of the house staff. The Company's property, however, was less fortunate. Most of the buildings in Bunhill Row were burned out on the night of 28th/29th December, 1940, and the remainder were badly damaged both in this raid and on 11th May, 1941, when several fatal casualties occurred in Armoury House and its surroundings.

In July, 1941, Lord Fortescue's tenure as Colonel-Commandant having expired, Lord Galway, who had recently returned from New Zealand, resumed command of the Company.

At the invitation of the military authorities, an H.A.C. Cadet Battalion was formed and recruited in 1942, with head-quarters at Armoury House. This unit took over the functions of the Battalion in supplying guards of honour at Guildhall and the Mansion House on many official occasions. They even trained gun detachments which fired salutes at The Tower during the absence of the Batteries overseas and during the period of "suspended animation."

Lord Galway made every possible effort to induce the authorities to sanction the formation of an Infantry Battalion for service overseas, as it was felt that the Infantry traditions of the Company were in danger of being overshadowed since the disappearance of the Battalion into the 162 O.C.T.U. It was hoped that a Reconnaissance Battalion might be given the title of H.A.C. (even in brackets) and that to such a unit as many H.A.C. Infantry officers as were available could be posted. Unfortunately, the only concession the War Office would make was to offer to name a battalion of Royal Fusiliers the *n*th Battalion The Royal Fusiliers (Honourable Artillery Company), and it was felt that such a nomenclature was devoid of any rhyme or reason. Therefore nothing was done and the tradition of the H.A.C. Infantry was, for a time, carried on by the Cadet Battalion.

In March, 1943, Lord Galway died, to the great regret of all members. In the same year the King was graciously pleased to appoint Field-Marshal The Viscount Gort, V.C., G.C.B., C.B.E., D.S.O., M.V.O., M.C., to the vacant post of Colonel-Commandant. All members were most gratified that the appointment should have been given to so distinguished a soldier. Lord Gort being at the time in Malta as Governor, the Captain-General decided that, in his absence, a Deputy Colonel-Commandant should be appointed, and this honour fell to the senior officer on the Regimental Reserve of Officers.

The Colonel-Commandant, Lord Gort, returned home from Malta in August, 1944, and at once proceeded to take the keenest interest in Regimental affairs. In October of the same year, however, he was appointed High Commissioner for Palestine and Transjordan and left to take up this extremely onerous and difficult task. Unfortunately, his health broke down, and, returning to England in November, 1945, he went into hospital and died on 31st March of the following year, to the deep regret of all who knew him.

The Company had thus lost two distinguished and devoted Colonel-Commandants in the short space of two years, and it was feared that difficulty would be found in replacing Lord Gort. However, in September, 1946, the Deputy Colonel-Commandant, after conferences between senior officers of the Company and the Court of Assistants, approached the Captain-General and His Majesty appointed no less a personage than the former Chief of the Imperial General Staff, Field-Marshal The Viscount Alanbrooke, G.C.B., O.M., D.S.O., to the vacancy. This selection gave the greatest satisfaction to members of the Company, who felt that the appointment of this

342

most distinguished officer as Colonel-Commandant was a mark of appreciation of the war effort of the Regiment.

In September, 1944, members of the Company read with pride of the award of the Victoria Cross to Major R. H. Cain, South Staffordshire Regiment (a member of the Company since 1928), for outstanding gallantry while serving with the 1st Airborne Division at Arnhem.

MAJOR R. H. CAIN, V.C.
South Staffordshire Regiment
(late No. 2 Company, H.A.C.)

Honours and decorations won by members of the Company and by other officers and men serving with H.A.C. units included 1 V.C., 1 G.C., 1 K.C.B., 3 C.Bs., 12 C.B.Es., 28 D.S.Os. or bars, 11 O.B.Es., 100 M.B.Es., 2 D.S.Cs., 215 M.Cs. or bars, 23 D.F.Cs. or bars, 1 A.F.C., 5 G.Ms., 1 D.S.M., 4 D.C.Ms., 40 M.Ms., 4 B.E.Ms., 1 A.F.M., and 62 foreign decorations. More than 3,800 members were granted commissions. The Roll of Honour records the names of 723 who lost their lives.

At the Victory Parade in London in June, 1946, the Company was represented by a detachment of 1 Officer and 11 other ranks, of artillery and infantry mixed, and a Colour Party of 2 Officers and 1 Sergeant-Major. The Colour Party marched with the massed Colours of British Infantry, and the detachment, for a reason impossible to fathom, in rear of the Essex Regiment (44th Foot) in the Infantry column.

It was not until May, 1947, that the War Office came to the decision to reconstitute the Territorial Army and accordingly the regiments which were in a state of suspended animation were revived, with some alterations of nomenclature.

The 11th, 12th and 13th (H.A.C.) Regiments, R.H.A., faded into history and their successors became the 1st Regiment, H.A.C. (R.H.A.), comprising "A," "B" and "C" Batteries, each armed with 25-pounder self-propelled guns on tank chassis, the establishment being identical with that of an R.H.A. Regiment. To these, however, was added an entirely new unit in the form of "G" Locating Battery, H.A.C., equipped with special survey instruments and radar sets and recruited from personnel with experience in Locating and Survey units.

The 86th (H.A.C.) H.A.A. Regiment, R.A., was revived as the 2nd Regiment, H.A.C. (H.A.A.), a mobile regiment armed with 3.7-in. H.A.A. guns, the two initial batteries being named "D" and "E." "F" Battery was included in the establishment, but not raised for the time being.

1st Regiment H.A.C. formed part of the 56th (London) Armoured Division, T.A., and 2nd Regiment H.A.C. part of No. 1 Anti-Aircraft Group, both new formations.

The Infantry Battalion alone did not undergo a change of name, but was revived as a lorried infantry battalion of 56th (London) Armoured Division, to take up once more its proud position as the senior infantry unit of the Territorial Army and, in point of age, the senior unit of the British Army.

CHAPTER XVI

ATOMA PACIS FULCRA

THE revival of the Company's pre-war units in their old form took place in a very new world. In a century of constant invention and rapid change and the immense upheavals of two major wars, nothing had such a powerful effect on mankind as the dramatic revelation of the Atom Bomb. Its sudden arrival caused the almost immediate cessation of the war and abruptly interrupted and stopped what had become a normal way of life!

The euphoria which followed the end of hostilities faded slowly. It took many months for all the men and women, spread across the world, to return home, to gain their release and to pick up civilian life again. Rationing and shortages were the order of the day; everything seemed to have been used up and the reorganization of the creation of wealth was an even slower process, and a more painful one, than the previous concentration of effort on war purposes.

Despite all this, it was a very happy time. There was the great relief of the lifting of personal danger, there was the joy of reunion with family and friends, and not least there was the sense of comradeship and achievement between service men who had won, and survived. Gone for many was the anxious awareness of yet another campaign to be fought; they knew that the better the regiment, the more it had seemed to foster an "indecent scramble for death". Now they could relax, cheerfully recall past battles and dangers, and discuss the disasters caused by the uninspired decisions of some of their commanders, with studied British nonchalance. Of course, it had been a great victory but everyone knew how close we had been to defeat, how much we owed to our ally, the U.S.A., how much to one of our own citizens, and how much to Hitler's obstinacy.

But there was no real peace. The three major allies had failed to agree on how peace should be organized or shared. In conference they had used the same words with different meanings. The Iron Curtain had replaced the front lines of war. Mutual trust was not achieved. The Cold War had begun. The Bomb soon ceased to be the monopoly of one power group and, to this day, there is no certainty as to whether it stabilizes or endangers peace; whether it is a Peacemaker or a Pacemaker. "Arma pacis fulcra" became "Atoma pacis fulcra".

In such a political climate NATO was born, the American presence in Europe remained, and because the Bomb could be counterproductive, and thus unlikely to be used, only conventional forces could prevent a Russian army of bayonets marching to the Atlantic, as they had marched in other directions. Missing was the firm hand of the mighty Churchill on the tiller. A new era in the world's history had begun.

More than four centuries had passed since the Fraternity of St. George had begun its voluntary duty of nurturing skill-at-arms for the "better defence of this our realme", and of training citizens to lead the trained bands (the best reserve force of its day). After all those years of "setting out of soldiers"—fortuitously a charity under the sagacious Good Queen Bess—came fulfilment. The Company became a part of the new Territorial Force in 1908 and this opened the door for it to provide officers in plenty for the army, and operational units wearing its own cap badge, throughout two world wars. It emerged with tradition firmly rooted, its own Battle Honours, and a very special *esprit de corps*—no mean achievement for "Saturday afternoon soldiers".

Between the two wars the authorities had expressed a not unreasonable reluctance to waste as "cannon fodder" officer potential which could benefit the whole army. It was not generally known in the late thirties how near the Company was to losing its operational role and becoming solely officer producing. That it kept its dual role was almost entirely due to the far-sighted perseverance of its regular Artillery Adjutant Captain Richard Goodbody R.H.A. who persuaded the War Office that the gunner element of the Company could both sponsor an O.C.T.U. and train field units. By the irony of fate Goodbody became both an H.A.C. Commanding Officer, and our Colonel-Commandant many years later. Another irony of history was Hitler's failure to pursue victory in the West after the fall of France, obsessed as he was with this *Drang nach Osten,* thus enabling the full H.A.C. programme to be completed.

At long last the Government decided that the international situation called for the strengthening of our depleted standing army by reviving the Territorial Force in its conventional and pre-war pattern. It was a separate force of twelve infantry and two armoured divisions which would move overseas on mobilization as it had before.

The units reformed on 5th May, 1947 had been in "suspended animation"—an apt official phrase but an unhappy state smacking too much of Damocles sitting with the sword hanging over his head. They were manned, as in the twenties, mostly by seasoned soldiers many of whom had served in the Company's artillery units or as officers throughout the forces. The long delay had reduced potential numbers and since most members had been officers there were several who understandably were reluctant to drop their pips and to start again at the bottom. However, there were quite enough to "get the show on the road", which they did with the confidence born of experience and no little regimental pride.

The post-war social climate had changed. The Welfare State, an ideal carefully pre-planned by the non-party wartime government, had come into being. The citizen was to be protected against all hazards from womb to tomb. Did that include protection for him against the King's enemies? A Recruiting Week in October, 1947 was formally opened by the Lord Mayor at a luncheon at H.Q. presided over by the Colonel-Commandant, Lord Alanbrooke. The Commanding Officer of 1st Regiment H.A.C. (R.H.A.), Lieut.-Colonel John Barstow, D.S.O., who had led 12th Regiment H.A.C. throughout its active war service, made a widely reported speech detailing the needs of the new units. At one point he questioned the success of volunteer soldiers in the future under "the artificial manure of socialism". He was not being political so much as foreseeing the possible effect of changed social conditions, but there was a howl of anguish next day from the *Daily Mirror* and others.

The Commanding Officers of the other two Regiments were: 2nd Regiment H.A.C. (H.A.A.)—Lieut.-Colonel E. R. G. Heath, M.B.E. (later to be Prime Minister) and H.A.C. Infantry Battalion—Lieut.-Colonel (late Brigadier) A. D. McKechnie, D.S.O., who had commanded the Buffs and then a Brigade. The Cadet Battalion, under the care of Major H. F. A. Jackson, M.B.E., continued to carry out ceremonial duties until

1948 and remained in being until 1958. The mounting of guards of honour at Guildhall by the Battalion and the firing of salutes at the Tower by 1st Regiment were naturally taken on again as soon as numbers permitted.

Recruiting was very much the first priority. The seasoned pre-war officers in charge were all too conscious of the unreality of the training of the thirties, despite the keenness of the volunteers and their awareness of the imminence of war. Now, much as numbers were needed, the would-be members were very thoroughly screened, and warned of the demanding nature of their commitment. The result was cadres of high quality, a great deal of actual experience and tough training. One example in these early years was "B" Battery's march from London to Brighton, led by Major Robin Smith, M.C. & Bar, one weekend, to prove that not only the Infantry wore boots.

While the military were still in suspended animation, the Court of Assistants had begun and continued the formidable task of restoring the Company and its properties to peacetime conditions. The House had been de-requisitioned in 1946, but the Artillery Garden was still under the control of the War Office at the end of 1947. A request was made by Finsbury Borough Council for the use of the ground for sporting purposes for young people from the borough. The legal authorities of the War Office advised that our Charter and Lease permitted only military purposes, and the request was refused. The Court sanctioned the use of the House by all serving in the Company's active units who were not also members, while on military duty. It also promulgated rules of eligibility for admission and re-admission. Now qualified were all those who had served in the Company's units during the war. It also decided to discontinue the appointment of a Chairman and Vice-Chairman and to revert to ancient custom, whereby the Senior Civil Chief present presided over meetings of the Court, or in the absence of Civil Chiefs, a member elected for the meeting.

Thanks to the devoted work of the groundsman, Ray Warner, cricket was played again in the summer of 1947 and soccer and hockey in the winter, and the Golfing Society also operated. Returfing of the southern part by the War Office and making good of the site of the trenches was also undertaken (see plate opposite p. 339). Sutling still suffered severely as rationing became even more severe and functions above 100 persons required the special permission of the Court. Rationing was finally removed in 1953.

Back in May, 1945 the Court had entrusted the formation of an Old Comrades Association to an ad hoc committee headed by Lieut.-Colonel J. Bamford Smith, O.B.E. T.D. Over 40 years later, in his 101st year, this grand old man set down an account of it in his own words: "I am happy to remember that I wrote personally to all our senior commanding officers abroad before the end of the War—to be certain to retain the names and addresses of their command—so that I could include them on the lists to be circulated and 'kept in touch' with after the War—and right up to the present time (I have now passed my 100th birthday!!)—I often add a copy to my current file!!" It was stated at the time that "the primary object of the Association is to promote and keep alive that spirit of happy comradeship which has been so marked during the present war, and which indeed has been the very basis of the Regiment's efficiency and service".

With such a start the O.C.A. flourished. The first reunion at Armoury House on 11th January, 1946 was attended by 240 of all ranks of H.A.C. units. It quickly reached a membership of nearly 3,000. Under the dedicated secretaryship of Captain G. T. L. Dowdney, former R.S.M. of 11th H.A.C., R.H.A., more than 1,000 were found employment, 800 applications for financial aid were met, and over 1,100 requests for help were dealt with, during the first 12 years. Over 200 reunions and other events had taken place. In 1961 the H.A.C. Benevolent Fund was widened to make Old Comrades and their dependants eligible, and the invaluable social and welfare work continues to this day.

One such event was the Westmeath Lunch. Time passes and the number of members attending falls slowly but inevitably. By 1985 not one of the survivors was fit enough to come to London. After all she did sail in 1914!

The end of 1947 saw the retirement of the Company's Secretary, the popular and indefatigable Major G. Goold Walker, D.S.O., M.C. His 25 years of service had seen the completion of the reorganization after the First World War, the historical display at the Royal Tournament, our 400th Anniversary, visits to and from the Ancient and Honourable Artillery Company, the conduct of some First World War battlefield tours, and the full term of the Second World War. He was a gifted historian (the author of most of this book), and editor of *The H.A.C. in the Great War*, with a remarkable capacity to unearth our traditions and privileges. After a not very happy interlude, he was finally replaced on 22nd November, 1948 by another most capable and industrious Secretary, Brigadier E. Foster Hall, M.C. (late the Buffs).

Among the several Regimental activities which were making steady progress was the "Maynetennce of the Science & Feate of Shoting in . . . Handgonnes". The Open Range Meeting was held at Bisley in September, 1948 with an almost record attendance. The Hut was coming back into regular use including a ten-day stay by the XIVth Olympiad competitors from Portugal, Italy, Brazil, Cuba, Monaco and Belgium. This precedent was later extended to housing university and public school teams attending the N.R.A. meetings. The Metropolitan Special Constabulary Detachment which, like the Windmill, had never closed down, continued its good work. The Company of Pikemen and Musketeers went from strength to strength to full strength, and their ceremonial role of attending on and escorting the Lord Mayor became indispensable to the ritual of the City. In effect they consolidated the traditional protection which the H.A.C. had provided for the Corporation in more troublous days. In 1950 they played a memorable part in the pageantry of the Royal Tournament.

The restoration and rebuilding of the Company's properties, and recovery of their rents, were major preoccupations of the Court. The House itself had escaped major damage but had suffered six years' neglect. All the property on Chiswell Street and Bunhill Row, except one commercial building and the flats, had been destroyed by bombing and the ensuing fires. War damage payments began to come in during 1947 and went on until 1950. The surplus above immediate repair requirements was placed in a Redevelopment Fund. After protracted negotiations and after the area of 21/23 Chiswell Street had been in temporary occupation by the City of London T. & A.F. Association, all the areas were relet on long leases, including the Bunhill Row flats pending a long-term development plan.

The floor of the Long Room was found to be unsafe for large gatherings and had to be supported with steel girders. For some time the Annual General Court and events like dances had to be held in the Albert Room.

Naturally the Court had been concerned with the increasing strains on our finances. As related in Chapter x, see p. 220, the subscription had stood at two guineas since 1803, except for two short periods (1816 and 1934–1858) when it had been reduced to one guinea. A proposal to increase it was rejected by the Annual General Court of 1949. Instead, the Treasurer exhorted members to add a voluntary donation to their dues and to make Sutling more profitable by fuller use of its improving facilities. Both appeals had some effect though only 500-odd members increased their subscriptions. More potent was the decision to exploit our charitable status dependent on the statute of Queen Elizabeth I relieving bodies engaged in the "setting out of soldiers" of taxation. In 1950 Counsel's opinion was sought as to whether subscriptions could be made under Deed of Covenant with tax deducted, and whether such tax could be reclaimed by the Company. The answer to both questions was "Yes", and a guinea-pig member successfully tested the procedure, which was then made available to everyone. All this helped to stave off an increase for a few years but by 1955 the reserves accumulated during the war years and the interest on claims for war damage had been exhausted. The subscription was raised to three guineas.

During 1950 the first National Servicemen were posted to the Regiment. One of them had joined before his National Service and returned as a volunteer afterwards. In the following year the units were allotted their quota of "Z" reservists and both their quality and quantity greatly enhanced the scope of annual training.

When Colonel H. W. O'Brien, M.C. resigned his appointment as Deputy Colonel-Commandant, Lieut.-Colonel J. A. T. Barstow, D.S.O., lately commanding 1st Regiment, took his place. The Captain-General had done the Regiment a great honour by appointing Lord Alanbrooke, the top soldier of the day, our Colonel-Commandant, and then by extending his tour, but a deputy was needed to deal with the many matters not requiring a Field-Marshall's attention. In human terms "Brookie" was the least pompous of men, easily approached and a born raconteur. To enable him to meet the many new officers, and they him, it had been decided in 1949 to institute an Active Officers' Dinner—with no guests allowed—which became an annual event. It was a happy occasion when he also become Constable of the Tower, whose Master-Gunner within was traditionally an H.A.C. senior artillery officer. Another matter of great satisfaction to the Company was Captain R. Corfield's "fiftieth" when he presented to us in 1949 a full-length portrait of His Majesty King George VI in Field Marshall's uniform with Garter Robes, painted for the Regiment by Maurice Codner, R.P.

The impressive entrance hall and staircase of Armoury House were greatly enhanced by the unveiling and dedication in 1952 of the Memorial stained glass windows and attendant panelling. The work included a new cabinet for a second Roll of Honour to be placed alongside that of the 1914–1918 War, while the South African Roll has been inscribed on the oak panelling. To complete our Memorials, a Roll of Honour was placed in a new cabinet in St. Botolphs, Bishopsgate.

The Regiment received with the deepest sorrow news of the death of His Majesty George VI, our Captain-General on 6th February, 1952. Appropriate messages sent to Her Majesty the Queen and to Her Majesty Queen Elizabeth the Queen Mother were gracefully acknowledged. On ascending the throne, Her Majesty assumed the title of Captain-General of the Honourable Artillery Company and on 12th May Her Majesty graciously intimated that she would receive a deputation on 17th December and sign the Roll of Members in its presence. A diamond and ruby brooch in the shape of the Company's crest was duly presented to her at Buckingham Palace and the Vellum Roll signed and the Vellum Books inspected. Lord Alanbrooke led the deputation which comprised the Vice-President, the Treasurer, the Deputy Colonel-Commandant, the Officers commanding the 1st and 2nd Regiments and the Battalion, and the Secretary.

An application was made to the Sovereign through the War Office for the Company to retain its privilege to parade in full strength next to the Brigade of Guards at the coming Coronation. The request was repeated by the Colonel-Commandant direct to the Secretary of State in 1953. The Army Council did not dispute its validity but stated that it was not possible to uphold all the privileges of the past. The Company was able only to be given token representation in the procession and on the route.

THE H.A.C. DELEGATION TO BUCKINGHAM PALACE, 17TH DECEMBER, 1952.

Back row: the Secretary, Colonel Barstow, Major Hill and Colonel Jackson. Front row: Major Pettit, Colonel Armstrong, Lord Alanbrooke and Colonel Davis

The next royal occasion—the first major event since re-forming—was the presentation of new Colours in July, 1955. Although A.A. command ceased to exist in that month—and with it 2 Regt. H.A.C., the active side, padded still with N.S. men, had sufficient numbers, and, of course, adequate training to put on an impeccable performance. The scene will never be forgotten by those present and no less the splendid greeting to Her Majesty delivered by the Senior Officer commanding the parade, Lieut.-Colonel H. F. A. Jackson, O.B.E., the Infantry C.O. at that time.

After the ceremony Her Majesty also presented in person to the Colonel-Commandant and President the Royal Warrant establishing the Company of Pikemen and Musketeers as a "formed body armed and accoutred . . . and carrying the Cross of St. George as part of the Military Parade on great occasions of state and other ceremonial occasions". The Warrant also regulated their command, numbers and occasions and, of

353

course, permitted the wearing of service decorations, medals and insignia.

A feature of the post-war years has been the various visits abroad during which the Pikemen have either accompanied the Lord Mayor or paraded abroad with his approval. The first of these visits was to Helsinki in 1957 and since then to Zurich, Oslo, Brussels and to participate in military tattoos in Berlin and Ghent. In 1971 they visited the U.S.A. to escort the Lord Mayor at the opening of the old London Bridge on its transfer to Lake Havasu. At home presentations have been made at the Royal Tournament and the Festival of Remembrance.

It was perhaps the close relationship of the Pikemen with the City hierarchy that prompted the court to remind the Honorary Members (the Lord Mayor, Sheriffs, Aldermen and Recorder) that they were entitled to attend meetings of the Court. It is a matter of history that the hint was taken and the tradition has continued ever since.

The Court decided that one old custom should be given very special attention: to wit, the traditional feast of the Company on St. George's Day. Accordingly, on 23rd April, 1953 no less a personage than the Prime Minister, Sir Winston Churchill, honoured us with his presence and proposed the Toast of England. He was accompanied by the three wartime Chiefs of Staff and the Archbishop of Canterbury. As the years passed, many other royal and famous figures have graced the occasion including, in chronological order, the Dukes of Gloucester and of Kent, Prince Michael of Kent, the Prince of Wales and the young Duke of Gloucester.

Historically there has always been a delicate balance in the control of the Company between Civil and Military authorities, and earlier chapters have recorded in detail such disastrous periods as 1888/1889, and the more recent reluctance of the Battalion in 1937 to accept the imposition of an Officers' Mess, as a matter of discipline. In 1953 the able and popular Vice-President, Major J. A. Hill, resigned from his important post because he felt the Court were becoming too involved, contrary to his views, in the discussion and conduct of military matters. His going was deeply regretted by all, but was a salutary reminder of the sensitivity of our peculiar constitution.

In the autumn of 1954 the Ancient and Honourable Artillery Company of Massachusetts broke with precedent and carried out the Fall Field of Duty outside America. A large contingent came to fraternize in London and to visit Boston in Lincolnshire. The two companies entertained one another with banquets. This visit was repeated in 1959 and the H.A.C. reciprocated with a strong detachment, active and veteran, going to Boston for their June Day Election in 1963.

Lord Alanbrooke's extended tour came to an end in August, 1954 and sadly as he was missed we were now to enjoy the leadership of Major-General Sir Julian Gascoigne, K.C.V.O., C.B., D.S.O. until 1959. His warm and genial personality rapidly endeared him to the Regiment and his tour coincided with a smooth period in our affairs but with many significant happenings. National Service was running out, the units became 100% volunteers, though most were young and inexperienced and needed more and more instruction. Divisional formations still remained and regular training culminated in large-scale exercises. His Royal Highness Prince Philip became a member in 1957, signing the Roll brought to him by a deputation which visited Buckingham Palace.

Battle Honours awarded to the H.A.C. were published in Army Order No. 20 in the same year. Those selected to be borne on the Colours are in heavy type, viz:

"Bourgebus Ridge", "Antwerp", "Le Havre", "**Rhine**", "**North-West Europe, 1944–45**", "**Knightsbridge**", "**El Alamein**", "**El Hamma**", "Sbiba", "**Thala**", "Tunis", "North Africa, 1941–43", "**Sicily, 1948**", "**Cassino II**", "**Coriano**", "Senio", "Italy, 1944–45".

The Territorial Army celebrated its golden jubilee the following year with a Royal Review in Hyde Park. The Company was represented by a composite detachment with Colour and the Band and the same day the Battalion mounted the Queen's Guard at the Palace.

The Second World War history, *Regimental Fire!*, written by a veteran member, Brigadier R. F. Johnson, and dedicated to the Captain-General was published. A portrait of Her Majesty by Anthony Devas, A.R.A., R.P., commissioned and presented by Sir Julian Gascoigne, was exhibited at the Royal Academy and afterwards hung in the Long Room. In 1959 at the end of his tour, Sir Julian was appointed Governor of Bermuda and he was most fittingly succeeded by our old and valued member and friend Lieut.-General Sir Richard Goodbody, K.B.E., C.B., D.S.O., one time Commander of 11th Regiment in Africa, and pre-war Artillery Adjutant. Colonel J. A. T. Barstow, D.S.O., resigned his post as Deputy Colonel-Commandant and was not replaced.

On 8th April, 1960, the young Prince of Wales visited Armoury House and signed the Vellum Book. He also sat in the layer's seat of a 25 pounder under the personal instruction of the Colonel-Commandant. At 11 he was the same age as Prince Charles, later King Charles II, when he signed in 1641.

THE WINDS OF CHANGE

Austerity was still with us and inflation had raised its ugly head although its future rake's progress could not be foreseen. One major Government reaction was to cut defence expenditure and, in particular, the Territorial Force. On 1st May, 1961 the establishments of the Company's units were severely reduced and their roles modified. "G" Locating Battery disappeared but a new Officer Training Wing was started and a Regimental Headquarters created under its own H.A.C. Colonel. The entire set-up came under command of 54 (E. Anglia) Divisional/ District—except for the O.T.W. which was vested in the Regimental H.Q. The first Colonel was Colonel J. M. Austin-Smith, M.C. who had replaced Colonel A. G. P. Lincoln, M.C. The commanding officers were determined to make up for lack of numbers by increased efficiency and more realistic training. One example was 1st Regiment's 1,200-mile march round England shooting its guns at one artillery range after another.

On the property side a very important matter securing the Company's future was resolved by the efforts of the Estate and Finance Committee. The freehold of that part of the ground leased to the City Lieutenancy and mostly subleased to the Company was bought from the Church Commissioners for £10,000. The area comprised the site of the House and Gun Park, the whole Parade Ground and the eastern half of the ground. All except Finsbury Barracks remained subleased to the Company. In the event of development the conveyance provided that any profit would be divided with the Church Commissioners. Three years later freehold of the vicarage and garages was also acquired from the Church Commission. The remaining half was still held on the 2,000-year lease from the City of London.

The short term lease of the Bisley Hut was converted into a 99-year lease in 1963.

The security of the premises, and the related expansion of car parking, were reviewed in 1961. The gates were locked at night, a ground keeper was employed and parking controlled and charged for.

An actuarial study of the membership trend showed that, based on 700 active members, no significant decline in numbers was likely for some years.

From time to time it has been customary for the Guild of St. George to display its particular skill in "The Science & Feate of Shoting . . .". There being no longer a Daily Telegraph Cup to interest the "handgonners" the "better defence of this our Realme" was demonstrated in 1962 by "C" Battery H.A.C. who won the Queen's Cup for artillery at Larkhill. The trophy was presented to the Regiment at the Mansion House by H.R.H. Princess Alice Countess of Athlone before a Guard of Honour under Major D. S. Morpeth, the Battery Commander (and future C.O. of the Regiment).

Another gunner trophy might here be mentioned—the Jock Cup—competed for annually by the six troops of guns of the Regiment in a "Quick Action" competition. One of the most important aspects of the artillery role during the war, and since, was the ability to bring a troop of guns on the move into action with maximum speed, particularly when supporting armour. Bogey time for an accurate salvo on to a target was four minutes or less.

The title has no connection with General "Jock" Campbell of "Jockcol" fame but was chosen to commemorate a much loved character—Jock Lovibond—who had been 11th Regiment's Medical Officer at the outbreak of war and who rejoined on reforming. He was the friend of all and helped enormously to revive and maintain the old spirit and traditions. Sadly he died young in 1957 but all who knew him were delighted at his being so aptly remembered in the sporting competition named after him.

The Benevolent Fund was reconstituted to cover the needs of everyone connected with the Company, viz. members, ex-members, old comrades, staff and the dependants of all of them. The Colonel-Commandant launched an Appeal to raise £50,000 —a substantial target in those days. Over £30,000 had been given or promised by May, 1962. Her Majesty the Queen graciously subscribed, as did the Lord Mayor. A Staff Pension Fund was inaugurated in 1964 and the Company was formally registered as a Charity.

The title of "1st Regiment H.A.C. (R.H.A.)" was changed to "1 Field Regt. H.A.C. (R.H.A.)", in common with the rest of the Royal Artillery in order to indicate the operational role in the titles. About this time, an application to the L.C.C. for outline permission to redevelop the Bunhill Row flats site was turned down and in 1965, when inflation was beginning to escalate, the subscription rose to five guineas.

A project intended to further our military standing and to interest all members, was the series of lectures devised as a Memorial to our late Colonel Commandant Viscount Alan-brooke (1946–1954). A total of nine talks on military or politico-military subjects were given by eminent people of great experience within their subject, ranging from Professor Michael Howard to Sir Richard Hull over a six-year period.

The Secretary Brigadier E. Foster-Hall, M.C., who had served the Company and its members so conscientiously for over 16 years, retired in 1965 and his place was taken by Lieut.-Colonel P. Massey, M.C. (late the Royal Dragoons).

During that summer the Government had been having a drastic re-think on the future nature and role of our armed forces. Economy, as well as the most practicable way to meet our NATO (and Irish) commitments, called for highly professional, well equipped and trained, and instantly available units and formations with more integrated reinforcement facilities. The nuclear age meant that the day of massed armies with their slow mobilization and deployment was over.

The under-strength, divisionally organized and geographically orientated Territorial Force was no longer appropriate. The role, size and shape of the Reserve Army was to be recast, with reserve battalions and brigades directly affiliated to their regular counterparts. The tours of duty in Ireland, where each unit in turn was subjected to the *real* experience of coming under fire, demanded a higher standard of self-discipline than normal peacetime soldiering called for.

This brief history cannot record in full the protracted debate. Suffice it to say that the Colonel-Commandant Sir Richard Goodbody, and the Regimental Colonel Norman Young successfully fought, with the support of the Army Commander, for a place for the H.A.C. in the new Orbat from which it had at first been omitted. At long last, in December, 1966 our volunteer categories were formalized thus:

Army Volunteer Reserve II. Sub-unit reinforcement called out without Royal Proclamation. Includes Officer Pool.
A.V.R. III. Called out for Home or Civil Defence.
A.V.R. IV. Bandsmen.

Our reorganization (see diagram) was finalized with effect from 1st April, 1967 as a Headquarters, a Training Wing and two Companies and two Batteries, while "C" Battery formed part of a non-H.A.C. composite artillery unit known as the Greater London Regiment.

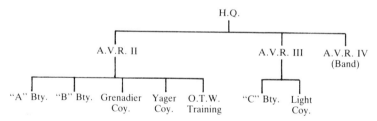

Although the whole concept seemed as near *Reductio ad absurdum* as could be devised, the challenge was taken up by the very capable officers in charge of the active units and it was made to work. Colonel G. D. Spratt, successor to Colonel Norman Young, M.C., was an ex-Guards officer who had joined the Battalion as a private. Lieut.-Colonel the Lord Freyberg, O.B.E., M.C. was a serving Guards officer specially picked to help the H.A.C. in the crisis, as C.O. of the mixed unit. One inspired innovation by Lieut.-Colonel Freyberg was to get his unit overseas to Malta for annual training in 1966. A change is as good as a tonic.

The weak point was "Too many Chiefs and not enough

Indians". The base was too narrow to provide a viable major unit such as a battalion or artillery regiment which could operate realistically in the field—particularly with the extra role of officer production. On the credit side, A.V.R. II was well equipped, given better and better training facilities, and was even a good example in miniature of the all-arms battle group which had replaced the strictly Divisional. The A.V.R. III element was greatly assisted by its erstwhile H.A.C. comrades but it died quickly and was quietly reabsorbed

It was fitting that a portrait of General Richard Goodbody, G.C.B., K.B.E., D.S.O., which was commissioned from Mr. Carlos Sancha and had been heavily oversubscribed, should be unveiled in the Long Room in 1967 by his successor, General Sir Rodney Moore, G.C.V.O., K.C.B., C.B.E., D.S.O., appointed on 1st October, 1966. "Richard", as he was affectionately known to all fellow members, had spent most of his distinguished career in contact with the Company in many different capacities.

According to a public statement made by Mr. Enoch Powell, "the British Army had suffered three hammer blows at the hands of the Administration . . . the third possibly the worst blow being the halving of the Territorial Army". While the fate of our own active units was in the melting pot, the Court set up a Policy Committee in 1969, chaired by Colonel G. R. Armstrong, D.S.O., M.C., to consider how best the Company should be organized to weather the years ahead when, temporarily at least, there might be no military role. It was an interesting but unspectacular exercise involving the scrutiny of its corporate and charitable status, its economy and membership trend, the efficiency of its management and its numerous ancillary activities. Its report did more to confirm the soundness of the Company's present objectives than to suggest radical change, but it did stress the need to simplify committee and office routines, to develop long-term property plans, to rationalize the layout of the house for military use and to meet inflation by raising charges to the users as necessary. An inevitable but not disastrous decline in membership was expected, but with or without an active role for the "setting out of soldiers" the basic Charter object of "defence . . . of the realme by maynetennce of the Science . . . of Shoting" would still justify our existence. As a result some streamlining of Court and office work was achieved and house charges and the subscription were raised to match inflation, i.e. from five guineas to eight pounds. Legal advice a few months later approved "trading" with non-members and outside bodies under certain conditions. Finally a study was begun for redeveloping parts of the Company's premises.

On 31st July the Metropolitan Special Constabulary contingent celebrated its Jubilee. The Commissioner for the Metropolis, Sir John Waldron, K.C.V.O. inspected and took the salute at the march past. Before an audience of some 200, including many original members of the Division, the detachment, led by the Regimental Band, marched on to the field at Armoury House. Then as the shadows lengthened across that historic ground, 50 years to the hour when the first members were attested, Inspector North reported to the Colonel-Commandant Sir Rodney Moore, "Sir, the Regimental Detachment of the Metropolitan Special Constabulary is ready for inspection."

This day perhaps marked the high point in the "FLAT 'ATS" post-war service. Membership stood at nearly 100. The unit had made a notable contribution to Civil Defence and to general policing throughout the war. In common with other Company activities there were many ups and downs in the years that followed. The authorities wanted a fuller programme of training and seemed to set too little store by the H.A.C. connection.

Fortunately reorganization within the Division enabled our detachment to change place with the Specials at City Road station which then took only H.A.C. recruits. The Court was able to provide accommodation at H.Q., so the unit came back home. It was now to renew its enjoyable duties at all the principal state functions in London and of course to participate in the Regimental ones.

The sixties saw the growth of the "Demo" tendency, involving the police in extra duties and the need for "special" assistance. There were the inevitable changes in organization, administration, uniform and equipment which affected all Government services. The introduction of personal radios for policemen was perhaps the most significant.

Over succeeding years the place and image of the police in the life of the nation has undergone a subtle change. Crime and violence have increased and, just as the military faced a call for

HIS ROYAL HIGHNESS THE PRINCE OF WALES ADMITTED A MEMBER AT THE
ST. GEORGE'S DINNER, 23RD APRIL, 1970

fewer but better trained and equipped men, so the Force has
become more professional with a corresponding fall in the role
of the part-timer. Recruiting has fallen and time alone will show
how this trend will develop.

His Royal Highness the Prince of Wales, having graciously
expressed his willingness to join the Company, was duly elected
by the Court on 20th April, 1970. Three days later he attended
the St. George's Dinner where, after proposing the "Toast of
England", he made the customary declaration and signed the
Vellum Roll. In the previous November, His Royal Highness
Prince Philip, Duke of Edinburgh, had also attended a held-over
St. George's Dinner in 1969, and now to complete a unique trio
of royal visits, to everyone's great satisfaction Her Majesty, our
Captain-General, inspected the Company on 11th June in the
Artillery Ground. It was a particularly happy occasion and in a
message afterwards the Queen said how much she had enjoyed
meeting so many members and their wives at the garden party
which followed the parade. When a veteran expressed the

Company's great pride in seeing her wearing the Regimental brooch, she quickly replied, "I adore it"; and then, noticing his wife wore a similar brooch, Her Majesty pointed to it with the wicked remark, "Mine's bigger".

At the next St. George's Dinner it was the turn of a veteran member Lieut.-Colonel The Rt. Hon. Edward Heath, M.B.E. to propose "England". His portrait, also by Carlos Sancha and presented by Colonel F. J. N. Davis, now hangs in the House. In the "Fall" a strong detachment from the "Ancients" came for their Tour of Duty. They had the honour of being received at Buckingham Palace by the Captain-General and their visit included a reception at Armoury House, morning service at St. Paul's, followed by a buffet at H.Q. and finally thei˙ own banquet at Grosvenor House. Another occasion which gave us more than usual satisfaction was the attendance of Her Royal Highness Princess Margaret as the Guest of Honour at the Mess Club Ladies' Dinner in May, 1972. Her Royal Highness was very warmly received.

TROOPERS ALL

The age of inflation was also the age of the explosion of sophisticated technology. The V1 pilotless flying bomb and the terrifying V2 rocket, which appeared on the scene near the end of the Second World War, were blunt instruments compared with the guided missiles of the seventies. Computerization and the micro chip control not only the supermarket check-out but also the super-power weapon systems.

It was in this new and fast changing background that the rather hotchpotch set-up of the Company's A.V.R. Active unit dragged to an end. There had been a visit to Cyprus in 1970 and in 1973 great glory was won by a team from the newly combined Grenadier/Yager Company which, under the inspired leadership of Captain Tim Lloyd Davies, won the "Cambrian Marches" in Wales in competition with Paratroopers and Marines. It was a very tough exercise and a great tribute to them. The last conventional camp took place on the Plain. Immediately afterwards, following a stern address by the Commanding Officer, Lieut.-Colonel Gilchrist, warning of the extra burdens to come, the Regiment began to reorganize into four squadrons with a new operational reconnaissance role in B.A.O.R. in the event of war.

In the words of one serving officer at the time, "the post camp period of 1973 saw the Active unit management suffering the Swan Syndrome—all calm and serene on the surface but paddling like hell underneath".

A milestone in our history was reached when gunners and privates all became troopers wearing the same cap badge. The longstanding gulf between Batteries and Battalion went at a stroke. The term "squadron" was not new to us and was chosen to avoid confusing the veteran affiliations of Infanteers and Gunners.

The Index to this work contains no fewer than 42 references to uniform, and the post-war years have seen no reduction in the H.A.C.'s often criticized obsession with it. Not surprisingly, therefore, during the summer recess of 1973, the Dress Committee of the Active unit met regularly to produce the new form of dress. Hours were spent in discussion with representative veterans to arrive at an acceptable compromise. The final paper went off to the Colonel-Commandment for his comments. Back came the reply: "The matter of dress for the H.A.C. has been discussed with the Captain-General and attached is the approved order of dress". It bore little resemblance to that suggested by the Committee.

Months later there arrived at Armoury House a formal letter which began: "The Army Dress Committee note with some displeasure that the H.A.C. has taken upon itself to introduce new forms and order of dress without first seeking the approval of this committee. Please advise by return the circumstances which have brought this about." The reply, sent by return, said simply: "The new form and order of dress have been set out by our Captain-General and our Colonel-Commandant. Please take up the matter of approval with them." No more was heard of the subject, and the Quartermaster registered the sealed patterns.

In 1973 the Vice-President, Captain W. D. Pryke had chaired a sub-committee to settle the vexed question of how veterans could be nominally affiliated to active squadrons. The Members List published at the time remained very much on an "original unit" basis. A later list in 1980 attempted to place veterans as belonging to the various squadrons but it is doubtful if the old practice can usefully be changed or superseded. The membership has always consisted of "chronological layers" of successive generations who identify and recognize their comrades from the sub-units they served in.

The new establishment also envisaged the formation of a Gun Troop so as to provide fire for observation practice. Apart from manning guns, the new training entailed expertise in the use of small arms, the mastery of all infantry skills and the handling of modern communication techniques and advanced radio equipment. It also included all aspects of mobility and rapid deployment. The operational task was more demanding than any previous role in the Regiment's history. Training just had to be tough and arduous and called for the utmost in enthusiasm, tenacity and determination.

The recruits at this time were necessarily devoid of military experience and were therefore subject to very testing training courses. After a year those who survived were indeed top quality troops.

The training of officers, including those from other units, continued on one-year courses, and the H.A.C., and the R.M.A. Sandhurst remained the only officer producing units in the Regular or Territorial Army. We were thus the only T.A. unit able to commission our own officers.

Annual training in 1975 and 1976 took place in B.A.O.R., followed by a special intensive camp in the U.K. in 1977. At this point the unit achieved its first main goal—it was declared "operational". It was a landmark in the Company's history and an exceptional performance for part-time soldiers.

On 6th May, 1974 the 50th anniversary of the Company's first Royal Salute at the Tower of London was celebrated by a gathering at Headquarters of all available Master Gunners within the Tower. The custom of appointing a senior artillery officer from the H.A.C. to this post began in 1931.

Those present were:

Major J. McDermid, T.D.	1943–47
Lieut.-Col. J. A. T. Barstow, D.S.O., T.D.	1947–51
Lieut.-Col. E. R. G. Heath, M.B.E., M.P.	1951–54
Col. G. R. Armstrong, D.S.O., M.C., T.D.	1954–57
Col. A. G. P. Lincoln, M.C., T.D.	1957–60
Col. J. M. Austin-Smith, C.B.E., M.C., T.D.	1960–64

Col. A. N. Young, M.C., T.D.	1964–67
Lieut.-Col. D. S. Morpeth, T.D.	1967–68
Col. B. L. Davis, T.D.	1968–71
Lieut.-Col. G. E. Gilchrist, T.D.	1971–74

The post has since been filled by:

Col. C. B. Powell-Smith, T. D.	1974–77
Col. B. A. Kay, T.D.	1977–80
Col. C. H. M. Martin, O.B.E., T.D.	1980–82
Lieut.-Col. R. A. Burford, T.D.	1982–84
Col. S. A. Sellon, O.B.E., T.D.	1984–86

A pleasant task, not without honour but, alas, with no pay!

The Company now found itself in the grip of rampant inflation, which, in the decade 1965/75 had amounted to 143% or 13½% per annum. Most western countries, with their free economies, had reacted by adjusting prices and wages as necessary. Despite inflation the fact was that the standard of living and the distribution of wealth had greatly improved since the thirties, not always evenly it is true. Most families had a car, television and subsidized medical care, etc., and it was in the context of this "better" world that the Regiment had to review its special problems. For centuries it had been sustained by the "quarteridge" paid by all members. Earlier chapters relate the many ups and downs in numbers and finance. In more modern times the small active element which used the House and its facilities were supported by a larger number of veterans who, through age or geography, rarely visited it. There was now a yawning gap between Income and Expenditure, multiplied by inflation. Since neither Rents nor Investment income could be quickly expanded, the other two main sources, Subscriptions, and "Trading", had to be increased. A Planning Committee under the Chairmanship of Colonel R. R. St. J. Barkshire was appointed in 1975 "to consider how the Company was to survive and continue to achieve its object . . . in view of its acute financial difficulties."

It soon came out with the interim recommendation that, subject to legal approval, the membership should be widened to include a limited number of persons whose military service had not been with H.A.C. units. Though well aware of the risk of a possible loss of traditional Regimental spirit and veteran support, the proposal was agreed by a Special General Court in

HER ROYAL HIGHNESS PRINCESS ANNE INSPECTING THE GUARD OF HONOUR AT THE
GUILDHALL WHEN THE FREEDOM OF THE CITY WAS CONFERRED UPON HER,
27TH FEBRUARY, 1976

July. Thereafter legal advice was taken as to the possible consequential effect on our charitable status and the exemption from Rates arising from the Crown's occupation of the premises. Meanwhile the Committee re-examined all aspects and activities of the Company which had mostly been covered by the Policy Committee in 1969. Its broad conclusion was that we were faced with the running of a large commercial enterprise which was under-capitalized. Its final report was approved at another Special General Court in September. One necessary and immediate step was the raising of the subscription from £8 and £15, seemingly a near 90% increase but, in fact, greatly reduced because of the concessions to the young and the old.

Legal approval for the wider membership having been received, the Planning Committee's proposals were accepted at the Annual General Court in March, 1976. Thus began the

367

process of converting what had always been a strictly military institution, into a combination of a West End club and the Connaught Rooms. The H.A.C. had always provided its soldiers with a much higher standard of "barrack" accommodation than other volunteers and way beyond that laid down for the T.A. generally. It was intended that this policy should continue but the main part of the House would be available on commercial terms to the public—or to selected portions of the public— for social occasions.

Henceforth there would be two categories of members: Regimental Members who had done appropriate terms of service in the Company's units or its Metropolitan Special Constabulary, and Members who had served for two years as Regulars or three years as Volunteers elsewhere. Such non-Regimental Members could not vote on changes in the Rules and Orders nor could they be Members of the Court. Basic subscriptions were to be £40 for Town Members and £20 for Country plus an entrance fee of £10 for the new category. Sixty-three were accepted in 1976 and by 1985 the number had reached nearly 300.

In May the Regiment said farewell with very great regret to the Colonel-Commandant, General Sir Rodney Moore, G.C.V.O., K.C.B., C.B.E., D.S.O. His never failing charm and tact had won him innumerable friends. He had thrown himself heart and soul into our affairs and steered us through the troubled waters of T.A.V.R. into the exciting and challenging new operational role. In his place the Captain-General appointed a doughty warrior in the person of General Sir Victor FitzGeorge-Balfour, K.C.B., C.B.E., D.S.O., M.C.

In the following year the genial Lieut.-Colonel Massey, M.C., retired and was succeeded by Captain G. C. Lloyd, C.B.E., R.N., who had participated in the Korean War. One of the first things the new Secretary became involved in was the action being planned to modernize the House which could not be delayed much longer. Armoury House is an imposing old building which had expanded on a patchwork basis. It has always invoked the affection of successive generations of members but, like Versailles, it was inconvenient functionally and expensive to run and to maintain. Some parts were wearing out.

The Court of Assistants decided to launch an Appeal to raise funds for a rebuilding project and sought professional advice for

LORD MAYOR'S DAY, 1977

The Right Honourable the Lord Mayor escorted by the Company of Pikemen and Musketeers

both. The resulting "Rationalization" Committee was chaired by the Treasurer (later Vice-President), Captain R. B. Tiley, and an Outline Plan, prepared at the Royal College of Art Project Office, was approved by a Special Court on 17th January, 1978.

The anticipated cost of rebuilding was in excess of £400,000 and the Appeal target was set at £500,000. It was a bold venture because the wider basis of membership had not yet produced the expected numbers, financial viability had not been achieved, and the success of the Appeal was still unpredictable. Inevitably the Company was committing itself to an expensive life-style depending on large scale "trading" to pay its way. The size, and indeed the very existence of the Active side could never be controlled or influenced by the Civil side and would always be subject to military needs themselves dependent on international politics and economics. The doubts of many veterans were expressed in the words of one who was well versed in large-scale financing and was also a life long supporter of the Company: "Are we satisfied that having spent this large sum to make the buildings cosy and warm for the members who use it, they can afford to run it?"

Unfortunately, the first estimate was not borne out by more detailed examination by the quantity surveyors engaged who calculated that the finance required would be double the original amount quoted. This led to protracted and agonising re-appraisals which the Rationalization Committee wrestled with for 18 months. The product of these deliberations was a decision to phase the planned work into three, the first two dealing with essential repairs to roofs, including the Albert Room, relocation of the Sutling Room, modernization of the kitchens and servery, refurbishment of the Drum Room, the creation of up-to-date M.S.C. office and Pikemen's store and changing rooms. Later the General Office was moved to the top floor of the east wing. There is no doubt that phasing greatly increased the overall cost of the works, but this course was forced upon the Committee as they were unable to proceed without sufficient finance which was not forthcoming initially from the Appeal. The subsequent result was that Phase III—the building of new changing rooms for the Active unit in the area occupied by the east end of the Albert Room was never undertaken, and temporary changing rooms were provided instead in the west wing of the House itself and in the west wing of the Albert Room.

Throughout the programme of works begun in May, 1979, the Committee was indebted to the professional knowledge and expertise of Colonel B. L. Davis, T.D., who made many useful suggestions which were gratefully accepted. A professional team of fund raisers was employed, headed by Mr. F. A. G. Rider whose efforts on behalf of the Company led to his being awarded Honorary Membership on completion of his work. Some 50% of the membership contributed generously, and together with £150,000 odd from a special Appeal to the City Institutions and a grant of £87,000 from the Territorial Army Volunteer Reserve Association for the Albert Room roof, nearly enough was raised for Phases I and II.

At this stage, in order to raise money the Court even went to the length of recommending the auctioning of the Company's greatest treasure, the Greenwich Suit of Armour. This outrageous proposal was withdrawn at a Special General Court on 15th October, 1979, requisitioned by the veterans, but only then because, in the words of the President, "offers of an unspecified number of interest-free loans had been made by Members . . . so that a special meeting of the Court had decided that it was inopportune to sell the Armour at this stage". Members were then appalled to learn that the cost of withdrawal from auction would be approximately £5,000: a terrible blunder which should never be repeated—talk about the family silver!

About three-quarters of the project was completed by the end of 1980, when rebuilding ceased. There had been a long period of discomfort endured by members and staff, particularly in the catering area where the whole operation had been contracted to a specialist firm in October, 1979.

Several assistants had been urging a new look at property possibilities and it so happened, rather suddenly it seemed, that the Courst sold the head lease of Friendly House during the year for the not inappropriate sum of £747,000.

Laughter in Court perhaps!

Unfortunately it was the Active side which suffered most from the curtailment of the building project. Their new changing rooms under the Albert Room roof never materialized. A couple of years later, when trading seemed almost the main occupation of the Company, the soldiers could not even be fed on drill nights in the well set-up "public" rooms. After the usual prolonged investigation, a hole was knocked in the wall of the Sutling Room to give them access to the R.A.M.C. Mess in the barracks next door. Time will show whether the huge expense of the Rationalization programme, though it was a great improvement, was justified. There were many who thought that "never had so much been spent on so few". Half the membership had "voted with their feet" and not subscribed. Possibly the bogey of the "barrack room economy" had been a myth, and there had after all been a middle course, relatively unexplored. It is certainly ironic that quite soon the soldiers had to eat in the barracks, there being "no room for them in the inn".

Now that is all over the silent majority of older veterans look back sadly to the days when the Long Room was a real clubroom, spacious and splendid—the Sutling Room was in its proper place, with the dining and cold rooms adjacent, the Secretary and staff were just through the door, accessible and in touch with members. Let us hope that this lost tribe will overcome such nostalgic prejudices and, hopefully, be able to afford to use the new facilities.

The Regiment had returned to B.A.O.R. in 1978 for the next three camps. In 1979, "Ex Trusty Halberd" was created to search in depth the strengths and weaknesses of training and that of equipment. Throughout this time, one of the remarkable features of progress was the enormous support of the regular forces. The 1979 operational test exercise that B.A.O.R. dedicated to the H.A.C. alone, utilized Corps resources at a level which would be unimaginable to anyone who had not witnessed the big exercises of N.S. days.

In September, 1980 the unit, again in B.A.O.R., took part in the huge reinforcement programme "Ex Crusader". U.S. forces were flown across the Atlantic, dropping directly into the operational zone. The U.K. regular and Territorial forces crossed the Channel. Whatever problems of mobilization had been anticipated for the H.A.C., these were fully realized but provided the basis for further progress.

By now the Regiment had completed seven years in its new role and, appropriately, the new Gun Troop created in 1974 duly carried off the National Artillery Association's Queen's Cup.

Meanwhile, to digress for a moment, in June, 1978 nearly 100 members visited Boston to attend the Ancient and Honourable Company's traditional Drum Head election on Boston Common. After a bad start in an aeroplane which somehow landed at Philadelphia, they reached Boston and were nobly entertained in true Ancient fashion, including, of course, a "surfeit of lampreys" or maybe clams. The tour wound its way back via Montreal, some even took in New York, with fraternal visits to 2nd Regiment Royal Canadian Artillery and the Grenadier Guards of Canada.

The great event of 1980 was not however the civic tumult of Rationalization but the honour we were to receive from our Captain-General. Our last visit from Her Majesty had been a brief call to the House in 1978, after the Royal Party including His Royal Highness the Duke of Edinburgh had attended a

THE CAPTAIN-GENERAL ARRIVES TO PRESENT NEW COLOURS FOR THE SECOND TIME IN HER REIGN, 25TH JUNE, 1980

service at John Wesley's re-opened chapel; they then crossed City Road to take tea with 230 members of the congregation. But it was 25 years since the last Presentation of Colours and on 25th June it happened again.

It was a splendid occasion, blessed with reasonable weather, expertly rehearsed and beautifully presented by the Commanding Officer, Lieut.-Colonel Clive Martin. He was afterwards congratulated by the Court for "not only organizing a superb parade but making a small profit as well"—for charity of course!

There was even enough sun to dazzle the huge crowd of spectators with the shine from 200 pairs of boots. All present will remember the Captain-General's address to Her Regiment, Lieut.-Colonel Clive's well delivered reply, the precision and turnout of the troops and the surge of anticipation to squadron markers by those who were, hopefully, to meet the Queen. After photographs and luncheon with the officers there was the signing of the Vellum Book and the Regimental Fire given by each squadron in turn as the Queen's car drove slowly through the East Gate.

GUN SALUTE AT THE TOWER, 1980

Among those who also honoured us with their presence that day were three ex-Colonel-Commandants: Major-General Sir Julian Gascoigne, General Sir Richard Goodbody and General Sir Rodney Moore, who each met their many old friends. With the inherent modesty of all distinguished old soldiers, and because protocol demanded it, none was wearing his medals, as the members would have wished them to do. A guest on this occasion—well met for the first time—was General Sir Richard Trant, later to be our next Colonel-Commandant.

It was a year of royal occasions. Major Basil Bicknell, living up to "C" Battery's reputation as the "Sloane Street" or "champagne battery", and aided by Colonel Norman Young, took advantage of the Appeal to organize a ball in New York City. The occasion was graced by the presence of Their Royal Highnesses Prince and Princess Michael of Kent and eight members and their wives as well as 165 willing guests wined and dined at the Union Club on Park Avenue. Among those present were General Sir Rodney and Lady Moore and two past

Captains of the Ancients. A great time was had by all, not least Mr. Rationalization who got about £6,000.

No, cricket was not invented in the West Indies, but much more likely by the Guild and Fraternity of St. George tired no doubt of the twang of bow strings and hearing instead the thonk of willow on leather. As related in Chapter VII, see pp. 140–3, the game is referred to as far back as the reign of Elizabeth I, and the Company's records show that cricket was being played in the Garden as far back as 1725—15 years earlier than Hambledon records. The first match of which there is a positive record took place in 1730 when London beat Surrey by six notches and earned 20 guineas. The 250th anniversary of this notable event was duly celebrated in 1980 with three special games 6th to 8th June when, despite a very wet season, the weather was kind.

After archery, cricket, and after cricket, football in its two disguises; then hockey, golf, squash, shooting—all these clubs had been resuscitated by 1947. The teams were naturally based on pre-war old sweats and it took some time for the clubs to build up to two or more elevens, or fifteens. Sport is a natural adjunct to soldiering, but the military commitment comes first and as happens in civilian life business often interferes with pleasure! Apart from the greatly increased training obligations of the post-war volunteer, other obstacles to attracting a viable sports club membership and thus worthwhile fixture lists were the limited numbers in the right age group, and the spread of the five-day week. This last nullified the pre-war advantage of an inner City ground. There was also a distinct trend towards field sports at the expense of team games. However, the Company has a long tradition of harbouring talent in its ranks. In the early thirties "A" Battery alone had three rugger internationals serving at one time. None could play for the Regiment because all necessarily performed in a higher league!

The Clubs have had to resort to guest players to maintain their sides and the Court of Assistants has always been sympathetic to the inevitable infiltration by non-members provided they pay their way.

The Ski Club developed naturally from the practice enjoyed by the Army in Austria after the war. The Saddle Club was set up by the indefatigable enthusiast Richard Edmonston-Low, a pre-war member who stayed on afterwards as a regular. Sailing had always been the hobby of many others. The clubs epitomize the spirit of the Regiment and with the reunions and other social activities play an important part in binding the members together.

In the last chapter (p. 309) a brief account has been given of the gallant but futile action of "H" Troop, "E" Battery, 11th (H.A.C.) Regiment R.H.A., in the Western Desert in 1942. The recommendation of General Koenig for the award of the Croix de Guerre to all who took part had not materialized. G.H.Q. Middle East declared at the time that the General as a Free Frenchman had no authority to make awards in the name of France. This decision was never accepted by "E" Battery's Commander, Major R. C. Croxton, but he himself was wounded shortly after and sent home, whilst the Troop Commander Captain R. C. Colley was "in the bag".

In fact, unknown to all concerned, the decision had been rescinded and the awards made and approved in 1943.

It was not until May, 1980 that the widow of one of those killed unexpectedly received her husband's medal. Through Major Roger Croxton's intensive efforts and one or two strokes of luck more medals were issued and received, and by 1982 all 12 of those concerned had been traced.

Justice was done at last.

The Court had to find a replacement for Mr. Arthur Grimwade who had for so long acted as Honorary Curator. After consultation with the Director of the National Army Museum, Mr. Stephen Wood was appointed and immediately began a survey of the Company's treasures. He reported that there existed more than enough colours, uniforms, swords and other weapons to produce a first-class Regimental Museum. A programme of work was agreed, beginning with the creation of an Acquisition Book; Mrs. Linda Shelley was appointed to carry out extensive conservation on a part-time basis. In 1983 Mr. David Smurthwaite replaced Mr. Wood who had left London for an appointment in Scotland. Plans by then were well advanced for the opening of the Museum in 1987. The Company was also indebted to the voluntary labours entered into by Mrs. Jean Tsushima, the granddaughter of a member of the Regiment. Her prodigious task of sorting, cleaning and accessioning the large volume of archival material that had accumulated over the years was daunting, and the Company now has a functioning Archival Department with a great deal of outstanding work.

Apart from weaponry the Company's much neglected library of antiquarian militaria had been catalogued, assessed and renovated under the aegis of Colonel Geoffrey Armstrong, himself an antiquarian bookseller, in 1972. Thereafter Colonel H. F. A. Jackson spent long hours collating and sorting the store of Regimental photographs.

One last matter in this crowded year of 1980 was a change in the scope and responsibilities of the Secretary. Planning committees, particularly that of the Vice-President Colonel Gilchrist in 1980, had stressed that the carrying out of Court decisions was not the function of part-time committee members. In future the "Secretary", though a much revered word in our vocabulary, would be entitled "Chief Executive" and would act as such. Hopefully this did not necessarily imply even more work, probably less. Records of membership and subscriptions had been computerized, and Direct Debit Mandates introduced in 1979.

The Company, in common with all similar organizations, had learned to live with the scourge of inflation. Now it had to accept another rapidly escalating horror—terrorism. Not only was H.Q. inherently vulnerable as a military centre but even more so as a place of general resort which could be hired, by respectable people no doubt, but open to infiltration particularly at night and at weekends. For hundreds of years a wall had been a necessary protection, but in the new era of terrorism were added membership cards, admission and parking passes, closed gates and gatekeepers and an access telephone line. Our eyes have to be kept open and our fingers crossed. The extra expense became a big drain on funds.

Another source of infiltration, and not everyone accepted it as necessary, was the increasing access allowed to the ladies. They had always been present on appropriate occasions, properly escorted, and they even had the benefit of a powder room—a suitably sounding name in an artillery headquarters. But they began to penetrate the innermost male sanctums. Outraged veterans found that the Long Room was no longer sacred and there were even tales of the invasion of the Sutling Room. The entertainment of a female Lord Mayor seemed to be the final act of submission to women's rights—or was it merely the return to the days of camp followers and "show a leg"? Whichever it was, like terrorism we shall have to live with it.

In October, 1982 the City of London saluted representatives of the Falkland forces who formed up in the Artillery Garden for their march to Guildhall. The whole South Atlantic operation had been an enormous inspiration to the volunteer forces and had demonstrated the worth of elite units, well versed in military skills, supremely fit and determined. It emphasized and justified the need for tough training and the value of that aptly named quality—guts. Apart from the spit and polish and nostalgia that day there was a very cheerful and happy spirit abroad, exemplified by much good natured chaff and many unexpected encounters with old friends. In case Battalion veterans think their day and age had a monopoly of bootshine, there was seen approaching H.Q. on his way to parade a young marine, very smartly turned out except for his shabby "jogging" shoes. He carried his beautiful glossy parade boots in a plastic bag, obviously not trusting the cleanliness of British Rail.

In 1981, following the improvements to the House, a successful marketing exercise was undertaken to encourage outside functions to use the Sutling facilities. "Trading" revenue grew steadily and in 1983 the Court of Assistants set up H.A.C. Enterprises Ltd. "for all profit-making aspects from external non-member sources . . . the annual net surplus to be covenanted back to the Company".

The appointment of Colonel G. E. Gilchrist, T.D. to be Honorary Colonel-Commandant Royal Artillery in 1983 was a signal honour both to him and to the Regiment.

The Court Minutes reveal continued anxiety over the potential diminishing of numbers, i.e. from 3,310 in 1947 to 2,400 in 1983 (excluding 260 non-Regimental), an average drop of 25 a year or 18 if the new members were included.

It was made known in 1983 that the T.A. was to be expanded, and in the following year the formation of a Home Service Force was announced. It was to consist of independent companies, each sponsored by a T.A. unit. Two of the six to be raised in London were allotted to the H.A.C. The operational role would be key point protection in an emergency and eligibility limited to those men below the age of 50 who had completed not less than two years' military service. The annual commitment would be three obligatory and two voluntary weekends, some of the time likely to be spent at Bisley. The companies were soon to be fully recruited.

Obviously we were getting a much needed shot in the arm as well as a probable small bonus for the Hut, suffering hard times. In the past—the middle fifties—the National Rifle Association had objected to the use of the Bisley Hut for military training. Our trucks were regarded as a blot on the neat, social club atmosphere of the ranges. It was also hard on the N.R.A. that our annual musketry classifications were shot, at least by the gunners, on the nearby Pirbright ranges. Times changed and the revival of training at the Hut (accommodation being paid by the M.O.D.) gave our premises new life and hope. Alas, the M.O.D. enjoy the benefit of hawk-eyed army auditors. The much needed funds were withheld and the Company realized that without active usage the Hut would not be viable.

Bisley holds a warm place in the hearts of most veterans particularly from the days between the wars when the "Science and Feat of Shoting . . ." and the art of winning the Daily Telegraph Cup had been perfected. It would be sadly missed, and strong efforts were made to keep it going including the recent provision of a two-roomed lecture annexe.

All good things come to an end and in the autumn of 1984 General Sir Victor's tenure as Colonel-Commandant expired. Although a very experienced fighting soldier, it happened that his tour of duty did not require him to wrestle with the fate or even the very existence of the Active unit. Instead he had to weather the financial storms and nurse his charges through the traumas and decisions of Rationalization. On his own admission he had had no experience of City affairs, or of the Territorial Army, which probably made it easier and might well have been the reason for his happy and successful stewardship!

In his place the Company was glad to welcome the imposing figure of General Sir Richard Trant, K.C.B. whose first acquaintance with the Regiment had been as a V.I.P., M.O.D. guest at the Presentation of Colours in 1980. Thereafter he was deeply involved in the conduct of the Falklands campaign.

The media gave great prominence to Exercise "LIONHEART", billed as the biggest outing for the Army since

The scene at dawn on 30th June, 1984, as balloons ascend from the Artillery Garden to mark the 200th anniversary of Lunardi's first aerial flight in England

the Second World War. As might be expected, the H.A.C. Active unit were there. No doubt they stole the show, but as can be observed from the jottings in the Journal they were too modest to boast about it. It can however be calculated, from a careful analysis of the figures, just how many kilos or litres or pints of food and drink a sleepless man, loaded with an hundredweight of equipment, requires per pound per day and per mile to restore his erstwhile vitality. So nothing much has really changed on the active front in 40 years! At least in the logistics.

London's greatest ball, to wit, the Flank Companies', was "heightened" by an extra item on its colourful agenda, a celebration to mark the 200th anniversary of Lunardi's balloon ascent in 1784. The original event, and the centenary in 1884 have been described in Chapters IX and XII, see pp. 188–92 and p. 249. On 28/29th June, five balloons duly took off heavenwards and the wind decreed that they should land at Streatham Common, Croydon Airport and Redhill, instead of Hertfordshire. It should be recorded that on his landing near Ware in 1784 Lunardi was taken home by the local M.P. Mr. William Baker to recuperate for a week at his palatial mansion, Bayfordbury. It is of interest that this Baker was the son of Sir William Baker, Alderman and M.P., who had been elected Vice-President of the Company in 1762. Two of his great- (very great-great-) granddaughters were the wives of members of the Company in 1984.

The period of nearly 40 years described in this chapter was one of such vast economic change that it is hard to comprehend the succession of problems which arose, and to evaluate the steps taken to solve them, without recourse to the basic facts and figures.

Brief facts:

1. Premises ravaged by war had to be rebuilt.

2. Military units in "suspended animation" had to reform and later to reorganize several times.

3. The non-military activities which bond all members together had to be restarted.

4. The unpredictable scale of the fall in the value of money had to be met from limited and variable resources.

5. Nothing could be done which might prejudice the next four centuries.

The narrative relates most of the significant happenings as they occurred and in the context of their time.

The background figures summarized overleaf show the progress of income from various sources, the rise of expenditure, the growth of our assets, the decline in membership and the overwhelming effects of the fall in the value of money. They provide an outline only to the full information in the Annual Accounts.

Old timers from the thirties nostalgically recall their two-guinea subscription and the 10p a day pay plus £1.50 bounty received for a fortnight's exposure to the ice on the horse

Brief figures:

	1946	1948	1965	1970	1985
INCOME (£'000)					
Subscriptions		5		15	117[1]
Rents		2		16	70[2]
Investments		1		6	64[3]
Total (inc. etc.)		9		40	350[4]
EXPENDITURE		12		44	297
FUNDS		85		150	1075[5]
PURCHASING POWER	£1		49p	11p	5p

	1947	1948	1965	1970	1975	1985
MEMBERSHIP	3310	3101	3153	2895	2782	2674
ANNUAL SUB. CHANGES	2 gns	2 gns	5 gns	£8	£15	£58

Notes
1. The annual subscription is now virtually index-linked
2. Rents are mostly fixed until 21st century
3. Investments are roughly one third each property, gilts and equities at time of writing
4. "Trading" is now a substantial contributor
5. Funds include proceeds of Friendly House and the newly established "21st-Century Fund"
6. Numbers reflect the "W.W.II bulge", wastage and include 277 "new" members

troughs. They find it hard to believe that the 20p a day reached in 1947 has become £18 a day, with a bounty of £400 (though it has to be earned), a mileage allowance and something extra to buy a crust. On the other hand, the annual subscription has become £58. No wonder local recruiting posters read "Enjoy yourself and get paid—Join the Territorial Army".

And what of 1987? Business today in the City Road continues much as usual and there is no truth in the rumour that the

FLOTATION TRAINING ON THE BATTLE SELECTION COURSE, 1985

Company runs the Artillery Arms in Bunhill Row. The Actives have a growing establishment and a tough role—why not? The tougher the better if real men are to be attracted. The new H.S.F. companies are well manned, the premises are well used by members and customers, trade is profitable. There are ancillary pursuits for veterans of all tastes and clubs for most games and pastimes and hobbies, the City Fathers love us—we try hard to deserve our royal patronage. The old soldiers just fade away as they always did, but as one Chairman of the Court used to say to the new ones "You will never be able to repay to the Regiment what it will give you, however hard you try."

Let that still be true 450 years on.

EGYPT & NORTH AFRICA

Algiers 320 m.
Philippeville 170 m.
Bizerta
TUNIS
Medjez
Teboursouk
Dj Kournine
Bou'Arada
Le Kef
Thala
Sbiba
Kasserine
Kairouan
Hammam Lif
Hammamet
Bou Ficha
Enfidaville
Sousse
Cape Bon
Pantelleria
Palermo
SICILY
Catania
Messina
ITALY
IONIAN
SEA
MALTA
Valetta
MEDITERRANEAN
Mezzouna
W. Akarit
El Hamma
Mareth
Sfax
TRIPOLI
Misurata
Sirte
Benghazi
Charr
M
Antel
Agedabia
Marsa Brega
El Agheila
TRIPOLITANIA
C

Scale of Miles
0   50   100   200   300   400

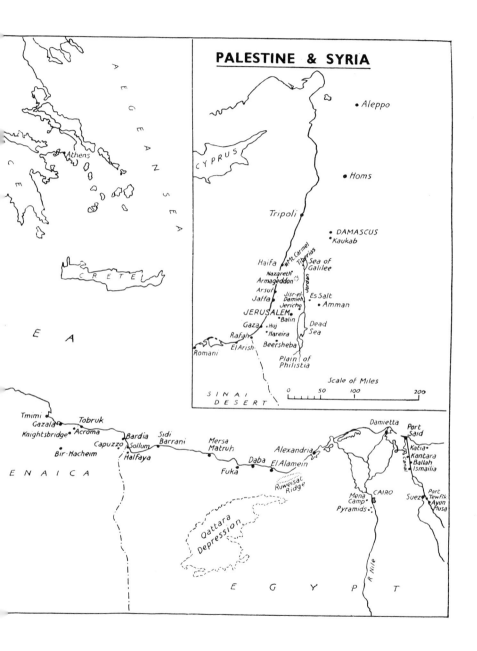

PALESTINE & SYRIA

• Aleppo

CYPRUS

• Homs

Tripoli

• DAMASCUS
• Kaukab

Haifa
Mt Carmel
Tiberias
Sea of Galilee
Nazareth
Armageddon
Arsuf
Jaffa
Jisr-el-
Damieh
Jericho
Es Salt
• Amman
JERUSALEM
• Balin
Gaza
• Huj
Rafah
• Hareira
Dead Sea
El Arish
Beersheba
Romani
Plain of Philistia

Scale of Miles

0   50   100   200

SINAI DESERT

AEGEAN SEA

Athens

CRETE

SEA

Tmimi
Gazala
Tobruk
Knightsbridge
Acroma
Bardia
Sidi Barrani
Mersa Matruh
Damietta
Port Said
Capuzzo
Sollum
Bir-Hacheim
Halfaya
Alexandria
Daba
El Alamein
Fuka
Katia
Kantara
Ballah
Ismailia

CYRENAICA

Ruweisat Ridge

Qattara Depression

Mena Camp
Pyramids
CAIRO
Suez
Port Tewfik
Ayun Musa

E G Y P T

R Nile

385

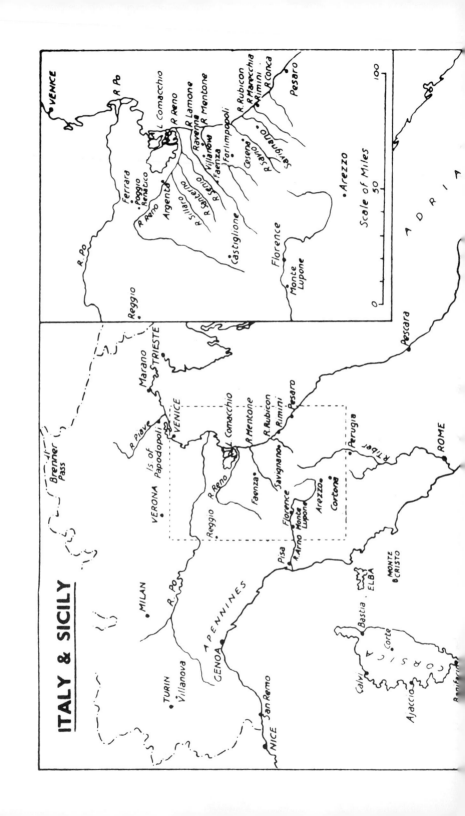

ITALY & SICILY

Scale of Miles

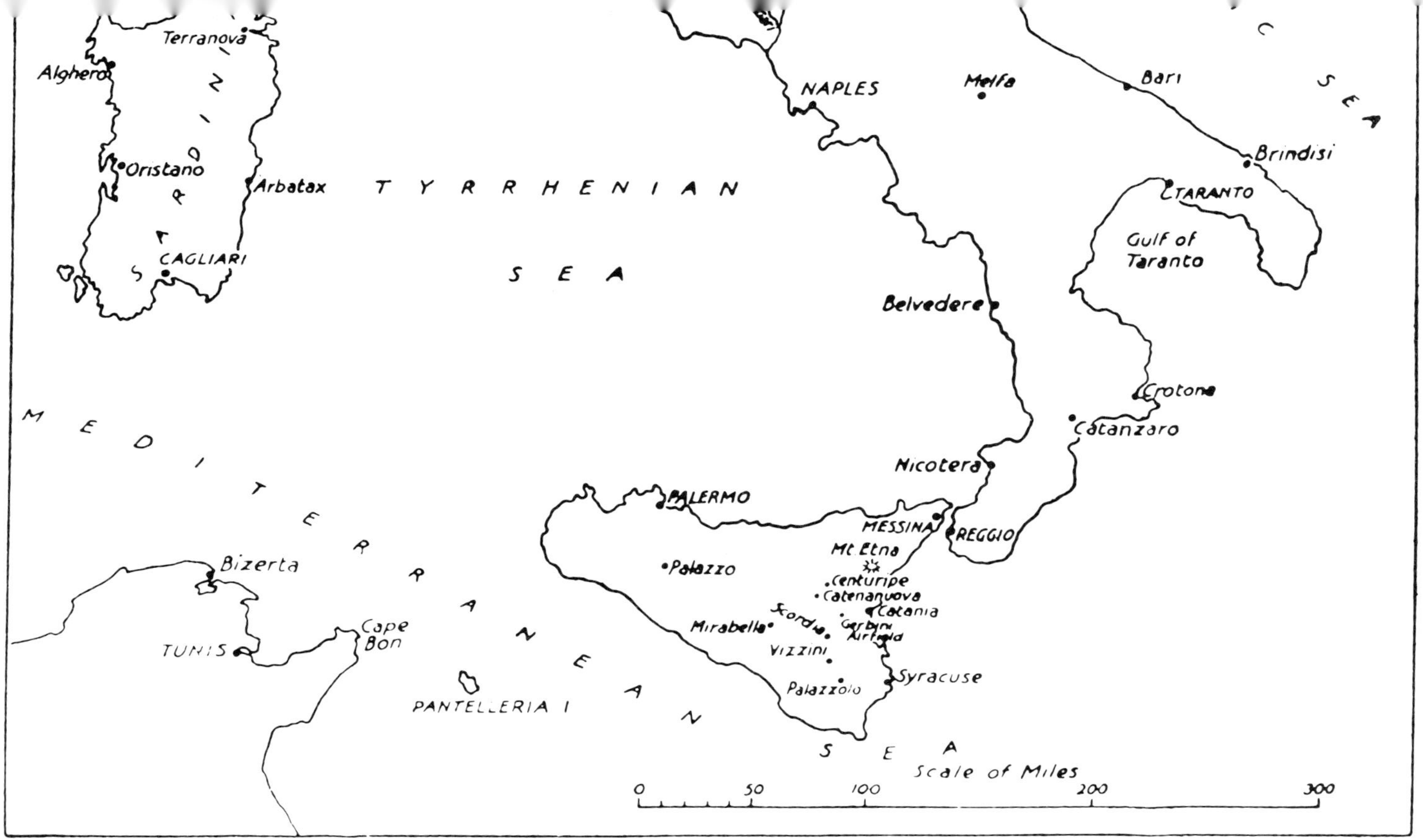
Terranova
Alghero
Oristano
Arbatax
CAGLIARI
SARDINIA
TYRRHENIAN
SEA
NAPLES
Melfa
Bari
Brindisi
TARANTO
Gulf of Taranto
Belvedere
Crotone
Catanzaro
Nicotera
PALERMO
MESSINA
REGGIO
Mt. Etna
Palazzo
Centuripe
Catenanuova
Catania
Scordia
Gerbini
Airfield
Mirabella
Vizzini
Palazzolo
Syracuse
MEDITERRANEAN SEA
Bizerta
TUNIS
Cape Bon
PANTELLERIA I
Scale of Miles
0
50
100
200
300

NORTH-WEST EUROPE

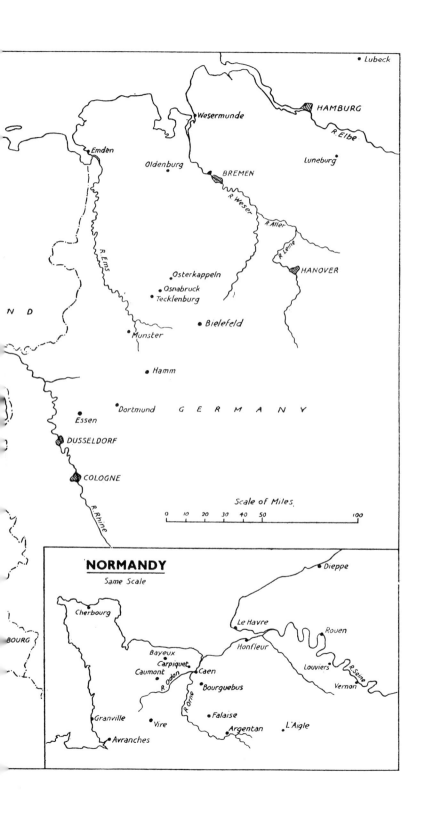

ROLL OF HONOUR, 1900-1902

Pte. R. S. Hutchings, City Imperial Volunteers
Lieut. B. Moeller, 2nd Bn. The Middlesex Regiment
Lieut. D. G. Robbins, Imperial Yeomanry
Lieut. R. H. Tremearne, 5th (Militia) Bn. The Royal Warwickshire Regiment
Lieut. H. H. Ward, Imperial Yeomanry
Lieut. J. S. Watney, Imperial Yeomanry

APPENDIX "B"

ROLL OF HONOUR, 1914-1918

1ST BATTALION

Les Lobes
Pte. F. J. Milne

Wulverghem
Sergt. A. E. Thomas
Pte. A. V. Jones
Pte. C. A. Webster

Kemmel
Capt. W. S. Newton
Sergt. J. C. Dale
Cpl. S. J. Fabian
Cpl. T. H. Fowler
Cpl. R. S. Tate
L./Cpl. P. S. Lampard
L./Cpl. P. W. Pakeman
Pte. W. H. Chittick
Pte. T. W. Dowsett
Pte. A. C. Drysdale
Pte. P. C. Ellis
Pte. J. L. Elmslie
Pte. C. R. Fowler
Pte. M. M. Fuchsbalg
Pte. H. A. Godby
Pte. G. Goodman
Pte. G. G. Heywood
Pte. P. Holman
Pte. L. Inskipp
Pte. M. G. Jameson
Pte. C. H. Kray
Pte. E. H. Lindeman
Pte. S. C. Lindsey
Pte. A. C. Parry
Pte. A. D. Paull
Pte. H. E. Percy
Pte. K. Powell
Pte. H. J. Sandle
Pte. C. S. Smallman
Pte. P. C. Stone
Pte. G. V. White
Pte. J. A. H. Woodhouse

Dickebusch
Pte. L. J. F. Benham
Pte. C. E. King
Pte. H. H. Laste
Pte. W. Oldham

Elzenwalle and St. Eloi
C.S.M. J. C. Browne
C.S.M. R. U. Green
L./Sergt. E. Hoyle
Cpl. S. D. Allan
Cpl. A. C. Johnson
Cpl. A. F. Vertue
L./Cpl. E. Buckney
L./Cpl. C. R. East
L./Cpl. W. M. Phillips
Pte. F. Archard
Pte. F. W. Barnes
Pte. F. M. Bateman
Pte. F. E. Clark
Pte. H. E. Coomber
Pte. A. L. Davies
Pte. F. H. B. Fawley
Pte. G. ffrançon-Davies
Pte. P. Fitch
Pte. E. F. Gardiner
Pte. J. G. Grahame
Pte. M. Green
Pte. G. S. Grundy
Pte. D. V. Harris
Pte. L. G. Harris
Pte. R. Y. Hedderwick
Pte. C. C. Keelan
Pte. F. D. Lenton
Pte. H. H. Parsons
Pte. J. Roberts
Pte. N. P. Russell
Pte. A. L. Skinner
Pte. O. S. Stembridge
Pte. T. L. G. Turnbull
Pte. A. H. Welsford
Pte. R. Williams

Hooge, 16th June, 1915
Lieut. C. Tatham
2/Lieut. W. G. Hoare
C.S.M. H. B. Pitts
Sergt. S. A. K. Money
Sergt. S. N. C. K. Whitehead
Cpl. J. C. Jobling
Cpl. B. J. Moorat
L./Cpl. K. S. Boyd
L./Cpl. G. H. Capel

L./Cpl. H. H. Hatton
L./Cpl. C. L. Henry
L./Cpl. R. F. Kent
L./Cpl. E. R. Munt
L./Cpl. F. A. Openshaw
L./Cpl. J. B. Reid
L./Cpl. W. A. Smith
L./Cpl. C. Sturt
L./Cpl. H. Tindall
Pte. R. F. W. Abbott
Pte. R. H. Ballard
Pte. E. Barrett
Pte. C. E. Chaland
Pte. D. J. Clare
Pte. F. T. Derry
Pte. L. A. I. De Weck
Pte. F. H. Fisenden
Pte. T. H. Godfree
Pte. S. L. Grix
Pte. H. D. Jones
Pte. F. Lashmore
Pte. O. H. Lewis
Pte. J. H. Morum
Pte. G. I. Neal
Pte. G. E. Pearse
Pte. H. R. Poulain
Pte. E. H. Russell
Pte. A. C. H. Sims
Pte. E. J. Snow
Pte. W. A. G. Southwell
Pte. E. L. Sprunt
Pte. A. H. Wigg
Pte. E. R. Withers

Ypres Salient, June-September, 1915
Capt. W. C. Hayden
Lieut. G. M. Bazin
Lieut. A. N. V. H. Ommundsen
2/Lieut. J. S. Leeds
Sergt. R. L. Corry
L./Sergt. S. A. Gard
Cpl. F. H. Hockey
Cpl. C. A. James
Cpl. A. F. B. Littlewood
L./Cpl. G. A. Mascord
Pte. E. N. Bluemel
Pte. W. G. Bunnett
Pte. S. C. Collings
Pte. J. A. J. Gale
Pte. R. Gilman
Pte. L. S. Glunning
Pte. H. C. A. Gravatt
Pte. A. Jennings
Pte. L. P. Jones
Pte. C. W. King
Pte. N. Landsby
Pte. M. H. Lemmon
Pte. E. H. Medhurst
Pte. H. F. Paterson
Pte. W. Pearson
Pte. L. Peniston-Bird

Pte. L. J. D. Pepperday
Pte. P. Pilgrim
Pte. J. D. Savidge
Pte. H. E. Smith

Souchez
Pte. J. J. Eley
Pte. B. Rosbrook
Pte. M. Thomas

Calonne
2/Lieut. H. A. Link
Cpl. C. G. Prescott
L./Cpl. I. G. Holden

Mailly Maillet
Pte. A. D. Freeman
Pte. S. J. White

Hebuterne
Pte. A. D. Garrett
Pte. P. E. Lewis

Mesnil
Pte. R. D. King
Pte. H. Morgan
Pte. A. P. Spanton

Beaucourt
Lieut. D. P. Bonham
Lieut. E. G. Trewhitt
2/Lieut. C. B. Ellis
2/Lieut. L. P. Humphreys
2/Lieut. A. F. S. Smallman
C.S.M. L. P. Charles
C.S.M. L. Swallow
Sergt. H. E. Gentle
Sergt. E. J. Layton
Sergt. W. T. Nickels
L./Sergt. H. T. S. Green
L./Sergt. W. Timms
Cpl. P. R. Baly
Cpl. L. L. Huggins
L./Cpl. W. C. Dew
L./Cpl. G. W. Fishbourne
L./Cpl. A. H. Garrad
L./Cpl. R. D. Hart
L./Cpl. W. J. M. Maisey
L./Cpl. J. Millburne
L./Cpl. L. J. Pointing
L./Cpl. J. H. Roberts
L./Cpl. L. H. Roberts
L./Cpl. W. C. Spelman
L./Cpl. W. J. Taylor
L./Cpl. R. J. Wright
Pte. J. E. Ball
Pte. S. H. Barnard
Pte. O. J. Barnes
Pte. F. J. Baxter
Pte. R. D. Beavis
Pte. J. A. Beggin

Pte. H. T. Bevan
Pte. E. I. Butler
Pte. C. H. Carpenter
Pte. A. G. A. Carter
Pte. F. G. Commings
Pte. L. Davidson
Pte. H. J. Dunford
Pte. J. L. Eldrid
Pte. S. J. Evans
Pte. F. A. Fillmore
Pte. G. J. Garnett
Pte. J. W. Gooderham
Pte. J. W. A. Goulding
Pte. C. W. Gradwell
Pte. G. R. Hammond
Pte. J. V. Heaseman
Pte. A. J. Hill
Pte. H. E. Hooper
Pte. A. W. Hopkins
Pte. A. W. Hull
Pte. F. W. Kimber
Pte. S. B. King
Pte. W. G. King
Pte. R. C. Kingston
Pte. H. C. Larder
Pte. H. L. Leaver
Pte. M. W. Lloyd
Pte. N. C. Mondy
Pte. W. E. Morgan
Pte. R. C. Morsley
Pte. A. J. Newman
Pte. J. G. S. Nops
Pte. H. T. Prebble
Pte. J. P. C. Quin
Pte. H. Reeves
Pte. S. C. Riddick
Pte. G. G. Robertson
Pte. H. C. Rowe
Pte. J. A. Samworth
Pte. A. Sharp
Pte. L. G. A. Soper
Pte. T. E. D. Southwick
Pte. G. A. Stephens
Pte. C. E. Tautz
Pte. C. F. Thorpe
Pte. C. E. Trevers
Pte. T. T. Underwood
Pte. S. W. Waldridge
Pte. F. Waterman
Pte. C. Webb
Pte. E. R. Wedlake
Pte. P. A. Wooten

Beaumont Hamel

Lieut.-Colonel E. C. P. Boyle, D.S.O.
Capt. S. J. Bryan
Sergt. E. A. Emes
Cpl. E. S. Marrs
L./Cpl. J. F. W. Alsford
L./Cpl. W. G. Chandler
L./Cpl. A. Johnstone

L./Cpl. H. W. Smith
L./Cpl. A. N. Woolston
Pte. A. A. Aylett
Pte. J. Blue
Pte. A. W. Bradley
Pte. A. C. Clackett
Pte. D. H. Davies
Pte. H. H. Davies
Pte. T. M. Dow
Pte. A. Dowdeswell
Pte. C. E. Garnham
Pte. W. J. George
Pte. S. W. Goldstein
Pte. A. E. Gravatt
Pte. H. F. L. Greaves
Pte. H. Gregory
Pte. J. H. Hargreaves
Pte. P. L. Hooker
Pte. C. H. Hubbard
Pte. N. E. Kipling
Pte. W. T. Knight
Pte. E. E. Large
Pte. A. T. Matthews
Pte. W. J. Morris
Pte. H. T. Nicklin
Pte. W. H. Ostler
Pte. W. J. Pywell
Pte. N. Smart
Pte. L. G. Smith
Pte. S. C. Smith
Pte. B. A. Stacey
Pte. S. E. Symons
Pte. A. G. Tye
Pte. H. E. Valentine
Pte. E. W. Wetherall
Pte. E. R. Williams
Pte. C. Williamson
Pte. P. G. Winterbourne
Pte. L. H. Worssam

Bailleul

2/Lieut. G. E. Brown
Cpl. T. B. Walker, M.M.

Oppy and Gavrelle

Capt. G. R. Thorpe
2/Lieut. J. Newton
Sergt. R. Malyn
Sergt. G. L. Nicole
Sergt. E. S. Sims
Sergt. H. E. Tombs
Cpl. A. H. Deane
Cpl. R. S. Goddard
Cpl. P. Roderick
Cpl. A. S. Warner
Cpl. W. L. Winn
L./Cpl. E. S. Allsop
L./Cpl. F. H. Alston
L./Cpl. W. J. Bendry
L./Cpl. F. N. Bennett
L./Cpl. J. B. Bishop

L./Cpl. W. A. Cole
L./Cpl. C. W. Collins
L./Cpl. D. N. Ebben
L./Cpl. A. Fergusson
L./Cpl. A. Harvey
L./Cpl. A. H. Heall
L./Cpl. C. Larsson-Nils
L./Cpl. J. L. Morey
L./Cpl. H. J. Riggs
L./Cpl. C. H. Rose
L./Cpl. G. E. Smyley
Pte. F. G. H. Allum
Pte. G. E. Barnes
Pte. E. J. Bartlett
Pte. E. Battersby
Pte. C. H. Bennett
Pte. D. H. Bennett
Pte. F. W. Brookes
Pte. C. M. Bush
Pte. S. E. Chappell
Pte. P. Cole
Pte. S. Cornell
Pte. R. T. Cranefield
Pte. V. E. Cummings
Pte. E. H. Davis
Pte. C. F. L. Fearn
Pte. C. D. Francis
Pte. C. V. Frith
Pte. J. Grinstead
Pte. F. V. Hanley
Pte. L. E. Harris
Pte. W. E. Harrison
Pte. W. H. Holland
Pte. S. G. Hyland
Pte. S. S. Jenkins
Pte. E. V. Jenkins
Pte. J. C. Johnstone
Pte. H. C. Kendrick
Pte. F. C. Keogh
Pte. J. E. Langridge
Pte. W. F. Lee
Pte. W. H. Lewis
Pte. J. V. Luke
Pte. S. Mathew
Pte. J. W. M. Millard
Pte. G. Moir
Pte. F. W. Morin
Pte. H. G. J. Peavot
Pte. C. M. S. Peters
Pte. T. P. Purser
Pte. L. G. Rabbett
Pte. J. Riddey
Pte. M. Rowse
Pte. S. J. Shattock
Pte. E. G. Shears
Pte. R. T. Stapley
Pte. D. H. Starkey
Pte. J. H. Stephens
Pte. R. Swannell

Pte. W. H. Thomas
Pte. J. B. Williams
Pte. J. W. Wilson
Pte. H. Young

Belle Eglise

L./Cpl. F. Orchard
Pte. E. G. King

Accidentally killed overseas

2/Lieut. W. D. Robinson
Sergt. E. A. Barton
L./Cpl. C. Smart
Pte. T. A. Fraser
Pte. R. L. Knatchbull

Accidentally killed in England

L./Cpl. W. R. Jonas*
Pte. D. G. Moss

Died in hospital overseas

L./Cpl. J. H. Elton
L./Cpl. W. J. M. Merrington
L./Cpl. F. W. Strutt
Pte. W. H. Barrett
Pte. E. H. Beach
Pte. F. K. Bill
Pte. S. Bristowe
Pte. F. J. Brown
Pte. A. S. Caley
Pte. A. Cann
Pte. B. S. Cooper
Pte. H. Davey
Pte. R. O. Dilworth
Pte. T. R. Edwards
Pte. P. B. Geldard
Pte. E. B. Hurst
Pte. A. L. Jenner
Pte. S. Jones
Pte. G. B. Kitson
Pte. F. Maddison
Pte. W. E. G. Mein
Pte. W. H. Page
Pte. A. W. Seager
Pte. S. L. Skelton
Pte. C. V. Tebbitt
Pte. M. Walker

Died in hospital in England

Pte. F. D. Bishop*
Pte. P. George*
Pte. E. Haigh*
Pte. S. R. Hitchcock*
Pte. W. Hoyle*
Pte. F. W. Prestwich*
Pte. H. S. Richmond*
Pte. W. A. Tyrrell*
Pte. C. J. Woollard*

* After service overseas.

"A" BATTERY

Es Salt

Capt. C. L. Harris
Sergt. P. C. Millar (died of wounds as P.o.W.)
Bdr. V. V. Wearing (died at sea during repatriation from P.o.W.)
Dvr. N. H. Phillips
Dvr. F. R. Reynolds
Dvr. F. R. Smith

Drowned at sea

Dvr. R. G. Hopkinson
Dvr. H. F. S. Williams

Died of sickness overseas

Capt. C. N. Dyer
S./S./Cpl. C. L. Millar
Gnr. E. F. Funston
Dvr. A. E. E. Hill
Dvr. E. C. B. Key
Dvr. J. L. Morris

"B" BATTERY

Balin, Palestine

Bdr. F. J. Eglington

Es Salt, Palestine

Wheeler W. V. Saunders

Drowned at sea

Dvr. R. G. A. Austin
Dvr. T. W. Rudledge

Died at sea

A./S./Sergt. Whittle

Accidentally drowned in Egypt

Dvr. J. Jacobs

Died of sickness overseas

Sergt. J. S. Edmondson
Cpl. J. F. Howkins
Bdr. G. R. Sanson

L./Bdr. R. C. Lupton
Dvr. H. L. Cruse
Gnr. H. K. Cunnington
Dvr. A. S. Gill
Gnr. L. P. Hinton
Gnr. A. J. Le Guet
Gnr. J. S. Mitchenson
Gnr. F. S. White

Accidentally killed in England

Fitter/S./Sergt. E. O. Ardley
Dvr. S. W. Jackson

Died of sickness in England

Gnr. D. W. Cruttwell
Gnr. R. S. Preeston*

Died in England after being invalided

Lieut. and Q.M. A. J. Norris

2ND BATTALION

Ploegsteerte

Sergt. E. W. J. Potter
L./Cpl. C. J. Dolwin
Pte. E. G. Bowman
Pte. S. H. Claxton
Pte. A. Cohen
Pte. W. Jallings
Pte. E. R. Johnson
Pte. H. C. Love
Pte. A. W. Sharpe

Beaumont Hamel

2/Lieut. C. J. Byron
Sergt. W. C. Feaviour
Sergt. R. W. Wright
Cpl. J. L. P. Gifford
Cpl. A. Kemp

Cpl. F. W. Peet
L./Cpl. S. H. Woodward
Pte. E. Aldersley
Pte. R. H. Ashford
Pte. L. J. Buckingham
Pte. H. Butler
Pte. J. E. T. Cass
Pte. A. F. Chauntler
Pte. H. E. Corin
Pte. H. E. Ebsworth
Pte. F. Fisher
Pte. W. H. Giles
Pte. R. F. Heeley
Pte. E. C. Henzell
Pte. L. A. Hitchcock
Pte. R. O. A. Holmes
Pte. J. F. Kennedy
Pte. J. Lane

* After service overseas.

Pte. P. S. Levy
Pte. J. Lewis
Pte. H. Limon
Pte. F. J. Newton
Pte. C. F. Osman
Pte. T. W. Parfitt
Pte. C. H. Pullen
Pte. C. C. Reed
Pte. F. A. Scott
Pte. J. V. Stanborough
Pte. H. E. Tebbitt
Pte. J. A. P. Tibbs

Bucquoy and Ecoust

2/Lieut. E. W. Brass
2/Lieut. E. H. Gray
2/Lieut. A. W. Jones
Sergt. P. M. Bonner
Sergt. P. C. Phillips
Cpl. W. H. Davidson
L./Cpl. J. L. Cresswell
L./Cpl. S. F. Hutchinson
L./Cpl. E. J. Knight
L./Cpl. A. E. Livett
L./Cpl. A. Parsons
L/Cpl. T. E. Redrup
Pte. W. T. Abbott
Pte. F. P. Amor
Pte. J. G. Barney
Pte. E. J. Barrett
Pte. H. A. Beaumont
Pte. B. H. Britton
Pte. W. C. Brooks
Pte. W. B. Buck
Pte. A. L. Charrington
Pte. P. S. Churchill
Pte. W. Clemishaw
Pte. R. E. Clubb
Pte. E. R. Cooke
Pte. S. F. Cramp
Pte. C. L. Doughty
Pte. T. H. J. Doyle
Pte. R. B. Godfree
Pte. F. C. P. Green
Pte. L. W. Greenwood
Pte. P. J. Hale
Pte. H. L. Hodge
Pte. J. R. Hodge
Pte. I. P. Jones
Pte. H. E. Lawrence
Pte. W. H. N. Marples
Pte. F. H. Masham
Pte. F. C. Mitchell
Pte. L. G. Moss
Pte. F. G. Pilcher
Pte. W. W. Rainer
Pte. M. H. Scannell
Pte. R. G. Seale
Pte. C. V. Smethurst
Pte. H. A. Stephenson, M.M.
Pte. H. B. Swann

Pte. J. L. Sworder
Pte. A. G. Taylor
Pte. H. C. Trinder
Pte. H. G. Tucker
Pte. H. V. Turnbull
Pte. N. P. Vincent
Pte. W. F. Vizer
Pte. T. E. F. Waller
Pte. W. G. Walton
Pte. E. A. West
Pte. A. G. Wicks
Pte. C. J. Wilson
Pte. J. K. S. Zealley

Bullecourt

Capt. J. H. Pritchard
Capt. F. H. S. Satchwell
Lieut. E. W. F. Hammond, M.C.
2/Lieut. A. M. Beck
2/Lieut. H. A. P. Bocket
2/Lieut. G. F. C. Brown
2/Lieut. C. E. Ellis
2/Lieut. G. F. Farmiloe
2/Lieut. R. H. Fedden
2/Lieut. R. J. Flory, M.C.
2/Lieut. G. A. Fraser
2/Lieut. L. F. Gandar-Dower
2/Lieut. C. J. St. Quintin
C.S.M. G. S. M. Robinson
Sergt. A. J. Brayfield
Sergt. N. A. E. Brown
Sergt. J. C. Drinkwater
Sergt. A. M. Dunn
Sergt. W. H. Jackson
Sergt. J. E. H. Mann
Sergt. N. E. Woodger
L./Sergt. R. L. Evans
L./Sergt. G. W. Pugh
Cpl. J. M. Crosby
Cpl. C. H. Franklin
Cpl. N. S. Robertson
L./Cpl. C. A. Cryer
L./Cpl. P. R. Farrow
L./Cpl. E. J. Forrest
L./Cpl. W. J. Gatward
L./Cpl. R. J. Grant
L./Cpl. A. F. Gray
L./Cpl. C. N. Heryet
L./Cpl. W. O. Hill
L./Cpl. R. P. Jeaffreson
L./Cpl. D. F. G. Selby
L./Cpl. E. B. Tilleard
L./Cpl. L. A. Walker
Pte. P. M. E. Abbott
Pte. A. E. Arnold
Pte. T. L. Ayling
Pte. L. W. Bailey
Pte. P. F. Bex
Pte. C. S. Beyfus
Pte. H. R. G. Bishop
Pte. F. W. Blake

Pte. L. F. Braddick
Pte. J. Bruster
Pte. E. G. Buckeridge
Pte. M. W. Calder
Pte. S. Clemmetson
Pte. J. Colley
Pte. H. D. Copps
Pte. J. E. Cornish
Pte. F. H. Couling
Pte. W. Coulson
Pte. E. Court
Pte. D. Cowan
Pte. A. L. Crawford
Pte. R. H. Crawford
Pte. J. V. Criswick
Pte. C. S. Crompton
Pte. C. H. Cutting
Pte. G. L. Davies
Pte. F. G. Davis
Pte. M. J. B. Dickson
Pte. S. H. Dix
Pte. D. G. Dodds
Pte. H. Double
Pte. J. D. Dowden
Pte. A. E. Edwards
Pte. C. D. Elphick
Pte. R. L. Fowles
Pte. E. T. Friend
Pte. H. B. Garrad
Pte. F. G. Gentry
Pte. J. G. Gordon
Pte. R. M. J. Greig
Pte. G. A. Greville
Pte. F. Grocott
Pte. H. F. Gulden
Pte. A. E. Gunn
Pte. L. H. Haime
Pte. R. C. Haley
Pte. A. J. Hanford
Pte. F. F. Hardingham
Pte. F. Harsant
Pte. B. E. Hart
Pte. R. H. Hawkins
Pte. J. M. Hedgecock
Pte. F. W. Heggie
Pte. M. L. Hubbard
Pte. N. B. Hulse
Pte. A. G. Humphrey
Pte. H. C. Hunt
Pte. G. Jenkins
Pte. R. Johnson
Pte. F. W. King
Pte. W. T. Laming
Pte. T. G. Lee
Pte. C. D. Le Gros
Pte. E. B. Leigh
Pte. A. V. Lindley, M.M.
Pte. A. T. Lockerbie
Pte. G. A. Lowther
Pte. C. A. H. Lufkin
Pte. A. H. Mahr

Pte. J. L. Mann
Pte. E. G. Meech
Pte. W. M. Moffat
Pte. A. S. Monroe
Pte. W. S. Morrell
Pte. E. W. Morris
Pte. J. W. Morton
Pte. L. J. S. Moysey
Pte. N. T. Norman
Pte. R. R. Oldreive
Pte. H. T. Page
Pte. P. F. Parry
Pte. H. G. Payne
Pte. A. T. Peal
Pte. T. E. Pearson
Pte. E. Peel
Pte. W. J. Pipe
Pte. N. J. Price
Pte. S. E. Proverbs
Pte. H. E. Pulleyn
Pte. H. E. R. Ribstone
Pte. F. G. Rogers
Pte. H. A. Salter
Pte. A. W. Scarf
Pte. H. R. Seamark
Pte. W. P. Seymour
Pte. D. G. C. Sheppard
Pte. S. F. Sherrington
Pte. C. W. Shurrock
Pte. T. Simpkin
Pte. V. L. Simpson
Pte. A. A. Smith
Pte. J. C. Smith
Pte. E. Spears
Pte. R. W. Springfield
Pte. L. H. Straw
Pte. J. C. O. Sullens
Pte. R. R. Summers
Pte. F. E. Taylor
Pte. R. Taylor
Pte. H. J. Thomas
Pte. H. S. Thomas
Pte. S. Thornton
Pte. C. H. Trubshawe
Pte. S. L. Wade
Pte. C. F. Watkins
Pte. T. T. Watson
Pte. R. M. Whear
Pte. C. W. H. White
Pte. G. L. White
Pte. E. A. Whiting
Pte. H. C. Wild
Pte. S. Wiles
Pte. A. G. Wilson
Pte. H. C. Wise
Pte. C. E. Wood
Pte. B. J. Wright

Passchendaele

Capt. D. Brunton
Capt. E. F. H. Murray, M.C.

2/Lieut. P. C. Blisset
2/Lieut. S. C. East
2/Lieut. R. G. Goddard
2/Lieut. R. Meldrum
2/Lieut. R. C. D. Moore
C.S.M. W. H. T. Worth
Sergt. H. G. Creasey
Sergt. E. J. Harland
Sergt. R. A. J. Hunt
Sergt. H. J. Longhurst
Sergt. H. C. Stroud
L./Sergt. H. Reed
Cpl. H. A. Clark
Cpl. F. T. Cox
Cpl. J. Gibson
Cpl. D. Lawrence
Cpl. G. W. Ratcliffe
Cpl. B. Smith
Cpl. M. Wilson
L./Cpl. C. J. Dowley
L./Cpl. F. H. P. Ellis
L./Cpl. C. Gilham
L./Cpl. F. R. Green
L./Cpl. F. S. Mager
L./Cpl. R. Mitchell
L./Cpl. R. E. Oldham
L./Cpl. W. G. Payne, M.M.
L./Cpl. J. J. Polson
L./Cpl. A. E. B. Shirley
L./Cpl. T. C. Spencer
L./Cpl. C. G. Ward
Pte. S. N. Allaway
Pte. T. G. Allen
Pte. W. E. Allin
Pte. A. Armstrong
Pte. C. A. Ashman
Pte. W. J. Barnes
Pte. F. G. Barnett
Pte. A. R. R. Bartlett
Pte. S. P. Beale
Pte. L. W. Boiteux
Pte. H. Bower
Pte. W. Bradley
Pte. W. Breden
Pte. J. W. Brooks
Pte. A. G. Brown
Pte. P. K. Brown
Pte. R. C. Brown
Pte. E. S. Child
Pte. H. L. Christmas
Pte. E. Clapp
Pte. N. K. Coles
Pte. H. R. Cornford
Pte. W. A. Curry
Pte. R. L. Davis
Pte. A. H. De Broeck
Pte. W. J. E. Denny
Pte. R. J. Donovan
Pte. A. P. Dyall
Pte. J. B. Errington
Pte. V. W. Fletcher

Pte. S. J. Forfar
Pte. G. A. Forman
Pte. D. A. Fowler
Pte. A. Frost
Pte. G. Gent
Pte. E. J. Goodwin
Pte. S. J. H. Gough
Pte. G. S. Hall
Pte. G. M. Heath
Pte. H. N. Hewitt
Pte. W. Hicks
Pte. W. L. Hillier
Pte. L. S. Holland
Pte. H. B. Hort
Pte. E. F. Houghton
Pte. M. Howard
Pte. J. T. Hutton
Pte. F. H. Inns
Pte. W. Johnson
Pte. R. J. Joint
Pte. H. O. Jones
Pte. J. W. Jopling
Pte. M. P. Joseph
Pte. A. W. Jukes
Pte. P. A. Kemp
Pte. W. Kershaw
Pte. L. H. Levy
Pte. H. J. Lewis
Pte. E. Lowden
Pte. H. C. Margetts
Pte. C. J. B. McGeorge
Pte. F. P. Monahan
Pte. E. P. Olliffe
Pte. F. W. Patterson
Pte. G. Pearson
Pte. J. L. Perren
Pte. L. A. Peters
Pte. G. S. Planner
Pte. W. S. F. Poole
Pte. A. W. Porter
Pte. C. A. Pye
Pte. L. A. Rayner
Pte. W. A. Redman
Pte. R. A. Roe
Pte. C. A. Roffey
Pte. F. L. Samuel
Pte. H. T. Shurmur
Pte. A. T. Smith
Pte. H. L. Southall
Pte. E. V. Stacey
Pte. A. G. Steel
Pte. E. K. Still, M.M.
Pte. L. F. Stroud
Pte. F. S. Symmons
Pte. J. M. Tatton
Pte. A. E. Tayler
Pte. R. M. Taylor
Pte. L. Thomas
Pte. L. C. Thomas
Pte. W. J. Thomas
Pte. A. W. Thompson

Pte. S. J. Thompson
Pte. F. C. Tout
Pte. S. M. Treharne
Pte. J. H. B. Tristram
Pte. E. H. Waldron
Pte. H. L. Way
Pte. T. Widdowson
Pte. A. J. Winterbourne
Pte. C. A. Wood
Pte. F. W. Young

Nervesa

Sergt. H. N. Verrels
Pte. H. C. Franklin

Asiago Plateau

2/Lieut. J. S. Reeve
Sergt. D. F. Vieweg
L./Cpl. H. T. Bennett
L./Cpl. W. A. Percival
Pte. H. A. Castle
Pte. W. G. Daw
Pte. F. A. East
Pte. E. W. Fisher
Pte. U. R. C. Gardner
Pte. H. L. Greenaway, M.M.
Pte. J. Hall
Pte. V. W. Henderson
Pte. W. V. Hickman
Pte. W. E. Hore
Pte. H. A. How
Pte. E. A. Kates
Pte. A. E. Long
Pte. C. H. Martin
Pte. N. B. Nash
Pte. W. E. Powell

Papadopoli

2/Lieut. D. P. Sims
Cpl. B. W. Barker
L./Cpl. H. L. J. Cassini
L./Cpl. E. Horton
L./Cpl. A. H. O. Lea
Pte. L. D. Allan
Pte. F. H. Blackford
Pte. J. W. Brandon
Pte. E. Butler
Pte. E. V. Evans
Pte. A. D. Grieve
Pte. A. Hall
Pte. N. J. W. Helliwell
Pte. W. C. G. Hollands
Pte. E. T. Jones
Pte. L. Lepper
Pte. E. E. Moore
Pte. G. W. Nicholson

Pte. D. F. Seear
Pte. W. F. Smith
Pte. A. Thompson

Tagliamento

Sergt. C. E. Fowler

Died of sickness overseas

Lieut. D. T. L. Curtis
Lieut. D. S. Davis
2/Lieut. R. S. B. Porter
L./Cpl. P. H. Bloor
L./Cpl. J. F. Clark
L./Cpl. W. Taylor
Pte. H. T. C. Barkham
Pte. H. Beer
Pte. E. C. Brown
Pte. A. H. Ford
Pte. S. L. L. Gover
Pte. J. M. Hinton, M.M.
Pte. J. A. Hodson
Pte. O. Lake
Pte. R. G. Low
Pte. J. H. Medlock
Pte. J. F. L. Parsons
Pte. C. H. Rawlings
Pte. J. Reeves
Pte. H. B. Ruff
Pte. R. D. Sadd
Pte. V. E. T. Salmon
Pte. R. L. Spear
Pte. B. Stackhouse

Drowned at sea

Pte. A. Lazarus

Accidentally killed overseas

Pte. A. H. Williamson
Pte. H. W. Rattenbury

Died of sickness in England

Major C. F. Nesham*
C.S.M. J. W. H. Kent*
Sergt. W. J. Norwood*
Cpl. F. W. Willis
L./Cpl. W. H. Whitehead*
Pte. G. A. Martin*
Pte. S. S. Murrin*
Pte. J. H. Pooley
Pte. A. C. Springate*
Pte. L. L. Van der Bergh*
Pte. G. M. Watkins*
Pte. H. Whitby
Pte. V. M. Woodman

* After service overseas.

309 (H.A.C.) SIEGE BATTERY

Ypres and Passchendaele
2/Lieut. G. Sheppard
Gnr. E. P. Bannister
Gnr. A. M. Behar
Gnr. F. C. Cherry
Gnr. C. H. Earley
Gnr. H. E. Fitness
Gnr. G. L. Fogden
Gnr. T. H. Green
Gnr. F. P. Heathcote
Gnr. A. T. Maylam
Gnr. R. Oulsnam
Gnr. C. E. Read
Gnr. D. R. Upsdale

Somme
Capt. W. Elliott
Lieut. P. H. Edmondson, M.C.
2/Lieut. B. P. Baugh

2/Lieut. J. B. Glover
Gnr. A. Burningham
Gnr. F. W. Downes
Gnr. F. G. Essex
Gnr. W. Leech
Gnr. H. T. Parkinson
Gnr. D. S. Pollack
Gnr. C. E. Smith

Died of sickness overseas
Lieut. W. R. Mortleman
Gnr. R. G. Baker
Gnr. W. G. C. Lane
Gnr. L. A. Pollard

Died in hospital in England
Gnr. J. C. Menzies*
Gnr. G. W. Watkins*

"2/A" BATTERY

Passchendaele
Bdr. S. F. Chattey
Gnr. W. D. Darvill
Gnr. L. S. Lennon
Gnr. W. S. Saville
Dvr. J. C. Starkie
Gnr. L. Wright

Loos
Cpl. J. H. J. Fowles
Gnr. D. E. Brock
Gnr. D. J. Horn
Dvr. G. A. Rice

Arras and Vis en Artois
Major J. K. L. Fitzwilliam, M.C.
Lieut. G. Rogers
2/Lieut. A. Chaventré
Gnr. V. F. Mummery

Died of sickness overseas
Sergt. A. F. Earnshaw
Bdr. C. F. W. Carter
Dvr. C. Burrell
Dvr. E. H. S. Gomme
Gnr. H. G. Smith

Died in hospital in England
Dvr. J. P. Williams

"2/B" BATTERY

Passchendaele
Sergt. G. A. Frymann
Bdr. A. Beach
Dvr. W. D. C. Cooper
Gnr. F. H. Dyer
Gnr. L. E. Jones
Gnr. C. A. Longcroft

Loos
Dvr. J. L. Unwin

Vis en Artois
Cpl. W. A. White
Dvr. G. E. Bloxham

Dvr. S. G. Cardnell
Dvr. J. R. Cowans
Dvr. C. E. Pond
Dvr. J. W. Wooldridge

Died of sickness overseas
Major Sir Arthur L. Lucas-Tooth
Dvr. F. C. Carnaghan
Gnr. J. H. Fairweather
Gnr. P. Smith

Died in hospital in England
Dvr. J. H. F. Tweddle*

* After service overseas.

401

RESERVE BATTERIES

Died in hospital in England
2/Lieut. E. C. Philp
Gnr. R. Ansell
Dvr. C. J. Bladworth
Dvr. L. Brotherton
Gnr. R. G. Coates

Dvr. W. G. Crawford
Dvr. H. T. Hiland
Gnr. P. C. B. Machin
Gnr. T. H. Roe
Gnr. B. Steer
Gnr. G. D. Unthank

RESERVE BATTALIONS

Accidentally killed in England
Pte. H. W. Finch
Pte. W. A. Tolley

Died in hospital in England
Pte. R. J. Barker
Pte. A. E. Colberry
Pte. C. Cuss
Pte. C. E. W. Davison
Pte. J. D. J. Ennever

Pte. F. E. Grantham
Pte. R. H. E. Hill
Pte. P. S. Jenkin
Pte. G. A. Priest
Pte. H. Riddle
Pte. P. G. Scholey
Pte. C. P. Steed
Pte. E. A. F. Stone
Pte. L. H. S. Torrie
Pte. E. Vialls
Pte. J. L. E. White

MEMBERS OF THE HONOURABLE ARTILLERY COMPANY WHO FELL IN ACTION OR DIED WHILE SERVING WITH OTHER UNITS.

Royal Naval Volunteer Reserve
Lieut. F. O. Forrester, M.C. (Anson Battalion, R.N. Div.)
Lieut. E. W. L. Hulbert
Lieut. L. T. Taylor
Lieut. L. E. Tucker (Collingwood Battalion, R.N. Div.)
Sub-Lieut. F. Wild
2/Lieut. C. A. Richards, M.C. (Anson Battalion, R.N. Div.)
P.O. S. H. Cripps (Drake Battalion, R.N. Div.)

Royal Marine Artillery
Lieut. T. E. Hulme
Lieut. C. N. B. Rigby

Royal Naval Air Service
2/Lieut. W. G. Parry

Reserve of Cavalry
Lieut. G. F. J. Jarvis

Royal Field Artillery
Brig.-General A. C. Lowe, C.M.G., D.S.O.
Lieut.-Colonel J. N. Sinclair, D.S.O.
Major V. S. Longman
Major J. C. O'Callaghan, M.C.
Major H. V. Ramsey
Major C. O. von Treuenfels, D.S.O.
Major G. B. Winch, D.S.O.

Capt. A. P. G. Beale
Capt. H. Beckton
Capt. G. Belas
Capt. G. A. O. Berridge, M.C.
Capt. B. Catling, M.C.
Capt. F. C. Dawkins, M.C.
Capt. M. Gliddon, M.C.
Capt. A. W. Hame
Capt. R. G. Hitchings
Capt. R. P. Nathan, M.C.
Capt. P. R. Phillips
Capt. L. L. Reeves
Capt. N. G. Shepard
Capt. H. E. Shepherd
Capt. S. H. Stroud
Capt. L. Woods
Lieut. B. A. Boyton
Lieut. S. N. Budgen
Lieut. N. N. Caton, M.C.
Lieut. R. G. Clarke
Lieut. L. V. Desborough (att. R.F.C.)
Lieut. J. H. M. Dunn
Lieut. J. R. Eagleton
Lieut. G. P. Edwards, M.C.
Lieut. F. Eggleton
Lieut. D. Fiske
Lieut. S. P. Fryer
Lieut. C. S. Gaskain
Lieut. B. G. Hill, M.C.
Lieut. G. S. Hodgkinson
Lieut. M. Howkins
Lieut. A. A. Johnston
Lieut. F. J. Long
Lieut. H. B. MacPherson, M.C.

Lieut. A. C. O. Morgan
Lieut. C. St. J. Neville
Lieut. D. O'Brien
Lieut. R. H. Pickering
Lieut. L. W. Porterfield
Lieut. A. D. W. Scott, M.C.
Lieut. T. A. Turner
Lieut. A. L. D. Wheeler
Lieut. J. M. S. Wright
2/Lieut. J. N. Anderson
2/Lieut. E. S. Armitage
2/Lieut. W. J. Baker
2/Lieut. C. H. Baxter
2/Lieut. F. C. Boully
2/Lieut. H. K. Briggs
2/Lieut. H. M. Brocklesby
2/Lieut. C. A. Button
2/Lieut. K. W. Calder
2/Lieut. E. Carter
2/Lieut. T. W. Caslon
2/Lieut. C. B. Clarke
2/Lieut. W. H. Collinson
2/Lieut. W. H. G. Compton
2/Lieut. F. H. Dyer
2/Lieut. J. A. E. Frend
2/Lieut. N. Grant
2/Lieut. W. Gutmann
2/Lieut. D. S. Hicklenton
2/Lieut. G. B. Hone
2/Lieut. B. T. Howse
2/Lieut. R. C. Ireland
2/Lieut. H. S. L. Jordan (att. R.A.F)
2/Lieut. L. S. Last (att. R.A.F.)
2/Lieut. H. D. Lee
2/Lieut. E. Lucie-Smith
2/Lieut. G. A. Nicholls (att. R.H.A.)
2/Lieut. V. Page, M.C.
2/Lieut. W. S. B. Parry
2/Lieut. C. S. Peerless
2/Lieut. L. M. S. Prior
2/Lieut. B. Sherrard
2/Lieut. C. T. Smith
2/Lieut. E. St. C. Smith (att. R.A.F.)
2/Lieut. A. L. Tongue
2/Lieut. G. S. Whitehead
2/Lieut. H. A. Whittard
2/Lieut. C. W. Wise
2/Lieut. L. S. Witt

Royal Garrison Artillery

Capt. V. F. Carr
Capt. J. L. Isaacson
Lieut. D. J. Aherne
Lieut. N. H. Aste
Lieut. J. C. Carroll
Lieut. G. W. Gotch (att. R.A.F.)
Lieut. S. Johnson
2/Lieut. J. O. Abbott
2/Lieut. H. G. Dennison
2/Lieut. E. R. Free

2/Lieut. G. H. Grellier
2/Lieut. J. A. Hedderwick
2/Lieut. H. C. Henman
2/Lieut. W. J. Horner
2/Lieut. F. J. O. Lamb
2/Lieut. H. G. Porter
2/Lieut. E. J. Quaife
2/Lieut. H. F. Schall
Gnr. F. A. Burnett

Royal Engineers

Lieut. W. W. Moore
Lieut. A. K. Newland
Lieut. I. T. V. Norman
2/Lieut. P. Coates
2/Lieut. C. P. Lewis
2/Lieut. J. H. M. Phillips
2/Lieut. W. H. Slight
Spr. H. W. Waterman

Royal Engineers (Signals)

Lieut. M. Hill, D.C.M.

Grenadier Guards

Capt. T. T. Pryce, V.C., M.C.
2/Lieut. A. S. Corkran
Pte. J. F. Pollard

Scots Guards

Capt. D. G. Stephenson
Lieut. M. N. Schiff

Welsh Guards

Lieut. N. Newall
2/Lieut. V. E. Foot
2/Lieut. H. B. Trotter, M.M.

The Queen's Regiment (Royal West Surrey)

Major L. E. Andrews, M.C.
Lieut. J. R. A. Balchin, M.C.
Lieut. H. T. Batson
2/Lieut. C. L. Borst
2/Lieut. R. H. Curtis
2/Lieut. J. M. Foord-Kelcey
2/Lieut. J. A. Harvey (att. T. M. Bty.)
2/Lieut. C. A. Hine
2/Lieut. F. H. L. Roberson

The Buffs (East Kent Regiment)

Major G. F. Pragnell, D.S.O.
Capt. G. T. Neame
Capt. D. G. Pearse
2/Lieut. E. G. Bungard
2/Lieut. F. H. Dungey
2/Lieut. P. Freedman

The King's Own (Royal Lancaster Regiment)

2/Lieut. J. V. W. Eccles

The Northumberland Fusiliers
Major C. J. H. Adamson
2/Lieut. S. V. Chapman
2/Lieut. F. C. Jarvis
2/Lieut. M. G. Klean

The Royal Warwickshire Regiment
Capt. P. H. Hollick
Lieut. C. T. Cockle
2/Lieut. F. Devis
2/Lieut. T. L. Goode
2/Lieut. L. Jackson
2/Lieut. B. A. Shepard
2/Lieut. G. H. Turner
2/Lieut. R. V. Wilson

The Royal Fusiliers (City of London Regiment)
Capt. M. I. Christie, D.S.O.
Capt. B. Spence
Lieut. W. G. Blackwell
Lieut. R. A. Butchard
Lieut. W. W. Edwards
Lieut. L. R. Howard
Lieut. A. W. Savours
Lieut. H. D. Sumner
2/Lieut. C. Blackwell
2/Lieut. W. L. Bridgman
2/Lieut. W. A. Bullock
2/Lieut. G. E. Bungey
2/Lieut. C. Gill
2/Lieut. L. A. Green
2/Lieut. J. C. Manson
2/Lieut. W. D. Scott
2/Lieut. A. J. Stiles
2/Lieut. J. Stringer
2/Lieut. D. M. Ullman
2/Lieut. L. T. Westaway
L./Sergt. N. U. Porter

The King's (Liverpool Regiment)
2/Lieut. E. N. Goldspink
2/Lieut. G. S. Horbury
2/Lieut. C. A. Peters
2/Lieut. P. G. Statton

The Norfolk Regiment
2/Lieut. L. Edwards
2/Lieut. L. W. Last
2/Lieut. W. T. Nancarron
2/Lieut. J. Soddy
2/Lieut. T. Whitty

The Lincolnshire Regiment
Lieut. A. W. Hadrill
2/Lieut. G. W. H. Applin
2/Lieut. L. C. Coath
2/Lieut. R. L. Courtice
2/Lieut. L. J. E. C. Fairweather

The Devonshire Regiment
2/Lieut. C. G. Carlton
2/Lieut. W. H. Sandford

The Suffolk Regiment
Lieut. A. H. Woodgate
2/Lieut. A. K. Baylis
2/Lieut. J. L. Fish
2/Lieut. H. C. Franks
2/Lieut. A. Hubbard
2/Lieut. A. C. Shears
2/Lieut. C. F. Sworder
2/Lieut. H. W. Whatling

Prince Albert's (Somerset Light Infantry)
2/Lieut. L. Hopkins
2/Lieut. P. C. Knight
2/Lieut. A. L. Springfield
2/Lieut. L. H. Vaughan

The Prince of Wales's Own (West Yorkshire Regiment)
Capt. C. E. A. Long
Capt. L. G. Peters
Lieut. F. J. Hicking
2/Lieut. R. A. Evans
2/Lieut. A. F. A. Patterson
2/Lieut. E. S. Poole

The East Yorkshire Regiment
2/Lieut. A. T. Sawdon

The Bedfordshire Regiment
Lieut. J. L. Ash
Lieut. G. Lenton
2/Lieut. R. N. Balding (att. M.G.C.)
2/Lieut. G. A. Binns
2/Lieut. R. D. J. Brighten
2/Lieut. F. L. Sharpin

The Leicestershire Regiment
Capt. G. F. Grogan
Lieut. D. C. Flood
2/Lieut. W. G. Robinson

The Lancashire Fusiliers
Capt. M. P. Gamon
2/Lieut. E. H. Fryer
2/Lieut. J. B. Lupton
2/Lieut. J. L. Townsend

The Cheshire Regiment
2/Lieut. F. B. Gadson
2/Lieut. B. H. Shaw

The South Wales Borderers
Lieut. E. A. Griffiths
2/Lieut. G. H. Bowyer
2/Lieut. P. E. Burrell
2/Lieut. R. H. Cole
2/Lieut. G. B. Jones

The Gloucestershire Regiment
Capt. A. H. Jones
Capt. F. W. C. Stiliman
Lieut. L. S. Griffin

The Worcestershire Regiment
Lieut. E. N. Finney
Lieut. T. H. S. Senior
2/Lieut. C. H. D. Banks
2/Lieut. R. G. Cook
2/Lieut. H. E. Ginn
2/Lieut. W. L. Perks
2/Lieut. B. W. Pigg
2/Lieut. R. W. Powell
2/Lieut. A. M. Scougall
2/Lieut. E. E. Vaile

The East Lancashire Regiment
Lieut. D. Walker
2/Lieut. E. A. Dothie
2/Lieut. H. G. Raphael
2/Lieut. J. W. Redding
2/Lieut. H. M. Webster

The East Surrey Regiment
Capt. A. A. Collinson
Capt. J. B. Raymond, M.C.
Lieut. P. P. Kelly
2/Lieut. F. T. Harrison
2/Lieut. H. J. Newland
2/Lieut. J. A. B. Paul, M.C.
2/Lieut. H. B. Roe
2/Lieut. P. J. Seater
2/Lieut. M. A. Stimson

The Duke of Cornwall's Light Infantry
Lieut. V. C. W. Bennett
Lieut. L. C. Coombe
2/Lieut. H. G. Barnes
2/Lieut. E. R. Chillwell
2/Lieut. R. H. Kelynack
2/Lieut. W. P. Martin
2/Lieut. J. Outram
2/Lieut. W. A. Rooke
2/Lieut. E. M. Vowler

The Duke of Wellington's (West Riding Regiment)
Capt. H. M. S. Carpenter
Capt. T. Coulthurst
Lieut. J. E. Raphael
2/Lieut. A. Gunn

The Border Regiment
2/Lieut. J. H. Dothie
2/Lieut. W. K. Sanderson

The Royal Sussex Regiment
Major W. T. Heagerty
Major W. G. B. Humble-Crofts
Capt. H. C. Barnes, M.C.
Capt. A. S. Fabian
Capt. C. M. Humble-Crofts
Lieut. R. Cornford
Lieut. F. S. Gillespie
Lieut. H. C. Langdale
Lieut. G. F. Sogno
Lieut. C. Sparks
Lieut. C. T. Squires
Lieut. A. B. Wilkinson
2/Lieut. C. P. Burley
2/Lieut. F. Burton
2/Lieut. A. C. Cushen
2/Lieut. E. W. Dudley
2/Lieut. J. M. Field
2/Lieut. R. S. Oxley, M.M.
2/Lieut. L. K. Rayner
2/Lieut. W. F. Scandrett
2/Lieut. E. W. Tice

The Hampshire Regiment
Lieut. S. E. Haddy
Lieut. C. F. Wilson
2/Lieut. W. F. Keep
2/Lieut. H. C. Scoggin
2/Lieut. C. H. Stock

The South Staffordshire Regiment
Lieut. S. W. Brettell
Lieut. F. S. Creasey
2/Lieut. J. J. Fisher

The South Lancashire Regiment
Lieut. R. S. Carlton
Lieut. J. E. T. Strickland (att. M.G.C.)
2/Lieut. E. A. Daniels
2/Lieut. A. C. Handyside
2/Lieut. R. L. Viner

The Welsh Regiment
Lieut. C. H. Davies
2/Lieut. D. L. S. Gaskell

The Black Watch (Royal Highlanders)
2/Lieut. H. West

The Oxfordshire and Buckinghamshire Light Infantry
Capt. W. C. Trimmer
2/Lieut. J. P. Copinger
2/Lieut. R. A. Cresswell
2/Lieut. J. W. H. Fussell

2/Lieut. K. I. T. Morland
2/Lieut. A. C. Skoulding
2/Lieut. N. H. Talbot

The Essex Regiment
Capt. E. N. Balme, M.C.
Capt. J. W. Bell
Capt. W. R. Fish
Capt. I. H. Linford, M.C.
Lieut. S. C. Harrison
Lieut. H. Taylor (att. M.G.C.)
2/Lieut. L. F. Cooke
2/Lieut. J. C. Gardom
2/Lieut. W. G. Hartley, M.M.
2/Lieut. T. E. C. Haworth
2/Lieut. L. R. Hodge

The Sherwood Foresters (Nottingham-shire and Derbyshire Regiment)
Lieut. S. E. Cairns, M.C.
Lieut. J. W. C. Taylor
2/Lieut. F. H. Chappell
2/Lieut. D. F. Don
2/Lieut. R. N. Lakeman
2/Lieut. E. H. Lifetree

The Loyal North Lancashire Regiment
Capt. A. E. Osborne
Lieut. E. U. Green, M.C.
Lieut. R. Willis
2/Lieut. C. C. Trippe

Princess Charlotte of Wales's (Royal Berkshire Regiment)
Major D. Tosetti, M.C.
Capt. R. Holland
Lieut. L. D. Fanshawe
Lieut. V. D. W. Pitt
2/Lieut. S. H. Bedford
2/Lieut. C. H. Chambers
2/Lieut. E. J. Druitt
2/Lieut. H. S. Griffin
2/Lieut. V. A. Lavers, M.C.
2/Lieut. A. R. Tarrant

The Queen's Own (Royal West Kent Regiment)
Capt. J. O. Heath
Capt. P. Stevens
2/Lieut. W. D. Cornford
2/Lieut. C. T. Davies
2/Lieut. C. E. M. Dillon
2/Lieut. H. W. File
2/Lieut. C. J. Fox
2/Lieut. J. K. Ground
2/Lieut. E. D. Harrison
2/Lieut. G. Mansfield
2/Lieut. A. Martin
2/Lieut. R. W. S. Meakins
2/Lieut. H. R. Pracy

2/Lieut. V. C. W. Sutton
2/Lieut. C. P. Wright
2/Lieut. F. G. Yeo

The King's Own (Yorkshire Light Infantry)
2/Lieut. J. E. Cundall
2/Lieut. A. J. Liddell
2/Lieut. A. D. Maconachie
2/Lieut. H. P. C. Rawlins
2/Lieut. E. B. Yardley

The King's (Shropshire Light Infantry)
Lieut. G. F. D. Artaud
2/Lieut. E. M. Hannah, M.C.
2/Lieut. A. E. Lewis

The Duke of Cambridge's Own (Middle-sex Regiment)
Lieut. H. A. Godfrey
Lieut. D. Holman
2/Lieut. H. J. Barker
2/Lieut. H. G. Blaxall
2/Lieut. A. Brewerton
2/Lieut. C. J. Crawford
2/Lieut. C. B. Grundy
2/Lieut. R. E. Grundy
2/Lieut. W. W. Hardwick
2/Lieut. W. F. Parriss
2/Lieut. C. A. White

The King's Royal Rifle Corps
Capt. J. S. Ryan
Lieut. E. W. B. Maggs
Lieut. W. P. Morris
2/Lieut. K. G. Dennis
2/Lieut. L. W. Lewis (att. M.G.C.)

The Duke of Edinburgh's (Wiltshire Regiment)
Capt. L. H. Horncastle, M.C.
Capt. L. Stansfield-Smith
Lieut. D. W. Gosden
Lieut. L. J. F. O'Brien
2/Lieut. S. F. G. Jones
2/Lieut. W. E. Scott

The Manchester Regiment
Capt. E. Ross
Lieut. F. Leach
2/Lieut. A. Copley
2/Lieut. F. A. Eminton
2/Lieut. H. S. Grimshaw
2/Lieut. E. F. Smith

The Prince of Wales's (North Staf-fordshire Regiment)
Capt. W. O. Russell
Capt. G. H. Tortoishell
Capt. C. C. B. Ward

2/Lieut. E. N. Coxe
2/Lieut. R. P. Harker
2/Lieut. D. H. Krauss

The York and Lancaster Regiment
Capt. T. E. Sanderson
Capt. S. F. Smith
Lieut. G. R. Eddie
2/Lieut. O. W. Dodwell
2/Lieut. D. W. McIntyre

The Durham Light Infantry
Capt. C. R. Gold, D.S.O.
Capt. H. G. Legg
2/Lieut. S. F. Bobby (att. T.M. Bty.)
2/Lieut. C. L. G. Hill

The Highland Light Infantry
Lieut. E. H. Wuensch
2/Lieut. C. H. Shipton

Seaforth Highlanders (Ross-shire Buffs, The Duke of Albany's)
Capt. A. Irving
Lieut. H. Macaulay

The Queen's Own Cameron Highlanders
Capt. D. Methvin

The Royal Irish Rifles
2/Lieut. J. G. Bland
2/Lieut. H. S. Davy

Princess Victoria's (Royal Irish Fusiliers)
2/Lieut. R. N. Wood

The Connaught Rangers
2/Lieut. J. R. Moore

Princess Louise's (Argyll and Sutherland Highlanders)
2/Lieut. R. M. S. Scott

The Prince of Wales's Leinster Regiment
Lieut. H. Pearman (att. R.A.F.)
2/Lieut. W. J. A. Blatchly
2/Lieut. T. Hickman
2/Lieut. E. Kahn

The Royal Munster Fusiliers
2/Lieut. A. E. Male

The Royal Dublin Fusiliers
2/Lieut. J. J. A. Coyne

The Rifle Brigade (Prince Consort's Own)
2/Lieut. W. H. Blades
2/Lieut. G. C. Dalgoutte
2/Lieut. R. S. Hansford
2/Lieut. W. R. H. Merriman
2/Lieut. H. J. R. Moseley
2/Lieut. C. E. Southgate

The Motor Machine Gun Corps
Lieut. P. Jeffries

The Machine Gun Corps
Lieut. E. R. A. Wagstaffe
2/Lieut. H. Jackson
2/Lieut. E. Manger
2/Lieut. C. Nichols
Pte. J. I. C. Boswell
Pte. T. W. Peters

The Tank Corps
Lieut. G. H. Adney, M.C.
2/Lieut. L. A. Evans

Army Service Corps
Capt. A. C. Estall
Capt. C. F. Pavitt, M.C.
Lieut. S. Austin
Lieut. J. H. Heyman
Lieut. L. M. Matthews
Lieut. N. S. Smith

Army Ordnance Department
Lieut. J. H. Sanders

Army Pay Department
Pte. W. T. Perrott
Pte. R. W. H. Smith

Special List (Interpreters)
Lieut. F. V. Thicke

Labour Corps
Pte. H. Beer

The Nigeria Regiment (West African Frontier Force)
Capt. J. M. Bales

The King's African Rifles
Capt. P. M. Pascall, M.C.

The Imperial Camel Corps
Capt. A. F. Newsam

16th Rajputs (Indian Army)
Capt. K. Morfey

407

35th Sikhs (Indian Army)
Lieut. R. P. L. Adams

57th Wilde's Rifles (Indian Army)
Lieut. B. L. Amsden

63rd Palamacotta Light Infantry (Indian Army)
Capt. A. L. Smith

Honourable Artillery Company
Capt. J. T. Catley (att. Royal Field Artillery)
Capt. E. M. Ellis, M.C. [att. 18th London Regiment (London Irish Rifles)]
Capt. S. Hawkins, M.C. (att. Staff)
Capt. F. W. E. Hoare (att. Royal Fusiliers)
Capt. L. W. McArthur, M.C. (att. R.A.F.)
2/Lieut. H. P. Chaffey (att. Royal Fusiliers)
2/Lieut. C. Caudle (att. Royal Fusiliers)
Cpl. C. G. S. Ward (att. R.F.C.)
L./Cpl. A. Mann, M.M. (att. R.A.F.)
Pte. E. G. B. Farrow (att. Field Survey Co., R.E.)

Westmorland and Cumberland Yeomanry
2/Lieut. G. W. Bennett

Derbyshire Yeomanry
Capt. L. W. Mansell

1st County of London Yeomanry
Lieut. G. J. P. Holton

Surrey Yeomanry
Capt. A. O. Shalders
Lieut. J. H. Dodgshon (att. R.F.C.)

The Hertfordshire Regiment
Capt. C. S. Cautherley
Capt. F. McN. Drury

The Cambridgeshire Regiment
Capt. A. S. Armstrong
Capt. F. W. Ford, M.C.

The London Regiment
Capt. S. R. Chapman (London Rifle Brigade)
Capt. E. D. Rose (2nd City of London Bn.)

Lieut. L. F. Aberdein (3rd City of London Bn.)
Lieut. L. T. Cheney
Lieut. C. G. R. Cracknell (24th Bn. The Queen's)
Lieut. O. H. Garrud (3rd City of London Bn.)
Lieut. F. G. Goodyear, M.C. (24th Bn. The Queen's)
Lieut. W. S. Hall (20th Bn. Blackheath and Woolwich)
Lieut. H. V. Orris (1st City of London Bn.)
Lieut. W. H. Parker
Lieut. H. F. Stapleton (1st City of London Bn.)
Lieut. A. Starr
Lieut. G. F. Trenow, M.C. (London Rifle Brigade)
Lieut. G. A. Westlake (1st City of London Bn.)
2/Lieut. A. W. Adkin (20th Bn. Blackheath and Woolwich)
2/Lieut. E. J. Battersby (London Irish Rifles)
2/Lieut. C. T. Booth (Poplar and Stepney Rifles)
2/Lieut. C. J. Brodie (4th City of London Bn.)
2/Lieut. J. H. Chamberlain (1st City of London Bn.)
2/Lieut. A. G. Costello (Poplar and Stepney Rifles)
2/Lieut. H. Dawson (7th City of London Bn.)
2/Lieut. J. F. Elders (Queen's Westminster Rifles)
2/Lieut. D. T. Forbes (Poplar and Stepney Rifles)
2/Lieut. W. S. Halford (20th Bn. Blackheath and Woolwich)
2/Lieut. B. T. Haselgrove (Queen Victoria's Rifles)
2/Lieut. R. B. Heagerty (2nd City of London Bn.)
2/Lieut. J. V. Jeffree (3rd City of London Bn.)
2/Lieut. E. A. O. Jones (Queen's Westminster Rifles)
2/Lieut. F. W. Lane (Post Office Rifles)
2/Lieut. F. J. Larkin, M.C. (22nd Bn. The Queen's)
2/Lieut. J. K. Nowell (Post Office Rifles)
2/Lieut. H. F. Segnitz (19th Bn. St. Pancras)
2/Lieut. C. A. Speyer (4th City of London Bn.)
2/Lieut. G. E. Stirling (Post Office Rifles)

2/Lieut. F. A. Thew (22nd Bn. The Queen's)
2/Lieut. H. L. Thorn (20th Bn. Black-heath and Woolwich)
2/Lieut. P. C. Townend (4th City of London Bn.)
2/Lieut. P. A. Vaile (19th Bn. St. Pancras)
2/Lieut. A. W. Wallis (10th Bn. Hackney)
Cpl. W. J. F. Bull (13th Kensington Bn.)
Pte. H. C. Atkinson (13th Kensington Bn.)
Pte. E. S. Eastment (13th Kensington Bn.)

Royal Flying Corps or Royal Air Force
Capt. G. K. Smith, M.C.
Capt. F. J. H. Thayre, M.C.
Capt. N. W. W. Webb, M.C.
Capt. O. B. W. Willis
Lieut. C. B. B. Cockman
Lieut. N. H. Crow
Lieut. L. N. Franklin
Lieut. G. Harwood, A.F.C.
Lieut. F. A. Hewens

Lieut. C. Seymour
Lieut. J. G. Will
2/Lieut. J. Armstrong
2/Lieut. J. C. H. Barfield
2/Lieut. C. R. Brice-Halley
2/Lieut. F. Cawley
2/Lieut. D. Clarke
2/Lieut. R. W. Follit
2/Lieut. W. N. Hicks
2/Lieut. G. C. Hoskins
2/Lieut. R. R. Humphreys
2/Lieut. L. E. J. Lonnen
2/Lieut, C. T. Lovell
2/Lieut. J. Mill
2/Lieut. D. P. Ogilvie
2/Lieut. A. E. Parks
2/Lieut. J. Thompson, D.C.M.
2/Lieut. C. G. Ward

Units Not Known
2/Lieut. F. D. Bishop
2/Lieut. H. A. Hope
2/Lieut. C. H. Hussey
2/Lieut. V. S. Lovell
Pte. J. Adams
Pte. J. Hill

ROLL OF HONOUR, 1939-1945

11TH (H.A.C.) REGIMENT, R.H.A.

Calais
Gnr. L. J. A. Crouch (att. East Riding Yeomanry)

Agheila
Lieut. J. L. F. Armitage
2/Lieut. W. M. Hart
2/Lieut. H. F. C. Tompson
Sergt. M. J. T. Town, M.M.
L./Sergt. H. J. Harold
L./Bdr. G. A. Colwell
Gnr. D. Godfrey
Gnr. D. Grindey
Gnr. E. L. K. Hill
Gnr. W. E. Hughes
Gnr. A. Shea
Gnr. R. A. G. Steels
Sigmn. E. J. Dorney

"H" Troop Action
Lieut. J. W. Venning
Sergt. V. B. M. Banbury
Sergt. J. E. Steventon
L./Bdr. V. C. Buckland
L./Bdr. A. H. Russell
Gnr. H. F. Brazington
Gnr. H. L. V. House
Gnr. T. Lloyd
Gnr. L. Sheldon

Pre-Knightsbridge
Cpl. C. Fell
Gnr. A. T. Hughes

Knightsbridge
Major H. Bourne
Major J. R. O. Charlton, M.C.
Major J. W. Hopkins, M.C.
Lieut. M. V. Boys
Lieut. A. F. Worthington
2/Lieut. F. C. Haldin
2/Lieut. C. G. A. Leechman
2/Lieut. R. Leftwich
2/Lieut. R. H. McDonald
B.S.M. J. H. Thorns
B.S.M. S. A. J. Trotman

S./Sergt. A. Goodman
Sergt. J. W. Deakin
Sergt. G. M. Nicoll
Sergt. H. Rowntree
Sergt. A. D. Sneddon
Sergt. B. J. Swingler
Sergt. S. M. Tompkinson
Sergt. J. W. Villette
L./Sergt. L. R. Callaghan
L./Sergt. G. T. Dando
L./Sergt. D. Maddox
L./Sergt. N. Rishton
L./Sergt. G. Terry
Bdr. W. J. R. Boardman, M.M.
Bdr. C. P. Brown
Bdr. G. H. Clark
Bdr. N. S. Donaldson
Bdr. A. W. Farquhar
Bdr. J. E. Hayward
Bdr. E. C. Holcroft
Bdr. F. J. Ironton
Bdr. G. J. Lawley
Bdr. L. J. Nunn
Bdr. H. R. Parry, M.M.
Bdr. A. C. Smith
Bdr. J. C. Tinsley
L./Bdr. R. Best
L./Bdr. H. Cook
L./Bdr. H. D. Crutchley
L./Bdr. C. M. Davies
L./Bdr. H. J. Noble
L./Bdr. S. G. Spaull
L./Bdr. N. Whittingham
L./Bdr. J. H. Williams
Gnr. G. T. Allan
Gnr. S. Baker
Gnr. E. G. Balding
Gnr. L. Barker
Gnr. A. K. Chappell
Gnr. H. Chaytors
Gnr. A. J. Crowe
Gnr. G. J. Dodd
Gnr. G. Goltenboth
Gnr. D. W. Griffiths
Gnr. C. F. Haywood
Gnr. G. Helm

Gnr. T. W. Hills
Gnr. J. Hingley
Gnr. E. Hobson
Gnr. F. A. Hodge
Gnr. H. A. Jeffreys
Gnr. A. Johnson
Gnr. G. A. Jones
Gnr. R. Jones
Gnr. F. Knight
Gnr. F. J. Mann
Gnr. G. L. O'Neill
Gnr. W. H. Parker
Gnr. A. L. Pratchett
Gnr. S. J. Radley
Gnr. C. Rogers
Gnr. J. C. Smith
Gnr. F. G. Wakelin
Gnr. R. F. Watts
Gnr. J. T. Webb
Gnr. E. A. Willis

Alamein

Capt. S. A. G. Watt
Sergt. J. E. Baird
Bdr. W. J. Black
Bdr. G. C. Jeffries
L./Bdr. R. S. Williams, M.M.
L./Cpl. W. E. Glennon
Gnr. A. G. Aldridge
Gnr. C. R. Bailey
Gnr. W. S. Cockburn
Gnr. H. C. Downie
Gnr. J. Goldston
Gnr. E. E. Hargreaves
Gnr. G. L. Hemming
Gnr. J. Malcolm
Gnr. S. A. Payne
Gnr. E. W. Rogers
Gnr. A. Shanks
Gnr. W. E. Smith
Gnr. L. Viney
Gnr. W. F. Walton
Gnr. F. W. White
Gnr. L. Williams

Tunisia

Capt. T. F. Butler-Stoney, M.C.
Lieut. A. S. Humphreys
Lieut. B. H. S. Laskey
Sergt. J. R. Kettle (att. 1st Corps)
Bdr. E. Watson
L./Bdr. C. Edge
Gnr. J. W. Busby
Gnr. J. W. Shaw
Gnr. T. C. Smith
Gnr. F. B. Wilson

Sicily

Major D. Rowlandson
Capt. J. H. McAllum, M.C.
L./Bdr. R. Harper

Gnr. A. A. Philip
Gnr. G. E. Pryke
Gnr. G. W. Richardson
Gnr. R. Stanford
Gnr. F. Wookey

Gothic Line

Capt. L. Q. Drage, M.C.
Capt. A. W. Grant
Sergt. G. W. Smith
Bdr. A. M. Pennington
Bdr. H. L. G. Ward
L./Bdr. W. T. Holloway
Gnr. R. Hartley
Gnr. M. H. Harty
Gnr. W. E. Heslop
Gnr. H. L. Hills
Gnr. D. Jenkins
Gnr. D. C. Webber

Senio to the Po

L./Bdr. A. M. Duckworth
Gnr. W. Morrison

Lost at Sea as Prisoners of War

B.Q.M.S. H. A. Murray
Sergt. W. G. Battle
Sergt. A. E. Chaplin
Sergt. P. E. Farrell
Sergt. A. H. Godden
L./Sergt. B. F. Dummott
L./Sergt. B. Edwards
Bdr. E. F. Cadman
Bdr. C. S. Lemon
L./Bdr. J. M. Green
L./Bdr. G. D. F. McGrath
Gnr. C. W. Bale
Gnr. J. A. Bestwick
Gnr. J. Bettany
Gnr. F. J. Biddulph
Gnr. G. Brown
Gnr. L. C. Chard
Gnr. F. W. Cheeseman
Gnr. M. B. Edge
Gnr. N. W. Erry
Gnr. J. Finbery
Gnr. R. Gibson
Gnr. A. Groden
Gnr. J. E. S. Hatley
Gnr. E. N. Hayes
Gnr. A. V. Hennessy
Gnr. J. E. Hopton
Gnr. G. W. Hurley
Gnr. P. D. Jackson
Gnr. D. M. Jones
Gnr. L. Lane
Gnr. M. J. Larner
Gnr. J. G. Mills
Gnr. A. C. Munro
Gnr. E. W. Nye
Gnr. F. J. Nye

Gnr. J. E. P. O'Brien
Gnr. D. A. Osborn
Gnr. T. E. Pearman
Gnr. J. J. Prosser
Gnr. W. R. Rangecroft
Gnr. J. Seel
Gnr. H. D. Simmons
Gnr. F. Sims
Gnr. T. Smith
Gnr. G. W. Snelling
Gnr. E. L. Stone
Gnr. A. A. H. Stretch
Gnr. J. A. Turner
Gnr. C. R. Willingham
Gnr. C. W. Wilson
Gnr. G. Worcester
Gnr. H. P. Wright

Died as Prisoners of War

Sergt. A. Straiton
L./Bdr. R. Graves
Gnr. C. A. S. Beer
Gnr. J. A. Cole
Gnr. S. Corden
Gnr. J. M. Griffiths

Gnr. W. Jones (of wounds)
Gnr. O. G. Lewis
Gnr. J. McCracken
Gnr. E. Moxon
Gnr. W. Preshous
Gnr. R. M. Taylor (of wounds)

Killed on Active Service

Capt. C. D. Earle
Sergt. H. B. Wright
L./Bdr. V. Clegg
Gnr. H. I. Dorell
Gnr. S. J. Macallan
Gnr. E. W. Robinson, M.M.
Gnr. W. Rooney

Died on or as a result of Active Service

Sergt. E. Weaver
L./Bdr. A. E. Gardner
Gnr. D. Campbell
Gnr. E. D. W. Daniel
Gnr. C. H. Pearce
Gnr. C. A. Porter
Gnr. G. Treharne
Gnr. J. L. Whitehouse

12TH (H.A.C.) REGIMENT, R.H.A.

North Africa

Major M. J. V. Perry
Lieut. G. W. M. Swallow
Lieut. H. C. Swift
B.S.M. R. Mackenzie
Sergt. F. S. Davies
Sergt. C. G. Hughes
Sergt. J. C. Lawrie, D.C.M.
Sergt. R. Temple
L./Sergt. D. L. Hodson
L./Sergt. T. A. Stott
Bdr. P. W. R. McGregor
Bdr. R. E. B. Neish
Bdr. J. Rennie
Bdr. D. Strain
L./Bdr. J. C. Keddie
L./Bdr. F. V. Lander
L./Bdr. T. S. Rowan
L./Bdr. A. Williams
L./Bdr. S. Winter
Gnr. G. P. Bright
Gnr. D. Cooper
Gnr. A. J. Cooper
Gnr. J. W. Dickerson
Gnr. F. Forth
Gnr. G. H. Gould
Gnr. D. Hagyard
Gnr. T. Kenny
Gnr. E. Miles
Gnr. J. H. Newton
Gnr. P. E. Pickersgill

Gnr. S. Rimmer
Gnr. E. Ryan
Gnr. W. K. Sharpe
Gnr. R. W. F. Sheppard
Gnr. R. F. Sutton
Gnr. H. Tate
Gnr. J. W. Thompson
Gnr. H. A. Voss
Gnr. J. Walsh
Gnr. J. Ward
Gnr. W. V. White
Gnr. T. L. Wilkinson
Gnr. R. R. Wilson
Gnr. E. Wroth

Italy

Lieut. E. C. Freeman
Lieut. G. N. Holbrook
Lieut. W. H. M. McNicholas
L./Sergt. S. T. Powell
L./Sergt. B. Preston
Bdr. W. Bennetts
Bdr. W. A. J. Lambert
Bdr. T. White
L./Bdr. C. Clough
L./Bdr. S. Gilchrist
L./Bdr. C. H. Holding
L./Bdr. G. V. Leech
L./Bdr. S. V. Leach
L./Bdr. H. H. Mash
Gnr. H. Binnie

Gnr. R. A. J. Blackwell
Gnr. D. A. Broadbent
Gnr. G. S. Collins
Gnr. J. J. Crosbie
Gnr. W. S. Dring
Gnr. E. Gent
Gnr. A. Glascoe
Gnr. A. Goldberg
Gnr. W. Gustard
Gnr. A. H. M. Haynes
Gnr. T. Hodson
Dvr. D. J. Jones (R. Sigs.)
Gnr. F. E. Jones
Gnr. L. Lyon
Gnr. A. G. Maskell
Gnr. J. A. Mease
Gnr. H. H. Morley
Gnr. D. E. Morris
Gnr. T. M. O'Brien
Gnr. J. Ormrod
Gnr. A. Patching
Gnr. E. V. Phillips

Gnr. D. C. Probert
Gnr. P. Ricketts
Gnr. P. R. Sketchley
Gnr. A. F. Stansfield
Gnr. F. Thomson
Gnr. C. Turner
Gnr. H. Turpin
Gnr. D. Veevers
Gnr. W. Young

Killed on Active Service
Bdr. G. V. Brown
Gnr. F. Baller
Gnr. C. J. Cocks
Gnr. G. E. R. Duncombe

Died as Prisoner of War
L./Bdr. G. E. Johnson

Died of sickness on Active Service
R.S.M. D. S. Macleod
Bdr. L. T. Clive

13TH (H.A.C.) REGIMENT, R.H.A.

Normandy
Capt. C. P. Vivian
Lieut. E. A. Barson, M.M.
Lieut. A. P. Stanford
Sergt. J. Clark
Sergt. V. D. McGill
Sergt. S. S. Woolger
L./Sergt. P. Willis
Bdr. M. H. W. Fraser
Bdr. J. Hallinan
Bdr. C. Pyle
Gnr. S. A. Blackburn
Gnr. J. W. Cawte
Gnr. A. F. Edmonds
Gnr. R. H. Ellicott
Gnr. F. E. Enever
Gnr. E. T. Jones
Gnr. F. Kirkham
Gnr. F. S. Morriss
Gnr. P. O'Malley
Gnr. J. O'Rourke
Gnr. H. W. T. Percival
Gnr. H. J. Shaw
Gnr. N. Weir
Gnr. J. E. Wood

Amiens and Antwerp
Lieut. A. P. G. Bluett
Bdr. L. W. Hudson
Gnr. W. H. Bawn
Gnr. E. Dawson
Gnr. T. A. Graham
Gnr. G. J. Halladay
Gnr. D. McDonald

Belgium and Holland
Bdr. L. J. Flack
L./Bdr. W. J. Giles
Gnr. L. F. Adams, M.M.
Gnr. G. H. W. Bannister
Gnr. B. J. Clare
Gnr. H. T. Cook
Gnr. J. W. Nash
Gnr. J. Smith
Gnr. R. Tothill
Gnr. C. Willis

Germany
Capt. G. D. H. Budgen, M.C.
B.S.M. E. C. Watts
Cpl. W. R. Robinson (R. Sigs.)
Gnr. A. Bulman
Gnr. F. Cownie
Gnr. H. Stansbury
Sgmn. R. J. Bentham (R. Sigs.)
Sgmn. W. Connell (R. Sigs.)

Accidentally killed on Active Service
L./Bdr. J. Moran
Gnr. W. R. Buchanan
Gnr. W. Lockett

Died of sickness on Active Service
L./Bdr. A. Blackith
Gnr. T. W. Culshaw
Gnr. T. Ellis

86TH (H.A.C.) HEAVY ANTI-AIRCRAFT REGIMENT, R.A.

Major W. A. Clark
B.S.M. J. H. Shepherd
Sergt. H. Wright
Gnr. A. W. Boxell
Gnr. L. A. Breeze

Gnr. L. M. Bullwinkle
Gnr. C. Crowther
Gnr. W. D. Toms
Gnr. A. Young

275 (H.A.C.) HEAVY ANTI-AIRCRAFT BATTERY, R.A.

Major H. J. Finch
B.S.M. J. W. T. Grimshaw
Cpl. L. Farrell
Gnr. A. O. Brown
Gnr. C. Corby
Gnr. C. F. Curtis

Gnr. C. H. Gabrielson
Gnr. W. Hough
Gnr. W. Hudson
Gnr. P. W. S. Selby
Gnr. G. Walsh

446 (H.A.C.) HEAVY ANTI-AIRCRAFT BATTERY, R.A.

Gnr. T. Smith

H.A.C. COMPANIES 13TH (HOME DEFENCE) BATTALION, THE ROYAL FUSILIERS

Killed in Action
Cpl. J. O'Mahony
Cpl. F. A. P. Wright, M.B.E.
Fus. C. P. Meadows
Fus. G. E. Spicer

Died on Active Service
Capt. A. J. Beaumont
Fus. D. Kirby

MEMBERS OF THE HONOURABLE ARTILLERY COMPANY WHO FELL IN ACTION OR DIED WHILE SERVING WITH OTHER UNITS

Royal Navy
C.P.O. S. W. Snelling, D.S.M.

Royal Naval Volunteer Reserve
P.O. E. S. English
Lieut. G. B. Pudney (Fleet Air Arm)

Royal Marines
Lieut. T. B. Carothers

The Queen's Bays (2nd Dragoon Guards)
Capt. I. P. Goold Walker

3rd The King's Own Hussars
Capt. R. H. Le Bas

8th King's Royal Irish Hussars
Lieut. G. F. F. Douse

13th/18th (Royal) Hussars (Queen Mary's Own)
Lieut. M. A. Ritchie

24th Lancers
2/Lieut. J. H. Crane

Royal Armoured Corps
2/Lieut. N. Carman

Royal Tank Regiment
Capt. A. O. Lott
Capt. W. B. Sant
Lieut. G. Bullett
Lieut. C. L. Cowan
2/Lieut. B. R. Cushing
2/Lieut. L. J. Hotson
2/Lieut. A. Rhodes

Reconnaissance Corps
Capt. S. C. Fordham

Royal Wiltshire Yeomanry (Prince of Wales's Own)
2/Lieut. C. G. Kirkby

Staffordshire Yeomanry (Queen's Own Royal Regiment)
Capt. J. G. Tyrell, M.C.

Royal Regiment of Artillery
Brig. W. A. Sheil, C.B.E., D.S.O.
Lieut.-Colonel J. M. Davies, M.C.
Major J. T. M. Appleby
Major O. C. H. Burton
Major J. D. C. Ellison
Major A. W. Ellis
Major P. Hazell, M.C.
Major C. M. Ogden-Smith, H.A.C.
(att. Special Air Service)
Major L. V. Stribling
Major C. E. M. Wiggins
Major E. V. E. White
Capt. P. R. Alexander
Capt. B. E. Allan
Capt. K. E. Allanson
Capt. C. C. Ballyn, D.F.C.
Capt. P. M. Bennett, R.H.A.
Capt. P. M. Britton, H.A.C., R.H.A.
Capt. D. G. Castle
Capt. P. Cohen
Capt. D. Cooper
Capt. R. G. Course
Capt. G. C. Daniel
Capt. G. S. de Jonge, M.C., R.H.A.
Capt. G. H. Dickie
Capt. A. R. Forster, R.H.A.
Capt. P. S. Y. Garrett, M.C.
Capt. J. C. Gaye
Capt. W. H. Gill
Capt. R. A. Harrison-Austin, R.H.A.
Capt. N. Hayes
Capt. S. A. Heald
Capt. P. Hoare
Capt. A. E. Howorth
Capt. R. B. Hutt
Capt. F. M. Jackson
Capt. E. G. Jamieson
Capt. E. A. Knight
Capt. J. D. Landale
Capt. G. W. Lloyd, M.C.
Capt. J. S. Loram, M.C.
Capt. C. H. Lucy
Capt. R. H. Mills
Capt. W. S. Molison, D.F.C.
Capt. P. H. Newson-Smith
Capt. R. C. Nightingale
Capt. C. W. R. Oddie
Capt. G. W. D. Ormerod
Capt. I. G. Pattison
Capt. H. D. Peal, R.H.A.
Capt. W. J. Potter
Capt. W. G. Reader
Capt. F. C. K. Rowland
Capt. R. V. Seddon
Capt. G. J. S. Slinn, M.C., R.H.A.
Capt. E. M. Stevens, R.H.A.
Capt. R. H. Stevens
Capt. V. B. Throndsen
Capt. J. K. Tobutt
Capt. J. P. Townend

Capt. D. D. Tweddle
Capt. W. J. Underhill
Capt. R. C. Whorlow
Capt. K. B. M. Wright
Lieut. L. D. Andrew, M.C.
Lieut. H. Bonsall
Lieut. D. V. J. Boys
Lieut. T. P. Cokayne
Lieut. P. W. Crocker
Lieut. G. H. Evison
Lieut. E. A. P. Forward
Lieut. M. F. Fulcher
Lieut. T. H. Gates
Lieut. A. F. Gray
Lieut. G. R. Horne
Lieut. R. Jutsum
Lieut. G. H. Johnson
Lieut. P. A. Keech, R.H.A.
Lieut. F. F. Leroy
Lieut. G. J. Macphee
Lieut. L. W. Marten
Lieut. J. C. May
Lieut. R. M. Monkhouse
Lieut. J. L. Moore
Lieut. H. D. Mordle
Lieut. J. R. Moritz
Lieut. G. A. C. Newton
Lieut. B. L. Olley
Lieut. D. A. Pickup
Lieut. C. F. Robinson
Lieut. C. J. Saunders
Lieut. R. E. A. Stebbing
Lieut. J. O. Timms, R.H.A.
Lieut. R. H. F. Truman
Lieut. W. C. O'D. Waddington
Lieut. R. A. C. Webster
2/Lieut. G. B. Cocollis
2/Lieut. G. Cook
2/Lieut. E. J. Dainty
2/Lieut. H. P. Davies
2/Lieut. A. H. Jones
2/Lieut. J. A. Macintosh
2/Lieut. F. B. Mitford, R.H.A.
2/Lieut. J. R. W. Monk
2/Lieut. S. M. Parker
2/Lieut. R. C. Pitt
2/Lieut. G. N. Symons
2/Lieut. J. B. Timewell
2/Lieut. D. E. Waterman
2/Lieut. J. G. Wynne
L./Bdr. F. D. Gifford, R.H.A.
L./Bdr. P. D. H. Pierson, R.H.A.
Gnr. J. N. Ingram
Gnr. G. G. Mackay

Corps of Royal Engineers
Major T. C. Baillon, M.B.E.
Major R. C. Bingham
Capt. J. B. Iceton
2/Lieut. R. C. Allen

Royal Corps of Signals
Capt. S. L. Blatch
Lieut. H. D. Jack

Irish Guards
Major A. R. Eardley-Wilmot, M.C.

Welsh Guards
Sergt. F. B. Eames

The Queen's Royal Regiment (West Surrey)
Major R. Elliott
Major J. R. Walker
Capt. E. R. C. Mayer
Lieut. D. S. S. Bullock
Lieut. R. T. Shaw
2/Lieut. H. M. C. Candy
2/Lieut. O. Holmes
2/Lieut. R. L. Hopkins
L./Cpl. S. G. Turner

The Buffs (Royal East Kent Regiment)
Lieut. N. J. Mander

The King's Own Royal Regiment (Lancaster)
Capt. F. F. Winmill (att. Chindits)
Lieut. R. J. T. Ewin

The Royal Warwickshire Regiment
2/Lieut. M. A. Gammidge
2/Lieut. D. E. Widmer

The Royal Fusiliers (City of London Regiment)
Capt. O. B. S. Gray
Capt. E. G. Head, T.D.
Capt. F. G. Kahl (att. Commandos)
Capt. A. J. Lake, H.A.C.
Capt. J. C. Rhodes

The Lincolnshire Regiment
Lieut. G. C. George
2/Lieut. J. C. Burrell
2/Lieut. H. L. Burridge

The Somerset Light Infantry (Prince Albert's)
Lieut. G. B. S. Wilson

The East Yorkshire Regiment (The Duke of York's Own)
Major F. F. Robins, M.C.
Capt. G. D. Wood

The Bedfordshire and Hertfordshire Regiment
Lieut. D. H. Jackson
Lieut. B. O. Kesby
2/Lieut. G. E. Robers-Medway

The Leicestershire Regiment
Lieut. J. M. Bonell
2/Lieut. C. A. Botibol

The Green Howards (Alexandra, Princess of Wales's Own Yorkshire Regiment)
2/Lieut. A. J. Capps

The Lancashire Fusiliers
Capt. A. M. Doyle-Davidson

The Royal Scots Fusiliers
Major C. T. Korts
Capt. F. S. Ripper
2/Lieut. H. A. F. F. McGrath

The Royal Welsh Fusiliers
Lieut. G. V. R. Davies

The South Wales Borderers
Capt. D. M. Davidson, M.C. (att. Commandos)
Capt. W. R. Gwillim
Lieut. D. A. Dutton (att. Commandos)

The Cameronians (Scottish Rifles)
Capt. N. R. Munn

The Gloucestershire Regiment
Capt. L. Leese (att. Commandos)

The East Surrey Regiment
Lieut. D. K. Smith
2/Lieut. J. F. L. Williams
Pte. G. L. Sharples

The Duke of Cornwall's Light Infantry
Capt. A. Lehmann
2/Lieut. M. E. Arnold

The Duke of Wellington's Regiment (West Riding)
Major P. P. Benson, M.C.
Lieut. E. P. Locatelli

The Royal Sussex Regiment
Capt. D. W. Gaylard, M.C.
Lieut. L. C. Armstrong
2/Lieut. P. J. V. Nolan
2/Lieut. E. P. Slowe

The Hampshire Regiment
Major E. C. Henley
Capt. C. J. Cresswell

The Dorsetshire Regiment
Major R. E. Harris
2/Lieut. G. R. E. Follett
2/Lieut. E. V. Ingram

The South Lancashire Regiment (The Prince of Wales's Volunteers)
2/Lieut. B. O. Warren

The Welsh Regiment
Lieut.-Colonel J. S. Morrison-Jones, M.C.
Capt. G. C. Williams
2/Lieut. K. R. Mattey

The Black Watch (Royal Highland Regiment)
Capt. C. S. Higgins

The Oxfordshire and Buckinghamshire Light Infantry
Capt. E. A. Moy-Thomas

The Essex Regiment
Capt. B. J. Cornelius
2/Lieut. A. J. Baines

The Sherwood Foresters (Nottinghamshire and Derbyshire Regiment)
Major L. C. Hunter

The Loyal Regiment (North Lancashire)
Major G. W. York

The Northamptonshire Regiment
Capt. H. W. Morgan
Lieut. M. E. Handon
Lieut. D. P. Passmore
Lieut. J. Perry

The Royal Berkshire Regiment (Princess Charlotte of Wales's)
Capt. J. M. Bedford
2/Lieut. M. H. Holme

The Queen's Own Royal West Kent Regiment
Major G. M. Dyas, M.C.
Capt. L. T. Mead
Capt. P. M. Peerless
2/Lieut. A. T. V. Pine
Pte. B. A. W. Penn

The King's Own Yorkshire Light Infantry
Major W. G. Haughton, H.A.C.

The King's Shropshire Light Infantry
Lieut. J. L. Stride
2/Lieut. R. W. Morgan

The Middlesex Regiment (Duke of Cambridge's Own)
Capt. J. R. Asling
Capt. F. B. B. Buckbarrow
Capt. D. West

Lieut. C. Cheesewright
Lieut. K. E. Young
2/Lieut. K. D. Tarr

The King's Royal Rifle Corps
Major F. de R. Dawson

The Wiltshire Regiment (Duke of Edinburgh's)
Capt. B. G. Widnell, M.C.
Lieut. W. E. Halse-Hearne (att. Commandos)

The Manchester Regiment
Major J. M. North

The Durham Light Infantry
Major P. P. Kelly, H.A.C.
Major F. S. Manford
Lieut. D. R. Prince
2/Lieut. G. H. Blakey
2/Lieut. T. A. Graham

The Seaforth Highlanders (Ross-shire Buffs, The Duke of Albany's)
Lieut. H. F. S. Mackenzie
2/Lieut. P. C. Fleming

The Gordon Highlanders
Capt. P. D. Kebbell

The Queen's Own Cameron Highlanders
Capt. R. D. M. Emmerson
Capt. J. B. J. Houghton, M.C. (att. Commandos)

The Royal Ulster Rifles
Capt. J. A. O'R. O'Flynn
Lieut. R. Quinn

The Argyll and Sutherland Highlanders (Princess Louise's)
Lieut. R. Carswell

Glider Pilot Regiment
Capt. N. G. Hardie

Parachute Regiment
Lieut. D. S. Catlin

Royal Army Service Corps
Major K. A. W. Charnaud
Capt. R. H. Carr
Capt. D. S. Haigh
Capt. E. H. Notson

Royal Army Medical Corps
Major R. Edwards
Major R. A. Foucar

417

Royal Army Ordnance Corps
Major J. A. C. Barlow
Lieut. C. C. Ingram

Royal Army Pay Corps
Lieut. E. M. G. Cartledge
Lieut. L. W. Plumb

General List
Major W. W. Burton, D.L.
Capt. E. R. Wakefield
Lieut. S. J. Thomson

5th Mahratta Light Infantry
Major D. D. Higgins

9th Jat Regiment
Lieut.-Colonel W. M. Morgan, M.C.

18th Royal Garhwal Rifles
Lieut. J. S. Hogan

19th Hyderabad Regiment
Major A. D. Brown

25th Ajmer Regiment
Capt. F. B. Chambers

Indian Ordnance Mechanical Engineers
Capt. F. D. Deakin

The Lincoln and Welland Regiment (Canadian Army)
L./Cpl. T. M. Griffiths

New Zealand Field Artillery
2/Lieut. J. P. Dill

Hong Kong Volunteer Defence Corps
Bdr. J. M. Houghton
Pte. J. C. Eager

Singapore Volunteer Corps
Pte. L. F. D. May

Royal Air Force
S./Ldr. J. C. Betts
S./Ldr. R. L. J. Fitch, D.F.C.
S./Ldr. A. V. Gowers, D.F.C.
S./Ldr. J. B. Parnall
S./Ldr. P. J. E. Ritchie, D.F.C.
S./Ldr. R. M. Sanders
F./Lt. A. R. Brown
F./Lt. F. G. H. Chalk, D.F.C.
F./Lt. R. P. Garnett
F./Lt. F. D. Holdsworth
F./Lt. P. J. Lea
F./Lt. E. R. Muller-Rowland
F./Lt. P. E. Raw, D.F.C.
F./Lt. N. M. Tucker
F./Offr. R. C. Greenlees
F./Offr. P. U. M. Gordon-Crosby
F./Offr. C. A. Hobson
F./Offr. J. M. Vaughan
P./Offr. E. W. Blackwell
P./Offr. K. C. W. Cope
P./Offr. P. L. G. Davies
P./Offr. R. A. Duce
P./Offr. G. C. R. Franks
P./Offr. G. I. Jerdein
P./Offr. T. S. Lewis
P./Offr. S. MacHugh
P./Offr. V. J. Norman
P./Offr. J. G. Perry
P./Offr. A. Petty
P./Offr. A. Swainston
P./Offr. K. G. Webb
P./Offr. P. G. Wilson
L.A.C. L. G. Washington

Merchant Navy
2nd Radio Officer J. L. Price

Home Guard
Lieut. E. F. Stanford, T.D. (**Lieut.-Colonel H.A.C.**)
R. B. Hobson

Civil Defence
Air Raid Warden A. F. Ettlinger

APPENDIX "D"

HONOURS AND AWARDS, 1900-1902

COMPANION OF THE ORDER OF ST. MICHAEL AND ST. GEORGE
Major G. McMicking, City Imperial Volunteers

DISTINGUISHED SERVICE ORDER
Lieut. A. C. Lowe, City Imperial Volunteers

DISTINGUISHED CONDUCT MEDAL
Sergt. W. Dixon, City Imperial Volunteers
Sergt. P. Taylor, City Imperial Volunteers
Sergt. A. E. Wood, City Imperial Volunteers

HONOURS AND AWARDS, 1914-1918

1st BATTALION

VICTORIA CROSS, MILITARY CROSS AND BAR AND DISTINGUISHED CONDUCT MEDAL
Lieut. A. O. Pollard

VICTORIA CROSS
Lieut. R. L. Haine

COMPANION OF THE ORDER OF ST. MICHAEL AND ST. GEORGE AND OFFICER OF THE ORDER OF THE BRITISH EMPIRE
Lieut.-Colonel E. Treffrey

DISTINGUISHED SERVICE ORDER

Lieut.-Colonel E. C. P. Boyle*   Major A. Lambert-Ward
Lieut.-Colonel C. F. Osmond

MEMBER OF THE ORDER OF THE BRITISH EMPIRE
Pte. G. M. Chantry

MILITARY CROSS

Major M. G. Douglas	Capt. R. Spicer
Major G. H. Mayhew	Capt. W. A. Stone
Capt. N. Baines	Lieut. P. F. Finch
Capt. D. G. Collins	Lieut. R. J. Fowles
Capt. E. M. Ellis*	Lieut. A. W. Hawes
Capt. H. P. G. Maule	Lieut. H. F. Kent
Capt. F. M. Merson	Lieut. B. Petley
Capt. F. P. Morphy	Lieut. F. Rowcliffe
Capt. R. S. Morshead, Royal Army	Lieut. E. L. Samuel
Medical Corps	Lieut. N. Viney
Capt. G. F. T. Murnane	2/Lieut. L. W. McArthur
Capt. H. W. O'Brien	R.S.M. A. G. S. Huddart
Capt. A. G. Simmons	R.S.M. J. Wall

DISTINGUISHED CONDUCT MEDAL AND MILITARY MEDAL
Cpl. R. Hughesdon

DISTINGUISHED CONDUCT MEDAL

C.S.M. M. H. Boyd	Cpl. M. Hill*
C.S.M. E. F. H. Murray*	Cpl. D. T. Jones
Sergt. W. M. Frampton	L./Cpl. R. W. Cryer
Sergt. A. L. Laskie	Pte. R. Cutler
Sergt. S. E. Sandle	Pte. J. Thompson*
Sergt. J. Tyrie	Dmr. A. J. Stiffen

MILITARY MEDAL AND BAR

Sergt. C. H. Perry   Cpl. T. B. Walker*

* Killed in action.

C.S.M. L. H. Sugden
C.Q.M.S. W. Doran
Sergt. J. F. W. Cully
Sergt. C. Freter
Sergt. D. W. Mackrell
Sergt. F. Mighell
Sergt. C. Rowe
Sergt. R. A. Welstead
L./Sergt. A. Bates
Cpl. H. S. Chamberlain
Cpl. J. G. Gillanders
Cpl. H. W. Lowe

MILITARY MEDAL

Cpl. V. G. Scarlett
Cpl. S. L. Squires
L./Cpl. R. A. Cartledge
L./Cpl. A. Mann*
L./Cpl. R. S. Oxley*
Pte. J. W. Greene
Pte. W. G. Hartley*
Pte. J. G. Hoodless
Pte. G. H. E. Kime
Pte. C. A. Pitt
Pte. A. W. Richards
Pte. C. Wolfenden

MERITORIOUS SERVICE MEDAL

R.Q.M.S. F. Adams
C.Q.M.S. J. H. Chick
Sergt. J. A. V. Rumbold
Sergt. F. J. White
L./Sergt. A. E. Clarke

L./Cpl. G. E. Allard
Pte. P. Carlile
Pte. H. S. Rackham
Pte. H. W. Soar

MEDAILLE MILITAIRE (FRANCE)

Sergt. H. H. Aitken

Sergt. J. A. V. Rumbold

BRONZE MEDAL FOR VALOUR (ITALY)
L./Cpl. R. S. Oxley, M.M.*

"A" BATTERY

MEMBER OF THE ORDER OF THE BRITISH EMPIRE
Lieut. J. C. L. Barnes

"B" BATTERY

DISTINGUISHED SERVICE ORDER
Major The Hon. R. M. P. Preston

MILITARY CROSS

Capt. D. J. McAndrew

2/Lieut. C. Phillips

DISTINGUISHED CONDUCT MEDAL

B.S.M. G. G. Holloway
Sergt. M. E. Barrett

Sergt. A. J. Clark

MILITARY MEDAL

Sergt. H. W. Davies

Wheeler-Sergt. H. E. Wright

MERITORIOUS SERVICE MEDAL
Cpl. G. M. Priest

2ND BATTALION

COMPANION OF THE ORDER OF ST. MICHAEL AND ST. GEORGE
Lieut.-Colonel L. R. C. Boyle

BAR TO DISTINGUISHED SERVICE ORDER
Lieut.-Colonel R. N. O'Connor, D.S.O., M.C.

* Killed in action.

421

The Honourable Artillery Company

DISTINGUISHED SERVICE ORDER

Major J. Snape, M.C.   Capt. F. B. Garrard

MILITARY CROSS AND MILITARY MEDAL
Lieut. E. F. Gaud

MILITARY CROSS

Capt. D. M. Bluett   Lieut. L. Montgomery
Capt. T. C. Bower   Lieut. S. E. Sandle, D.C.M.
Capt. M. B. Brown   Lieut. A. S. Williamson
Capt. F. A. Garrett   2/Lieut. R. J. Flory*
Capt. E. F. H. Murray, D.C.M.*   2/Lieut. S. E. L. Foster
Capt. E. B. Woollan   2/Lieut. J. C. Hennis
Lieut. J. E. England   2/Lieut. F. A. Kup
Lieut. E. W. F. Hammond   R.Q.M.S. C. Glanville
Lieut. R. Heather

DISTINGUISHED CONDUCT MEDAL AND BAR
Sergt. H. Jenkinson

DISTINGUISHED CONDUCT MEDAL AND MILITARY MEDAL
Sergt. W. J. Bradley

DISTINGUISHED CONDUCT MEDAL

C.S.M. J. R. Hockridge   L./Sergeant. J. A. Clarke
C.S.M. T. C. Wilkinson   Pte. S. A. Bent
Sergt. H. E. Hibbard

MILITARY MEDAL AND BAR
Pte. J. W. Jones

MILITARY MEDAL

C.S.M. F. J. C. Wordley   L./Cpl. V. E. Jarvis
C.Q.M.S. F. M. Davies   L./Cpl. A. Lines
Sergt. W. G. Abor   L./Cpl. A. Platt
Sergt. H. C. Armstrong   L./Cpl. J. Robb
Sergt. A. Barlthrop   L./Cpl. G. J. Roberts
Sergt. H. W. C. Bartlett   L./Cpl. C. T. Southgate
Sergt. R. S. Billingham   Pte. J. G. Anyan
Sergt. G. Burnett   Pte. C. Cassidy
Sergt. W. E. Eagling   Pte. A. R. Childs
Sergt. C. O. Foster   Pte. F. W. Dixon
L./Sergt. P. J. Goult   Pte. K. A. Dyall
L./Sergt. C. Petley   Pte. A. J. L. Ead
L./Sergt. S. Tonkin   Pte. S. Fraser
Cpl. T. J. H. Carey   Pte. C. S. Gavin
Cpl. R. C. Doyle   Pte. C. W. Gearing
Cpl. H. T. Gilbert   Pte. H. L. Greenaway*
Cpl. C. H. Hodgson   Pte. J. M. Hinton†
Cpl. E. E. H. Kendall   Pte. R. Huskinson
Cpl. D. N. Shepherd   Pte. A. W. Jones
Cpl. T. E. Wall   Pte. R. Laird
Cpl. T. Woodcock   Pte. A. V. Lindley†
L./Cpl. G. S. Brampton   Pte. S. C. Noakes
L./Cpl. E. Cook   Pte. W. J. Parry-Morris
L./Cpl. J. Dowsett   Pte. H. G. Payne
L./Cpl. F. J. Gilson   Pte. W. E. P. Richards
L./Cpl. C. J. Harvey   Pte. L. F. Rowsell
L./Cpl. J. C. Humphrey   Pte. A. W. Russell

* Killed in action.   † Died of wounds.

422

Pte. C. Scandrett
Pte. E. K. Still*
Pte. H. B. Trotter†
Pte. E. A. Tyzack
Pte. W. Wadden

Pte. W. V. Ward
Pte. A. Watson
Pte. C. Watson
Pte. A. E. Williams
Pte. C. A. Young

MERITORIOUS SERVICE MEDAL

C.Q.M.S. S. E. Goodricke
Sergt. H. J. Pallett
Sergt. M. A. Walsh
Cpl. A. H. Nicholls

Cpl.-Dmr. W. B. Blair
L./Cpl. T. L. Alexander
Pte. J. H. Haigh
Pte. W. J. J. Robins

SILVER MEDAL FOR VALOUR (ITALY)

Lieut.-Colonel R. N. O'Connor, D.S.O., M.C.
Capt. D. M. Bluett, M.C.

CROCE DE GUERRA (ITALY)

Capt. R. W. Cryer, D.C.M.
Capt. S. E. Sandle, M.C., D.C.M.
Lieut. E. H. Gaud, M.C., D.C.M.
Lieut. R. Heather, M.C.

Sergt. H. C. Armstrong, M.M.
L./Cpl. E. W. Golding
Pte. W. S. Thorn

CROIX DE GUERRE (FRANCE)

Capt. R. W. Cryer, D.C.M.

CROIX DE GUERRE (BELGIUM)

Major J. Snape, D.S.O., M.C.

Sergt. H. Jenkinson, D.C.M.

BRONZE MEDAL FOR VALOUR (ITALY)

Lieut. J. E. England, M.C.

Sergt. S. A. Bent, D.C.M.

309 (H.A.C.) SIEGE BATTERY, R.G.A.

MILITARY CROSS

Major J. H. Knox

Lieut. P. H. Edmondson*

MILITARY MEDAL

B.Q.M.S. H. J. Tansley
B.Q.M.S. F. Woodcock
Sergt. F. C. Bishop
Sergt. L. H. Hay
Sergt. P. M. Keen
Sergt. G. R. Seton
Cpl. C. K. Bird
Bdr. A. S. Challis

Bdr. R. P. Green
Bdr. R. W. Moss
Gnr. W. W. Green
Gnr. A. J. Griffiths
Gnr. H. Hammond
Gnr. A. H. Lough
Gnr. R. T. Slinn
Gnr. T. H. Williams

CROIX DE GUERRE (BELGIUM)

Sergt. N. Fulford-Brown

"2/A" BATTERY

MILITARY CROSS

Major E. C. Ellen

Major W. A. S. Turner

DISTINGUISHED CONDUCT MEDAL

Cpl. A. W. Moss

* Killed in action.

† Died of wounds.

423

MILITARY MEDAL

Sergt. J. C. Coombe
Sergt. A. E. Harris
Sergt. L. C. H. Hobday

Sergt. J. A. Lingwood
Bdr. F. Lymbery

MERITORIOUS SERVICE MEDAL
Sergt. W. G. Cook (A.V.C.)

"2/B" BATTERY

MILITARY CROSS
Lieut. D. E. Brackenbury

MILITARY MEDAL

Cpl. G. A. Darby
Dvr. G. H. Booker
Gnr. A. S. Diamond

Dvr. L. P. Howarth
Gnr. H. E. Long
Gnr. T. W. Rees

MERITORIOUS SERVICE MEDAL
Cpl. G. C. Pooley

RESERVE BATTALION

MEMBER OF THE ORDER OF THE BRITISH EMPIRE

Capt. J. G. Gibson
Lieut. J. B. Monk

MERITORIOUS SERVICE MEDAL

Sergt. W. F. Bishop
Pte. M. Lock

ORDER OF ST. STANISLAUS (RUSSIA), 3RD CLASS
Lieut. W. G. F. Clare

CADET BATTALION

MEMBER OF THE ORDER OF THE BRITISH EMPIRE
Lieut.-Colonel E. C. Ouvry

H.A.C. OFFICERS SERVING WITH OTHER UNITS

COMPANION OF THE ORDER OF THE BATH
Colonel R. J. Reece, Royal Army Medical Corps

COMPANION OF THE ORDER OF ST. MICHAEL AND ST. GEORGE
Brig.-General A. C. Lowe, D.S.O.*

BAR TO THE DISTINGUISHED SERVICE ORDER
Lieut.-Colonel The Hon. R. M. P. Preston, D.S.O.

DISTINGUISHED SERVICE ORDER AND MILITARY CROSS
Major R. O. Ward (att. Royal Field Artillery)

* Killed in action.

DISTINGUISHED SERVICE ORDER

Lieut.-Colonel J. F. Duncan (att. Royal Field Artillery)
Lieut.-Colonel O. L. Eugster (att. Royal Horse Artillery)
Lieut.-Colonel R. C. Hawkins (att. XIII Corps)
Major M. G. Douglas, M.C. (att. XXII Corps)
Major H. V. Landsberg (att. Royal Horse Artillery)
Major G. Lomer (att. Royal Field Artillery)
Capt. T. Carnwath, Royal Army Medical Corps
Capt. H. P. G. Maule, M.C. (att. V Corps)

OFFICER OF BRITISH EMPIRE ORDER

Capt. V. C. Montague (att. Fifth Army)
Capt. B. W. Noble (att. XIII Corps)
Capt. H. H. Stephens (att. Fifth Army)

MILITARY CROSS

Major P. Forrester (att. Royal Field Artillery)
Major J. L. Gow (att. Royal Field Artillery)
Major R. D. Russell (att. Royal Field Artillery)
Major J. S. Stranaghan (att. Third Army)
Capt. S. Hawkins (att. 7th Brigade)*
Lieut. C. J. F. Abbott (att. 22nd Infantry Brigade)
2/Lieut. J. H. Mosley (att. XIII Corps)

ORDER OF THE NILE (3RD CLASS)

Lieut.-Colonel O. L. Eugster, D.S.O. (att. Royal Horse Artillery)

ORDER OF THE CROWN OF BELGIUM

Major M. G. Douglas, D.S.O., M.C. (att. XXII Corps)

ORDER OF AVIZ (PORTUGAL)

Lieut. J. E. Morgan (att. Portuguese Troops in France)

CROIX DE GUERRE (FRANCE)

Major E. Garnsey (att. Fourth Army)
Major J. S. Stranaghan, M.C. (att. Third Army)

CROIX DE GUERRE (BELGIUM)

Major M. G. Douglas, D.S.O., M.C. (att. XXII Corps)
Capt. S. Hawkins, M.C. (att. 7th Brigade)*

H.A.C. OTHER RANKS SERVING WITH OTHER UNITS

MEMBER OF THE ORDER OF THE BRITISH EMPIRE

Sergt. E. M. Magor

DISTINGUISHED CONDUCT MEDAL

Cpl. W. C. Channing (att. Machine Gun Corps)

MILITARY MEDAL

Cpl. G. Waddington (att. The Tank Corps)

CROIX DE GUERRE (FRANCE)

Sergt. C. Rowe, M.M. (att. Intelligence Corps)
Pte. E. A. Barton (att. Second Army)

* Killed in action.

425

THE HONOURABLE ARTILLERY COMPANY

HONOURS AWARDED TO MEMBERS OF THE H.A.C. SERVING WITH OTHER UNITS

VICTORIA CROSS, MILITARY CROSS AND BAR
Capt. T. T. Pryce, Grenadier Guards*

COMPANION OF THE ORDER OF THE BATH AND COMPANION OF THE ORDER OF ST. MICHAEL AND ST. GEORGE
Major-General C. E. Budworth
Brig.-General J. C. Wray

KNIGHT COMMANDER OF THE ORDER OF THE BRITISH EMPIRE AND DISTINGUISHED SERVICE ORDER
Lieut.-Colonel F. Hall, Royal Field Artillery

COMPANION OF THE ORDER OF ST. MICHAEL AND ST. GEORGE AND DISTINGUISHED SERVICE ORDER
Lieut.-Colonel J. D. Mitchell, The Sherwood Foresters

COMMANDER OF THE ORDER OF THE BRITISH EMPIRE
2/Lieut. T. O. Willson, General List

DISTINGUISHED SERVICE ORDER, MILITARY CROSS AND TWO BARS
Capt. F. R. W. Jameson, Royal Engineer Signals

DISTINGUISHED SERVICE ORDER, MILITARY CROSS AND BAR
Major G. Huskisson, Royal Field Artillery
Capt. P. S. Barber, The Dorsetshire Regiment

DISTINGUISHED SERVICE ORDER AND MILITARY CROSS
Lieut.-Colonel P. L. Lincoln, The Northumberland Fusiliers
Lieut.-Colonel S. S. Mallinson, Royal Engineers
Lieut.-Colonel E. T. Peel, The Wiltshire Regiment
Major F. G. Tollworthy, 1st London Regiment
Capt. G. D. Henderson, The Queen's Own (Royal West Kent Regiment)
Capt. H. A. Pallant, Royal Army Medical Corps
Capt. C. E. V. K. Peberdy, The West Yorkshire Regiment

DISTINGUISHED SERVICE ORDER
Lieut.-Colonel H. Bayley, Royal Field Artillery
Lieut.-Colonel D. Cookes, Royal Field Artillery
Lieut.-Colonel C. H. Fair, 19th London Regiment
Lieut.-Colonel J. N. Sinclair, Royal Field Artillery*
Major H. Barter, Royal Field Artillery
Major A. W. Bird, The East Surrey Regiment
Major G. C. J. Brady, Royal Field Artillery
Major B. S. R. Cunningham, Royal Army Service Corps
Major J. G. Gillam, Royal Army Service Corps
Major G. A. Grounds, The Leinster Regiment
Major B. H. N. H. Hamilton, Royal Air Force
Major H. F. Mason, Royal Garrison Artillery
Major G. F. Pragnell, The Buffs*
Major A. L. A. Swann, Royal Army Service Corps
Major C. O. von Treuenfels, Royal Field Artillery*
Major G. B. Winch, Royal Field Artillery*
Capt. M. I. Christie, The Royal Fusiliers†
Capt. C. R. Gold, The Durham Light Infantry*
Capt. P. F. Knightley, The Royal Welch Fusiliers

---

* Killed in action.   † Died of wounds.

Appendices

OFFICER OF THE ORDER OF THE BRITISH EMPIRE AND MILITARY CROSS
Lieut.-Colonel R. H. Andrew, General List

OFFICER OF THE ORDER OF THE BRITISH EMPIRE
Lieut.-Colonel J. Dodds, Royal Army Ordnance Corps
Lieut.-Colonel G. G. Jessiman, Royal Army Service Corps
Lieut.-Colonel D. M. McRae, Royal Engineers
Major C. G. Coates, Royal Army Service Corps
Major P. V. Cotton, The Middlesex Regiment
Major G. J. Reed, The North Staffordshire Regiment
Capt. A. F. Baker, Royal Army Service Corps
Capt. J. L. Bradley, Royal Army Service Corps
Capt. J. W. Butters, Intelligence Corps
Capt. E. W. Camp, The Durham Light Infantry
Capt. V. C. Cook, Royal Army Service Corps
Capt. C. K. Davidson, Royal Field Artillery
Capt. E. D. A. Herbert, Royal Garrison Artillery
Capt. J. J. W. Herbertson, Intelligence Corps
Capt. W. N. Musgrave, Royal Army Service Corps
Capt. R. W. Romer, Royal Field Artillery
Capt. S. B. Winch, Royal Army Ordnance Corps
Lieut. A. S. Ellyatt, Royal Garrison Artillery

MEMBER OF THE ORDER OF THE BRITISH EMPIRE AND MILITARY CROSS
Lieut.-Colonel H. A. Mann, Royal Engineers

MEMBER OF THE ORDER OF THE BRITISH EMPIRE
Major P. C. Hoyland, Royal Air Force
Capt. H. A. Lloyd, Staff
Capt. W. R. Matthews, Labour Corps
Capt. H. W. Mirehouse, The South Lancashire Regiment
Capt. H. P. Tate, Royal Air Force
Capt. W. M. Young, General List
Capt. C. B. Rolfe, Royal Army Service Corps
Lieut. W. G. Kewley, Royal Air Force
Lieut. F. H. Postlethwaite, Royal Air Force
Lieut. L. A. Spall, The Herefordshire Regiment
2/Lieut. H. E. Marks, The Duke of Cornwall's Light Infantry

MILITARY CROSS AND THREE BARS
Lieut. H. A. Gilkes, 21st London Regiment

MILITARY CROSS AND TWO BARS
Capt. V. G. Stokes, The Royal Berkshire Regiment

MILITARY CROSS AND BAR AND AIR FORCE CROSS
Capt. P. W. S. Bulman, Royal Air Force

MILITARY CROSS AND DISTINGUISHED FLYING CROSS
Lieut. E. R. H. Pollak, Royal Air Force

MILITARY CROSS AND BAR
Major S. H. Blakey, 22nd London Regiment
Major G. J. L. Burton, The King's Royal Rifle Corps
Major A. G. Griffiths, The Tank Corps
Major J. C. O'Callaghan, Royal Field Artillery*

* Killed in action.

427

Major W. G. Pringle, Royal Field Artillery
Major J. Wells, The Sherwood Foresters
Capt. N. M. Benton, Royal Field Artillery
Capt. W. O. Field, Royal Warwickshire Regiment
Capt. G. E. Gunning, 8th London Regiment
Capt. S. A. Macey, The Devon Regiment
Capt. G. E. Porter, The Devon Regiment
Capt. N. W. W. Webb, Royal Air Force*
Lieut. G. F. Doble, The Queen's Own (Royal West Kent Regiment)
Lieut. S. F. Webb, Royal Field Artillery
Lieut. W. A. C. Wilkinson, Coldstream Guards
Lieut. H. W. E. Williamson, Royal Engineers

MILITARY CROSS

Lieut.-Colonel C. G. Allen, Royal Army Service Corps
Major W. T. Anderson, The Middlesex Regiment
Major L. E. Andrews, The Queen's Regiment*
Major W. M. Barfoot, The East Surrey Regiment
Major G. C. Beloe, The Gloucestershire Regiment
Major E. L. Bowley, Royal Field Artillery
Major P. Brachi, Royal Garrison Artillery
Major J. L. Bryan, The Manchester Regiment
Major A. R. Carr, Royal Garrison Artillery
Major J. S. Casey, The Royal Sussex Regiment
Major H. Crone, Royal Engineers
Major T. H. Davison, Royal Field Artillery
Major H. Dowson, The King's Royal Rifle Corps
Major J. R. Dudin, Royal Field Artillery
Major G. V. Dudley, Royal Field Artillery
Major R. E. A. Duthy, Royal Field Artillery
Major A. W. Fish, The Royal Welch Fusiliers
Major F. T. Galloway, Royal Garrison Artillery
Major D. Gilchrist, Royal Engineers
Major D. F. Grant, Royal Field Artillery
Major G. L. Hawes, Royal Field Artillery
Major W. E. Hewett, Machine Gun Corps
Major R. R. Hoare, Royal Field Artillery
Major L. F. Horne, Royal Field Artillery
Major D. V. Johnson, The Middlesex Regiment
Major F. J. Lambert, The Tank Corps
Major L. G. N. Langmead, The Rifle Brigade
Major E. A. McKechnie, The Argyll and Sutherland Highlanders
Major G. E. Mager, Royal Field Artillery
Major I. J. H. Malone, The North Staffordshire Regiment
Major H. M. Moore, Royal Army Service Corps
Major F. Morgan, Royal Garrison Artillery
Major F. W. Morgan, Royal Field Artillery
Major H. P. Nesham, Royal Field Artillery
Major H. L. Owen, The East Lancashire Regiment
Major F. Y. Prout, The Loyal North Lancashire Regiment
Major E. A. W. Rogers, Royal Field Artillery
Major G. G. Shiel, The Northumberland Fusiliers
Major A. H. Square, Royal Field Artillery
Major J. F. Stephenson-Jellie, Royal Army Ordnance Corps
Major C. H. Tebay, Royal Field Artillery
Major D. Tosetti, The Royal Berkshire Regiment*
Major H. B. Viney, Royal Army Service Corps
Major A. S. Waley, General List
Major G. E. Weber, Royal Field Artillery

* Killed in action.

Major J. E. W. Wheatley, Royal Garrison Artillery
Major F. C. Williams, Royal Army Ordnance Corps
Capt. T. C. Allan, 22nd London Regiment
Capt. G. R. G. Alston, Royal Field Artillery
Capt. I. Anderson, The Seaforth Highlanders
Capt. F. K. Artis, Royal Field Artillery
Capt. P. R. Asprey, The Buffs
Capt. C. Atkinson, Royal Field Artillery (att. R.A.F.)
Capt. A. H. Ayscough, The Royal Fusiliers
Capt. A. Baines, The Middlesex Regiment
Capt. E. N. Balme, The Essex Regiment†
Capt. E. A. Baring-Gould, Royal Engineers
Capt. J. H. V. Barker-Mill, The Wiltshire Regiment
Capt. H. C. Barnes, The Royal Sussex Regiment and Trench Mortar
   Battery*
Capt. C. H. Bazeley, The King's Royal Rifle Corps
Capt. A. Beal, Royal Field Artillery
Capt. J. R. Beall, The South Lancashire Regiment
Capt. A. Bedford, The Sherwood Foresters
Capt. N. W. Beeson, Royal Field Artillery
Capt. T. F. Bentley, Royal Field Artillery
Capt. A. Berliner, Royal Garrison Artillery
Capt. G. A. O. Berridge, Royal Field Artillery†
Capt. G. M. Bonnin, Royal Field Artillery
Capt. D. J. Brass, The Lincolnshire Regiment
Capt. R. Brennan, The Royal Irish Fusiliers
Capt. T. B. Brown, The Rifle Brigade
Capt. W. C. Brown, The Durham Light Infantry
Capt. K. R. G. Browne, The Essex Regiment
Capt. W. F. Burman, The Essex Regiment
Capt. J. Carr, Royal Army Medical Corps
Capt. S. M. Castello, Intelligence Corps
Capt. J. R. Cater, Royal Field Artillery
Capt. B. Catling, Royal Field Artillery†
Capt. L. A. Chadwick, Royal Field Artillery
Capt. R. W. Clark, The Sherwood Foresters
Capt. E. A. N. Cleveland, The King's Regiment
Capt. R. E. Clilverd, Royal Field Artillery
Capt. E. Coster, The Royal Welch Fusiliers
Capt. V. H. Couldrey, The Royal Sussex Regiment
Capt. A. D. G. Courage, Royal Field Artillery
Capt. R. F. Craighead, Royal Army Ordnance Corps
Capt. W. N. Crosby, The Green Howards
Capt. E. Cumberland, The Norfolk Regiment
Capt. A. J. Dainty, Royal Field Artillery
Capt. A. J. F. Danielli, The Border Regiment
Capt. R. J. Davies, The Welsh Regiment
Capt. A. J. Davis, Royal Field Artillery
Capt. L. Davis, The King's Royal Rifle Corps
Capt. H. W. Dennis, 4th London Regiment
Capt. L. H. C. Dermer, Royal Engineers
Capt. R. P. Elwes, Coldstream Guards
Capt. J. J. Emberton, Royal Field Artillery
Capt. H. G. Evans, The Queen's Own (Royal West Kent Regiment)
Capt. R. Evans, The Royal Horse Guards
Capt. S. T. Evans, Royal Garrison Artillery
Capt. R. Fischel, Royal Garrison Artillery
Capt. D. H. Fish, Royal Field Artillery
Capt. F. W. Ford, The Cambridgeshire Regiment*

---

* Killed in action.   † Died of wounds.

Capt. A. R. Fraser, The Bedfordshire Regiment
Capt. H. McA. Frearson, The East Lancashire Regiment
Capt. E. R. M. Fryer, Grenadier Guards
Capt. J. H. Gibbons, Royal Field Artillery
Capt. L. H. Gilman, Hedjaz Armoured Car Battery
Capt. C. A. Glaeser, Staff
Capt. M. Gliddon, Royal Field Artillery†
Capt. E. C. Goddard, Royal Field Artillery
Capt. J. D. Goldie, Royal Field Artillery
Capt. C. M. Goodall, The Northumberland Fusiliers
Capt. S. M. Gow, Royal Garrison Artillery
Capt. M. R. Graham, Royal Engineers
Capt. H. Grindall, The Queen's Own Cameron Highlanders
Capt. J. Hall, The West Yorkshire Regiment
Capt. S. G. Hart, Royal Field Artillery
Capt. E. B. Haynes, Royal Engineers
Capt. R. S. Hedderwick, Royal Garrison Artillery
Capt. C. J. Henry, Royal Field Artillery
Capt. H. E. Hibbard, 9th London Regiment
Capt. C. Hill, The Royal Dublin Fusiliers
Capt. P. C. Hollingsworth, Royal Air Force
Capt. L. F. Holt, Royal Field Artillery
Capt. L. H. Horncastle, The Wiltshire Regiment*
Capt. J. T. House, The East Lancashire Regiment
Capt. A. R. Howlett, Royal Engineers
Capt. F. M. Hughes, The Royal Welch Fusiliers
Capt. S. D. Hutchinson, 20th London Regiment
Capt. G. F. Illingworth, Royal Field Artillery
Capt. R. D. James, Royal Garrison Artillery
Capt. P. Jeffs, Royal Field Artillery
Capt. O. C. Johnsen, Staff
Capt. J. R. C. Jorgensen, Royal Field Artillery
Capt. C. W. R. Knight, The Queen's Own (Royal West Kent Regiment)
Capt. C. McM. Laing, The Royal Scots (att. R.A.F.)
Capt. H. T. Lawden, The Royal Scots Fusiliers (att. M.G.C.)
Capt. A. D. Layton, The East Lancashire Regiment
Capt. D. H. Layton, The East Yorkshire Regiment
Capt. P. Light, The Cheshire Regiment
Capt. A. C. Lindley, The Essex Regiment
Capt. I. H. Linford, The Essex Regiment*
Capt. C. W. Longley, Royal Field Artillery
Capt. C. D. Lovering, The Herefordshire Regiment
Capt. F. C. Lovett, The Queen's Own (Royal West Kent Regiment)
Capt. A. N. Mackean, Royal Garrison Artillery
Capt. H. F. Magnus, 24th London Regiment
Capt. G. V. H. Mansell, Royal Horse Artillery
Capt. H. G. Mansfield, The Essex Regiment
Capt. H. W. Marsh, The Wiltshire Regiment
Capt. J. M. Miller, Royal Field Artillery
Capt. F. Mills, Royal Field Artillery
Capt. H. T. Morgan, The Wiltshire Regiment
Capt. R. P. Nathan, Royal Field Artillery†
Capt. A. J. Nation, Royal Garrison Artillery
Capt. F. C. G. Naumann, Royal Field Artillery
Capt. S. Neale, The Middlesex Regiment
Capt. J. H. B. Nihill, The Royal Munster Fusiliers
Capt. F. A. Nutter, Motor Machine Gun Corps
Capt. E. N. R. Oates, Royal Field Artillery
Capt. W. H. Parker, The Suffolk Regiment

---

* Killed in action.   † Died of wounds.

Capt. L. E. Parsons, The Royal Berkshire Regiment
Capt. P. M. Pascall, The King's African Rifles*
Capt. C. F. Pavitt, Royal Army Service Corps (*died*)
Capt. R. H. Pavitt, Royal Field Artillery
Capt. C. E. Peat, City of London Yeomanry
Capt. G. H. Plummer, The Royal Irish Regiment
Capt. B. Pontefract, The King's Own Yorkshire Light Infantry
Capt. E. W. Poynter, Royal Field Artillery
Capt. F. A. Preston, Royal Field Artillery
Capt. I. P. H. Preston, Royal Field Artillery (att. R.A.F.)
Capt. L. Price, The West Yorkshire Regiment
Capt. D. G. O. Priestley, Royal Engineers
Capt. H. K. Prosser, The Gloucestershire Regiment
Capt. A. C. Rawles, Royal Field Artillery
Capt. J. B. Raymond, The East Surrey Regiment*
Capt. C. Roberts, Royal Field Artillery
Capt. H. H. Robinson, Machine Gun Corps
Capt. J. C. Ross, The Black Watch
Capt. E. A. Rudd, The King's Royal Rifle Corps
Capt. A. J. Samut, The Wiltshire Regiment
Capt. J. B. Saul, The King's Own Yorkshire Light Infantry (att. M.G.C.)
Capt. D. M. Saunders, The Bedfordshire Regiment
Capt. W. Sewell, The Royal Warwickshire Regiment
Capt. E. A. Shingleton, The Royal Welch Fusiliers
Capt. S. H. Shoveller, The Rifle Brigade
Capt. R. J. Sims, Royal Garrison Artillery
Capt. A. J. Sington, Royal Field Artillery
Capt. G. K. Smith, Royal Air Force (*died in hospital*)
Capt. K. Smith, The Durham Light Infantry
Capt. D. V. Sutherst, The Queen's Own (Royal West Kent Regiment) (att. T. M. Bty.)
Capt. D. Sutton, 7th London Regiment
Capt. F. K. Sutton, Royal Horse Artillery
Capt. H. Tayler, Royal Field Artillery
Capt. F. J. Taylor, Royal Field Artillery
Capt. F. J. H. Thayre, Royal Air Force*
Capt. S. C. Theophilus, Tank Corps
Capt. W. H. Thompson, Royal Field Artillery
Capt. W. Tyrer, The York and Lancaster Regiment
Capt. F. L. Vanderpump, The South Wales Borderers
Capt. E. R. Venables, Royal Field Artillery
Capt. H. H. H. Walshe, Royal Field Artillery
Capt. D. G. Watson, The Highland Light Infantry
Capt. S. A. Webb, Royal Field Artillery
Capt. A. W. Wells, The Middlesex Regiment
Capt. C. G. Williams, Royal Field Artillery
Capt. G. D. Williams, General List
Capt. T. Wingate, Royal Field Artillery
Capt. H. W. Wooley, Royal Field Artillery
Capt. B. M. Woolf, Tank Corps
Capt. G. L. Worlock, The Royal Berkshire Regiment
Capt. H. M. Worsley, The Oxfordshire Hussars Yeomanry
Lieut. H. M. Achilles, Royal Horse Artillery
Lieut. G. H. Adney, Tank Corps*
Lieut. G. L. Allardyce, The Gordon Highlanders
Lieut. J. Anderson, Nigeria Regiment
Lieut. A. P. Atkinson, The Middlesex Regiment
Lieut. G. Auten, The Durham Light Infantry
Lieut. P. S. Ayers, Royal Field Artillery

---

* Killed in action.

431

Lieut. A. J. Bailey, Royal Field Artillery
Lieut. K. S. Bain, The West Riding Regiment
Lieut. J. R. A. Balchin, The Queen's Royal West Surrey Regiment†
Lieut. D. D. Bassett, Royal Field Artillery
Lieut. E. A. J. Bilham, Royal Engineers
Lieut. F. A. C. Burditt, Royal Field Artillery
Lieut. S. E. Cairns, The Sherwood Foresters*
Lieut. C. S. Callingham, Royal Field Artillery
Lieut. K. E. Candy, The Lancashire Fusiliers
Lieut. N. N. Caton, Royal Field Artillery*
Lieut. C. E. T. Cooper, The Seaforth Highlanders
Lieut. L. E. Cooper, 1st London Regiment
Lieut. C. H. Cork, The King's Royal Rifle Corps
Lieut. N. D. Dalton, The Middlesex Regiment
Lieut. E. E. Davies, The King's African Rifles
Lieut. F. C. Dawkins, Royal Field Artillery †
Lieut. C. F. Doncaster, The Royal Fusiliers
Lieut. L. A. Draper, The Royal Fusiliers
Lieut. I. J. Edell, Royal Field Artillery
Lieut. G. P. Edwards, Royal Field Artillery†
Lieut. B. Evans, The Suffolk Regiment
Lieut. C. H. K. Fisher, Royal Garrison Artillery
Lieut. F. O. Forrester, Anson Battalion, Royal Naval Volunteer Reserve*
Lieut. R. Foulkes, The King's Own Yorkshire Light Infantry
Lieut. B. G. Fox, West African Frontier Force
Lieut. B. Francis, Royal Garrison Artillery
Lieut. D. H. D. Freeman, Royal Field Artillery
Lieut. L. C. Gane, Royal Field Artillery
Lieut. C. E. Garland, The Sherwood Foresters
Lieut. L. C. Gates, 13th London Regiment
Lieut. H. C. Geer, Machine Gun Corps
Lieut. L. A. Gibson, The Northumberland Fusiliers
Lieut. G. H. Y. Gilbey, The Hampshire Regiment
Lieut. C. H. Golding, The Welsh Regiment
Lieut. F. G. Goodyear, 24th London Regiment†
Lieut. E. U. Green, The Loyal North Lancashire Regiment*
Lieut. D. A. Hamilton, Royal Field Artillery
Lieut. A. W. Hammond, Royal Garrison Artillery
Lieut. G. Harris, The Royal Fusiliers
Lieut. G. S. A. Hawkins, Royal Field Artillery
Lieut. B. G. Hill, Royal Field Artillery†
Lieut. H. E. Hirschland, Royal Field Artillery
Lieut. P. K. Hobson, Royal Air Force
Lieut. N. Hone, Royal Field Artillery
Lieut. F. R. M. Irwin, Royal Field Artillery
Lieut. E. C. Jones, Royal Field Artillery
Lieut. F. R. Jones, Royal Field Artillery
Lieut. R. H. Keeping, Royal Field Artillery
Lieut. A. C. Kingham, Royal Field Artillery
Lieut. R. H. Kingham, Royal Field Artillery
Lieut. W. S. Knowles, The Gurkha Rifles
Lieut. J. H. Langdon, The Gloucestershire Regiment
Lieut. P. W. Laverick, Royal Garrison Artillery
Lieut. V. A. Lavers, The Royal Berkshire Regiment†
Lieut. E. P. Le Heup, The Essex Regiment
Lieut. D. E. Liddell, Royal Field Artillery
Lieut. G. M. Liddell, Royal Field Artillery
Lieut. F. W. Lovell, The East Surrey Regiment
Lieut. H. Lumsden, Royal Field Artillery

---

* Killed in action.   † Died of wounds.

Lieut. H. B. McPherson, Royal Field Artillery*
Lieut. A. M. Mackintosh, The East Surrey Regiment
Lieut. L. J. Mann, Royal Air Force
Lieut. L. D. Marks, Royal Field Artillery
Lieut. G. F. Marsh, The Royal Berkshire Regiment
Lieut. F. A. Martin, Royal Field Artillery
Lieut. H. C. Mathew, The Suffolk Regiment
Lieut. H. L. Matthew, The King's Own Yorkshire Light Infantry
Lieut. F. R. Mee, The Leicestershire Regiment
Lieut. H. A. V. Moreton, 13th London Regiment
Lieut. D. W. Morgan, The Royal Welch Fusiliers
Lieut. G. W. T. Morgan, Royal Field Artillery
Lieut. W. M. Morgan, 42nd Devli Regiment
Lieut. E. A. Mortleman, Royal Field Artillery
Lieut. W. A. Moss, Royal Field Artillery
Lieut. W. N. Murch, 11th London Regiment
Lieut. G. H. Norman, Royal Garrison Artillery
Lieut. D. K. Paris, Royal Air Force
Lieut. H. H. Payne, Royal Field Artillery
Lieut. C. N. Poynton, Royal Marine Artillery
Lieut. I. C. Price, Royal Army Service Corps
Lieut. W. Price, Royal Garrison Artillery
Lieut. L. H. Pullen, London Rifle Brigade and Machine Gun Corps
Lieut. A. S. Pulley, Machine Gun Corps
Lieut. A. H. Pullin, Royal Field Artillery
Lieut. P. C. Richards, Royal Field Artillery
Lieut. J. S. Roffey, The Oxfordshire and Buckinghamshire Light Infantry
Lieut. W. Rosen, 4th London Regiment
Lieut. A. D. W. Scott, Royal Field Artillery†
Lieut. A. J. Shipton, The Royal Berkshire Regiment
Lieut. E. A. Shipton, Royal Field Artillery
Lieut. A. R. Sienesi, 4th Gurkha Rifles
Lieut. H. S. Smallman, Royal Field Artillery
Lieut. R. B. Solomon, Royal Field Artillery
Lieut. E. A. Stocken, Royal Field Artillery
Lieut. J. Stratton, The Cameronians
Lieut. C. L. Symonds, Tank Corps
Lieut. F. S. Symondson, Royal Air Force
Lieut. R. Thorn, Royal Field Artillery
Lieut. A. C. Timms, The Essex Regiment
Lieut. L. H. Tirrell, The Essex Regiment
Lieut. M. Tomson, Royal Engineer Signals
Lieut. G. F. Trenow, London Rifle Brigade*
Lieut. R. H. Unwin, Royal Field Artillery
Lieut. L. R. Ward, Royal Field Artillery
Lieut. W. E. Warden, Royal Air Force
Lieut. R. Watling, The Essex Regiment (att. R.A.F.)
Lieut. W. R. Weller, Royal Field Artillery
Lieut. H. R. Williams, Royal Field Artillery
Lieut. T. Williams, Machine Gun Corps
Lieut. G. T. Worn, The Norfolk Regiment
2/Lieut. C. B. M. Abbott, The Hampshire Regiment
2/Lieut. E. H. B. Clarke, Royal Field Artillery
2/Lieut. H. H. E. Q. Coles, The Royal Irish Fusiliers
2/Lieut. H. J. Crane, The Loyal North Lancashire Regiment
2/Lieut. J. C. Derlien, The Royal Fusiliers
2/Lieut. E. M. Hannah, The Shropshire Light Infantry†
2/Lieut. S. J. W. Holcombe, 11th London Regiment
2/Lieut. C. A. Jakeman, Machine Gun Corps

* Killed in action.   † Died of wounds.

2/Lieut. F. J. Larkin, 22nd London Regiment*
2/Lieut. V. Page, Royal Field Artillery
2/Lieut. J. A. B. Paul, The East Surrey Regiment*
2/Lieut. C. A. Richards, Anson Battalion Royal Naval Volunteer Reserve*
2/Lieut. A. J. Riley, The Royal Fusiliers
2/Lieut. W. F. Smith, The Royal Fusiliers

DISTINGUISHED SERVICE CROSS
Major L. H. Wilkins, Royal Air Force
Capt. H. G. Travers, Royal Naval Air Service

DISTINGUISHED FLYING CROSS
S./Cmdr. H. G. Dean, Royal Air Force
Capt. T. C. Angus, Royal Air Force
Capt. L. W. Baker, Royal Air Force
Capt. N. A. Bolton, Royal Air Force
Capt. E. R. Pennell, Royal Air Force
Lieut. C. A. Bourchier, Royal Air Force
Lieut. G. Davis, Royal Air Force
Lieut. H. F. Longbottom, Royal Air Force
Lieut. W. O'R. Patey, Royal Air Force
Lieut. R. D. G. Pizey, Royal Air Force

AIR FORCE CROSS
Capt. H. W. Kendall, Royal Naval Air Service
Lieut. G. Harwood, Royal Air Force*
Lieut. F. G. Taylor, Royal Air Force
2/Lieut. E. Priest, Royal Air Force

MILITARY MEDAL
Sergt. W. H. Godfrey, 13th London Regiment

MERITORIOUS SERVICE MEDAL
Cpl. W. Pike, Machine Gun Corps

ALBERT MEDAL
Capt. H. W. Sewell, Royal Engineers
Lieut. W. M. Morgan, 42nd Devli Regiment

ORDER OF LEOPOLD (BELGIUM)
Capt. N. A. Bolton, Royal Field Artillery (att. R.A.F.)

ORDER OF THE CROWN OF BELGIUM
Major H. L. A. Swann, D.S.O., Royal Army Service Corps
Lieut. W. W. Moore, Royal Engineers
2/Lieut. T. O. Wilson, C.B.E., General List

ORDER OF ST. ANNE (RUSSIA)
Lieut. C. A. Bourchier, D.F.C., Royal Air Force

ORDER OF AVIZ (PORTUGAL)
Major W. A. Collins, Royal Army Service Corps

ORDER OF THE NILE (EGYPT), 3RD CLASS
Lieut.-Colonel R. H. Andrew, O.B.E., M.C., General List*

---

* Killed in action.

CROIX DE GUERRE (FRANCE), AVEC PALME

Capt. A. Beal, M.C., Royal Field Artillery
Capt. J. M. Johnson, The East Surrey Regiment
Capt. A. E. Osborne, The Loyal North Lancashire Regiment
Capt. E. R. Pennell, D.F.C., Royal Air Force
2/Lieut. C. A. Button, Royal Field Artillery*

CROIX DE GUERRE (FRANCE)

Major B. F. Huggins, Royal Garrison Artillery
Major A. C. Neal, Royal Garrison Artillery
Major E. A. W. Rogers, M.C., Royal Field Artillery
Capt. R. E. Clilverd, M.C., Royal Field Artillery
Capt. E. D. A. Herbert, O.B.E., Royal Field Artillery
Lieut. G. Cockburn, Royal Field Artillery
Lieut. L. E. Cooper, M.C., 1st London Regiment
Lieut. A. W. Edmondson, Middlesex Yeomanry
Lieut. B. E. Goulder, Royal Field Artillery
Lieut. D. A. Hamilton, M.C., Royal Field Artillery
2/Lieut. F. O'Brien, Machine Gun Corps

SILVER MEDAL FOR VALOUR (ITALY)

Lieut. F. S. Symondson, M.C., Royal Air Force

BRONZE MEDAL FOR VALOUR (ITALY)

Capt. C. C. Durston, Royal Air Force

CROIX DE GUERRE (BELGIUM)

Lieut.-Colonel J. D. Mitchell, C.M.G., D.S.O., The Sherwood Foresters
Major C. G. R. Boreham, Royal Garrison Artillery
Major H. L. A. Swann, D.S.O., Royal Army Service Corps
Capt. N. A. Bolton, D.F.C., Royal Field Artillery (att. R.A.F.)
Capt. L. E. Cooper, 1st London Regiment
Lieut. W. W. Moore, Royal Engineers
2/Lieut. T. O. Wilson, C.B.E., General List

MEDAILLE AGRICOLE (FRANCE)

Lieut.-Colonel S. S. Mallinson, D.S.O., M.C., Royal Engineers

HONOURS AND AWARDS, 1939-1945

11TH (H.A.C.) REGIMENT, R.H.A.

DISTINGUISHED SERVICE ORDER

Lieut.-Colonel R. W. Goodbody, Royal Horse Artillery
Lieut.-Colonel W. M. Leggatt, Royal Horse Artillery
Lieut.-Colonel J. H. Slade-Powell, Royal Horse Artillery
Major J. R. Richmond, T.D.

MEMBER OF THE ORDER OF THE BRITISH EMPIRE

Capt. G. C. Tills   R.Q.M.S. J. Singleton

BAR TO THE MILITARY CROSS

Major D. M. Morris, M.C.   Capt. R. N. Smith, M.C.
Capt. J. W. Hopkins, M.C.*

MILITARY CROSS

Major G. R. Armstrong   Capt. E. Dudley Smith
Major J. P. Charles   Capt. J. D. Henderson
Major F. B. S. Maclaren   Capt. J. H. McAllum*
Major E. C. Mansel   Capt. J. S. Martin, Royal Army
Major D. M. Morris   Medical Corps
Major J. P. Sworder   Capt. J. M. Page
Capt. K. E. Bolton   Capt. J. A. F. Sewell
Capt. T. F. Butler-Stoney*   Capt. R. N. Smith
Capt. G. N. Chastel de Boinville   Capt. D. Young
Capt. L. Q. Drage*   Lieut. J. P. Thomson-Glover

GEORGE MEDAL

Lieut. G. F. Moore   Gnr. J. Waters

DISTINGUISHED CONDUCT MEDAL

L./Sergt. C. B. Dornton-Duff, M.M.   Gnr. D. B. Simpson

MILITARY MEDAL

B.S.M. R. Hall   Bdr. H. R. Parry*
Sergt. S. F. Kirk   Bdr. R. S. Williams*
Sergt. G. T. A. Knight   L./Bdr. H. D. Simmons
Sergt. V. H. Quinney   L./Cpl. J. M. Holder, Royal Corps of
Sergt. M. J. T. Town†   Signals
L./Sergt. C. B. Dornton-Duff   L./Cpl. J. McA. Morans, Royal Corps
L./Sergt. D. Tomlin   of Signals
Bdr. P. Bennett   Gnr. E. W. Robinson*
Bdr. W. J. R. Boardman*   Gnr. S. R. Westwood
Bdr. F. Gilbert

BRITISH EMPIRE MEDAL

Sergt. W. J. Binney

---

* Killed in action.   † Died of wounds.

436

APPENDICES

BRONZE STAR (U.S.A.)
B.S.M. G. W. Flutter

MENTIONS IN DESPATCHES
12 Officers and 25 Warrant Officers and Other Ranks

COMMENDATION CARDS
4 Officers

12TH (H.A.C.) REGIMENT, R.H.A.

DISTINGUISHED SERVICE ORDER
Lieut.-Colonel J. A. T. Barstow

MILITARY CROSS

Major J. Grose
Major D. E. Hughes
Major C. Middleton
Major S. N. Rae
Capt. J. M. Austin Smith
Capt. H. N. Atherton

Capt. J. G. Bagnall
Capt. J. G. H. Banks
Capt. T. P. Cracknell
Capt. K. Hunt
Capt. J. S. Pirie
Lieut. A. D. A. Newbury

DISTINGUISHED CONDUCT MEDAL
Sergt. J. C. Lawrie*

MILITARY MEDAL

B.S.M. F. J. Hunt
Sergt. T. B. Ainslie
Sergt. C. Farnsworth
Sergt. J. W. C. Hodkisson
L./Sergt. G. A. Ferrari
L./Bdr. H. Dickinson

L./Bdr. R. W. Griffin
L./Bdr. E. C. Howes
L./Bdr. R. H. Newell
Gnr. J. D. Kerr
Gnr. L. J. Peters
Gnr. S. G. Searle

SILVER STAR (U.S.A.)
Capt. T. P. Cracknell

MENTIONS IN DESPATCHES
12 Officers and 20 Warrant Officers and Other Ranks

COMMENDATION CARDS
1 Other Rank

13TH (H.A.C.) REGIMENT, R.H.A.

BAR TO THE DISTINGUISHED SERVICE ORDER
Lieut.-Colonel R. B. T. Daniell, D.S.O.

DISTINGUISHED SERVICE ORDER
Major R. Gaunt

MILITARY CROSS

Major G. V. de C. O'Grady (The O'Grady)
Major G. W. Smythe-Osbourne
Capt. R. T. C. Addington
Capt. A. N. Bicket
Capt. G. D. M. Budgen*

Capt. H. G. S. Davidge
Capt. P. Kinnersley
Capt. A. N. Young
Lieut. E. Mather
B.S.M. E. A. Powdrill

* Killed in action.

437

MILITARY MEDAL

Sergt. R. M. L. Dunbar
Sergt. R. Duncan
L./Bdr. F. Buckley
Gnr. L. Adams*
Gnr. A. M. Gillies

Gnr. A. Meylan
Gnr. A. Shaw
Gnr. R. Sutton
Gnr. N. Tait

ORDER OF LEOPOLD, WITH PALM
Lieut.-Colonel R. B. T. Daniell, D.S.O.

ORDER OF LEOPOLD, CLASS II
Capt. H. T. Fost

ORDER OF THE CROWN OF ITALY
Lieut.-Colonel H. R. L. Hodges

SILVER STAR (U.S.A.)
Capt. W. A. Taylor

CROIX DE GUERRE (FRANCE)
Major K. R. Farquhar

BRONZE CROSS (NETHERLANDS)
Lieut. P. de F. Delaforce

CROIX DE GUERRE (BELGIUM)

Lieut.-Colonel R. B. T. Daniell, D.S.O.
Lieut.-Colonel H. R. L. Hodges

Capt. H. T. Fost
Gnr. P. W. Foster

MENTIONS IN DESPATCHES
14 Officers and 10 Warrant Officers and Other Ranks

COMMENDATION CARDS
1 Officer and 12 Warrant Officers and Other Ranks

86TH (H.A.C.) H.A.A. REGIMENT, R.A.

OFFICER OF THE ORDER OF THE BRITISH EMPIRE
Lieut.-Colonel G. H. Champness

MEMBER OF THE ORDER OF THE BRITISH EMPIRE

Major E. R. G. Heath
Major C. Robinson

Capt. The Rev. J. C. T. Downes, Ch.F.
B.S.M. W. R. Newman

BRITISH EMPIRE MEDAL

B.S.M. J. R. Martin

B.S.M. R. C. Richardson

BRONZE STAR (U.S.A.)

Sergt. C. W. Britton
Sergt. H. T. W. Manning

L./Bdr. E. N. H. Oldrey

CHEVALIER OF THE ORDER OF LEOPOLD (BELGIUM)
Lieut.-Colonel G. H. Champness, O.B.E., T.D.

CHEVALIER OF THE ORDER OF LEOPOLD (BELGIUM) CLASS II
Capt. R. E. Stevens

* Killed in action.

APPENDICES

CROIX DE GUERRE (BELGIUM) WITH PALM
Lieut.-Colonel G. H. Champness, O.B.E., T.D.
Capt. R. E. Stevens

CROIX DE GUERRE (BELGIUM)
B.Q.M.S. G. W. M. Davies   L./Cpl. D. G. Y. Payne, R.E.M.E.
L./Bdr. R. S. Oatway

DECORATION MILITAIRE (BELGIUM) 2ND CLASS
B.S.M. J. Hanks   Bdr. F. Astridge
Sergt. W. Barclay

MENTIONS IN DESPATCHES
12 Officers and 2 Warrant Officers and Other Ranks

275 (H.A.C.) H.A.A. BATTERY, R.A.
MEMBER OF THE ORDER OF THE BRITISH EMPIRE
Capt. A. M. F. Williams

MILITARY MEDAL
Sergt. T. W. Rose

H.A.C. COMPANIES, 13TH BN. ROYAL FUSILIERS
OFFICER OF THE ORDER OF THE BRITISH EMPIRE
Lieut.-Colonel J. Bamford-Smith, T.D.

MEMBER OF THE ORDER OF THE BRITISH EMPIRE
Cpl. F. A. F. Wright*

METROPOLITAN SPECIAL CONSTABULARY (H.A.C. DIVISION)
BRITISH EMPIRE MEDAL
H. I. G. Pothecary

HONOURS AWARDED TO MEMBERS OF THE COMPANY WHILE
SERVING WITH OTHER UNITS, 1939-1945
VICTORIA CROSS
Major R. H. Cain, The South Staffordshire Regiment (Airborne)

GEORGE CROSS
Lieut. B. S. T. Archer, Royal Engineers

KNIGHT COMMANDER OF THE ORDER OF THE BATH
Lieut.-General R. N. O'Connor, D.S.O., M.C.

COMPANION OF THE ORDER OF THE BATH
Major-General R. Evans, M.C.
Major-General J. A. Sinclair, O.B.E.
Colonel The Earl Fortescue, O.B.E., M.C.

* Killed in action.

439

THE HONOURABLE ARTILLERY COMPANY

COMMANDER OF THE ORDER OF THE BRITISH EMPIRE (MILITARY DIVISION)

Brigadier W. A. Ebbels, M.C., Royal Artillery
Brigadier A. I. Irons, D.S.O., Pioneer Corps
Brigadier F. L. McNaughton, D.S.O., Royal Artillery
Brigadier J. G. S. Ross, O.B.E., Royal Artillery
Brigadier W. A. Sheil, D.S.O., Royal Artillery*
Brigadier T. Smith, O.B.E., T.D., H.A.C. H.A.A. (att. R.A.)
Brigadier T. C. Usher, D.S.O., Royal Artillery
Colonel A. R. Rees-Reynolds, The Queen's Royal Regiment
G./Capt. H. E. Hills, O.B.E., Royal Air Force

COMMANDER OF THE ORDER OF THE BRITISH EMPIRE (CIVIL DIVISION)

F. W. Brundle, Esq. C.C., City of London Air Defence Committee
K. G. J. Headington, Esq.
Capt. H. H. Payne, M.C.

BAR TO THE DISTINGUISHED SERVICE ORDER

Lieut.-Colonel W. A. Sheil, D.S.O., Royal Artillery*
Lieut.-Colonel T. C. Usher, D.S.O., Royal Artillery

DISTINGUISHED SERVICE ORDER

Brigadier H. C. Phipps, Royal Artillery
Lieut.-Colonel G. R. Armstrong, M.C., H.A.C. R.H.A. (att. R.A.)
Lieut.-Colonel J. R. E. Benson, Royal Artillery
Lieut.-Colonel A. J. C. Block, Royal Artillery
Lieut.-Colonel C. G. Buttenshaw, M.B.E., Royal Artillery
Lieut.-Colonel R. D. Judd, M.C., Royal Artillery
Lieut.-Colonel A. D. McKechnie, H.A.C. Inf. (att. The Buffs)
Lieut.-Colonel J. H. Mason, The Queen's Royal Regiment
Lieut.-Colonel W. A. Sheil, Royal Artillery*
Lieut.-Colonel T. C. Usher, Royal Artillery
Lieut.-Colonel W. A. C. Wilkinson, M.C., G.M., Royal Artillery
Lieut.-Colonel J. F. Young, H.A.C. H.A.A. (att. R.A.)
Major D. A. Beckett, The Essex Regiment
Major J. E. F. Linton, Royal Artillery
Major D. V. Mackay, Royal Artillery
Major R. S. Paterson, Skinner's Horse
Major P. Pettit, H.A.C. R.H.A. (att. R.A.)
Capt. P. B. Watson, Green Howards
Lieut. D. R. Schofield, Royal Fusiliers

OFFICER OF THE ORDER OF THE BRITISH EMPIRE

Lieut.-Colonel R. P. W. Adeane, H.A.C. H.A.A. (att. Staff)
Lieut.-Colonel P. Hodder-Williams, H.A.C. H.A.A. (att. R.A.)
Lieut.-Colonel A. O. Maclean, H.A.C. H.A.A. (att. R.A.)
Lieut.-Colonel A. Mills, M.C., H.A.C. H.A.A. (att. R.A.)
Lieut.-Colonel F. Mills, M.C., H.A.C. H.A.A. (att. R.A.)
Lieut.-Colonel E. J. Riseley, T.D., H.A.A. (att. R.A.)
Lieut.-Colonel T. Smith, H.A.C. H.A.A. (att. R.A.)
Lieut.-Colonel J. A. Tallent, H.A.C. H.A.A. (att. R.A.)
Lieut.-Colonel H. G. Virtue, H.A.C. Inf. (R. of O.) (att. R. Fus.)

MEMBER OF THE ORDER OF THE BRITISH EMPIRE

Colonel J. H. Bentley, Pioneer Corps
Lieut.-Colonel A. K. Brown, Royal Army Ordnance Corps
Lieut.-Colonel J. B. Griffiths, Pioneer Corps
Lieut.-Colonel H. J. Sandle, Royal Army Ordnance Corps
Lieut.-Colonel H. N. Whitehead, General List
Lieut.-Colonel F. D. Williamson, H.A.C. H.A.A. (att. Staff)

---

* Killed in action.

Major C. J. F. Abbott, M.C., The Manchester Regiment
Major J. E. Anderson, H.A.C. Inf. (att. Staff)
Major R. J. Attenborough, Royal Artillery
Major T. C. Baillon, Royal Engineers*
Major C. J. F. Barker, The Wiltshire Regiment
Major A. D. Baxter, Pioneer Corps
Major J. M. Beecham, Royal Artillery
Major F. R. G. Bell, Royal Artillery
Major W. H. Bennett, The Royal Fusiliers
Major T. W. Bonser, The Royal Fusiliers
Major E. Bowden, Pioneer Corps
Major A. F. Brown, Royal Army Service Corps
Major D. W. Brown, The Royal Fusiliers
Major L. W. Burtt, Royal Artillery
Major J. Carreras, Royal Artillery
Major E. Cawkell, J.P., Essex Home Guard
Major M. A. Chamberlain, The Lincolnshire Regiment
Major J. G. W. Charnaud, The Royal Fusiliers
Major P. L. G. Child, The Border Regiment
Major L. Chrimes, Royal Artillery
Major D. W. A. Clare, The Royal Welch Fusiliers
Major E. P. Clarke, Royal Artillery
Major D. Clitherow-Smith, The Queen's Own Royal West Kent Regiment
Major R. H. Coleman, Pioneer Corps
Major M. Y. Cobb, Royal Artillery
Major L. C. Downing, Royal Artillery
Major M. D. Dudley, Royal Corps of Signals
Major E. G. C. Flawn, Royal Artillery
Major R. H. Foster, Royal Artillery
Major F. I. Geddes, Royal Engineers
Major J. T. Griffiths, Royal Deccan Horse
Major N. L. Hall, The Lancashire Fusiliers
Major J. W. Hambly, Royal Artillery
Major G. W. Henderson, Royal Army Service Corps
Major J. C. S. Hester, Royal Corps of Signals
Major D. A. Hewat, The Lancashire Fusiliers
Major P. Hodder-Williams, H.A.C. H.A.A. (att. R.A.)
Major F. D. Hollick, Intelligence Corps
Major E. W. Horley, Indian Army
Major H. F. A. Jackson, H.A.C. Inf. (att. Sherwood Foresters)
Major C. F. Jacottet, Surrey Home Guard
Major C. R. Janvrin, The Royal Berkshire Regiment
Major H. D. Jay, Royal Army Service Corps
Major C. F. Journet, Royal Artillery
Major R. C. Laming, 3rd Gurkha Rifles
Major D. G. Lewis, Royal Artillery
Major E. H. E. Lydall, The Queen's Bays
Major E. L. G. McManns, Pioneer Corps
Major R. T. M. McPhail, Royal Artillery
Major P. G. E. Michaelis, Royal Artillery
Major W. R. Middleton, Royal Artillery
Major R. Moodie, Royal Engineers
Major K. F. Morrill, The Lancashire Fusiliers
Major E. A. Mounsey, Royal Army Service Corps
Major R. E. K. Norwood, Royal Electrical and Mechanical Engineers
Major T. W. F. Odell, Royal Army Service Corps
Major T. W. Peters, The Shropshire Light Infantry
Major T. F. Poole, Royal Artillery
Major W. F. Poole, Royal Army Service Corps

---

* Killed in action.

Major A. G. Robertson, The East Lancashire Regiment
Major S. C. Selwyn, Army Catering Corps
Major G. C. B. Shaddick, Royal Engineers
Major G. B. Smith, Army Catering Corps
Major W. R. L. Smith, Royal Army Service Corps
Major J. L. Spicer, Intelligence Corps
Major J. H. Thomson, The Rifle Brigade
Major Sir Geoffrey Tritton, Bart., The Rifle Brigade
Major K. L. Walmesley, Royal Artillery
Major P. L. Warren, Royal Artillery
Major T. A. Wilson, Royal Tank Regiment
Capt. N. Brownlow, The Royal Scots
Capt. G. Carew-Jones, Royal Artillery
Capt. C. R. Cook, Pioneer Corps
Capt. N. F. Daniel, Royal Artillery
Capt. A. E. Keech, London Home Guard
Capt. J. E. M. Maw, H.A.C. R.H.A. (R. of O.) (att. Pioneer Corps)
Capt. H. G. Oldman, H.A.C. R.H.A. (att. R.A.)
Capt. D. J. Owen, Royal Corps of Signals
Capt. F. J. Pinchen, Royal Army Service Corps
Capt. G. Power, Royal Artillery
Capt. I. S. Price, The Gordon Highlanders
Capt. J. L. Reed, Royal Artillery
F./Lieut. L. L. Hunt, D.F.C., Royal Air Force
Lieut. L. A. Rowe, Pioneer Corps
2/Lieut. R. H. B. Lord, M.C., Royal Engineers
2/Lieut. J. E. Radford, Royal Artillery

DISTINGUISHED SERVICE CROSS

Lieut.-Comdr. H. V. Gordon, Royal Naval Volunteer Reserve
Lieut. A. H. Maccoy, South African Naval Forces

BAR TO THE MILITARY CROSS

Capt. H. G. McFall, M.C., Royal Horse Artillery
Capt. G. J. S. Slinn, M.C., South Nottinghamshire Hussars, R.H.A.*

MILITARY CROSS

Lieut.-Colonel B. J. Brennan, Cameronians
Major B. L. Barber, H.A.C. Inf. (att. S. Staffs.)
Major P. Barnett, Royal Tank Regiment
Major P. P. Benson, Duke of Wellington's Regiment*
Major P. B. Bishop, Royal Horse Artillery
Major T. M. Brewis, Royal Artillery
Major W. K. Carson, Royal Artillery
Major R. M. Clarke, Royal Artillery
Major G. A. K. Collins, Royal Artillery
Major P. S. Crane, Royal Artillery
Major J. S. Cunis, Royal Artillery
Major G. F. Doggett, The King's Shropshire Light Infantry
Major E. N. Dominy, Royal Artillery
Major H. J. Drury, H.A.C. Inf. (R. of O.) (att. K.O.Y.L.I.)
Major R. H. W. Dunn, Royal Artillery
Major A. R. Eardley-Wilmot, Irish Guards*
Major A. T. Elsom, The East Yorkshire Regiment
Major R. Fox, Royal Artillery
Major J. L. Gebhard, The Royal Warwickshire Regiment
Major D. B. Girling, Royal Artillery
Major A. E. Greenhill, Royal Artillery
Major B. E. Gwyn, Royal Artillery

---

* Killed in action.

Major H. W. P. Harrison, The Royal Scots Fusiliers
Major P. Hazell, Royal Artillery*
Major R. S. W. Higgens, Royal Artillery
Major H. J. Jourdain, The Royal Sussex Regiment
Major R. D. Judd, Royal Artillery
Major N. L. Kind, 3rd Gurkha Rifles
Major D. G. Lahey-Bean, The Manchester Regiment
Major J. Lapthorn, Royal Artillery
Major D. O. Liddell, The Cameronians
Major A. G. P. Lincoln, H.A.C. R.H.A. (att. Ayrshire Yeomanry R.A.)
Major W. A. Livings, Royal Engineers
Major M. L. Macdona, Royal Artillery
Major J. S. Morrison-Jones, The Welch Regiment*
Major D. Neill, H.A.C. Inf. (att. Reconnaissance Corps)
Major P. E. Pettit, H.A.C. R.H.A. (att. Yeomanry R.A.)
Major V. E. Price, Royal Artillery
Major K. Richmond, Royal Artillery
Major D. L. V. Rowe, Royal Artillery
Major W. A. Russell, The Royal Scots
Major E. G. Scammell, Royal Artillery
Major N. S. Shields, Royal Artillery
Major H. J. T. Sills, The Duke of Wellington's Regiment
Major E. F. Thompson, The Middlesex Regiment
Major W. D. Tighe-Wood, The Royal Ulster Rifles
Major G. C. Wells, Royal Artillery
Major H. N. Whitmee, Royal Artillery
Major G. H. Wilford, H.A.C. Inf. (R. of O.) (att. K.O.Y.L.I.)
Major J. E. H. Wise, Royal Artillery
Capt. A. S. Allberry, The King's Own Yorkshire Light Infantry
Capt. D. J. Anderson, Royal Artillery
Capt. M. A. Ashton, The Royal Norfolk Regiment
Capt. M. C. Bailey, Royal Artillery
Capt. R. A. Baker, Royal Artillery
Capt. G. Ball, Royal Artillery
Capt. R. L. Banks, Royal Artillery
Capt. D. H. E. Barber, Royal Artillery
Capt. J. A. C. Baxter, Royal Horse Artillery
Capt. D. L. Benké, Royal Horse Artillery
Capt. H. P. N. Benson, The South Staffordshire Regiment
Capt. H. A. P. Blamey, Royal Artillery
Capt. M. G. Bond, Royal Artillery
Capt. B. G. Bonallack, Royal Artillery
Capt. I. L. Buck, Royal Artillery
Capt. I. F. Carpenter, Royal Artillery
Capt. R. E. Cartwright, Royal Artillery
Capt. M. W. Catesby, Royal Artillery
Capt. D. G. Clark, The Wiltshire Regiment
Capt. J. A. Connell, Royal Artillery
Capt. P. N. Cross-Brown, Royal Artillery
Capt. D. M. Davidson, The South Wales Borderers (att. Commandos)†
Capt. T. B. Davis, Royal Artillery
Capt. G. S. de Jonge, Royal Horse Artillery*
Capt. D. Dottridge, The Royal Fusiliers
Capt. V. Dover, Parachute Regiment
Capt. G. M. Dyas, The Queen's Own Royal West Kent Regiment*
Capt. D. F. Easten, The Queen's Own Royal West Kent Regiment
Capt. J. N. Fraser, 2nd Gurkha Rifles
Capt. W. M. Frost, The Queen's Royal Regiment
Capt. S. L. Garland, Royal Artillery

---

* Killed in action.   † Died of wounds.

Capt. P. S. Y. Garrett, Royal Artillery*
Capt. D. W. Gaylard, The Royal Sussex Regiment*
Capt. W. E. H. Grayburn, Royal Artillery
Capt. G. C. A. Greenwood, Royal Artillery
Capt. A. K. Guest, The Hampshire Regiment
Capt. T. P. Halford-Thompson, Royal Artillery
Capt. R. W. Harden, 27th Lancers
Capt. D. S. Harley, Seaforth Highlanders of Canada
Capt. W. G. Harris, Royal Horse Artillery
Capt. C. H. Harrisson, Royal Artillery
Capt. A. C. Hobson, Royal Artillery
Capt. F. R. Holdsworth, Royal Artillery
Capt. R. Holley, Royal Artillery
Capt. J. B. J. Houghton, The Cameron Highlanders (att. Commandos)*
Capt. R. D. Hunter, The King's Own Scottish Borderers
Capt. C. H. Jackson, H.A.C. Inf. (R. of L.) (att. The R. Sussex Regiment)
Capt. D. W. Jones, The South Lancashire Regiment
Capt. F. P. Keysell, Royal Artillery
Capt. G. W. Lloyd, Royal Artillery*
Capt. J. S. Loram, Royal Artillery*
Capt. D. A. Low, Royal Artillery
Capt. P. V. Lowe, Royal Artillery
Capt. H. G. McFall, Royal Horse Artillery
Capt. B. R. Marsh, Royal Artillery
Capt. J. G. Miller, Royal Artillery
Capt. E. E. Newbald, The Queen's Own Royal West Kent Regiment
Capt. J. F. B. O'Shea, Royal Artillery
Capt. J. F. Pearcy, Reconnaissance Regiment
Capt. K. A. Preston, Royal Artillery
Capt. D. L. Corbett-Price, Royal Artillery
Capt. F. F. Robins, The East Yorkshire Regiment*
Capt. F. R. Salinger, Royal Artillery
Capt. R. C. Seed, Warwickshire Yeomanry, Royal Armoured Corps
Capt. G. F. Senior, Royal Artillery
Capt. H. N. D. Seymour, London Irish Rifles
Capt. G. H. Shingleton, Royal Artillery
Capt. G. J. S. Slinn, South Nottinghamshire Hussars, R.H.A.*
Capt. W. O. Smedley, Royal Artillery
Capt. H. J. Stockings, The East Lancashire Regiment
Capt. D. E. Tacey, Royal Horse Artillery
Capt. J. B. Talbot, Royal Artillery
Capt. D. C. Turquand, 23rd Hussars
Capt. R. D. Tyler, Royal Artillery
Capt. J. T. Tyson, Royal Engineers
Capt. B. H. Valentine, The Queen's Own Royal West Kent Regiment
Capt. C. L. Warnock, Royal Artillery
Capt. F. H. Waters, The Hampshire Regiment
Capt. R. V. B. Webb, Royal Artillery
Capt. E. J. V. Williams, Royal Horse Artillery
Capt. D. V. Young, The York and Lancaster Regiment
Capt. H. J. Young, Essex Regiment
Lieut. L. D. Andrew, Royal Artillery†
Lieut. K. A. Attiwell, Royal Artillery
Lieut. D. Beck, Royal Artillery
Lieut. R. C. E. Cox, Royal Artillery
Lieut. L. B. Farmiloe, Royal Artillery
Lieut. R. E. Hampton, Royal Artillery
Lieut. A. F. Holland, 18th Royal Garhwal Rifles
Lieut. M. M. Johnstone, Derbyshire Yeomanry, Royal Armoured Corps

---

* Killed in action.   † Died of wounds.

Lieut. E. M. Kilbane, 5th Royal Inniskilling Dragoon Guards
Lieut. W. O. Lane, Royal Artillery
Lieut. J. C. S. Lepine, Royal Artillery
Lieut. I. K. McEachran, Royal Artillery
Lieut. A. G. Molison, East African Artillery
Lieut. R. A. Morrison, The Black Watch
Lieut. F. G. H. Murcutt, Royal Engineers
Lieut. D. M. Murray, 2nd Punjab Regiment
Lieut. F. Rowland, Royal Artillery
Lieut. A. E. W. Rumsey, Royal Artillery
Lieut. P. L. Russell, Royal Artillery
Lieut. The Hon. O. P. St. Aubyn, Army Air Corps
Lieut. G. A. Scaramanga, The King's Shropshire Light Infantry (att. Commandos)
Lieut. R. R. Seel, H.A.C. R.H.A. (att. R.H.A.)
Lieut. D. T. Smith, Royal Artillery
Lieut. R. A. P. Temple, The King's Royal Rifle Corps
Lieut. C. G. Toppin, Royal Artillery
Lieut. G. E. Townley, Reconnaissance Regiment
Lieut. J. B. Tyler, Royal Artillery
Lieut. J. G. Tyrell, Staffordshire Yeomanry, Royal Armoured Corps*
Lieut. P. M. Wand-Tetley, The Wiltshire Regiment
Lieut. O. M. Wentworth-Stanley, 11th Hussars
Lieut. P. C. Winton, The Gordon Highlanders
2/Lieut. C. J. L. Bennett, Royal Artillery
2/Lieut. R. A. J. Cheffins, The Middlesex Regiment
2/Lieut. D. W. Jones-Williams, 10th Royal Hussars
2/Lieut. R. H. B. Lord, The King's Own Yorkshire Light Infantry
2/Lieut. B. G. Widnell, The Wiltshire Regiment*

BAR TO THE DISTINGUISHED FLYING CROSS

Capt. C. C. Ballyn, D.F.C., Royal Artillery (Air O.P.)†
Capt. W. S. Molison, D.F.C., Royal Artillery (Air O.P.)†

DISTINGUISHED FLYING CROSS

S./Ldr. J. S. Adams, Royal Air Force
S./Ldr. R. J. L. Fitch, Royal Air Force (*killed on active service*)
S./Ldr. A. V. Gowers, Royal Air Force*
S./Ldr. P. C. Joel, Royal Air Force
S./Ldr. R. W. Quixley, Royal Air Force
S./Ldr. P. J. E. Ritchie, Royal Air Force*
F./Lieut. H. F. Burditt, Royal Air Force
F./Lieut. B. G. Carr, Royal Air Force
F./Lieut. F. G. H. Chalk, Royal Air Force*
F./Lieut. R. M. Curtis, Royal Air Force
F./Lieut. W. D. S. Jackson, Royal Air Force
F./Lieut. R. E. Knight, Royal Air Force
F./Lieut. P. O. Miles, Royal Air Force
F./Lieut. P. E. Raw, Royal Air Force*
Capt. C. C. Ballyn, Royal Artillery (Air O.P.)†
Capt. N. H. Chase, Royal Artillery (Air O.P.)
Capt. C. F. Huttenbach, Royal Artillery (Air O.P.)
Capt. W. S. Molison, Royal Artillery (Air O.P.)†
Capt. H. C. Salter, Royal Artillery (Air O.P.)
Capt. J. P. Stunt, Royal Artillery (Air O.P.)
F./Offr. L. L. Hunt, Royal Air Force

AIR FORCE CROSS

F./Lieut. J. R. Butler, Royal Air Force

---

* Killed in action.   † Died of wounds·

GEORGE MEDAL

Lieut.-Colonel W. A. C. Wilkinson, M.C., Royal Artillery
Major R. Chalkley, Royal Artillery
Capt. J. C. Nightingale, Royal Artillery

DISTINGUISHED SERVICE MEDAL

C.P.O. S. W. Snelling, Royal Navy*

DISTINGUISHED CONDUCT MEDAL

Sergt. B. W. Ogden-Smith, M.M., H.A.C. Inf. (att. Commandos)

MILITARY MEDAL

Sergt. B. W. Ogden-Smith, H.A.C. Inf. (att. Commandos)

AIR FORCE MEDAL

S./Sergt. D. A. Hall, Glider Pilot Regiment

LEGION OF MERIT (U.S.A.) DEGREE OF OFFICER

Lieut.-Colonel E. G. Rooney, Royal Artillery
Lieut.-Colonel T. Lubin-Silverston, Royal Artillery

SILVER STAR MEDAL (U.S.A.)

Lieut.-Colonel J. Harington, Royal Artillery

WAR DEPARTMENT BRONZE STAR (U.S.A.)

Lieut.-Colonel J. E. C. Fryett, O.B.E., Royal Artillery
Lieut.-Colonel E. H. E. Lydall, M.B.E., The Queen's Bays
Lieut.-Colonel E. P. K. Willett, Royal Artillery
Major C. H. Harmer, Intelligence Corps
Major Sir Geoffrey Tritton, Bart., The Rifle Brigade
Capt. A. Speed-Andrews, The King's Own Yorkshire Light Infantry

CROIX DE GUERRE (FRANCE) WITH PALM

Lieut.-Colonel E. J. Riseley, O.B.E., T.D., H.A.C. (att. R.A.)
Capt. F. C. K. Rowland, Royal Artillery*

CROIX DE GUERRE (FRANCE)

Major G. C. Wells, M.C., Royal Artillery
Capt. E. P. D. Cavendish, Royal Canadian Artillery

COMMANDER OF THE ORDER OF LEOPOLD (BELGIUM)

Brigadier J. G. S. Ross, C.B.E., Royal Artillery

CHEVALIER OF THE ORDER OF LEOPOLD (BELGIUM) WITH PALM

Lieut.-Colonel L. Chrimes, M.B.E., Royal Artillery
Major R. H. Forsyth, Royal Artillery
Major J. R. Turner, The Manchester Regiment
Major G. R. A. Wixley, Royal Artillery

CHEVALIER OF THE ORDER OF LEOPOLD (BELGIUM) CLASS II

Lieut.-Colonel J. F. Young, D.S.O., H.A.C. (att. R.A.)

CROIX DE GUERRE (BELGIUM)

Brigadier J. G. S. Ross, C.B.E., Royal Artillery
Lieut.-Colonel L. Chrimes, M.B.E., Royal Artillery
Lieut.-Colonel J. F. Young, D.S.O., H.A.C. (att. R.A.)
Major R. H. Forsyth, Royal Artillery
Major J. R. Turner, The Manchester Regiment
Major G. R. A. Wixley, Royal Artillery

---

* Killed in action.   † Died of wounds.

ORDER OF ORANGE NASSAU (NETHERLANDS)

Major E. L. C. Harding, The Duke of Cornwall's Light Infantry
Capt. A. G. L. Roberts, The King's Shropshire Light Infantry (att. Commandos)

BRONZE LION (NETHERLANDS)

Major R. L. Masters, Royal Artillery

BRONZE CROSS (NETHERLANDS)

Major I. H. McKechnie, Royal Artillery

HAAKON II FREEDOM CROSS (NORWAY)

S./Ldr. A. J. Goatly, Royal Air Force

MILITARY MEDAL OF HONOUR (CZECHOSLOVAKIA)

S./Ldr. A. Walsham, Royal Air Force

CHEVALIER OF THE ORDER OF THE CROWN OF OAK (LUXEMBOURG)

Capt. R. D. Spence, H.A.C. Inf. (att. Staff)

CROIX DE GUERRE (LUXEMBOURG)

Capt. R. D. Spence, H.A.C. Inf. (att. Staff)

MILITARY CROSS (POLAND)

Major A. C. Maxwell, Royal Artillery

MILITARY MEDAL FOR VALOUR (GREECE)

Capt. R. W. Harden, M.C., 27th Lancers

AIR FORCE CROSS (GREECE)

S./Ldr. P. F. Dawson, Royal Air Force

MEDAL OF HONOUR (REPUBLIC OF CHINA)

Capt. J. E. H. Wise, M.C., Royal Artillery

MENTIONS IN DESPATCHES

391 Members of the Company were Mentioned in despatches for service in other units. Of these, 27 were twice mentioned and 4 received three mentions.

ROLL OF THE VICTORIA CROSS

REGINALD LEONARD HAINE (1st Battalion, Honourable Artillery Company).

"Reginald Leonard Haine, Second-Lieut., Honourable Artillery Company. For most conspicuous bravery and determination when our troops, occupying a pronounced salient, were repeatedly counter-attacked. There was an ever-present danger that, if the enemy attack succeeded, the garrison of the salient would be surrounded. Second-Lieut. Haine organized and led with the utmost gallantry six bombing attacks against a strong point which dangerously threatened our communications, capturing the position, together with fifty prisoners and two machine guns. The enemy then counter-attacked with a battalion of the Guards, succeeded in regaining this position, and the situation appeared critical. Second-Lieut. Haine at once formed a block in his trench, and for the whole of the following night maintained his position against determined attacks. Reorganizing his men on the following morning, he again attacked and captured the strong point, pressing the enemy back for several hundred yards, and thus relieving the situation. Throughout these operations this officer's superb courage, quick decision, and sound judgment were beyond praise, and it was his splendid personal example which inspired his men to continue their efforts during more than thirty hours of continuous fighting." (*London Gazette*, 8th June, 1917.)

ALFRED OLIVER POLLARD (1st Battalion, Honourable Artillery Company).

"Alfred Oliver Pollard, M.C., Second-Lieut., Honourable Artillery Company. For most conspicuous bravery and determination. The troops of various units on the left of this officer's battalion had become disorganized owing to the heavy casualties from shell fire; and a subsequent determined enemy attack with very strong forces caused further confusion and retirement, closely pressed by hostile forces. Second-Lieut. Pollard at once realized the seriousness of the situation and dashed up to stop the retirement. With only four men he started a counter-attack with bombs and pressed it home till he had broken the enemy attack and regained all that had been lost and much ground in addition. The enemy retired in disorder, sustaining many casualties. By his force of will, dash and splendid example, coupled with an utter contempt of danger, this officer, who has already won the D.C.M. and M.C., infused courage into every man who saw him." (*London Gazette*, 8th June, 1917.)

THOMAS TANNATT PRYCE (Grenadier Guards, late 1st Battalion, Honourable Artillery Company).

"Thomas Tannatt Pryce, Lieut. (Acting Capt.), M.C., 4th Battalion Grenadier Guards. For most conspicuous bravery, devotion to duty and self-sacrifice, when in command of a flank on the left of the Grenadier Guards. Having been ordered to attack a village, he personally led forward his platoons, working from house to house, killing some thirty of the enemy, seven of whom he killed himself. The next day he was occupying a position with some thirty to forty men, the remainder of his company having become casualties. As early as 8.15 a.m. his left flank was surrounded and the enemy

448

CAPT. T. T. PRYCE, V.C., M.C.
Grenadier Guards
(late Private, 1st H.A.C.)

was enfilading him. He was attacked no less than four times during the day, and each time beat off the hostile attack, killing many of the enemy. Meanwhile the enemy brought up three field guns to within 300 yards of his line, and were firing over open sights and knocking his trench in. At 6.15 p.m. the enemy had worked to within sixty yards of his trench. He then called on his men, telling them to cheer and charge the enemy and fight to the last. Led by Captain Pryce, they left their trench and drove back the enemy with the bayonet some 100 yards. Half an hour later the enemy had again approached in stronger force. By this time Captain Pryce had only seventeen men left and every round of ammunition had been fired. Determined that there should be no surrender, he once again led his men in a bayonet charge, and was last seen engaged in a fierce hand-to-hand struggle with overwhelming numbers of the enemy. With some forty men he had held back at least one enemy battalion for over ten hours. His company undoubtedly stopped the advance through the British line, and this had great influence on the battle." (*London Gazette*, 23rd May, 1918.)

ROBERT HENRY CAIN (The South Staffordshire Regiment (Airborne), late Honourable Artillery Company.)

"In Holland on 19th September, 1944, Major Cain was commanding a rifle company of the South Staffordshire Regiment during the battle of Arnhem when his company was cut off from the rest of the battalion and during the next six days was closely engaged with enemy tanks, self-propelled guns and infantry. The Germans made repeated attempts to break into the company position by infiltration and had they succeeded in doing so the

THE HONOURABLE ARTILLERY COMPANY

whole situation of the Airborne Troops would have been jeopardized.

"Major Cain, by his outstanding devotion to duty and remarkable powers of leadership, was to a large extent personally responsible for saving a vital sector from falling into the hands of the enemy.

"On 20th September a Tiger tank approached the area held by his company and Major Cain went out alone to deal with it armed with a Piat. Taking up a position he held his fire until the tank was only 20 yards away when he opened up. The tank immediately halted and turned its guns on him, shooting away a corner of the house near where this officer was lying. Although wounded by machine-gun bullets and falling masonry, Major Cain continued firing until he had scored several direct hits, immobilized the tank and supervised the bringing up of a 75-mm. howitzer which completely destroyed it. Only then would he consent to have his wounds dressed.

"The next morning this officer drove off three more tanks by the fearless use of his Piat, on each occasion leaving cover and taking up position in open ground with complete disregard for his personal safety.

"During the following days, Major Cain was everywhere where danger threatened, moving amongst his men and encouraging them by his fearless example to hold out. He refused rest and medical attention in spite of the fact that his hearing had been seriously impaired because of a perforated eardrum and he was suffering from multiple wounds.

"On the 25th September the enemy made a concerted attack on Major Cain's position, using self-propelled guns, flame-throwers and infantry. By this time the last Piat had been put out of action and Major Cain was armed with only a light 2-in. mortar. However, by a skilful use of this weapon and his daring leadership of the few men still under his command, he completely demoralized the enemy who, after an engagement lasting more than three hours, withdrew in disorder.

"Throughout the whole course of the Battle of Arnhem, Major Cain showed superb gallantry. His powers of endurance and leadership were the admiration of all his fellow officers and stories of his valour were being constantly exchanged amongst troops. His coolness and courage under incessant fire could not be surpassed." (*London Gazette*, 2nd November, 1944.)